T0270678

HORSE SOLDIERS AT GETTYSBURG

A Cavalryman's View of the Civil War's Pivotal Campaign

DANIEL MURPHY

STACKPOLE BOOKS

Essex, Connecticut

Blue Ridge Summit, Pennsylvania

STACKPOLE BOOKS

An imprint of Globe Pequot, the trade division of
The Rowman & Littlefield Publishing Group, Inc.
4501 Forbes Blvd., Ste. 200
Lanham, MD 20706
www.rowman.com

Distributed by NATIONAL BOOK NETWORK

British Library Cataloguing in Publication Information Available

Library of Congress Cataloging-in-Publication Data

Names: Murphy, Daniel Kevin, author.
Title: Horse soldiers at Gettysburg : a cavalryman's view of the Civil War's
  pivotal campaign / Daniel Murphy.
Other titles: Cavalryman's view of the Civil War's pivotal campaign
Description: Essex, Connecticut : Stackpole Books, [2023] | Includes
  bibliographical references and index. | Summary: "In this new narrative of
  Civil War cavalry, author Daniel Murphy gets into the saddle and explores
  what it was like to be a cavalryman during the Gettysburg campaign. Horse-
  soldiering was a unique way of doing battle, and Murphy gives it more justice
  and nuanced description than any author has yet given it"— Provided by
  publisher.
Identifiers: LCCN 2022045644 (print) | LCCN 2022045645 (ebook) | ISBN
  9780811772716 (cloth) | ISBN 9780811772723 (epub)
Subjects: LCSH: Pennsylvania—History—Civil War, 1861-1865—Cavalry
  operations. | Gettysburg, Battle of, Gettysburg, Pa., 1863. | War horses—
  Pennsylvania—Gettysburg—History—19th century.
Classification: LCC E475.53 .M9455 2023 (print) | LCC E475.53 (ebook) |
  DDC 973.7/349—dc23/eng/20230308
LC record available at https://lccn.loc.gov/2022045644
LC ebook record available at https://lccn.loc.gov/2022045645

♾️™ The paper used in this publication meets the minimum requirements of
American National Standard for Information Sciences—Permanence of Paper
for Printed Library Materials, ANSI/NISO Z39.48-1992.

This book is dedicated to the best horse I ever had,
"Call Me Jet Man"

CONTENTS

PREFACE

I grew up with a fascination for all things cavalry. That interest continued into my adult life as I studied the Gettysburg campaign and the horse soldiers involved: John Buford, Jeb Stuart, George Custer, and John Mosby. I read an abundance of material on these individuals but always came away wanting to know more about the cavalry itself—how long could a regiment travel in a day, how was it formed, how did it maneuver, and just how did a cavalry charge work?

These questions led me to join a mounted reenacting troop, and over the next fifteen-plus years I learned about the equipment, the weapons, and the drill; above all else, I learned a great deal about horses. The more I discovered, the more I realized that most historians writing about cavalry knew few relevant details about the horses: what it took to care for them in the field, move them over terrain, or keep a group of fifty troopers in formation at a military gallop. Traditional historians knew a great deal about individual cavalrymen, their politics and the friends they made in school, but possessed little practical knowledge of horses, and even less knowledge of equine logistics. How much gear could a rider carry without taxing his mount, how much water did a horse drink in a day, how much grain did a working horse require before he risked muscle atrophy, and what was the shoeing cycle of a nineteenth-century cavalry mount?

When I compared this knowledge with the letters and diaries of the participants, I reached conclusions that varied from many standard interpretations. Most of these new conclusions were minor; however, others were significant, and explained why well-known participants of the campaign made the choices they did, and revealed how influential horses and equine logistics were on the campaign.

The goal of this work is to show the events from the participants' perspectives, with a similar practical knowledge, or horse sense, that the cavalry operated under in 1863. I offer the following in good faith and hope this work generates additional research, conclusions, and understanding.

ACKNOWLEDGMENTS

Few people write a book alone. I am certainly not one of those few, nor would I want to be. Foremost, I'd like to thank my wife, Jennifer, for her love and support. She has been a steadfast partner, fellow equestrian, and early encourager of my writing. Years ago, after listening to me complain about an article I was reading in a magazine, she looked at me and said, "Well, why don't you write one?" That spawned my efforts at writing articles and eventually brought me to this book.

Along the way, I had a long string of friends and support. Author Charles F. Price was an ardent supporter of my first writing attempts, and Chuck Campbell visited several battlefields with me and encouraged my early research on the Gettysburg campaign. I owe a special thanks to Dave Reisch at Stackpole Books, who believed in my manuscript and has been a great adviser. Also, I would like to thank Eric Lindblade, a licensed battlefield guide at Gettysburg, for his knowledge and expertise on the subject.

Much of my knowledge on cavalry is practical, and that began with Mike Kyle, who first put me on a horse at a reenactment. That started my cavalry hobby, and I made an entire "company" of friends whom I learned from and studied beside: Joel Anderson, Ron Crawley, Ed Harrelson, Bob Hoskins, Don Lyons, Henry McMillan, Burt Puckett, and Neill Rose. My heartfelt thanks also go out to author and historian Robert F. O'Neill, who continued to share his ideas, advice, and experience, even when we disagreed while walking over the battlefields.

Many outstanding authors have written on the Gettysburg campaign; a very short list of the great many who influenced me are: *They Met at Gettysburg* by Edward J. Stackpole; *Here Come the Rebels* by Wilbur S. Nye; *The Cavalry Fights at Aldie, Middleburg and Upperville*, by Robert F. O'Neil;

The Cavalry at Gettysburg by Edward Longacre; *"The Devil's to Pay" Gen. John Buford* by Michael Phipps; *Sabre and Scapegoat* by Mark Nesbitt; and *Retreat From Gettysburg* by Ken Brown.

Finally, I have to thank my former horse, "Call Me Jet Man" better know as "Mick" on, and off, the picket line. We rode together for fifteen years. I miss you every day, pal.

Daniel Murphy

LIST OF MAPS

1

MEN AND MOUNTS

Surviving photographs of Civil War cavalrymen leave us hundreds of tintype windows to another time. These images are sometimes familiar, and sometimes haunting, but all uniquely American; and the proud looks of these poised participants, many with weapons in hand, were common to both North and South. Most of these portraits were staged in studios with common props, but by blending studio portraits with equipment returns and images taken in the field, an accurate description of a nineteenth-century American horse soldier comes to light.[1]

He typically wore a simple shell jacket or fatigue blouse made from blue kersey or gray jean cloth. Head cover ranged from trim regulation kepis to broad-brimmed slouch hats with the latter preferred for protection from the elements. Issued footwear came in ankle-length brogans or flesh side boots with square-shaped toes. He often tucked spoons and toothbrushes through open buttonholes in his uniform jacket, and a tin cup became a near universal feature on campaign, quick strapped from a haversack or buttonhole.

The average private in the cavalry was twenty-five years old. Whether he fought for the North or the South, the two had many things in common. His lineage was typically western European, and the majority of horse soldiers serving in the Civil War were born in the United States.[2] Often raised on a farm, he grew up in an extended family, could read and write, was usually single, was a practicing Protestant Christian, and served in a volunteer regiment. Our American trooper grew up a product of the Victorian era, morally influenced by the Age of Industry and the Second Great Awakening—an evangelical fervor that swept America in the mid-nineteenth century advocating temperance, education, devotion to home, moral action, and, depending on regional location, the abolition of slavery, the continuation of slavery, or an indifference to what many considered an unpleasant and fading institution.[3]

If viewed through a twenty-first-century lens, the Victorian era was by no means a kind or charitable age but, rather, an abhorrent one. It was an age where human beings were legally held in bondage, and many leading countries found profit in conquest and colonialism; the subjugation and exploitation of less powerful peoples and cultures ran worldwide. Slavery still existed in America, and the ongoing removal and massed slaughter of countless Native American peoples and tribes was applauded from Maine to California all under the shining banner of Manifest Destiny. Most Victorians accepted these social proclivities, believed in a bootstrap code of self-worth, and encouraged upward social mobility through hard work and, with it, the promise of a better future.

American Victorians were extremely proud of their military heritage and the successful revolution their forefathers waged against Great Britain. Prior to the Civil War, militia units were formed in both the North and South, and in Massachusetts, officers in the mounted militia recalled the revolutionary actions of their ancestors at Lexington Green, Concord Bridge, and Bunker Hill. They even promised to hold themselves "ever ready to charge the enemy."[4]

This confidence carried over into the early days of the war, when new recruits were seen breaking ranks and recommending tactical maneuvers to passing field officers. One novice courier, while waiting for General Stonewall Jackson to write a dispatch, suggested Jackson "cut the answer short" as the courier's horse had a stone bruise, and it would take him a while to run it back![5] In fact, many Southern-born recruits believed their birthright gave them a natural edge in military matters, especially in mounted combat, often due to schoolroom lessons proclaiming the Revolutionary War deeds of Southern heroes like Francis "Swamp Fox" Marion, William Washington, and Henry "Lighthorse Harry" Lee.

Completing our mounted private's appearance was a sturdy leather waist belt with a brass embossed buckle displaying either a Federal Eagle or the seal of his home state. The belt supported a cartridge box and cap pouch, a horse sabre, and sword knot on the left hip, counterbalanced by a revolver on the right, carried butt forward in a flapped holster. A carbine sling of broad leather ran across the left shoulder and suspended a steel hook over the trooper's right hip, which captured a corresponding ring near the carbine's breech.[6] The arrangement and rigging of these three weapons—sabre, revolver, and carbine—were key to the troopers' combat system and allowed for one-handed operation—a crucial characteristic in a horse fight

Figure 1.1. Unidentified Federal trooper with carbine, revolver, and sabre.
Library of Congress.

as troopers rarely let go of the reins when their lives depended on control-
ling their horses' speed and direction.

The carbine sling allowed quick access to the carbine; the soldier
could raise the weapon to his shoulder, support the barrel with his left hand
while maintaining his reins, fire, and return the carbine to hang at his side
as needed. The butt-forward revolver allowed for ambidextrous draw, and
the sword knot was also an integral part of the system. Before drawing the

sabre, a trooper threaded his right hand through the knot, and this kept the trooper from losing the weapon during a melee. More important, once the trooper had drawn the sabre, he could drop the blade and let it hang from his right wrist. This left him free to draw and fire his carbine or revolver. In seconds, he could return either firearm and, with a flick of the wrist, have the sabre back in hand as the situation required.

Cavalry did not hone sabre blades razor sharp. Instead, they were edged like a cleaver, allowing the soldier to ride in close ranks with the blade dangling by the sword knot without cutting himself, his mount, or the mount or man beside him. The final two pieces of gear were a cloth haversack for rations suspended across the chest, as well as a tin, or sometimes wooden, canteen.

∼

Prior to the war, the United States Military Academy at West Point was ranked as the most prestigious martial academy in America, having been in operation since 1802. With an early emphasis on military engineering and artillery, the school formed to eliminate the need for foreign advisers in America's future wars. Over time, the curriculum expanded to cover practical instruction and advanced tactics in the three primary combat arms: infantry, artillery, and cavalry. Only two candidates were allowed from each state annually, and only one family member could attend per generation. Candidates often came from the "better families" of society and generally acquired a list of formal recommendations.

The U.S. Army offered graduating cadets a 2nd lieutenant's commission, with the branch based on class standing. Top slots went to the Corps of Engineers, then the artillery, followed by the cavalry, and then the infantry. While graduating cadets were qualified for a junior officer's commission, not all graduates had the proper temperament or acumen for active duty, nor did the academy inherently make them superior leaders or tacticians.[7] That said, the vast majority of general officers in the Civil War were former graduates of "The Point," and the tactics and organization learned at the academy shaped both the Federal and Confederate war efforts in dogma, training, and organization.

These aspects were especially true in the cavalry, where cadets studied a manual adopted by the U.S. War Department in 1841, named for the serving secretary of war, Joel Poinsett.[8] Privates formed in ranks two deep and maneuvered in fifty-man companies, commanded by a captain, with each company, or troop, composed of two twenty-man platoons commanded by a lieutenant. Two companies formed a squadron, multiple squadrons formed a battalion, and three battalions formed a twelve-company regiment. Multiple regiments then formed a brigade, and multiple brigades formed a division.[9] Officers called out the commands, and buglers transmitted the orders to the rest of the unit. Flags composed of regimental standards and swallow-tailed company guidons served as visual cues for the troopers to form upon and rally under when needed.[10]

At the start of the Civil War, five Federally funded regiments served in the Lilliputian-sized cavalry on the American frontier: 1st Dragoons, established 1833; 2nd Dragoons, established 1836; 1st Mounted Rifles, established 1846; 1st Cavalry, established 1855; and the 2nd Cavalry, also established in 1855. These units engaged in small-scale actions with the various native tribes along the frontier and defended the border with Mexico. Typical frontier service saw these units deployed to distant locations where they mostly fought in platoon- or company-sized engagements. Many of these frontier cavalry officers would later rise to prominent roles in the Civil War and go on to serve as general officers on their respective sides.[11]

These five units were redesignated in August 1861. To maintain seniority, the army redesignated the units in the following manner: the 1st Dragoons became the 1st U.S. Cavalry; 2nd Dragoons—the 2nd U.S. Cavalry; and 1st Mounted Rifles—the 3rd U.S. Cavalry. The prewar 1st Cavalry became the 4th U.S. Cavalry, and the prewar 2nd Cavalry became the 5th U.S. Cavalry. Outside of these "Regular" Federal units, the various states, both North and South, raised vast numbers of volunteer cavalry and designated them with a number declaring their volunteer seniority by date of organization, followed by their home state: 1st Massachusetts Cavalry, 2nd Virginia Cavalry, 3rd Pennsylvania Cavalry, and so on. Federal Regular and State Volunteer commissions were equivalent in the field, but rank in the Regular regiments counted as a true Federal commission during and after the war, where the state volunteer commissions did not transfer to the Regular Army.[12]

The pay for a private was $13 for Federals and $11 for Confederates, the key difference being an additional $12 bounty paid monthly to Confederate troopers who supplied their own horses, a common occurrence in Southern states.[13] This gave the Confederate cavalry a distinct advantage at the beginning of the war, as Southern recruits arrived on a sound horse the recruit knew in temperament and ability.[14] On the Federal side, the majority of the horses were owned and issued by the government, and many recruits received a green horse upon joining a Federal cavalry unit.[15] Some Northern recruits were not yet capable riders, and this combination of novice riders on green horses diminished the potential of some Union regiments at the onset of the war.[16] "We are drilling on horseback now,"

Figure 1.2.   Unidentified Confederate trooper with sabre. *Library of Congress.*

wrote one Union recruit. "When we draw sabres the horses run away and the Col. swears harder than ever."[17]

⁓

Horses were plentiful in America. In 1860, the horse population of the United States stood at 4.5 million and ranked near the top of the world.[18] The Thoroughbred contributed to the creation of all major American breeds east of the Mississippi and north of Florida, and this dated back to colonial times. New York, Virginia, and the Carolinas were all instrumental in American equine development, producing such breeds as the Old Canadian, Narragansett Pacer, Quarter-Running Horse, the Morgan, the American Saddlebred, and the American Standardbred.[19] Heros von Borcke, a European officer who served in the Confederate cavalry, appeared deeply impressed with Southern horses and described the typical Virginia cavalry mount during the war as descending from English Derby Thoroughbreds: "The horses were of medium size, very elegant in form, and extraordinarily efficient. They were also characterized by great docility and a very gentle nature."[20]

The Quarter-Running Horse, the ancestor of today's American Quarter Horse, also gained popularity in Southern circles. Like other breeds of the time, "Running Horses" were a blend of Thoroughbred, Hobby, and Narragansett Pacers, bred for quarter-mile sprints down small-town main streets on Sunday afternoons. Also popular in the South were hardy, gaited horses known today as the Tennessee Walking Horse and Missouri Fox Trotter. Both possessed smooth, mile-eating gaits popular on both sidetracks and turnpikes for traveling long distances.[21] The North did not breed as many gaited horses and tended to favor multifunctional breeds such as the versatile and resilient Morgan, capable of plowing, hauling, driving, and general riding. Many Federal officers preferred Thoroughbred-Morgan crosses for field duty.[22]

The Federal system of securing cavalry mounts relied on a wide web of purchasing agents dedicated to procuring horses for the government with mandated standards: six years old, 950 pounds, and no less than fifteen hands high. The price paid for a cavalry mount ranged from $150 to $185, the rough equivalent in today's economy of $3,500.[23] Military service was hard on mounts, and more than just cavalry mounts served. There were also artillery horses, as well as the horses and mules used for hauling food, ammunition, and equipment wagons. As the war continued, the armies used more and more mules for hauling wagons and artillery, and some rare troopers and officers preferred riding mules to horses.[24]

Whether by horses or mules, all Civil War armies moved by equine power on the march, and therefore the military required a great deal of animal stock. Due to the combustible engines of the twentieth century and asphalt-topped roads, we now take for granted the ease with which we move from point to point and can safely travel hundreds of miles per day on our highway systems. The nineteenth century was drastically different. Traveling twenty miles a day with a wagon was making good time in the 1860s. River crossings with formal bridges were found only on high-travel roadways and turnpikes, and the simple ford remained the most common way to cross a river. Most roads linked fords and bridges to one another and the numerous passes through mountain chains. Going up, over, and back

Figure 1.3.   Federal officer on cavalry mount. *Library of Congress.*

down a mountain pass on nineteenth-century roads not only slowed the pace but also taxed the horses, especially those pulling artillery and supply wagons.

Much like their human counterparts, Federal horses enlisted, trained, and deployed under the direction of the United States Army and, in particular, the quartermaster general of the Federal Army, Brigadier General Montgomery C. Meigs. The quartermaster general took responsibility for supplying almost everything but ordnance, medicine, and food. This left horses, mules, hay, grain, ambulances, wagons, hammers, nails, horseshoes, uniforms, boots, spurs, coffins, saddles, bridles, halters, and mobile forges.[25]

General Meigs struggled to supply the army with horses, and cavalry mounts in particular. Part of this difficulty came from simple graft, as evidenced in Pennsylvania in 1861, when the government purchased 1,000 horses. A second inspection showed that of the 1,000 horses, only 480 proved worthy: 35 were pregnant, 120 were too old, 86 were too young, 60 were too small, 8 were blind, 5 had debilitating conditions, and a number were sick and close to dying.[26] Meigs and his agents also battled a number of infectious diseases including: glanders, strangles, and distemper.[27]

Additional hurdles included keeping the horses properly groomed. Horses sweat, and when the sweat evaporates it cools the horse's body, allowing them to run great distances; however, sweat will not evaporate from a horse's back when wearing a saddle and blanket and carrying a rider. Therefore, properly grooming a horse's back was crucial to maintaining a working horse's health. Dust, dander, dirt, and dried sweat all form small particulates within the horse's coat that, under the collective weight of the saddle and rider, will grind through the horse's coat and create a skin abrasion if not consistently brushed and groomed. Abrasions led to painful saddle sores, flies, infections, and disease. In a perfect world, a cavalry horse would be fed, watered, groomed, saddled, and exercised. Afterward the saddle would be pulled, the coat brushed out, and the blanket shaken out and set up to dry while the horse was again watered, fed, and put up for the evening.

Frontline service was vastly different from the perfect world. The demands of a campaign did not usually allow for regimented grooming times, and horses often had to remain saddled for long periods of time. Sergeants and corporals had to be diligent in taking advantage of opportunities when their men could groom their mounts, and these often came at day's end when all were exhausted and only wanted to sleep, not attend to their horses. Noncommissioned officers also had to ensure the troopers did not overload their mounts on the march with extra cooking utensils, extra weaponry, extra ammunition, keepsakes, and scavenged items, as this taxed the horses beyond what was necessary. When wounded Confederates were captured in a makeshift hospital in 1862, they were interviewed by a reporter from the *New York Tribune* who asked the Rebels' opinions of their Federal counterparts: "The 8th Illinois, with whom they have frequently come in contact, they pronounced the best riders in [Federal] service, and said if they would carry less upon their horses, they would make splendid cavaliers."[28]

Along with proper care and grooming came food and water. Working cavalry mounts required between twelve and eighteen gallons of clean water a day, and this same horse required a daily supply of forage—hay or grass—as well as a daily issue of grain. Forage provided nutrition and the bulk needed for good digestion. Grain gave the high-energy calories needed to build muscle, maintain strength, and provide speed and stamina. Federal regulations called for fourteen pounds of hay for horses and mules, and eight pounds of grain, per horse, per day, every day; sadly, many horses suffered from want of nutrition.[29]

Sustained marches on slim rations or inadequate water would deplete a horse, weaken his immune system, and break him down without ever seeing the enemy. As large as they are, horses are fragile if not properly cared for. Officers could force their men ahead on short rations and make them *soldier on* in their belief of a cause, but horses are unaware of glory, duty, or social agendas. Their bodies and muscle structures are also far larger than humans' and require far more calories to maintain the muscle mass required to carry not just themselves but also a trooper, saddle, ammunition, and arms. Malnourishment, toxic plants, bad hay, dehydration, infrequent feedings, and tainted water all contributed to problems with horses' stomachs and their intestinal tracts. Horses cannot vomit and purge their stomachs as humans can, and if a horse ate the wrong thing, it could suffer a wide range of intestinal issues, from a simple colic, or stomach pain, to an intestinal blockage that can kill a horse.[30]

Another common problem with horses was their feet; proper care and attention had to be paid to ensure their hooves were trimmed and maintained or the horse would go lame. Many turnpikes and thoroughfares of the nineteenth century were macadamized with layers of crushed stone for shedding water; however, this surface proved extremely hard on the horses' feet. If the horse lacked metal shoes, the macadamized roads would erode the hoof wall and cripple the animal until the outer hoof could regrow.[31] Horses who couldn't keep up were left on the side of the road in droves. "I do my best for my horses and am sorry for them," wrote one Federal officer, "but all war is cruel and it is my business to bring every man I can into the presence of the enemy, and so make war short. . . . I have but one rule, a horse must go until he cannot be spurred any further, and then the rider must get another horse as soon as he can seize one."[32]

This may have been a slightly extreme view at the time, but it shows that horses were expendable, and their life and welfare valued less than that of the troopers who rode them. Estimated human deaths in the Civil War range from 618,000 to 630,000 or more, a monumental tragedy.[33] The estimated death toll for Civil War horses and mules sits between 1.3 and 1.5 million.[34]

Once in combat, the greater size of the horses made them better targets, and if wounded, the prospects for recovery were dire. Like humans, an abdominal wound to a horse tended to be fatal, and amputations were obviously out of the question. Perhaps the hardest service any animals saw in the war came in hauling field guns for the artillery. An additional team carried a caisson with one or two limber chests filled with ammunition

Figure 1.4.   Confederate artillery horses killed near Fredericksburg, Virginia, May 3, 1863. *Library of Congress.*

for the cannons. Artillery teams not only transported the guns and limbers but also maneuvered them during the battle and kept them supplied with ammunition. Therefore, gun and limber teams drew extraordinary amounts of fire during a battle, limiting a cannon crew's efficiency and capacity for action and movement.

Much like their human counterparts, horses could panic in battle, and the results could be catastrophic. "Riderless horses came thundering through the trees with empty saddles," recalled a Union lieutenant in 1862. "[A]rtillery horse with caissons attached ran through the squads of men, and striking trees, caused the percussion shells to explode, blowing horses, caissons and everything to atoms."[35] The problem of loose or wounded horses running wild did not stop with the artillery. Accounts of cavalry mounts bolting about with empty saddles were a common sight. The cry "loose horse" became a common concern in camp or in battle as a sprinting horse could flatten anyone in its path. The following account comes from a horse charge witnessed in 1863 Virginia: "the loud shouts, the sabers flashing . . . then the clash, the hewing strokes, the indescribable jumble and melee . . . horses overthrown, riders unhorsed and trodden underfoot . . . and constantly dropping out of the crush the rider-less horse, quivering with excitement, galloping a little to the rear and then turning instinctively to rejoin the troop."[36]

If a Union trooper lost his horse, he would normally serve dismounted within his regiment while waiting to receive a remount. If a Confederate trooper suffered the same fate, and the horse fell in battle, he would receive compensation for his loss by the government, and then be obligated to either find a replacement or enter a dismounted arm of the service.[37] If the Confederate's horse died through disease, or in a matter unrelated to combat, it became the trooper's responsibility to furnish another mount. As the war progressed, remounts became harder to find, and troopers were often taxed with finding serviceable substitutes. This self-contractor dynamic put the financial responsibility upon Southern troopers and may have aided the Confederate cavalry by forcing better grooming and hygiene practices.[38]

Whether Federal or Confederate, after receiving or purchasing a remount, the trooper brought the often-green horse back to his troop and introduced the animal to a new environment. Results varied, and not all horses had the temperament for cavalry service. Horses are social beings, and though not very vocal, they constantly communicate with one another in proximity. A stamped hoof, cocked ear, arched neck, or lowered head speaks volumes in equine parlance. Herd dynamics and structure, however, were soon bent to the will of the riders and the particular task at hand required by the troop.[39] This could cause kicking and biting in the ranks during drill evolutions where cavalry mounts had to work shoulder to shoulder with other horses, and new arrivals sometimes had to be shuffled about to avoid a spontaneous rodeo from occurring.[40] The break-in time for a cavalry mount lasted a month or two, and the more advanced the rider, the quicker the break-in time.

Another way of acquiring a new horse came from finding or capturing one on the battlefield. Corporal John Weston of Company C, 1st Massachusetts Cavalry, recalled such an incident at Aldie, Virginia, when his horse fell beneath him midcharge: "I had not gone 16 rods when a Minie ball went through [my horse] and killed him instantly. . . . I picked myself back up as lively as circumstances would permit and a [sergeant] of Co. A fell shot through the head, so I grabbed his horse and before he had hardly struck the ground I was in the saddle and skedaddling."[41]

Amid a storm of bullets and charging horses, Weston showed incredible poise and horsemanship by acquiring a new mount in those surroundings and returning to his lines. Another example of riding a found horse comes from Lieutenant Colonel Thomas Marshall of the 7th Virginia

Figure 1.5.   Private Levi F. Hocker, Company F, 17th Pennsylvania Cavalry.
Library of Congress.

Cavalry, who recalled an incident while pursuing a body of Federal cavalry across a narrow stone bridge with low shoulders and a rocky river far below: "As I was mounted upon a recently captured horse, about whose qualities I knew nothing, I did not endeavor to remain at the head of the column, but closed it up, sending back men when I found too many."[42]

Marshall's experience and horse sense shows here in spades. He knew better than to risk throwing his new mount into an environment where it could panic, kill them both, or possibly reverse any advantage won by his troopers—and leading a charge onto a high, narrow bridge spanning a river below, only to pitch into a bottlenecked mass of swinging blades, pistol fire, and rearing horses, presented a terrifically challenging situation for any horse. Instead, Marshall pulled back and continued to direct the action. Sometimes it was just as important to know what a horse wouldn't do as what it would. The bond between a trooper and his mount formed a crucial element in cavalry service; the better troopers were the better riders, and the better riders were those most in tune with their mounts.

2

WEAPONS AND TACTICS

The first recorded use of cavalry comes from the Middle East, where horse-drawn chariots pulled spearmen in range of the enemy in the 2nd millennia BCE.[1] Saddles, stirrups, and mounted archers followed, giving rise to metal breastplates, lamellar armor, chain mail, and the couched lance. Frankish charges proved brutally effective against shield walls of infantry. Mounted lancers bowled over the infantry, using the "shock" and "weight" of the charging horses to break the enemy's ranks, and then pursued the fleeing footmen with swords and battle axes.[2]

Similar shock tactics remained in use for centuries, with their success waning over time and giving way to gunpowder, matchlock muskets, and finally the flintlock musket. Horse tactics evolved as well, and in the seventeenth century, the flintlock pistol became the dominant cavalry weapon over the lance or sword. Caracole charges came in vogue, with horsemen charging up to the enemy and firing pistols as they turned about to ride away and reload. The shock of the horses breaking through the enemy vanished altogether, and the results proved mediocre at best.[3] Opponents soon countered by drawing swords, clapping spurs, and charging full speed through the weak pistol fire of their opponents to cleave them from the saddle. The cavalry had come full circle, and the shock of the horse charge reigned once again.[4]

At the same time, European generals were developing new infantry tactics to support the new infantry weapon of the time—the smoothbore musket. The musket was a single-shot weapon firing a single lead ball, with each charge rammed down the muzzle of the barrel in a series of rote movements. A well-trained infantryman could fire three rounds per minute in the stress of combat, and the most efficient use of these smoothbore flintlocks came from firing massed volleys at the enemy. Officers maneuvered large blocks of infantrymen by drum commands and deployed them in rigid lines whereby every soldier could bring his weapon to bear. This produced lethal volleys akin to naval broadsides with an effective range out to eighty yards on a man-sized target. Opponents would march and countermarch until one side closed in range, and both sides would hammer away until one gained an advantage through superior fire, a flanking action, or some turn of arms. The winning side then advanced to claim the ground with fixed bayonets.

The role of the cavalry naturally changed amid these smoothbore tactics. Because of the range of the smoothbore, and the time required to load the muskets, narrow windows of opportunity allowed for horse charges against infantry under the right circumstances. This dynamic created two distinct types of European cavalry: heavy and light. The heavy cavalry rode large, heavy-bodied horses and became known as Dragoon Guards, Cuirassiers, and Carbineers. The primary mission of the heavy cavalry, who were often equipped with metal helmets and breastplates, was to charge the enemy at a slow gallop and bull their way through opposing ranks of infantry and cavalry.

The second type of cavalry served a more strategic purpose. They rode light-bodied horses raised for speed and endurance, and ranged forward to gather intelligence and discover weak points in the opposition. Light horse units directed the advance of the army, guarded the flanks, engaged the enemy between the lines, and performed long-range reconnaissance missions. Frederick the Great's field generals, Hans von Ziethen and Wilhelm von Seidlitz, were wildly successful in forming units of light horse cavalry from native Hungarian horsemen. These units adopted the name of Hussars, for their Eastern European origins and curved cutting swords known as the sabre.[5] Later units of light cavalry based on the preceding Hussars were named Light Dragoons, Chevaulégers, and Chasseurs au Cheval. Napoleon's light horse commander, Antoine de Lasalle, won everlasting fame for the outstanding actions of his Hussars and their high-speed charges against enemy cavalry and infantry.[6]

The Victorian age arrived at the close of the Napoleonic Wars, and with it came new manufacturing techniques and a surge in new technologies. Two bellweather advances were the rifled musket and the minié ball, and this combination again altered the battlefield. Smoothbore muskets fired a round lead ball and had a rate of fire of three rounds a minute, with an effective range in combat of eighty yards. When at the charge, a cavalry squadron covered approximately thirty-three feet per second, or roughly one hundred yards in less than ten seconds, meaning a charging squadron could cover two hundred yards—far beyond the smoothbores' range in the time it took the infantry to reload. This meant a charging squadron would only suffer one fire in the course of their charge. Therefore, the use of cavalry charges in pitched battles against formed infantry could still produce victories if handled correctly, and the cavalry charge remained a viable option against smoothbore infantry.

That paradigm changed with the Minié ball and the rifled musket. Emerging in 1847, the Minié ball was a conical-shaped lead bullet with a hollow base. Soldiers still loaded from the muzzle, but the barrels had a concentric set of grooves cut into their surface known as rifling. When fired, the Minié ball's hollow base expanded to engage the rifling, which imparted a spin to the projectile, yielding greater accuracy and range. The expanding base also formed a tight seal between bullet and barrel and harnessed a greater amount of energy from the burning powder than a round ball.[7] These attributes tripled the range of the infantry's primary weapon. Now a squadron of cavalry would suffer two or three volleys when charging an infantry line; therefore, charges on prepared infantry were no longer a practical option.[8] The days of heavy cavalry battering their draft horses through the infantry were over. Field commanders would still need speed-bred horses for light cavalry to screen the enemy and range the advance, and light cavalry remained the best source for gathering reconnaissance available to Victorian generals.[9]

Likewise, Minié balls and rifled barrels delivered a new, far-ranging freedom for nineteenth-century horse soldiers. In the smoothbore wars, light cavalry used muzzle-loading carbines with truncated barrels short enough to be loaded from the saddle. Hussars and light dragoons could dismount and fight on foot if they absolutely had to, but the notoriously weak, clipped range of smoothbore carbines required a covering force of infantry with full-length muskets if cavalry wanted to take ground and hold it.[10] This curtailed the potential of smoothbore cavalry, but the combination of Minié balls and rifled barrels extended the range of the new carbines out to two hundred yards. Troopers could now dismount and hold their own ground against enemy cavalry charges and this made the Victorian light cavalry independent of slow-moving infantry support, meaning they could range far and wide at greater speed. This opened a new dynamic in cavalry operations and allowed for fast-moving, long-distance raids against supply lines, bridges, infrastructure, and even enemy cities.

The new light cavalry was meant to be bold in their work, to lead the advance, find the enemy, and range between the lines. During an advance, the cavalry would form a mobile screen to shield their own army's movements from the enemy. Opposing light cavalry would attempt to break past the enemy's screen and divine his intent. The better officers excelled in these maneuvers; they created opportunities, understood terrain, and seized the initiative whenever possible. During a retreat, the cavalry would form a rear guard to cover their armies' withdrawal and attempt to check the enemy's pursuit. If an enemy retreated in their front, light cavalry would vigorously pursue the enemy to create a rout, break the opposing rear guard, and keep up the pursuit until the enemy surrendered or scattered.

⌇

Cavalry actions were entirely different affairs than infantry fights with moving lines and constantly shifting flanks. The target of a mounted charge could be static, or it could be moving diagonally at more than thirty miles an hour. This made speed, timing, and formation the crucial elements to any mounted charge. Horse charges, often referred to as sabre charges, were not headlong gallops from start to finish. A well-led charge began at a walk, progressed to a trot, and then a canter or military gallop. The final sprint came as the ranks closed within fifty to a hundred yards of the enemy, and this maintained the necessary cohesion within the ranks to deliver the combined weight of the horses arriving in formation against the enemy. "The charge will be delivered against the enemy by squadrons, the gallop being taken when within 50 yards of the enemy's front, and the gait increased instead of diminished as the enemy is neared, so as to give the greatest possible force to the shock against the enemy's column. . . . Too much importance cannot be given to the shock of the charge, the furious impact of horse against horse, for in that will consist the success of the charge."[11]

The goal of a horse charge wasn't to kill the opponent outright, but to drive one's horses through the enemy formation, break their ranks apart, shatter their discipline, and create a rout.[12] Despite the misleading term *sabre charge*, the trooper's primary weapon in these affairs was his horse; the attending sabre blows were secondary.[13] The two went hand in hand; the short range of the sabre dictated the troopers' need to launch their mounts among the enemy, and the horses arriving en masse generated the weight, which broke the enemy apart, shattered their ranks, and wrecked their ability to fight as a unit. Once the enemy fled, the sabre saw its most effective use.[14]

There were two types of primary horse sabres listed in the US Ordnance Manual: the 1840 "Cavalry Sabre," often called the dragoon because of its early frontier service with the 1st and 2nd Dragoons; and the later

Figure 2.1.   Union officers from the 4th Pennsylvania Cavalry. Colonel James H. Childs, seen standing, was killed September 17, 1862. *Library of Congress.*

1860 "Light Cavalry Sabre," intended for the frontier 1st and 2nd Cavalry formed just before the war.[15] Individual blades varied slightly by manufacturer but were similar in weight and listed respectively at one pound, five ounces and one pound, six ounces in the manual, though the 1860 had a scabbard that weighed almost a pound less for a significant difference in day-to-day carrying.[16]

Intended primarily for the thrust, both blades could still manage an effective cut when needed. Their curved shape and single edge aided the trooper in wielding the weapon around his mount's head, neck, and shoulders, and the blade's curvature also helped with making a cut. The 1840 had a sturdy, flat-backed spine and a more forward "point of percussion" than the 1860. This gave the 1840 a slightly better cutting balance—a similar feel to a long-handled hammer—whereas the 1860 had a rounded spine, resulting in less material overall and was typically an inch shorter. This gave the 1860 a point of balance closer to the hilt, yielding a lighter, "faster-feeling" point for the thrust.[17] Proponents for both the point and edge argued the virtues of both; the thrust was certainly faster, more lethal, and best delivered at the charge, but the blade could become embedded in an opponent and prove difficult to withdraw. In contrast, a good cut offered greater knock-down power, was less likely to become entrapped, and rendered instant results in the swirling knee-to-knee melees once the lines mixed.[18] Killing the enemy wasn't necessary when wielding a sabre; the blades acted more like cleavers than scalpels and landed like steel whips that cracked skulls and splayed faces.[19] Though not usually lethal, a concussive wound to the head instantly forced an opponent out of the fight, and period accounts abound of troopers receiving head wounds in sabre fights during the war.

Officers could launch a charge in line or column. A line formation yielded a broad front two ranks deep, and this ranked as the preferred formation for combat. The line formation brought more weapons to bear against the enemy on contact, struck with a wider impact, and proved harder to contain. It also spread the enemy's fire over a broader area and potentially reduced casualties; however, the line charge required a large patch of open ground and became difficult to turn or maneuver once under way. The second option, charging in column, produced a narrower front and allowed greater maneuverability when charging down roads, threading wood lots, and passing fence gates. It also concentrated the entire force of the column on a single point. The drawback to the column charge was that it drew all opposing fire on its head, and if any of the front-rank horses were hit midcharge, it could retard the progress of all behind with an accordion-styled pileup.[20]

Officers responded with two options. The first was to maneuver their command in column, gain the range of the enemy, and, if terrain allowed, form the troops in line on a wide front prior to the charge and direct the horses straight ahead.[21] If circumstances or terrain wouldn't allow a broad front, horse commanders could charge in a group of columns, staged en echelon, whereby each succeeding group would offset right or left as dictated by bugle calls. This allowed the multiple columns greater maneuverability but still delivered much of the "weight" of a line charge as each column landed in league with the rest.

Given the rapid nature of cavalry fights and the short range and low killing power of the sabre, casualties were often slight in mounted combat, and a defeated force could quickly scatter, rally back, and reform to charge again.[22] In fact, the very act of charging through the enemy would disorder the victor as well as the vanquished, and experienced commanders rarely charged without a waiting reserve to support, or exploit, their actions.[23] Maintaining discipline throughout the entire charge was vital. If successful, troopers often experienced a surge of adrenaline as they barreled forward in triumph atop a herd of sprinting horses. Having cheated death, a rush of emotion and elation could engulf both man and mount resulting in headlong pursuits of the enemy, heedless of their officers and the bugle calls to rally back and reform. These reckless, post-triumph pursuits often ended poorly and to the detriment of the temporary victors.

Terrain played a crucial role in any horse charge. Steep creeks, swampy bogs, heavy woods, and ditches could easily wreck the boldest charge, no matter how determined the riders. Without good ground, the horses simply couldn't reach the target with any momentum, and momentum was essential in a horse charge. Fences were especially troublesome and common to almost every pasture, crop field, and road in nineteenth-century America. A typical horse could jump a three-foot fence with trooper aboard, but when it came to a two-hundred-man battalion vaulting a fence and maintaining the order required for a successful charge on the enemy, it proved extremely difficult; if attempted in any numbers above a platoon, it could easily end in failure.[24]

~

Samuel Colt's patented revolving cylinder pistol was yet another tremendous advance in technology for participants of the American Civil War. Colt's revolving pistols used a multichambered cylinder, allowing all chambers to be fired as quickly as one could cock the hammer and pull the trigger, all the while keeping the second hand free to manage the reins. Texas Rangers armed with Colts used the new weapons with outstanding success against the Comanche Nation, and these encounters gave way to a new tactic—the revolver charge.[25]

Horsemen could now gallop in on the enemy and quickly discharge multiple rounds at close range. This tactic enjoyed great success on the frontier against native horsemen bearing war clubs or bows and arrows; however, a drawback emerged against disciplined sabre-bearing opponents

Figure 2.2.   Confederate officer of the 43rd Virginia Cavalry Battalion.
Library of Congress.

when revolver-bearing troopers pulled up short and opened fire instead of riding through the enemy. When the troopers pulled short and fired, all momentum vanished, and the beneficial shock of the horses passing through the enemy and breaking their ranks evaporated.[26] One Confederate partisan countered this effect by ordering his troopers not simply to charge up to the enemy and fire but to drive through the enemy instead, firing as they went.[27] "When you are ordered to charge, I want you to go right through them. . . . [L]et every shot tell."[28] This preserved the shock of the charge as the men galloped through the enemy and fired point-blank, sometimes even shoving their barrels against the enemy when pulling the trigger.

Loading a percussion revolver took a bit of time, dexterity, and attention to detail. Each chamber in the cylinder had to be loaded one at a time and rammed down tight with a lever stored under the barrel. Each chamber then required seating a separate percussion cap on the nipple of each chamber.[29] Therefore, loading a revolver during combat never proved a practical option, and many officers preferred to charge their men with revolvers ready, and only switched to the sabre once the revolvers ran dry. Others took a different course and ordered their men to use the sabre first and keep their revolvers in reserve. Still others had the forward ranks close with revolvers in hand while the rear ranks stuck to the sabre, the intent being to blast an opening through the enemy with their revolvers and exploit the gap with sabre-bearing troopers coming up in the rear.[30] No one method worked for every situation, and every charge varied and held its own particular circumstances. Ultimately, using the speed and momentum of the horses, coupled with whatever weapon was at hand, produced the best results.[31]

Northern manufacturing gave the Federals a distinct advantage in their ability to produce a wide variety of revolvers. Colt and Remington were the most popular, followed by the Starr and the Smith & Wesson. Confederate manufacturing capacity was limited, and never truly geared toward revolvers. Instead, Southern forces relied primarily on seized arsenals before the war and battle captures after that. Other Southern sources were imports from France and England, including the popular French model LeMatt, along with the Kerr, and the excellent Beaumont-Adams revolvers from England.

The Federal advantage in weapons production also extended into carbine manufacturing and breech-loading carbines, in particular. The new breechloaders offered a faster rate of fire than muzzleloaders and allowed for much easier reloading from the saddle. When dismounted, breechloaders permitted the trooper to fire and reload from the prone position, negating the need to stand or kneel to handle the rammer of a muzzleloader. The Sharps, the Smith, and the Burnside were all Northern made and three of the most common models used in the war, with the Sharps using a combustible linen or paper cartridge, the Smith a rubber casing, and the Burnside a brass case housing the powder and projectile. All three were "capped" separately from the cartridge. Confederates prized the Sharps in particular, as they could manufacture the cartridges needed if they captured one. Another breechloading carbine popular among Southern troopers was the Maynard, which used brass cartridges to be kept and reloaded after each use.

While the breechloaders didn't have the power of muzzle-loading carbines, their higher rate of fire and ease of handling made them far more popular among the troopers. Still more popular were the Federal repeating carbines, which used self-contained metallic cartridges consisting of powder, ball, and a rimfire primer all in one. There were two types, the Henry and the Spencer. Each utilized an internal magazine holding fifteen rounds in the former and seven in the latter.[32] Each weapon had an incredible rate of fire, with the Spencer firing seven aimed shots in twenty-one seconds, and the Henry fifteen shots in eleven seconds. The Spencer was the more robust of the two weapons and fired a more powerful cartridge.[33] If either weapon fell to the Confederates, they were incapable of producing the ammunition, and therefore these repeaters had little value to Southern soldiers. One disadvantage of the repeaters was, paradoxically, their high rate of fire; per the manual, only forty rounds of ammunition were issued at a time, because of the danger of overweighting the mounts, and Spencer-bearing troopers could easily burn through forty rounds in an engagement before being resupplied.[34]

～

Beginning in the eighteenth century, specialized "flying batteries" of horse-drawn "light artillery" designed for rapid movement appeared on European battlefields.[35] By the nineteenth century, members of light batteries and horse batteries were either mounted, rode atop the battery horses, or sat atop the limber chests of guns and caissons, making all capable of keeping pace with mounted troops to provide close-range fire support.[36] Battery drivers would race forward and sling the guns about as gunners dismounted and unlimbered the piece. Once the horse team unlinked, the drivers would gallop the team out of range, while the gunners loaded and fired. This all occurred in under a minute, with ranges leading out to a mile. Horse artillery kept pace with the cavalry but also provided support during a charge or covered a retreat, and horse batteries often served as a mobile strong point where troopers could rally and reform under cover of the guns.[37] A skilled battery commander could direct the battle space from a mile away, effectively retarding an enemy advance, forcing him in a certain direction, or keeping an enemy from occupying a key piece of terrain.

There were two principal types of cannons used through the war—smoothbores and the newer rifled guns—which first saw widespread use in the Crimean War. Of the smoothbores, the lighter 12-pound howitzer, at 3,200 pounds, held sway with horse gunners for its lightweight, heavy payload and ease of transport, followed by the 12-pound Napoleon, at 3,800 pounds. Of the rifled variants, the Parrot saw the most service early on, and the three-inch Ordnance Rifle, or 10-pounder, surpassed the Parrot for safety and durability in the latter half of the war. The 10-pound Parrot weighed 3,190 pounds and the Ordnance Rifle 3,120 pounds, and this weight determined the number of horses needed to draw the piece and limber as well as the second ammunition wagon known as a caisson with its own team of horses.[38] Federal regulations stated an artillery horse could pull 600 pounds apiece, meaning a six-horse team was recommended for all the guns listed above.[39] These recommendations could not always be met on campaign.

Projectiles for smoothbores and rifles consisted of three types. The first was round shot, a single large-diameter iron ball, or rifled bolt, used at long ranges out to a mile to bounce through the ranks of enemy troops and smash the carriages, wheels, and limbers of enemy batteries across the field. The second type was shell and case—also known as shrapnel. Shell referred to a hollow iron projectile filled with powder and fitted with a timed fuse. The gun commander estimated the range on the fuse to burst the shell over opposing ranks and rain down lethal iron fragments. Case consisted of iron spheres filled with not only powder but also additional iron balls. Like shell, case was fixed with timed fuses and set to burst above enemy troops. The third type was grape and canister, held in reserve for close work of four hundred yards or less, with a preferred range of two hundred yards and closer. Grape shot typically came with a wooden sabot to extend the effect out beyond two hundred yards. Canister rounds were simple tin shells, or linen-wrapped cartridges, filled with dozens of iron balls that spread toward the target, effectively turning the guns into giant shotguns. Loading canister meant the enemy was expected inside two hundred yards—well within the range of rifled carbines and constituting an extermely dangerous situation for the gun crews.[40]

Horse gunners formed the most lethal arm in the mounted service, and the better battery commanders were true force multipliers who often determined the outcome of an engagement. A horse gunner needed a sharp

Figure 2.3.   A Federal artillery battery near Fredericksburg, Virginia, 1863.
Dickinson College.

eye for ground, a strong willingness to engage the enemy, and the foresight to know when to get his guns out of harm's way. The primary goal was to get a piece with the heaviest punch in the best range supported by the most ammunition while expending the least amount of wear on the horses.[41] Correctly managing the horse teams may have been the most crucial of all roles. If the horses were depleted through exhaustion, or hit by enemy fire when serving the guns, the battery became a static target until replacements arrived.

Four to six guns formed a battery, and each gun had a five-man crew and a gunner. Number one rammed and sponged the piece, number two handled the shell, number three plugged the vent, number four primed the gun and worked the lanyard, and number five brought ammunition up from the limber. The gunner, or chief of piece, did the aiming while an officer supervised the action, called the ordnance, and estimated range. Drill practice ended with anyone of the crew suddenly being called absent and repeated until down to the minimum of two men required.[42]

The unsung heroes of the war were the gun and caisson drivers. Just moving a horse team and gun over muddy roads at a gallop required a great deal of skill and nerve. To maneuver one under fire required an even greater degree of courage. The drivers rode "postillion" sitting on the left front of the horse teams, and each driver had a metal shield to keep their inside leg from getting crushed by the trace poles in tight turns. Everyone shot at artillery during a battle, especially when the guns and caissons were moving, and drawing greater attention. If even one horse in a team received a debilitating hit, the entire team came to a halt. The driver had to suffer the continuing fire until he could cut the dead or wounded horse—or horses—out of the traces and continue on before the rest of the team fell to the ongoing enemy fire.[43] Like good gunners, good drivers were essential to success in combat.

3

THE CONFEDERATES

By 1863, the American Civil War had ravaged the country for two years running. Predictions of a quick conflict proved wholly inaccurate, and casualties soared into the thousands and then tens of thousands as each side poured blood and treasure into the escalating conquest. Both sides won transitory victories, yet neither could capitalize on their gains. Federal wins in the west were offset by Confederate wins in the east, and the war rolled on with a reaping, scythe-like momentum. Early Federal cries of "*On to Richmond*" soon fell hollow in the killing fields of Virginia, and despite a distinct edge in numbers and material, the Federal war machine repeatedly ground to a halt far short of the eighty-three miles separating the two capitals.

In April 1863, the Federal Army of the Potomac attempted to outflank the Confederate Army of Northern Virginia outside Fredericksburg, Virginia. The opening moves went well for the Federals; General Joseph Hooker snuck his army out of their trenches, crossed the Rappahannock, and passed the Confederate lines. Hooker hoped to gain open ground beyond the Rebel flank by sending the majority of his own Federal cavalry on a deep raid toward the Confederate capital at Richmond, and thus force the Confederate cavalry to pursue the Federal cavalry and abandon Robert E. Lee's Army of Northern Virginia. Lee, however, was a former cavalry officer and refused the bait, choosing instead to keep plenty of his own troopers at hand, as he shifted his infantry and engaged Hooker at a wooded crossroads named Chancellorsville. As the two armies squared up in the heavy Virginia woods, watching Rebel horsemen discovered Hooker's right flank lay wide open with little mounted support.[1]

Lee considered the options and took a massive risk. Though outnumbered, he sent over half his troops on a day-long flanking march to strike Hooker's open flank. Hard-marching Confederate infantry arrived on the open Union flank in the late afternoon and quickly launched an attack. The Rebel assault shattered Hooker's Federal flank and led to one of the greatest tactical victories of the war. Hooker returned to his lines before Fredericksburg, and Lee's reputation soared into the ranks of Napoleon and Frederick the Great.[2]

~

Robert E. Lee grew up in the shadow of his father, Henry Lee III, a celebrated horseman and hero of the American Revolution. Highly intelligent and morally challenged, the elder Lee ended the revolution with a stain on his record that only continued to grow after the war.[3] After serving as the governor of Virginia, Robert's father fell from grace in a meteoric crash to the bottom involving deceit, debt, a prison cell, and finally a public beating before he abandoned his family and sailed for the West Indies.

Young Robert grew up determined to erase the mark of his father upon his family. Using the remains of his family name, he gained an appointment to the United States Military Academy at West Point and went on to graduate without a single demerit. Lee received a prestigious commission in the Corps of Engineers and then served as a staff engineer for General Winfield Scott in the war with Mexico. In Mexico, Lee scouted, discovered, and then guided American artillery batteries over the difficult passes at Jalapa, where the mountains ran so steep and rocky that the Mexican army judged them impenetrable. "The reconnaissances were conducted with vigor under Captain Lee at the head of the pioneers, and at the end of the third day a passable way for the light batteries was accomplished without alerting the enemy."[4] Lee's actions were key to the following American victory at Cerro Gordo, and he advanced rapidly from captain to colonel, serving in the battles of Contreras, Churubusco, and Chapultepec.[5] General Scott wrote Lee was "as distinguished for felicitous executions as for science and daring."[6]

Unlike his father, Robert impressed most everyone he met. Upon meeting him for the first time, an officer from Texas described him as "dignified without hauteur" and seemingly "possessing the capacity to accomplish great ends."[7] After the Mexican War, Lee served three years as superintendent of West Point, where he enjoyed the ability to share time with his wife and seven children. Afterward, he served as lieutenant colonel of the newly formed 2nd U.S. Cavalry and spent five years campaigning on the Texas frontier against the Comanche and Lipan Apache tribes.

Before leaving for Texas, Lee taught his son, Robert Jr., to ride a pony he'd purchased as a present for his youngest child. "We rode the dragoon seat, no posting," remembered Robert Jr., and though his new horse possessed a wonderfully smooth canter, his father insisted his son take the

Figure 3.1.   General Robert E. Lee, Army of Northern Virginia. *Library of Congress.*

rougher trot, forcing him at a young age to learn the rigid dragoon seat of the old guard frontier cavalry. Family or not, Robert E. Lee rarely wavered once he determined a course.[8]

In 1861, as Southern states began seceding from the Union, the Federal Army offered Lee command of the defenses of Washington, DC. Lee declined the offer, resigned his commission, and offered his services to the Confederacy. After first serving in southern Georgia and western Virginia, Lee took command of the Army of Northern Virginia in June 1862. Victories followed: the Seven Days, 2nd Manassas, Fredericksburg, and what many considered his greatest achievement, Chancellorsville.[9]

Lee had three sons, and all would serve in the Confederate army. The eldest, George Washington Custis Lee, attended West Point and served as aide-de-camp for the president of the Confederate states, Jefferson Davis. Lee's second son, William Henry Fitzhugh Lee, commonly known as "Rooney," attended Harvard, where he served as class president. Rooney then followed his father's inclination for mounted service and rose through the Confederate cavalry to command his own brigade. Lee's third son, Robert Jr., was only seventeen when the war broke out. Lacking an advanced education, "Rob" enlisted as a private in the Rockbridge Artillery and served eighteen months as a frontline gunner, seeing some of the heaviest fighting of the war.

In 1863, Robert Sr. secured Rob Jr. a commission in the cavalry. General Lee soon ordered Rob to take his famous horse, Traveller, on a day-long ride to Fredericksburg to help keep the animal in good condition. Remembering his father's prior riding lessons, Rob swung in the saddle with trepidation. "My misgivings were fully realized," recalled Rob, "for Traveller would not walk a step. He took a short high trot—a buck-trot, as compared with a buck-jump, and kept it to Fredericksburg, some thirty miles."[10] Two years of war had not changed his father's ways in the slightest.

∽

The Confederate war plan had always been based on quickly winning the war due to the North's distinct advantage in population, material resources, and manufacturing capacity. In the eastern theater, most all the fighting had occurred in Virginia, and after two years of campaigns, the state's food and forage reserves were critically low.[11] Scurvy flourished in the ranks, and many of Lee's artillery horses died over the winter of 1863, due to short supplies of fodder and grain. The problem became so severe that Lee had to scatter his cavalry and artillery to find them suitable provisions.[12] Until the spring grass renewed, Lee warned Confederate president Jefferson Davis that he could not form his army "for want of proper sustenance and forage."[13]

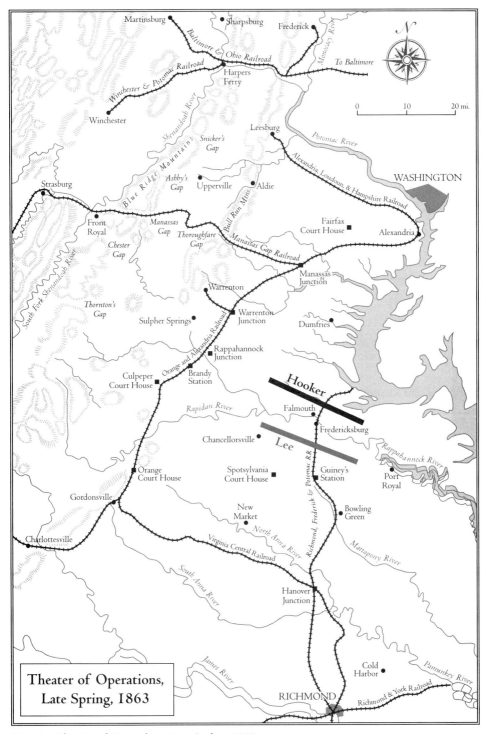

Map 1. Theater of Operations, Late Spring, 1863

Food grew scarce for civilians as well. Inflation ran rampant, and the women of Richmond rioted in the streets, brandishing axes and knives and yelling "Bread! Bread!" and "No more starvation!" Even President Davis couldn't quell the crowd.[14] The state of Virginia needed relief, and Lee petitioned Davis to take the war into Pennsylvania by slipping the Federal lines at Fredericksburg and marching north through the Shenandoah Valley behind the shielding peaks of the Blue Ridge Mountains. Lee's plan went beyond a simple invasion and resembled a raid of necessity; without securing food and horse grains the Army of Northern Virginia would either starve, lose the home front, or possibly both. A deep thrust across the Potomac to the fertile farmland of Maryland and Pennsylvania would also threaten the nation's capital in Washington and hopefully force the Federal army to withdraw from Virginia and protect their own capital in Washington City. Lee could then march up through the Cumberland Valley, collecting the needed supplies and sending them back to Virginia as he went.[15]

Lee had crossed the Potomac once before in 1862 and made rapid gains until a set of orders detailing his troops' whereabouts fell into enemy hands. Forced to cede the initiative, Lee was brought to battle before he could consolidate all his forces and fought the resulting Battle of Sharpsburg. Thousands died on both sides; though the fight ended in a tactical draw, it served as an overwhelming strategic reverse for the Confederates, and Lee retreated back across the Potomac. On Lee's second invasion, he would take extra steps to control the direction and momentum of the campaign and, as a security measure, issue fewer written orders and directives. Once in Pennsylvania, Lee would invite a battle of his choosing and hopefully plant a flag in victory. This might sway Northern opinions at the next election cycle, but the collection of Northern-grown foods and forage was needed straightaway, long before the November elections of 1864. Put simply: without an influx of supplies the Confederacy would soon fail. With an influx of supplies, they could survive the year, and if a crushing win occurred on Northern soil, the Northern population might view the war as unwinnable.[16]

This wasn't the only plan put forth. Others favored boarding the Army of Northern Virginia onto the railroad and shuffling the troops west to break the ongoing siege of Vicksburg, Mississippi. Still others called for moving Confederate troops to middle Tennessee and mounting a deep invasion into Ohio to reverse the course of western Union victories, and compel a Federal retreat in that sector.[17] In the end Lee's proposal won out, and Jefferson Davis gave the go-ahead.

Figure 3.2.   Robert E. Lee aboard his horse, Traveller. *Library of Congress.*

Lee summoned his three corps commanders to meet him in person: lieutenant generals James Longstreet, Richard Ewell, and A. P. Hill.[18] Lee's plan called for Ewell's II Corps to start the advance and move west from Fredericksburg for Culpeper Courthouse, followed by Longstreet's I Corps. A. P. Hill's III Corps would remain at Fredericksburg to keep Federal eyes occupied and hold the Federal forces in place. The three Confederate corps would then take turns entering the Shenandoah Valley, crossing the Potomac, and pushing into Pennsylvania.[19]

Lee's plan was not only a massive undertaking but also a massive risk. The plan required quick-marching seventy thousand men in a series of independent advances to get behind the Blue Ridge and disappear on the far side of the mountains. Lee presumed the Federals would stay east of the mountains to protect Washington from attack, and Lee would then secure the mountain passes leading to the Shenandoah Valley to keep his whereabouts and intentions hidden from the enemy. Once north of the Potomac, Lee would use the South Mountain and Catoctin Ranges of the Appalachians in Maryland and Pennsylvania to shield his march as he collected food and supplies west of the mountains in the Cumberland Valley.[20] Deception would play a key element in Lee's plan, and its origin likely came from a prior campaign.[21]

In June 1862, the Federal Army of the Potomac was driving on the Confederate capital in Richmond, in a slow but steady campaign designed to grind down the Confederate defenses and seize the Southern capital. At the same time, Confederate forces under General Thomas "Stonewall" Jackson advanced north through the Shenandoah Valley, threatening to attack Washington.

Jackson's forces never had the numbers to besiege Washington, D.C., but still loomed as a serious threat to the Federal capitol. However, President Lincoln kept thirty-seven thousand troops near Washington that were originally detailed to move south and support the attack on Richmond, Virginia, and the Federal assault on the Confederate capitol suffered a sharp reduction in personnel.[22] In 1863, Lee again hoped to drain resources away from the main Federal army.[23] By moving his three corps separately, Lee hoped to win the initiative, confuse the Federal response, flank the Army of the Potomac, and force the Federals to retreat and cover Washington.[24]

~

Major General James Ewell Brown Stuart led the cavalry of the Army of Northern Virginia. Known as "Jeb" by his contemporaries, he graduated West Point in 1854, placing thirteenth out of forty-five cadets. While at the academy, he earned a quixotic reputation after entering a fistfight against a much larger cadet. Stuart lost, as all expected, but the tenacity he displayed in the face of long odds appealed to many of his peers and instructors, including the serving superintendent, Robert E. Lee.[25] Lee continued to be impressed by Stuart after his black eyes faded, and he often invited Stuart over for meals with his family, where Stuart fawned hopelessly over Lee's eldest daughter, Mary.

Upon graduation, Stuart served in Texas campaigning against the Apache until he received a promotion to 1st lieutenant in the 1st United States Cavalry.[26] He transferred to Nebraska and took part in the Solomon Fork fight, where the 1st Cavalry made a sabre charge against some three hundred mounted Cheyenne warriors.[27] When the Cheyenne saw the formal line of flashing steel bearing down at a gallop, they turned and bolted across the prairie.[28] In the ensuing chase, Stuart and Lieutenant Lunsford Lomax, a fellow Virginian and West Pointer, spurred forward beyond the rest of their comrades in pursuit of the Cheyenne.[29]

Closing on the trailing warriors, they exchanged fire with a pistol-wielding warrior, but all shots went wide until Stuart charged in with his sabre and delivered a hard cut across the head of the warrior. At the same instant, the warrior pulled the trigger on his pistol.[30] The warrior fell to the deck; however, his shot hit the mark, and the ball struck Stuart in the chest. With both men bleeding profusely, the warrior somehow regained his feet, only to be shot down and killed. Lomax then helped Stuart to the ground, where he rigged a quick lean-to for a bit of shade with a blanket tied to a pair of sabres thrust in the dirt. Luckily for Stuart the bullet deflected on impact, ranged across his rib cage, and lodged between his ribs on the far side of his chest.[31]

While the main column continued on, the wounded stayed behind with some native mercenary scouts. The scouts soon abandoned the wounded, and, left to their own devices, Stuart and the others made a series of forced foot marches for Fort Kearney. The last was a grueling fifty-five-mile trek of dead reckoning led by Stuart with very little water, no compass, and only the stars as a guide. Despite the odds, the wounded reached Fort Kearney, where doctors drained Stuart's still festering wound and judged it nonlethal; he carried the ball between his ribs for the rest of his life. Stuart had excelled in an ordeal where many would have failed, and his reputation soared among his peers.[32]

Stuart grew into an intelligent, athletic officer described as "a middling tall man with a full reddish-brown beard," and one subordinate claimed the quick-witted Stuart "was as full of dash, as he was ambition."[33] Stuart was also

Figure 3.3.   Major General J. E. B. Stuart, the famed *Beau Sabre* of the Confederacy. *Library of Congress.*

vain, cocksure, and still a hopeless romantic: to say Stuart was a fop would be a disservice—Stuart was an extraordinary fop! A jocular, belly-laughing Victorian and first-class narcissist, he loved banjo music and musketeer-styled capes, and he enjoyed such popular sayings as "*Bully!*," "*Good Show!*," and

"*Ole boy!*"[34] Popular with some, disliked by others, Stuart never failed to make an impression on his fellow officers. "I never liked or admired Stuart," said Confederate staff officer Henry Kyd Douglas. "[H]e was vain and pretentious and overrated as a soldier." On the other hand, artillery commander Porter Alexander wrote, "Stuart never seemed to hesitate, or to doubt that he could just crash his way wherever he chose to strike. . . . [He] possessed the rare quality of being always equal to himself at his very best."[35]

Off the field, Stuart reigned as a first-class flirt and greatly enjoyed the company of women—particularly Southern belles. While stationed on the high plains, he married Flora Cooke, a smart and pretty young belle from one of the finest families in Virginia. Flora also happened to be the daughter of Colonel Philip Cooke of the U.S. 2nd Dragoons, a celebrated figure in the frontier military and renowned for publishing his own book on mounted tactics.[36]

At the start of the war, Stuart resigned his commission while his father-in-law remained in the Union. Stuart never looked back. He entered Confederate service and hit the ground running, quickly winning a string of small skirmishes that won him command of the 1st Virginia Cavalry. Where other commanders were flummoxed by the independence of their recruits, Stuart recognized the metal of their spirit and adapted it. "They are pretty good officers now," remarked a wry Stuart. "[A]fter a while they will make excellent soldiers."[37]

At 1st Manassas, Stuart received an order to guard Colonel Thomas J. Jackson's left flank. Riding forward in a column of fours, Stuart stumbled upon an advancing column of enemy infantry.[38] It was a classic meeting engagement, and Stuart, already well within rifle range, could either attack or retreat and suffer a volley. Equally surprised, the Federals rushed to form ranks and fire a volley. Stuart called for sabres and spurred forward, yelling, "On right, into line!" This directed each rank of four to first offset, and fall in on the right of the preceding set, creating a forward-moving column rushing to the front, in "echelon."[39] Quickly closing at the gallop, the Virginians weathered the hurried Federal fire and crashed through the infantry with sabres whipping down to break the Federal ranks and send the survivors fleeing for the rear. A Confederate battery and additional infantry followed Stuart's charge and shored up the Confederate flank. This action allowed Colonel Thomas J. Jackson to go on and earn his battle moniker, "Stonewall" Jackson.

The charge at Manassas gave Stuart a positive reputation, but what truly separated Stuart from other horsemen were his instincts for reconnaissance. Finding the enemy was only the first task; judging the enemy's plans lay at the heart of good reconnaissance: Was the enemy moving his base, or was he merely collecting supplies? If moving west, which route would he take? When would he arrive? Stuart excelled at this ability to divine his enemy's intent.[40] "I know of no one more competent than he to estimate the occurrences before him at their true value," wrote one Confederate field commander, and most others agreed.[41] Stuart might have been a fop—but he was a brilliant horse soldier.

During the Battle of the Seven Days, Stuart volunteered to lead his own reconnaissance beyond the Federal flank and determine the enemy's depth. Many officers would have rebuffed such a forward proposal from a twenty-nine-year-old subordinate, but Lee approved the plan and Stuart departed with twelve hundred troopers.[42] He soon determined the Federal flank lay ripe for attack, but rather than turn back, Stuart chose to loop the Federal army in a 150-mile circuit.[43] Hot on his tail came his own father-in-law, Phillip Cooke, now a brigadier general in the Federal cavalry. Cooke failed to catch his son-in-law as Stuart rode almost unchecked, skirmishing with Federal patrols, mapping enemy positions, dodging Union redoubts, and slashing Federal communications.[44]

Armed with Stuart's intelligence, Lee pushed out of Richmond and battered the Federals in a series of attacks. Southern casualties were horrendous, but Lee's aggressive assaults convinced the Union army they were facing a much larger enemy than actually existed and the Federals quit the campaign. Robert E. Lee received command of all Confederate forces serving in northern Virginia, and Stuart received a promotion to major general.

The reserved Lee and cape-wearing Stuart made an odd pairing but an excellent command team with Stuart repeatedly supplying Lee with accurate, actionable intelligence. In fall 1862, Lee's army sat near Harper's Ferry, while the Federals settled in western Maryland across the Potomac. Eager for intelligence, Lee sent Stuart on a deep raid across the Potomac to determine the footing and intent of the Federals: "You are desired to gain all information of the position, force and probable intention of the enemy which you can."[45] Stuart left with eighteen hundred men and drove north over the Potomac into Maryland. He continued into Pennsylvania, skirted Gettysburg, and dropped back down into Maryland.[46] The speed of the raid caught the Federals flat footed, and Stuart quickly shouldered past the Federal response and recrossed the Potomac, having once again looped the Army of the Potomac.[47] This time he covered 120 miles in three days and captured twelve hundred horses.[48] Stuart's losses were two men wounded. He wrote his wife that "it did me good to run" the Federal cavalry up

Figure 3.4.   A cannon-bearing redoubt overlooking a bridge in Virginia.
Library of Congress.

across the Potomac and back.[49] After debriefing Stuart, Lee judged the Federals were holding in place, and adjusted accordingly.[50]

The following spring at Chancellorsville, troopers from one of Stuart's brigades skirmished with the Federal advance and discovered the Union army had a wide-open flank.[51] Stuart shared the information with Lee and Jackson, and the pair began devising a plan of attack as Stuart's troopers found a route to lead the infantry around the Federal army. The following day twenty-eight thousand men followed Stuart's troopers, and Stonewall Jackson launched his attack in the afternoon, shattering the Union flank and driving the Federals more than a mile through the woods. Confused fighting continued into the night, and Jackson fell to an errant volley of Confederate infantry.[52]

Command of Jackson's II Corps devolved to Stuart, and Stuart continued the assault at dawn, hammering the Federal lines with combined attacks of infantry and artillery as he drove froward from the left, while Lee attacked from the right. The combination proved too much, and the

Federals retreated after a hard series of fights. Stuart had again played a major role in one of Lee's victories, but the death of Stonewall Jackson overshadowed Stuart's performance. Some thought Stuart's performance qualified him to replace Jackson and take command of Lee's II Corps.[53] Nevertheless, it's doubtful General Lee ever considered such a move. Stuart was too valuable as a reconnaissance officer; Lee wanted Stuart out front, screening the way forward and ranging the enemy.

Stuart began assembling his brigades for Lee's northern invasion in late May upon the rich pastures of Culpeper County, Virginia.[54] Sitting halfway between Washington and Richmond, this rustic county east of the Blue Ridge contained railheads running to both capitals, with the Orange and Alexandria Railroad running north for the Federals and the Virginia Central line running south for the Confederates. The Rappahannock River formed the northern border of Culpeper County, and the county held the first two natural fords in the river's rapid course down from the mountains. These elements combined to make Culpeper County an extremely valuable piece of terrain, as well as an excellent point for Lee to stage his army on the march from Fredericksburg to the mountain passes in the Blue Ridge.[55]

By early June, this county again sat in Southern hands as Confederate troops began staging in and around the county seat at Culpeper Court-house. Stuart, never one to pass on an opportunity to dazzle the local ladies, held a ball in the county courthouse on the evening of June 6. The fete had all the trappings of a two-penny novella as Stuart and his officers danced with the local belles beneath the glow of tallow candles perched overhead. The following day, Stuart held a review outside of town, and young women swooned in the crowd as he galloped past. A more stoic reporter judged the performance a "collection of pretty men," and stated, "I have no patience for such Tomfooleries."[56]

~

Stuart had five brigades under his immediate command at Culpeper.[57] Of the five brigade commanders, two were staunch allies, the third was an indifferent acquaintance, and the final two were unwanted.

The first brigadier, Fitzhugh Lee, was a good friend of Stuart's, and the nephew of Robert E. Lee. Short and trending corpulent, "Fitz" Lee became a noted prankster in his days at West Point, where he broke the family mold and graduated near the bottom of his class. Upon graduation, he accepted a commission in the frontier cavalry and saw action against the Comanche Nation on the Texas Prairie. In one instance, Lee found himself locked in a hand-to-hand struggle with a young warrior and, using

Figure 3.5. Brigadier General Fitzhugh Lee, Army of Northern Virginia. Fitz Lee was a close friend of Jeb Stuart. *Library of Congress.*

his considerable bulk, pinned his smaller enemy to the ground and killed him with two shots from his service revolver.[58] It was Fitz Lee's brigade that discovered the open Federal flank at Chancellorsville and screened

Jackson's corps on their flank march. However, Fitz could be superb one day and lagging the next.[59] Luckily, he commanded a solid brigade of veterans: the 1st, 2nd, 3rd, 4th, and 5th Virginia cavalries, plus the 1st Maryland Battalion.[60]

"Rooney" Lee, the second-born son of Robert E. Lee, commanded Stuart's next brigade. Outgoing and daring, Rooney left Harvard University before graduation to join the army and take part in the Utah War of 1857. He resigned his commission after two years and enlisted in the Confederacy in 1861, where he gained command of the 9th Virginia Cavalry. Stuart trusted the outgoing Virginian, and Rooney received his own brigade: the 9th, 10th, and 13th Virginia, plus the 2nd North Carolina Cavalry.[61] Like his cousin Fitz, the Lee name aided Rooney's path to brigade command, and Rooney proved he could hold his own in that position.

Stuart's next brigadier, Wade Hampton III, hailed from South Carolina and came from one of the wealthiest families in the South, with vast holdings of land and slaves. Tall and reserved, he had an erudite air and austere manners, but far from being a dandy, Hampton led from the front and had no qualms about mixing with the enemy in close combat.[62] A distance often existed between Hampton and Stuart, and part of this came down to age. Hampton was forty-five, while Stuart was only thirty, and Stuart's cape-clad antics and boisterous staff of twenty-year-old go-getters must have grated on Hampton's more conservative nature.

These feelings came to a head during the "Christmas Raid" in December 1862 across the Occoquan River. Stuart became frustrated with the intelligence Hampton provided, and Hampton grew angry when Stuart left a portion of Hampton's men in a temporary lurch.[63] Some hard feelings still existed between these two commanders in June 1863; however, Hampton always respected Stuart's rank, and both men trusted one another in the field. Hampton also held one of the strongest brigades in Stuart's command, composed of the 1st North Carolina, 1st and 2nd South Carolina, Cobb Georgia Legion, Phillips Georgia Legion, and the Jeff Davis Legion of Mississippi.[64]

Beverly Robertson was Stuart's fourth brigadier. A graduate of West Point in 1849, Robertson served ten years with the 2nd Dragoons on the American frontier. Robertson also courted Miss Flora Cooke before she married Stuart, and though Stuart won Flora's hand, the two officers remained rivals after the wedding. Outside of this rivalry, Stuart regarded Robertson as being too cautious for cavalry command, and he felt Robertson failed to inspire his men.[65] Stuart had briefly succeeded in having Robertson transferred to North Carolina to train recruits, but to Stuart's

Figure 3.6. Brigadier General Beverly Robertson, Army of Northern Virginia. Beverly Robertson and Jeb Stuart both courted Miss Flora Cooke before the war; Flora married Stuart. *Library of Congress.*

chagrin, Robertson didn't fit in with his commander in North Carolina either. Robertson returned to Virginia like a bad penny, but he brought two fresh cavalry units, the 4th and 5th North Carolina, for use in Lee's upcoming campaign.[66] Stuart happily received the troopers, but he advocated to have Robertson removed from the equation and placed in command of a recuperation camp behind the lines. In classic army parlance, Stuart cited Robertson as "a good disciplinarian" and an "excellent instructor" in his transfer request. Stuart's recommendation yielded no results.[67]

Stuart's fifth brigadier was William "Grumble" Jones, another graduate of West Point. Jones served in the prewar cavalry on the Texas frontier, where he watched his wife drown before his eyes in Matagorda Bay. Jones resigned his commission following his wife's death and returned to his native Virginia.[68] Though Jones was eight years Stuart's senior, his earlier resignation now put him behind Stuart in seniority of rank, a fact Jones forever regretted and often mentioned.[69] Overly frank and infamously profane, Jones often bordered on insubordination with superiors, particularly Stuart, whom Jones insisted on referring to as "that young whippersnapper." The upbeat Stuart disliked Jones's penchant for middling in lower-rank politics, an act Stuart perceived as detrimental to good leadership.[70] Stuart did, however, recognize Jones's superior ability at mounted combat and felt Jones was an excellent outpost officer. Grumble Jones's brigade contained the 6th, 7th, 11th, and 12th Virginia, plus the 35th Virginia Battalion.[71]

This left Stuart's horse gunners, formally known as the "Stuart Horse Artillery Battalion" and commanded by Major Robert Beckham. A native of Virginia, Beckham graduated West Point and first accepted a commission in the U.S. Corps of Engineers before resigning and entering Confederate service. At 1st Manassas, Beckham's battery drove forward in support of Stuart's charge and helped secure Stonewall Jackson's flank. Stuart's prior horse artillery commander, Major John Pelham, had been an exceptional gunner and a close friend of Stuart's before his recent death at Kelly's Ford.[72] Beckham had since replaced Pelham and still served in the former's shadow at the start of the Gettysburg campaign. Beckham's battery commanders were Captain James Breathed, Captain Roger Chew, Captain Wiley Griffin, Captain James Hart, Captain William McGregor, and Captain Marcellus Moorman.[73] Stuart's gunners enjoyed an excellent reputation, and one Confederate officer stated, "If there was any part of Lee's army gamer than the others it was the horse artillery of the cavalry corps."[74]

Stuart also benefited from a wide range of Confederate partisans and scouts specializing in operations behind enemy lines. These units included commissioned Confederate Rangers under John Mosby, as well as scouts from Company H, 4th Virginia Cavalry, known as the Black Horse Troop. In addition to these groups, a collection of hand-picked troopers from the 2nd South Carolina Cavalry, known as the Iron Scouts, operated from within Hampton's brigade.[75] These groups functioned like mounted commandos behind enemy lines, where they scouted Federal positions, attacked dispatch riders, ambushed patrols, and created general mayhem along the roads and railways.

Mosby operated mainly in the western space between the Bull Run Mountains and Washington, DC, while the Iron Scouts operated farther east, below Washington City and stretching south toward Fredericksburg. Most common were "running missions" meant to cover ground on fast horses and gain information on the enemy. Less common incursions centered on planned ambushes and attacking enemy picket posts.[76] Both units benefited from local citizens who gladly fed and housed them, and passed on information. Lee did not limit these operations to the Iron Scouts and Mosby's Rangers; a dispatch from the general records cites similar actions from multiple elements within Grumble Jones's brigade, Rooney Lee's brigade, and other units.[77] This constant harassment kept Federal cavalry commanders on high alert to defend against raids and attacks. It also forced the Federals to double and triple their patrols, which wore down their horses and curbed their ability to launch offensive operations against the enemy.[78]

As Stuart and his troopers turned in on the evening of June 8, they were expecting a busy day the following morning. Stuart and his cavalry would cross the Rappahannock in the morning, drive north through Rixeyville for Front Royal, and set the initial screen for Lee's infantry to march their way to Pennsylvania.[79]

4

THE FEDERALS

Major General Joseph Hooker won command of the Army of the Potomac in January 1863. Born in Massachusetts, Hooker could trace his roots back to his grandfather, who served as a captain in the American Revolutionary War. As a young man, Joseph first attended Hopkins Academy and graduated from West Point in 1837. Hooker's academics were excellent; however, he amassed a large number of demerits for minor infractions, and this dropped his standing to twenty-ninth out of fifty.[1] After graduation, he served in Florida's Seminole Wars as an artillery officer, and then as a staff officer for generals Winfield Scott and Zachary Taylor.

Hooker was good looking, bold in action, and possessed a magnetic personality. During the war with Mexico, he received three separate promotions for gallantry, with the first occurring at the Battle of Monterey during heavy street fighting. "I am under particular obligations to the chief of my staff, Lieutenant J. Hooker," wrote General Thomas Hamer, "[who] has been invaluable to me through the whole campaign; his coolness and self-possession in battle set an example to both officers and men."[2] At the later battle of Natural Bridge, the recently promoted Captain Hooker led two companies of infantry forward through a stream of hostile fire to carry an enemy position.[3] Hooker ended the war with a brevet promotion to lieutenant colonel, having served as a chief of staff for five different general officers.

Following the Mexican War, Hooker resigned his commission and moved to California, where he pursued an unsuccessful attempt at politics and enjoyed a reputation as a hard drinker and a ladies' man. He could also be combative in public affairs and revealed a flaw to his character in that he lost few opportunities to make a new enemy or irritate an old rival when the opportunity presented itself.[4]

Hooker traveled back east at the start of the Civil War and secured command of an infantry brigade through his prior record in the military. Once in the field, he distinguished himself in the Battle of Williamsburg, where he again showed a natural talent for leading men under fire.[5] Hard pressed by a series of Confederate attacks, Hooker ordered his bandsmen to play a tune to keep up morale in the middle of the fight. "Play, damn it! Play 'Yankee Doodle,' or any doodle you can think of!"[6] Three weeks later at Fair Oaks Station, his division fought on the Union left and repulsed two enemy brigades with the bayonet.[7] These performances gained Hooker the moniker "Fighting Joe" by the press, and he became an early hero of the war. Hooker next went on to lead his division at the Battle of Sharpsburg until he was shot in the foot and forced to leave the field.[8]

Hooker then served in the disastrous Federal attack on Fredericksburg, Virginia, under Major General Ambrose Burnside. Hooker's command made fourteen assaults against a prepared Confederate position and suffered massive casualties. Prior to the attacks, Hooker ridiculed Burnside's assault plan and afterward roundly criticized Burnside's actions in a second attempt to move over the Rappahannock against the Rebel army. Hooker clearly crossed the line with these comments, but President Lincoln now held little confidence in Burnside, and Lincoln soon cashiered his leading general and replaced him with the more popular "Fighting Joe."

Hooker rejuvenated the army and lifted its morale as soon as he took command. He passed new regulations improving the conditions in camp, revamped the quality of the soldiers' rations, diminished disease, and improved the overall health of his command.[9] He also curbed desertion and offered pardons to any soldiers who had remained at home past the expiration of their furloughs. Hooker then reordered the Grand Division command structure and returned the army to a more flexible Corps command structure.[10] With these changes made, he turned his attention to the Federal cavalry.[11]

Hooker's chief complaint with the mounted arm stemmed from the fractured use of the Federal cavalry. All armies had rivalries between the varying combat arms, but the Federal infantry and artillery often viewed the cavalry as a mere support arm to picket their supply lines, guard their camps, and run dispatches. This diminished the ability of the Union horsemen to take the fight to the enemy in large numbers and robbed the army of a potentially hard-hitting offensive arm.[12] Hooker meant to change that and reform the cavalry of the Army of the Potomac into its own sovereign corps, and he picked Brigadier General George Stoneman to command his new cavalry.[13]

~

Figure 4.1.   Major General Joseph Hooker, Army of the Potomac. Hooker earned a reputation for drinking alcohol and cavorting with loose women. *Library of Congress.*

Quiet in manner and diligent in action, Stoneman graduated from West Point in 1846, along with his friend and roommate, Thomas "Stonewall" Jackson. Upon graduation, Stoneman accepted a commission in the 1st U.S. Dragoons and saw action in California defending gold miners against the native Pomo Tribe; he later served along the Texas border under Lieutenant Colonel Robert E. Lee in the 2nd U.S. Cavalry.

As spring turned the corner in 1863, Hooker made plans to cross the Rappahannock River and attack Lee's forces near Fredericksburg. Prior to the main attack Hooker wanted Stoneman to take his newly minted Cavalry Corps, cross the Rappahannock and range behind Confederate lines, destroying railroad tracks and cutting Lee's communications with the Confederate capital—all designed to force Stuart to chase after Stoneman and ignore Hooker's main thrust at Lee's infantry.[14] With Stoneman on the loose, Hooker planned to pass around Lee's flank unnoticed while Stuart and his troopers chased after Stoneman.

Instead, Stoneman's raid started with a stumble. Heavy rains lifted the Rappahannock seven feet in twenty-four hours, negating any form of a quick start for Stoneman's new corps. "He has now been out three days," said President Lincoln, "yet he is not twenty-five miles from where he started."[15] Stoneman's raid eventually got under way but continued flooding retarded his efforts at every stream, and many roads remained flooded beyond use. Stoneman's raid gathered no momentum and therefore never created the level of distraction hoped for.[16] The Federal raiders wrecked miles of railroad tracks and burned a host of bridges but accomplished little else other than wrecking their horses in a brutal march through the mud. When Stoneman's command finally made it back to Federal lines, more than 60 percent of his horses were pronounced dead, missing, or unfit for further service.[17] Quartermaster Montgomery Meigs investigated and found the horses had carried too much weight, were not unsaddled or groomed at regular intervals, and suffered from a severe lack of watering and forage. The incredibly high rate of casualties hinted at neglect and drew the chief quartermaster's ridicule: "If we inflicted a proportionate loss on the enemy, he has suffered terribly."[18]

Instead of distracting Stuart and Lee, Stoneman's wretched pace allowed Stuart and extensive portions of his command to stay at Lee's side, and the absence of Stoneman's cavalry gave Lee a distinct advantage, which led to one of the greatest flanking actions in American history. Hooker largely scapegoated his infantry for the Chancellorsville defeat, but in the future, he determined to never again send his cavalry out beyond the range of his operations.[19] George Stoneman then suffered a debilitating bout of hemorrhoids, and Hooker granted him a medical leave. In Stoneman's absence, Hooker made the switch to Brigadier General Alfred Pleasonton.[20]

~

Born in Washington, DC, in 1824, Alfred Pleasonton grew up in the house of a minor celebrity in the State Department. Alfred's father, Stephen Pleasonton, saved the original copies of the Declaration of Independence and the Constitution from British capture during the War of 1812. For this meritorious act, Stephen Pleasonton earned a promotion to the Treasury office, and his sons all received appointments to the United States Military College at West Point.

Alfred Pleasonton graduated West Point in 1844, where he ranked seven out of twenty-five cadets. He accepted a commission in the U.S. Dragoons and saw his first action at Resaca de la Palma in the war with Mexico. The American infantry was encountering stiff resistance when Captain Charles May's 2nd Dragoons received orders to charge a line of Mexican cannons. "We charged entirely through the enemy's batteries of seven pieces . . . Lieutenants Winslip and Pleasonton leading the charge against the pieces on the left of the road. . . . The charge was made under a heavy fire . . . and gained the rising ground on the opposite side of the ravine."[21] Pleasonton and the dragoons boiled over the enemy guns, but their momentum carried them too far and they suffered a volley from the Mexican infantry. The charge, however, seized the initiative and screened the approach of the American infantry on the Mexican line. The Americans carried the position, and the Mexican army retreated into the chaparral. The dragoons then gave chase, cutting down the fleeing Mexican soldiers and creating a rout.[22] Pleasonton received a promotion to 1st lieutenant for gallant and meritorious service.

Captain May later drew criticism from his commanding officer for not directing the charge in a more efficient manner, but May countered with a successful campaign in the press where he took credit for capturing a Mexican officer that May's bugler actually corralled. May then received a promotion to lieutenant colonel due as much, if not more, to his writing than his actions. These exchanges may well have affected Pleasonton in his later career.

Following the Mexican War, Pleasonton served on the American high plains with the 2nd Dragoons. He took part in a number of campaigns against various Lakota tribes where he found his niche as an able administrator. The year 1861 found Pleasonton serving as a comfortable, thirty-seven-year-old captain in the 2nd Dragoons, as well as acting assistant adjutant-general of the regiment. When the war broke out, Pleasonton sensed an opportunity and marched his command straight across the plains to the gates of Washington.[23] If nothing else, Captain Pleasonton proved he had a fine sense of timing and poise. Shortly after his arrival, he won a promotion to major in the regular army.

Pleasonton next secured a position on General George McClellan's staff during the Peninsula campaign and quickly gained notice for his professional manner and confident swagger. When the Federal cavalry was floundering, and Stuart's troopers were riding rings around the army, Pleasonton projected nothing but perfect self-assurance. Smart, polished, and professional, Pleasonton thrived at headquarters, and most officers simply wanted to believe what he had to say. He also showed a good eye for ground and helped secure a base of operations on the James River during the campaign. This performance, plus his apparent drive and ambition, won Pleasonton a promotion to brigadier general in July 1862.

In the following Maryland campaign, the Confederates crossed the Potomac in early September, and Pleasonton first entered a checkered performance as he scouted the enemy and bombarded headquarters with a constant stream of fluctuating reports that read more like simple hearsay than gathered intelligence or reconnaissance.[24] Days later on September 8, Pleasonton's 3rd Indiana and 8th Illinois skirmished sharply with Stuart's cavalry at Poolesville, Maryland. The next day at Monocacy Church, Pleasonton drove the Confederates some distance and directed his troopers in several successful sabre fights.[25] On September 13, Pleasonton led his troopers forward along with his horse artillery, and pushed Stuart's screen up into Turner's Gap in South Mountain, where Pleasonton managed to secure a foothold before the mountain pass. The following day Pleasonton helped direct the advance of the Federal infantry.[26]

Pleasonton never actually cracked Stuart's screen, but his troopers acted as light cavalry should and maintained contact with the enemy until the infantry arrived to do the heavy lifting. Federal forces then pierced the Confederate line in a hard fight on September 14. The following morning Pleasonton again pressed the retreating enemy. "I started in pursuit of the enemy with a part of the Eighth Illinois Cavalry. The advance came up with the enemy's rear guard of cavalry on entering Boonsborough, charged them repeatedly, and drove them some 2 miles beyond the town."[27] At the Battle of Sharpsburg, Pleasonton supported Major General Edwin Sumner by advancing his skirmishers on foot and bringing a horse battery into play. The gunners swept the enemy clear with close blasts of canister, allowing additional artillery to come up and secure the line. Pleasonton then helped

Figure 4.2. Brigadier General Alfred Pleasonton, Army of the Potomac. Pleasonton was a capable officer and cunning politician. *Library of Congress.*

guide the fire of some eighteen guns, which beat back a Confederate attack threatening the Federal line.[28]

This proved Pleasonton could fight when he needed to. He just had a tendency to avoid a clash if unnecessary—especially if it might harm his reputation. A career officer from West Point, Pleasonton knew an officer could go far in life with success on the battlefield, and he also knew that the same officer's opportunities might well vanish with a defeat. Pleasonton was hardly alone in protecting the flanks of his career. Throughout history, many officers have used conflicts as stepping stones and still do. Pleasonton did indeed serve his country, but he also served himself and the image of himself. In this vein, he kept his mustache waxed, favored short-crowned straw hats known as skimmers, and liked jackboots and kid leather gloves. Eating hardtack and sleeping in the mud held little appeal for Pleasonton. Instead, he favored staff tents with tables, cooks, and servers.[29]

Following the Battle of Sharpsburg, the two armies sat idle, and Pleasonton dutifully pressed across the Potomac to feel out the enemy lines and sweep up hundreds of Confederate prisoners—most of whom were wounded and recuperating in civilian homes.[30] This was classic Pleasonton. He judged the wind, made an advance, reaped the rewards, and wrote a flattering after-action account. His luck changed in October 1862, when Lee sent Stuart on his Chambersburg raid into Pennsylvania. Pleasonton responded with a flurry of orders and hard marching but, in the end, failed to attack Stuart's rear guard as it slipped back over the Potomac.[31] Pleasonton then blamed George Stoneman for not covering the ford and bottlenecking Stuart. Stoneman wasn't having it; he called Pleasonton's claims ridiculous and demanded a court of inquiry.[32] The court of inquiry never materialized, but Pleasonton suffered considerable criticism for his tepid performance in pursuing Stuart, and he also made a lasting enemy in George Stoneman.

As always, Pleasonton landed on his feet. Following Stuart's raid, the Federal army crossed the Potomac into Virginia, and Lee countered by moving south through the Shenandoah Valley. Ordered out after the Rebels, Pleasonton soon ran into Stuart's screen of cavalry in the Loudoun Valley, and the fighting quickly came to a head around the hamlets of Philomont and Union, where Pleasonton and Stuart traded a series of heavy blows at the foot of the Blue Ridge Mountains. "Please direct that Pennington's battery be furnished with 1,200 rounds of ammunition as soon as possible. He is nearly out. Stuart brought up a fresh battery this afternoon, and we had considerable firing before he drew off." Adroitly wielding gunners and troopers in tandem, Pleasonton drove Stuart back to the mountain passes but failed to break the enemy line and reach Lee on the far side of the mountains.[33] Still, this performance patched up Pleasonton's standing and once again proved he could ably direct troops in the field. Pleasonton wasn't a coward; he was a career soldier who wanted to make it home for Christmas—hopefully with a promotion in rank.

Pleasonton also excelled as a writer, particularly in his after-action reports. All officers hedged their reports, but Pleasonton's reports were often outrageous and lacking in detail to camouflage his shortcomings.[34] A case in point came when Lee turned Hooker's flank at Chancellorsville. Pleasonton was still at odds with Stoneman, and therefore Pleasonton's division remained with Hooker's infantry while Stoneman departed on his raid across the Rappahannock with the lion's share of the Federal cavalry. Following the Confederate flank attack, and with Hooker's line still collapsing at dusk, Pleasonton ordered a charge from the 8th Pennsylvania Cavalry to slow the enemy in his front, and then formed a gun line from multiple batteries to meet the Rebel advance. The guns checked the Rebel advance in his portion of the field, and Pleasonton summed up his actions with a dramatic flair: "Such was the fight. . . . Artillery against infantry at 300 yards; the infantry in the woods, the artillery in the clearing. War presents many anomalies, but few so curious and strange in its results as this."[35]

In the fading light and surrounding panic, the enemy force Pleasonton checked was misidentified as Jackson's entire corps, and Pleasonton saw no reason to dispute the illusion. Several Federal officers questioned Pleasonton's report, but in the wake of the devastating loss at Chancellorsville, "Fighting Joe" Hooker needed to find something positive to lean on. When Abraham Lincoln came to the front to visit his field commander, Hooker introduced Pleasonton to the president as the officer who'd saved the Federal army from destruction.[36] Pleasonton did not bother to correct his commander. On May 22, Brigadier General Alfred Pleasonton received the appointment to lead the Cavalry Corps of the Army of the Potomac.[37]

~

On paper, Pleasonton's new corps made quite an impression with seven brigades parsed into three divisions for a grand total of fifteen thousand troopers.[38] In reality, the corps suffered drastically for want of horses, having lost some six thousand mounts in the Chancellorsville campaign. This obviously needed correcting and demanded prompt attention. Less than a week after Pleasonton took command, Army Quartermaster Meigs wrote, "I am using every exertion to procure [horses]. . . . [T]hey are beginning to come in."[39] Despite Meigs's reassurances, Pleasonton's corps had to play catch-up with remounts, and many of Pleasonton's units would arrive on the field astride green horses with only a day or two of service. Moreover, the Federal cavalry lacked its own positive identity, and despite winning a few engagements, it still suffered from a general lack of self-belief. It did, however, have some excellent field officers, and one of their best was a rough-hewn general from Kentucky, named John Buford.

Buford commanded the first of three divisions in Pleasonton's corps. He graduated from West Point in 1848 and served in the U.S. 2nd Dragoons with Alfred Pleasonton, where the pair hunted buffalo together on the high plains.[40] Buford, however, came cut from a different cloth than Pleasonton. Known to his men as "Honest John," Buford dressed plainly, preferring corduroy trousers, hickory shirts, and old field blouses to tailored uniforms and gleaming buttons.[41] "He don't put on as much style as most officers," remembered a trooper from Illinois, but he's "always on hand when there is fighting to be done."[42] Buford first saw combat against the Brulé Lakotas at the Battle of Blue Water Creek in 1855. The battle opened with a rifle volley that put the native camp in full flight; the 2nd Dragoons then gave chase for several miles, sabreing and shooting the survivors. Some seventy Lakotas were killed and one hundred wounded—many of them women and children. This showed war in its full, brutal reality, and Buford came away with a sobering glimpse of combat that erased all the romance often attached to warfare.[43]

Buford returned to Washington at the start of the war but could only allocate a staff position at the capital. He endured this post for several months until awarded a brigade of cavalry where he quickly came into his own. Many commanders pointed their men into combat, but few, like Buford, actually led them.[44] During the 2nd Manassas campaign of 1862, Buford's dismounted troopers helped fight the Confederate advance to a lengthy standstill at Thoroughfare Gap prior to the main battle.[45] Two days later, Buford covered the Federal retreat at Lewis Ford, where his brigade met a sweeping charge of Confederate cavalry. The Rebel attack generated initial success but the Confederates spurred up to a sprint from too great a distance and lost their formation as they closed on the main Federal body.[46] Buford's troopers from the 1st Michigan and 4th New York held their ranks, closed up in their charge, and broke through the loosening Confederate ranks. A sprawling sabre melee broke out across the field, with the Federals quickly gaining the advantage. "Our men charged upon the enemy with sabres only," recalled the commander of the 4th New York. "Throughout the entire affair my men behaved with the greatest coolness and gallantry."[47]

Two additional Southern regiments then rolled forward and plowed into Buford's troopers. The lines mixed, with the Rebels pouring out "a

Figure 4.3. Brigadier General John Buford, Army of the Potomac. An outstanding commander and horse soldier, Buford was also revered by his men.
Library of Congress.

hot fire from their revolvers, carbines &c."[48] Buford was struck on the knee, and his staff scattered; the fight eventually tilted in favor of the Confederates, and the Federals retired after a hard fight.[49] Yet despite the loss, the Federals could hold their heads high, knowing they had given as well as they'd got and briefly given even better than they'd received.[50] Buford had made his mark and earned his men's trust in mounted combat.[51]

Colonel Alfred Duffié commanded Pleasonton's 2nd Division. A native Parisian, Duffié served in both the French 6th Dragoons and 3rd Hussars and fought in the Crimean War. Lieutenant Duffié then deserted the French army and fled to New York with Miss Martha Ann Pelton, the daughter of a wealthy American shoe manufacturer, whom Duffié married soon after his arrival. Duffié spun an impressive web of lies about his war record, received a commission, and with his prior experience quickly rose to command the 1st Rhode Island Cavalry. "You no like me now," Duffié told his new command. "[Y]ou like me bye and bye."[52] His prediction proved correct as his men quickly mastered the drill under the French veteran. He spoke fractured English and filled in the voids with a host of accented expletives, which caused his troopers to affectionately call him a "bully little cuss."[53] Duffié performed well at Kelly's Ford in March 1863, leading his brigade in a series of charges against Fitz Lee's veterans.[54] Regarded as one of the best drill masters in the Federal cavalry, Duffié soon gained command of a cavalry division in the Federal reorganization following the Battle of Chancellorsville.

Pleasonton's 3rd Division fell under the command of Brigadier General David McMurtrie Gregg. Gregg graduated from West Point in 1855 and received his baptism of fire at the Battle of Tohotonimme. Commanding H Troop, 1st Dragoons, Gregg and four other companies engaged one thousand combined warriors from the Spokane, Palouse, Coeur d'Alene, and Yakama nations. The outnumbered dragoons fought a running battle; Lieutenant Gregg gained notice by first charging into the enemy, and he again distinguished himself in a breakout that evening.[55] At the start of the war, Gregg's experience quickly became apparent, and his family relations to the governor of Pennsylvania no doubt aided his promotion to command the 8th Pennsylvania Cavalry. Tall, extremely reserved, and popular with his troops, Gregg shunned the limelight and avoided both reporters and headlines. He did, however, prove to be a capable officer and showed a remarkable steadiness under fire.

On one occasion, enemy shells ripped up the ground about Gregg and his escort, and Gregg calmly trotted away as his companions sprinted past, lashing their horses for all they were worth. "Be calm, gentlemen," decried

Figure 4.4.　Brigadier General David M. Gregg, Army of the Potomac. Gregg was quiet, professional, and resolute in action. *Library of Congress.*

Gregg. "No occasion for haste!"[56] Gregg performed well during the Peninsula campaign of 1862 and again rendered steady service in the fall of that year opposite Stuart's cavalry.[57] A fellow officer wrote, "His modesty kept him from the notoriety that many gained through the newspapers; but in the army, the testimony of all officers who knew him was the same. Brave, prudent, dashing when occasion required dash, and firm as a rock."[58]

∽

By June 1863, General Hooker wanted his new cavalry corps to investigate reports of Confederate cavalry massing in and around Culpeper. Reports from Colonel George Sharpe's Intelligence Bureau predicted a Confederate assault would move north through the Shenandoah Valley against Winchester, and Stuart's cavalry would steal a march in league with this assault.[59] Other sources claimed Stuart's cavalry had massed at Culpeper to prepare for launching a great raid—but only to screen Lee's infantry onto rail cars bound for Mississippi to break the siege at Vicksburg.[60] There was even a Federal report dated May 20, 1863, where a Union operative in Virginia stated, "[H]e saw in Richmond a large number of our [Federal] coats, cleaned and [hanging] on a line to dry. There is a body of 1,500 picked cavalry intended for our uniforms and the countersign they expect to get from a disloyal [Union] colonel; they are to enter our lines, come into Washington and seize Mr. Lincoln and Secretary Seward and Stanton."[61] Rumors flew in all directions as soldiers and civilians alike braced for the next Confederate move. Most all Federals agreed on one thing: Stuart's cavalry would be key to any move Lee would take, and this prompted Hooker to draft a new set of orders. The cavalry corps would launch a massive reconnaissance in force on Culpeper, Virginia where Union spies reported Stuart was assembling his mounted brigades and artillery.[62]

Pleasonton would steal forward in two wings and attack at dawn.[63] One division under Buford would cross the Rappahannock at Beverly's Ford, while two more divisions under General Gregg would cross downstream at Kelly's Ford. Both Buford's and Gregg's wings would have a brigade of infantry attached to help alleviate the prior loss of horses in Stoneman's Raid, along with sufficient artillery in support. The two wings would advance separate of one another, rejoin at Brandy Station, and drive on for the county seat of Culpeper with orders to "disperse and destroy the rebel force assembled near Culpeper, and destroy his trains and supplies of all description to the utmost of your ability."[64]

Pleasonton and his cavalry corps were about to take the war in an entirely new direction.

5

THE ATTACK AT BEVERLY FORD

John Buford struck a match in the early morning darkness, drew on his pipe, and nudged his horse through the Union ranks above Beverly Ford. Buford's 1st Division bivouacked above the Rappahannock River the night before, having marched from Warrenton and then camped without fires in range of the ford. The troopers rose quietly, foregoing the typical morning bugles, and were soon staging by squadrons above the ford along the narrow road leading to the river. Buford didn't give fiery speeches or launch flame-throwing dialogues. He lifted his men's morale just by being at their side, and for the men of the 1st Division, having John Buford at your side was enough. Corporals counted files, sergeants shuffled sections, and letters passed between friends—letters to be sent home "in case anything should occur."[1]

Colonel "Grimes" Davis's 1st Brigade would lead the attack. Davis was a former captain of the frontier 1st Dragoons and a veteran of the Apache Wars. Despite having three brothers fighting for the Confederacy, Davis kept his Federal commission, shunned his brothers' politics, and remained with the Union. In September 1862, when Confederate forces were surrounding the Federal arsenal at Harper's Ferry, Davis refused to surrender and cut his way free by leading two regiments out through enemy lines.[2] Now, on the early morning of June 9, he brought his 8th New York Cavalry to the bank of the Rappahannock in a column of fours. Fog rolled over the river, and water could be heard rushing over a fish dam upstream. All else seemed quiet in the gathering dawn.[3] Corporals made a final count at the water's edge, and then came the hushed command to draw sabres; seconds later the horses bounded into the river.[4]

Guarding the south bank of the ford were two vedettes from the 6th Virginia Cavalry. The fog on the river and sound of water falling over the dam hid the Federal approach until the vedettes heard the horses strike the river. Bolting up, they sprinted for the rear while firing their revolvers in the air as a warning to the main picket.[5] Captain Bruce Gibson heard the shots and roused the rest of the picket above the river's bank.[6]

As the New Yorkers charged from the fog, the Virginians opened fire, killing Lieutenant Henry Cutler of the 8th New York and disrupting the Federal attack.[7] Gibson's men then sprinted back to join the main guard post on the Beverly Ford Road. They paused here, placing sharpshooters behind makeshift barricades and waiting to see if the Federals kept coming.[8] It proved a brief wait as the 8th New York rallied and spurred forward. The Rebels resumed firing, but Davis and his Federals kept coming, forcing Gibson to mount his command and spur for the rear as Federal bullets whistled through the air. Though brief, this sharp tempest stirred the camp of the 6th Virginia, whose horses "had been turned out unsaddled to graze. . . . It was with some effort that Major Flournoy was able to mount about 150 men and rush back to hold the enemy."[9]

Colonel Davis dashed up the road in pursuit of Gibson's picket, urging the column ahead against any mounting counterattack. Well known for his strict discipline and aggressive nature, Davis remained true to form and kept his men moving as dawn broke and the Confederates scrambled to assemble in the distance. The funneling ditches and thick woods bordering the road now allowed the outnumbered Virginians to rush up in quick formed columns that stunned the pressing Federals. Though smaller in depth, the Rebel columns were equal in frontage on the narrow roadbed, and the piecemeal assaults staggered the head of the larger Federal column and contained the Yankees' advance.[10] Horses slammed together, pistols cracked point-blank, and sabres screeched and scraped as the two sides clashed, reformed, and clashed again in brief combats for control of the road.

Lieutenant Robert Allen of the 6th Virginia pulled back into the trees following one of these narrow exchanges, where he noted a high-ranking Union officer charging forward from the Federal column. Allen spurred forward at the officer, ducked a vicious sabre cut, and fired the last load in his revolver.[11] The shot struck the Federal officer in the head, and Lieutenant Allen spurred clear without looking back. Colonel Davis dropped from his saddle and died moments later.[12]

∿

Blunt, bitter, and ornery were three of Grumble Jones's better personality traits. The gunfire coming from the ford sounded louder than any picket skirmish and kept rolling closer and closer to his unsaddled brigade. Worse still, Stuart's Horse Artillery lay camped between Jones's men and the river.

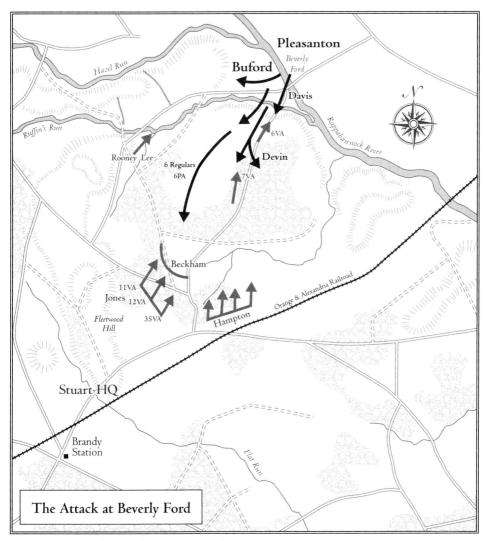

Map 2.   The Attack at Beverly Ford

If Jones didn't act quickly, the unknown Federal force might sweep over the Rebel artillery park any minute. Grabbing a horse, he swung in the saddle without coat or hat and headed for the fight, all the while yelling orders laced in high-pitched, rapid-fire expletives.[13]

Battery Captain James Hart hitched his guns as the Federal cavalry rode into view. Like the other gunners, Hart awoke to a mass panic with riders galloping past, carbines cracking in the woods, and bullets thrumming through camp. The gunners responded with their revolvers, and Hart pointed two guns from his battery into the attack. Major Robert Beckham then ordered Hart's two guns to buy time for the rest of the batteries to retire. Loading canister, Hart's gunners began blasting away at the head of the Federal column, while Beckham guided his other batteries beyond range of the Union attack.[14] At this point, Grumble Jones arrived with some troopers and ordered Hart's guns off the road. Hart refused, claiming he had orders to remain in the road, and the Federals were too many for Jones and his near troopers to reverse. Jones acquiesced, reformed, and took his men around the artillery before spurring straight ahead at the Federals. "Jones pushed around the guns and charged down the road," wrote Hart afterward, "but in less than two minutes was driven [back]."[15] Hart's gunners then opened with canister to keep the Federals at bay, with the drivers galloping forward and dragging the pieces back by *prolonge*, a quick technique of dragging the guns short distances with the prolonge rope, then firing in turn as the guns leapfrogged down the road to join Major Beckham and the rest of the artillery.[16]

With Davis down, and the Rebel guns retiring, the Federal attack slowed, reformed, and redressed for the next push, the advance passing to the next regiments in line, the 8th Illinois and 3rd Indiana. The 3rd Indiana now pressed into the swirling Confederates, whose numbers were increasing by the minute as more and more of Jones's men arrived. Major William McClure of the 3rd Indiana pitched forward against the Rebels and guided the Federal advance into the enemy horsemen with steady charges and repeated volleys of revolver fire. The Hoosiers drove the Confederates for a half mile and more, eventually gaining a wider section of road bordered by thinning pinewoods that allowed the Federal squadrons to spread to the west side of the roadbed.[17]

As McClure's troopers ranged forward, they ran into Southern reinforcements from the 7th Virginia Cavalry. Originally formed around Turner Ashby's Valley Cavalry, the veteran 7th pitched into McClure's right with a sharp charge through the open pines before falling back through the trees.[18] McClure's men counterattacked and drove ahead in the attack's wake, only to come under a blistering fire from dismounted sharpshooters posted behind a low stone fence running through the pines. Unbeknownst to the Federals, the Virginians had used their earlier charge to screen the deployment of additional men behind this fence, and these Rebel sharpshooters now emptied several Federal saddles with their carbines.[19] As one Federal recalled, "We drove the rebels back for a ways and took some prisoners. Then the rebels were reinforced, and drove us back."[20] This action again stalled the Union advance and a squadron of the 8th Illinois dismounted, sent their horses to the rear, and moved forward to continue the fight on foot.[21]

Colonel Thomas Devin commanded the 2nd Brigade of Buford's 1st Division. A former house painter from New York, Devin was born to Irish parents and turned a simple paint and varnish business into a distribution guild. He joined the mounted militia before the war, studied everything he could find on cavalry, and held the rank of lieutenant colonel in the state militia when the war began. Once in combat the self-taught Devin proved steady under fire: "Col. Devin knew how to take his men into action and also how to bring them out."[22] Upon reaching the fighting along the ford road, Devin dismounted additional squadrons and started establishing communications with General Buford as he prepared to make another advance.

Moving cavalry through wooded terrain required more than just waving a sword. Officers wrote orders and handed them to couriers, and the couriers fanned out in search of the right squadrons and battalions. Once a squadron was located, files needed recounting and ranks needed squaring, so men and mounts maintained their order and arrived ready to engage. Just the size of the horses created a space problem in the woods along the Beverly Ford Road. The average horse is 10 feet long from nose to croup, and 3.5 feet wide from knee to knee with rider aboard. Therefore, the space required to stage a single 128-man squadron in a column of fours required a footprint 14 feet wide by 384 feet long—not including officers.[23] That much space wasn't easy to find in a wooded environment, and officers had to adapt on the fly yet still maintain order to preserve any semblance of military effectiveness.

If called to dismount and fight on foot, the squadron counted off by fours; three men dismounted, linked their mounts' leads, and handed them to the number four who remained mounted. The number fours turned about and led the mounts to the rear so the next available squadron could move up, take the same ground, and wait as a mounted reserve for the skirmishers. In the meantime, the dismounted men readied their carbines and formed into foot platoons. This all occurred while stray bullets thrummed through trees, wounded men walked back to the rear, and loose horses charged through the woods in wild bursts of fear-fueled adrenaline that would flatten anyone standing in their path.

Devin remained composed through it all and directed traffic as the firing continued to escalate and a horse was shot beneath him.[24] Gaining another mount, he extended sharpshooters to either side of the road in conjunction with Major McClure, deployed two guns from Lieutenant Albert

Figure 5.1. Colonel Thomas C. Devin, Army of the Potomac. A civilian prior to the war, Devin joined the state militia and ardently studied everything he could find on cavalry. *Library of Congress.*

Vincent's 2nd U.S. Artillery, and began spreading troopers west from the Beverly Ford Road to link with Buford, who was now working to extend the Federal line to their right and secure the ford with troops from his Regulars Brigade.[25]

By now General Pleasonton had crossed the Rappahannock along with the rest of Buford's wing. He checked his watch and his frustration grew; the sun had been up for almost two hours, yet the column had barely advanced a mile past the river. His intelligence reports had clearly been in error; the Confederate cavalry had camped at the river rather than Culpeper Courthouse, and perhaps more enemy cavalry were headed his way. Worse still, General Gregg's wing had suffered a delay, and Pleasonton had yet to hear a single shot from Kelly's Ford. Pleasonton penned the following dispatch to a courier and had it wired to headquarters: "The enemy is in strong cavalry force here. We have had a severe fight."[26]

June 9 would prove to be a very long day for the new corps commander.

~

As the Federals shored up their lines, Major Beckham fell back with his Confederate batteries and created an artillery perimeter around St. James Church, a small country chapel two miles from the Rappahannock. The church sat close to the Beverly Ford Road; it overlooked an open field resembling a large bowl almost a half mile across and ringed with trees, with the church perched on the southern edge of the bowl, farthest from the Federal advance. Beckham knew good ground when he found it and began laying his guns along the southern edge of the field to create a crescent-shaped line just forward of the church.[27] As Beckham formed his guns, Grumble Jones brought up the 11th and 12th Virginia, plus the 35th Virginia Battalion, and placed them in support of Beckham's position. As Jones deployed, Wade Hampton also arrived with his brigade of Carolinians, Georgians, and Mississippians and formed his men east of the ford road.[28]

While the Confederates took their positions, Buford, Devin, and Pleasonton continued extending the Federal line out from the river and used General Adelbert Ames's infantry to form a bridge between Buford on the Federal right and Devin on the road.[29] The 1st Division and Ames's infantry now formed a broad line stretching across the road about a mile from the river and rolled back in a western arc to rest on the Hazel River just upstream from its confluence with the Rappahannock. Upon completing this line, the Federals began receiving an increase of fire along the road from Hampton's Confederates and Beckham's guns at St. James. To counter the threat, Buford ordered the Regulars Brigade to press forward west of the road, pass unseen through the dense woods, and attack the Confederate left.[30]

Commanded by Major Charles Whiting, the Regulars Brigade was unique, and composed primarily of regular army units: the 1st U.S., 2nd U.S., 5th U.S., and 6th U.S., plus one state volunteer regiment, the 6th Pennsylvania.[31] With the sun now breaking through the trees, the Regulars formed a column and marched forward. Unknown to Buford, Pleasonton was also feeding troops and guns forward to meet the mounting Confederate presence east of the road. As the Regulars moved forward, a courier found the column in motion and delivered a set of orders for the 2nd U.S. Cavalry. The new orders came from Pleasonton, who didn't know the 2nd Regulars were under separate orders; the new set directed the 2nd U.S. to report back to Pleasonton and support an advancing artillery battery. Unfortunately, the 1st U.S. still sat on picket duty north of the Rappahannock River, and the 5th U.S. was already supporting another battery. This meant only the 6th Pennsylvania and the 6th U.S. moved forward to make the charge on the enemy guns at St. James.[32]

Unfazed, the 6th Pennsylvania's commander, Major Robert Morris, kept going.[33] His column snaked through the heavy woods, causing the lengthy formation to get strung out, particularly the 6th U.S., who fell far behind Morris's Pennsylvania volunteers. Morris continued on, and his vedette soon found the edge of a clearing and halted in the shadows of the trees on the northern lip of the bowl. From here, the clearing dropped away and rose back to the church on the far side. Though largely free of trees, a creek crisscrossed the open bowl and gave way to a daunting crescent of Rebel batteries perched on the southern rim. As if divining the scouts' mission, the Rebel gunners opened fire, ranging the tree line and driving the vedette back into the woods, where they reported to Major Morris.[34]

Morris sent one company forward as skirmishers and followed with his remaining squadrons in columns of fours. The trailing 6th U.S. would follow Morris and offset to the left, en echelon.[35] The Pennsylvanians advanced through the cloaking woods with sabers drawn, "expecting each moment to hear the thunder of artillery."[36] When they reached the clearing, they spotted a skirmish line of Confederate cavalry headed their way. The leading Pennsylvanians dropped their sabres by the sword knots and swept up their carbines.[37]

~

Grumble Jones scanned the woods from the far side of the bowl. Earlier, Beckham's gunners had ranged the far tree line and driven off a handful of Federals, prompting Jones to make a reconnaissance of his own.[38] He sent a battalion of the 11th Virginia pressing into the woods beyond the bowl on the far Confederate left and ordered a separate squadron of the 12th Virginia to ride across the clearing for the far trees.[39] Captain Charles O'Ferrall of the 12th Virginia led his squadron forward in skirmish order, with six paces between the files and all going at a trot. O'Ferrall almost reached the tree line when the woods in his front erupted in a volley, dropping men and horses alike. "They let drive a galling fire, checking my advance, and killing and wounding several of my men and horses." After firing their volley, the Federals dropped their carbines by the hooks, snapped their sabres in hand, and spurred forward from the trees, "as thick as angry bees from a hive."[40] The Pennsylvanians slashed through O'Ferrall's squadron and scattered them in all directions.

Beckham's gunners now opened fire at the blue coats charging from the trees. Major Morris exited the woods at a canter in a column four troopers wide, and now needed to form a column of squadrons sixty-four men wide and two ranks deep to spread the enemy fire and best make the assault on the enemy guns. Moving at a canter, or military gallop of three hundred yards a minute, the front ranks first had to advance thirty paces, then check down to a slower trot to allow the rear ranks to clear the trees, catch up, and create a squadron front.[41] This was no simple thing to do on a parade field; to do it under artillery fire, when every instinct in men and horses screamed to sprint straight ahead, made it exponentially more difficult. On a parade field it took fifty seconds to complete the maneuver, and Poinsett's manual stressed that "the rapidity of the gaits should be increased only under extraordinary circumstances."[42] No one timed the maneuver on the day of the battle, but the 6th Pennsylvania seemed to have accomplished the task well below the allotted regulation time. "The wildest enthusiasm has seized our men," wrote one of their officers, "and at the full speed of their horses they dash forward."[43] To the men of the 6th Pennsylvania, enemy artillery fire clearly fell under "extraordinary circumstances."[44]

Southern shells streaked through the air, and Pennsylvania sergeants were bawling at the men to keep their dressings when the Federals encountered a second obstacle—a series of hidden ditches running across the bowl beneath the tall grass. The troopers vaulted the ditches with varying success as the enemy guns kept plowing shrapnel and shell through their ranks. "Never rode troopers more gallantly," recalled Captain Hart of the Southern horse artillery, but as the Pennsylvanians closed in, the Rebels reloaded with canister to separate the gallant Yankees from their saddles.[45] As the Confederates prepared to fire, the 6th Pennsylvania received a respite from unexpected quarters.

Figure 5.2.   Company 1, 6th Pennsylvania Cavalry, Army of the Potomac. Originally issued lances, the 6th Pennsylvania Cavalry was reequipped with breech-loading carbines prior to fighting at Beverly Ford. *Library of Congress.*

Upon seeing O'Ferrall's squadron of skirmishers run over, Grumble Jones ordered additional Rebel troops to charge forward in support. In the time it took these troops to come up, the Pennsylvanians had begun their charge on the guns and were now closing the distance when a single squadron of Lieutenant Colonel Elijah White's 35th Virginia Battalion spurred forward with their high-pitched hoops and yells that would soon earn them their Comanches moniker.[46] Gunner George Neese of Chew's battery wrote, "When within two hundred yards of us and the guns about to use canister, Lt. Col. White, commanding a small detachment of Virginia cavalry, led his force between our guns and the enemy. . . . Our fire ceased instantly."[47] In their rush to support O'Ferrall's squadron, White's troopers prevented the Rebel gunners from firing on the 6th Pennsylvania at the critical range of two hundred yards—the crossfire killing zone created by Beckham's crescent-lined batteries.

This godsend allowed the Pennsylvanians to shove White's men aside and roll on to the very mouths of the guns. After White's 35th Battalion, however, came squadrons of the 11th Virginia, followed closely by elements of the 12th Virginia, and both pitched headlong into the 6th Pennsylvania's right flank, driving the Federals sideways across the field toward a far Rebel battery that now opened at point-blank range.[48] The

Federals swerved clear of the guns, only to be pinned on the tree line by the Virginians. Jones's men were about to bag the entire 6th Pennsylvania when four squadrons of the trailing 6th U.S. Cavalry arrived at the gallop and countercharged the Virginians in turn.[49] The lines mixed, and the fight pitched back and forth through the clearing and over the guns. "It was warm work," recalled a Virginia trooper, "hand to hand, shooting and cutting each other in desperate fury, all mixed through one another, killing, wounding and taking prisoners."[50]

These fights were not the chivalrous fencing duels of the cavalry depicted in poems and paintings. Sabre fighting from the ground—true fencing—allowed for a whole series of foot feints, edge guards, sweeps, traps, and glides with the blade. But sabre fighting from the saddle made for an entirely different affair. A combatant's mount became his feet, and a combatant first had to maneuver his blade past the head and neck of his own horse, then past his opponent's animal before a blow could even land on his enemy. This negated all but the most basic cuts, thrusts, and guards. Therefore, mounted sabre melees were more akin to twenty-mile-an-hour knife fights, with men slashing, stabbing, and crashing off one another as they bowled in, struck a blow, and spurred clear. It was survival of the fittest, waged in packs of tens and twos, with troopers cleaving, cursing, and chopping one another from the saddle. "[A] rebel made a dash at me," wrote a Union lieutenant. "I cut at him twice and missed. . . . [A]s he passed, he [cut] his sabre at me. One of my men . . . thrust his carbine against the breast of the rebel and shot him dead."[51] Glittering duels between chivalrous opponents were few and far between.

The Regulars' sudden arrival occurred just in time to save the 6th Pennsylvania. Charging into the Virginia ranks, the Regulars' attack allowed the Pennsylvanians to break free as the Virginians rallied and turned to face the new threat. The Pennsylvanians sprinted for their lines, with many riding through the woods skirting the bowl and drawing artillery fire along the way. "Whistling shot and screaming shell fall all around us, sending a shower of limbs, twigs, bark, leaves and earth all over us. . . . [W]e lie close to our horses' necks, and hug still closer as the crashing shot and shell passes within a few feet or inches of us."[52] In the Pennsylvania's wake, the 6th U.S. also felt "compelled to retire" as the Virginians rallied, countercharged, and drove the Regulars back across the bowl.[53]

Jones's troopers began rallying back to Beckham's guns when General Stuart appeared on the field, perfectly dressed and appointed, with his staff trailing behind. Nerves remained tight and bullets still flew about, but Stuart coolly took in the situation as Beckham's gunners slowed their rate

Figure 5.3. Brigadier General William E. Jones, Army of Northern Virginia. Grumble Jones was a skilled officer and well known for his profanity-laced tirades. F. T. Miller and R. S. Lanier, eds., *The Photographic History of the Civil War in Ten Volumes*, vol. 4, *The Cavalry* (New York: Review of Reviews, 1911). Public domain/Wiki Commons.

of fire and prepared for the next action. Like many that morning, Stuart woke to the sound of gunfire coming from the river, which he could clearly hear from his headquarters atop Fleetwood Hill overlooking the rail depot at Brandy Station. The sustained fire convinced Stuart a fight was brewing, and dispatches soon arrived from Grumble Jones, confirming an enemy attack.[54] Stuart promptly ordered all supply wagons to the rear, called for a set of maps, and started dispatching a blizzard of orders. He sent Hampton's brigade to support Jones's command, and directed Rooney Lee's brigade to the west of St. James Church with orders to press the Federal right flank at Beverly Ford. Fitz Lee's brigade would also move for Beverly Ford from their current position across the Hazel River. Additional dispatches went to Robertson, whose brigade sat in the direction of Kelly's Ford, and Stuart warned Robertson to keep a sharp eye out for any enemy in that direction. Finally, Stuart sent couriers for General Lee's headquarters to warn him of the attack.[55]

East of the ford road, Hampton had dismounted a squadron of skirmishers from each of his regiments and sent them forward to secure the woods on the Confederate right. Finding the enemy proved swift work, and Hampton's sharpshooters—the period term for cavalry dismounted as skirmishers—soon engaged Federal sharpshooters from Buford's 1st and 2nd brigades, while Devin and Pleasonton continued funneling men and guns in as needed.[56] Carbine fire escalated, and Hampton reported the woods to his front were "infested with dismounted cavalry and the knapsack gentry" of Ames's Federal infantry. Hampton sent in additional sharpshooters, lengthening his front farther east of the road as his men advanced from tree to tree, fighting "in regular Indian style."[57] Devin likewise added more troopers to the mix until both sides were blazing away in close-range firefights that filled the surrounding woods with clouds of blue powder smoke.

Devin responded by calling forth a squadron of the 9th New York Cavalry and sending it charging against the advancing Confederates.[58] Major William Martin struck a gallop and pressed forward through a clearing in the woods, charging diagonally "left to right" against the Rebel line until a volley from Hampton's sharpshooters cut through the New Yorkers. Martin fell with a bullet through his shoulder, and the rest of his troopers turned about under the heavy fire.[59] Federal stretcher-bearers carried the major to the rear, but the charge effectively screened Devin's own sharpshooters, who drove forward at the Rebel line in league with the New Yorkers' horse charge and stalled the Southern drive in that section of the line.[60]

A lull settled over the field.

Buford's 1st Division had crossed the river and established a perimeter about the ford. All forward progress appeared checked, and there was little Pleasonton could do but wait for Gregg's wing to arrive from Kelly's Ford.[61]

From Stuart's point of view, the situation must have seemed well on the way to mending. Beckham and Jones held his center. Rooney Lee held his left, and Hampton had secured his right. Stuart felt his men had arrested the Union advance, and any looming crisis had passed for now. As the volume of fire diminished, Grumble Jones received a message that a large force of Federal cavalry was approaching Brandy Station from the south, likely via Kelly's Ford, and moving for Beverly Robertson's brigade. Jones sent a courier to tell Stuart of this new threat, but Stuart—who had been in repeated contact with Robertson that morning—knew Robertson had identified the Federals in his front, and felt that flank secure.[62] Having never been a fan of Jones's politics and intrigues, Stuart snapped back a stinging reply: "Tell General Jones to attend to the Yankees in his front. . . . I'll watch the flanks."[63]

The curt rebuff sent Jones into a tirade. "So, he thinks they ain't coming, does he? Well, let him alone, he'll damned soon see for himself!!"[64]

6

FLEETWOOD HEIGHTS

General David Gregg crossed Kelly's Ford at dawn and could already hear carbine fire sounding from upstream. Despite the battle noise, Gregg had to hold at the ford for two critical hours while he waited for the guides of Duffié's 2nd Division to find the ford. Once Duffié arrived, Gregg sent the tardy division on for Stevensburg, where Duffié would halt, secure Stevensburg, and contact Gregg before turning for either Brandy Station or Culpeper.[1] Gregg then took the direct route for Brandy Station with his 3rd Division. Colonel Percy Wyndham's brigade led this advance, followed by Captain Joseph Martin's 6th New York Light Artillery. Colonel Judson Kilpatrick's brigade brought up Gregg's rear, along with General David Russell's accompanying infantry.[2]

Gregg soon found his route checked by the 4th and 5th North Carolina of Beverly Robertson's brigade, posted two miles from the ford. Gregg countered by leaving Russell's infantry and one troop of the 10th New York Cavalry to deal with Robertson while Gregg turned west, trailing after Duffié for three miles before turning north for Brandy Station via the Fredericksburg Plank Road. Along the way, the sounds of cannon fire grew from Brandy Station, and Gregg received word from Pleasonton that, one, Buford's wing had encountered heavy enemy resistance and, two, Pleasonton believed he had met a larger force of the enemy than his own.[3]

As Duffié and Gregg continued their separate marches, Beverly Robertson seemed content to keep his distance from Russell's infantry and their three-band rifled muskets. This was a sizable force of infantry in Robertson's front. Robertson, however, failed to range or harass either Gregg's or Duffié's mounted columns. This behavior fell completely out of line with Stuart's expectations—especially after Stuart warned Robertson to remain vigilant.[4] Robertson's failure became Gregg's fortune as his 3rd Division

Figure 6.1. Colonel Percy Wyndham, Army of the Potomac. Wyndham was an accomplished pugilist and mercenary. *Library of Congress*.

trotted north, with every man in the ranks expecting a fight as they closed in range of the rail depot at Brandy Station.

Leading the march was Colonel Percy Wyndham, an Englishman with wide, flowing mustaches he kept waxed and trimmed like an extravagant country squire. Wyndham's starchy accent and refined dress could be deceiving; at thirty years of age, he had already served in the French Navy, the Austrian Lancers, and Garibaldi's Italian Army of Liberation in Sicily. The world-traveled mercenary was also a well-trained pugilist and loved a good fight in, or out, of the ring.[5] As Wyndham closed on the rail depot, he reined up to study a tall ridge rising on the far side of the tracks that overlooked the surrounding fields and open pastures. Wyndham saw no sign of Buford's men. Instead, there only appeared to be a large farmhouse atop the ridge. An orchard lay on one side of the farmhouse, and there were several tent flies pitched nearby and what looked to be a Confederate headquarters flag flapping in the breeze. A lone Confederate gun sat near the flag.[6]

Such a sight spawned a host of questions for Wyndham. Whose headquarters were perched on the hill? Was the lone gun part of the batteries he'd heard launching salvo after salvo? Had those been enemy batteries? If so, were they parked just on the far side of the ridge? Like any trained pugilist, Wyndham felt good footwork and a stiff jab was a better opener than two straight steps and a haymaker. Rather than order an all-out charge, Wyndham ordered the 1st Maryland Cavalry to prepare for an advance and brought up a section of two guns from Martin's battery.[7]

∽

Major Henry McClellan sat his horse beside Stuart's headquarters flag and watched the Federal column below. The young major could see a Union brigade approaching and instantly recognized the threat. If the Federals could take Fleetwood Heights, the high ground where Stuart's flag now flew, they would dominate Stuart's position at St. James and pin the Confederate cavalry between two Federal forces.[8] McClellan sent the last of his couriers galloping for Stuart with an urgent plea to send troops immediately, while the lone gun commander, Lieutenant John Carter of Captain Chew's battery, opened fire at the Federals across the tracks.

Back at St. James Church, Jeb Stuart sat watching the Federals in his front when a courier galloped in with an urgent summons from Major McClellan—Federal cavalry was approaching Brandy Station in force and about to roll over Stuart's headquarters. The sound of exploding shells from Lieutenant Carter's gun punctuated the report, and Stuart quickly ordered Grumble Jones to pull his 12th and 35th Virginia out of the line at St. James, and send them on for Fleetwood Heights post haste. After being stamped down by Stuart earlier, it's unclear exactly what Jones said in response to this new set of orders, but one can assume it peeled the paint from any near limber chests.

~

Percy Wyndham peered through his field glasses as a single squadron of his 1st Maryland Cavalry charged in and secured the depot at the railroad tracks.[9] This brought little change from the tent flies atop Fleetwood Heights, and Wyndham then advanced three guns from Martin's battery over the open ground between the depot and the heights.[10] While the guns prepared to move forward, Wyndham ordered up a second Maryland squadron, followed by the 1st Pennsylvania Cavalry.[11] Wyndham then shadowed the rest with the 1st New Jersey Cavalry, and all trotted forward to sweep the heights beyond the tracks.[12]

Atop the hill, McClellan watched the Federals coming forward. Lieutenant Carter fired his last round before hitching his piece and beating a quick retreat.[13] McClellan rode back to the crest of the hill, where he saw Colonel Harman's 12th Virginia Cavalry coming up from St. James at a canter. Growing desperate, McClellan waved them on, his arm spinning like a windmill in a hurricane as the Virginians charged up the slope.[14] "A hard gallop had enabled only the leading files of the 12th Virginia to reach the top of the hill," wrote McClellan afterward, "the rest of the regiment stretching out behind in column of fours." Deployed in such fashion, the 12th had little chance of success in the coming melee: "[T]he result of this charge has always been a mortification. . . . I should say even to this day that the whole responsibility rested with me and not Colonel Harman."[15]

On the other side of the hill, the 1st Maryland was but fifty yards from topping the ridge when they saw Harman's Virginians appear in their view. The two sides collided on the crest, and the Marylanders drove through the Virginians in this initial clash. The rest of the 12th Virginia arrived and gained a brief success before the 1st Pennsylvania closed and cut through the Virginians like a scythe.[16] Reeling, the Virginians turned back only to be shattered again when Wyndham and the 1st New Jersey hit them beside the farmhouse.[17] "On each side, in front, behind, everywhere on top of the hill the Yankees closed in upon us."[18] Assailed on multiple fronts, the 12th Virginia fell back in disarray.

Were it not for the fluid nature of mounted combat, the contest may have ended here, but the inherent ebb and flow of a horse charge allowed Harman to fall back, reform, advance, and charge in again by platoons, sections, and squads. These piecemeal attacks kept the Federals from clearing the hill and dismounting sharpshooters to hold the ground. Harman's men and mounts would never maintain this footing for long, and just as the Federal numbers began to take hold, White's 35th Virginia came rushing up the hill in two wings, one passing in front of the farmhouse and the other behind, to slam into the Federals and tilt the tables back about.[19]

"We would break their line on one side, and they would break ours on the other," recalled a trooper from the 12th Virginia. "[We] fought them singlehanded, by twos, fours and squads, just as the circumstances permitted."[20] This was not an endless combat of sprinting horsemen ceaselessly coursing the field; horses are incapable of such acts. If they were, the Kentucky Derby would last an hour rather than two minutes, and polo ponies would run entire matches as opposed to brief rounds lasting seven minutes.

Charges by platoons and companies would meet, crash, disintegrate, and fall away, and neither side could actually hold any ground until they made another attack. In between the actions, the troopers took hurried swigs from their canteens and let their horses have a blow while sergeants squared the ranks, corporals counted the ever-dwindling files, and the combat continued on along the crest. E Troop of the 1st New Jersey lost and retook their company guidon three times in these rolling piecemeal fights. "The third time, when all seemed desperate, a troop of the 1st Pennsylvania cut through the enemy and brought off the flag."[21]

As the struggle continued, Colonel Harman of the 12th Virginia could feel his men drifting; the repeated charges were taking their toll, and his men and horses were nearing their breaking point. Growing desperate, Harman called out to rally his men on the backside of the hill. "For God's sake, Form!" yelled Harman. "For my sake, Form!"[22] The plea worked, and the Virginians rallied about for what might be the last charge. Raising his sabre, Harman looked over his shoulder to see Major Cabell Flournoy and the 6th Virginia Cavalry galloping up from St. James.[23] Several guns from Stuart's horse artillery followed in his wake.[24]

Heartened by this sight, the Virginians spurred into the Federals. Captain O'Ferrall of the 12th Virginia shot a Union officer point-blank and clubbed him to the ground.[25] Colonel Harman suffered a cut across his neck and turned for the rear, blood pouring from the wound.[26] Major Broderick, 1st New Jersey, was shot and then cleft from the saddle in a rapid string of sabre blows. Meanwhile, Federal Marcus Kitchen lanced a Rebel from his saddle with the point of his sabre, then turned for a second target. As he closed, the next Rebel shot Kitchen's horse through the head. The horse leaped in the air and twisted sideways, "his feet never to touch the ground again." The horse crashed on his side stone dead, and Kitchen

**Figure 6.2.   *Cavalry Charge near Brandy Station* by artist Edwin Forbes.
*Library of Congress.***

lay stunned in the middle of the field, "arms and legs abroad, stretched out like a dead man."[27] Kitchen woke moments later, stood up in a daze, and somehow wandered through the ongoing fight unharmed until rescued by fellow members of his company.[28]

Farther up the ridge, three guns from Hart's Rebel battery galloped forward to join Captain William McGregor's section deploying north of the Carolina Road. As they closed, Federals from the 1st New Jersey came careening out of the smoke and dust atop Fleetwood and crashed into the charging guns. Major Shelmire of the 1st New Jersey waved his men ahead, and the Jerseys swarmed through the moving guns, slashing and cutting as they went.[29] Horse gunner LeGrande Guerry responded by shooting Major Shelmire with a revolver. Battery lieutenants C. E. Ford and William Hoxton were quick to follow, drawing and firing into the mass of swirling Union troopers and killing two men in rapid succession.[30] The Jerseys soon found their sabres a disadvantage amid the rolling cannons and wheels, and spurred clear of the guns as quickly as they appeared.[31]

It was this exact style of fractured, surging combat Stuart witnessed as he gained the heights with his staff in tow. Federal troopers were everywhere, rallying, reforming, and charging across the heights as Martin's Federal battery wreaked havoc from the plain below the heights. "Shrapnel, case shot and pistol balls hissed through the air. . . . [R]iderless horses were running about like scalded cats [and] men running away toppled over one another without sense or reason." Captain William Blackford rode beside Stuart as they pushed into the fray and mixed with the enemy. Blackford recalled having "some capitol pistol practice," as he emptied his revolver into the swirling chaos.[32] The newly arrived 6th Virginia gave a temporary edge to the Confederates, but Stuart could see more Federals waiting at the depot below and knew any advantage could change in a second.[33] If the Federals ever managed a massed charge that swept the heights complete, they could secure the position with guns and sharpshooters and rout Stuart's entire force. Turning from the fight, Stuart yelled to his staff, "Go for Hampton! For God's sake, get Hampton!"[34]

In the interim, a squadron of the 6th Virginia made for Martin's battery. Galloping forward with sabres in hand, they suffered a dose of canister and bowled over the guns.[35] The gunners ducked beneath their cannons, and the Virginia blades scraped by to clatter harmlessly off the barrels, gun wheels, and limber chests. Farther below, Federals were already rallying, and a squadron of Marylanders charged forward to defend Martin's section. The arriving Federals chased off the Rebel troopers, and Martin's gunners popped back up to resume firing at will—so long as Martin's battery held its ground, the Federal cavalry atop the ridge would continue to enjoy close support.[36] Stuart needed someone to knock the Federal battery down and keep it down. Looking about, he marked Colonel White's 35th Battalion and ordered them to take a pass at the Yankee guns.[37]

White's battalion reloaded and rolled forward in earnest. Streaming across the hill on the battery's lower left flank, they struck the covering Maryland cavalry and then spurred through the guns, firing as they went.[38] Once past, they wheeled about and unloaded, shooting down the battery horses and the Federal drivers in a one-sided gunfight.[39] "The[se] artillerymen fought like heroes," wrote one of White's troopers. "There was no demand for surrender, nor any offer to do so."[40] Crouching among the guns, a Union officer recalled, a single Rebel horseman dashed and darted between the pieces, his sabre cutting down a gunner with each pass in a chilling, almost "supernatural" manner until more Federal cavalry arrived and forced White to retire.[41] This charge damaged Martin's battery, and after killing the battery horses, no one could move the guns from the field.[42] The guns now sat static between the lines, still firing but immobile.

❧

Down near the depot, General Gregg strained to read the state of affairs atop the heights. Clouds of dust obscured his view, and he could make out little more than sections of men and mounts wheeling in and out of the dust or forming on the periphery of the cloud. The typically stoic Gregg had

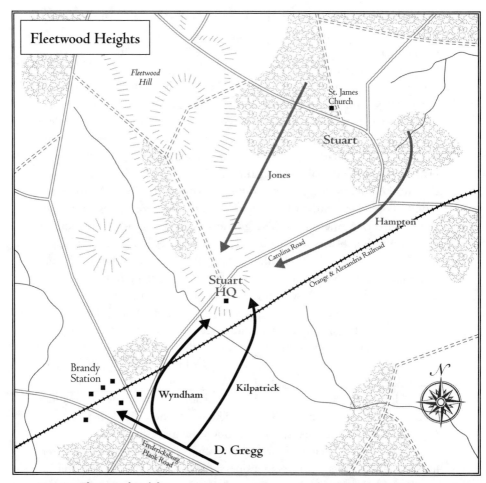

Map 3. Fleetwood Heights

pumped his fist in approval when he'd watched Wyndham's early success. Now he stared with sobering discontent as Union troopers darted loose about the field in scattered sections and platoons.[43] Wyndham's brigade was flagging, their horses were spent, and they needed support, but Gregg had no other troops to commit.

Help soon appeared from Colonel Hugh Judson Kilpatrick and his following brigade. A native of New Jersey, the unruly Kilpatrick had a peculiar habit of turning the brim of his slouch hat up on one side and down on the other, giving him an original, but decidedly uneven appearance.[44] Kilpatrick's sense of style matched his reputation. In January he'd served two weeks in Washington's Capitol Prison for fraudulently appropriating forage from the quartermaster, and then widely insulting the provost marshal while out on a drinking spree about town.[45] Along with his propensity for finding trouble, Kilpatrick displayed both a mercurial temper and a spitfire eagerness for combat that won the early confidence of his men. "He fights the Rebels as we expected to fight them," claimed one of his rankers.[46] This confidence was by no means universal; another member of his command described him as rash, capricious, ambitious, and reckless—just the sort of man General Gregg needed right now.[47]

Gregg gave the order to attack, and Kilpatrick unleashed his brigade in two waves. The 10th and then 2nd New York would cross the tracks in separate columns and aim for Stuart's left flank atop the heights, with Lieutenant J. Wade Wilson's section of artillery following in support.[48] For added weight, Kilpatrick would trail behind with the 1st Maine as a mobile reserve to see the job through. At Kilpatrick's command, the brigade started forward, with the front ranks carrying revolvers in hand and the rear ranks resting bare sabres on their shoulders.[49] Unbeknownst to Kilpatrick, General Wade Hampton's Confederate brigade came up the far side of Fleetwood at this very moment.

Like Jones, Hampton first had to disengage from the line near St. James Church, and Hampton left his dismounted men behind as he galloped for Fleetwood. His men rode just as they'd left the former line, with two squadrons from the Cobb Legion Cavalry out front, followed by the 1st South Carolina. Farther right came squadrons from the 1st North Carolina, and finally the Jeff Davis Legion of Mississippi.[50] Cobb's Georgians closed first, their commander yelling, "Sabres, boys, sabres, no pistols!"[51] The Georgians were disciplined troops, trained and led by Colonel Pierce Young, who learned his craft at West Point. Enjoying good, open ground, Young deployed at a gallop, taking his first squadron into the head of the Federal column, and sending the second squadron to offset left, en echelon, and strike the Federal column seconds later.[52]

The twin blows crashed into the 10th New York like a freight train. "The Rebel line that swept down on us came in splendid order," recalled a New Yorker, and landed with an "indescribable clashing, slashing, banging, and yelling."[53] The Georgians ripped through the Federal column from front to flank, effectively shattering the Yankee formation and scattering the remains.

Continuing on, the Georgians pursued the fleeing Federals down through a small orchard sitting between the farmhouse atop Fleetwood and the tracks below, where they galloped headlong into Wilson's horse battery, piling up, over, and through the drivers to knock the cannons out of play

Figure 6.3.   Unidentified Soldier of Company A "Richmond Hussars" Cobb Georgia Legion Cavalry. Subject armed with Sharps Carbine, Adams revolver, and horse sabre. *Library of Congress.*

before they ever dropped a trail.[54] Lieutenant W. C. Howard of the Cobb Legion came spurring down the ridge when his mare suddenly took the bit in her teeth and sprinted straight ahead despite his best attempts to turn her out: "I was carried *nolens volens* right amid the confused mass of jumbled up Yanks by my unruly mare, never stopping until she ran up against a piece of artillery." Howard finally regained control of his mare as Federal gunners jumped from their limber and began "running for dear life."[55]

Colonel John Black's 1st South Carolina landed the next blow on Kilpatrick's following regiment, the 2nd New York. Somehow, in approaching the railroad tracks, an officer of the 2nd New York gave an errant order and turned elements of the regiment sharply leftward, away from the 1st South Carolina.[56] This may have come from the fact that the 2nd New York was just crossing the railroad tracks when the Georgians struck the 10th New York. Railroad tracks are an obstacle to any horse, and this obstacle of wooden ties and steel tracks would have wreaked havoc on any mounted formation—especially one moving at speed and witnessing the destruction of a brother regiment before their very eyes. Whatever the cause, the New Yorkers' sudden turn served up a ruthless opportunity to the 1st South Carolina, who had just received a shipment of Enfield rifles.[57] As Black's first squadron charged deep, the trailing squadrons pulled to a stop at the railroad cut and delivered a volley into the rear of the 2nd New York, which landed "with effect."[58] The surviving New Yorkers scattered, and Black's first squadron swung down the tracks causing any remaining Federals to flee for the rear. Kilpatrick, the former commander of the 2nd New York, watched this second reverse unfold before his eyes and vented the loss in a rage described by a witness as "well-nigh uncontrollable."[59]

Meanwhile, farther up Fleetwood Hill, and following to the right of the Georgians, the 1st North Carolina and Jeff Davis Legion rolled over the truncated color guard of the 10th New York and captured their colors.[60] Rolling on, these Rebel squadrons slashed ahead in spreading columns, sweeping up prisoners and driving all before them until suddenly coming under friendly artillery fire from Fleetwood Hill, where new Confederate guns had just arrived. This friendly fire disordered Hampton's men and brought them to a sudden halt that checked any further gains of the brigade.[61]

Yet one man's loss is another's fortune, and the disorder in Hampton's ranks caused by the friendly artillery fire occurred just as the 1st Maine charged forward and slipped behind these halting regiments in a fluke of timing and place. The Mainers galloped into the same roiling dust clouds that caused the Southern gunners to target their own side, and the admonished gunners now held their fire as the 1st Maine rolled unhindered into the rear of Jones's 6th Virginia Cavalry. The shock was terrific as the New Englanders bowled through the Virginians at the gallop, breaking the Rebel ranks apart, and sabering all in reach.[62]

Led by Colonel Calvin Douty, the 1st Maine kept rolling to the far side of the hill, where they turned about, reformed, and charged back through, this time coming under fire from the rallied Southern gunners now reopened for business. Marked by the enemy cannons, Douty sagely turned his men out and galloped back across the tracks, followed by the scattered remains of Kilpatrick's New Yorkers.[63] Meanwhile, General Hampton reformed his brigade, dressed his ranks, and prepared to charge down upon Kilpatrick's scattered troopers when Stuart ordered him to stand down, hold his position, and cover the hill.[64]

The final play came from the 11th Virginia Cavalry, headed by Stuart's former Plains War compatriot, Colonel Lunsford Lomax. Summoned from St. James, Lomax's 11th Virginia charged past the heights and made straight for Martin's static battery, now guarded by a squadron of sharpshooters from Wyndham's brigade. Lomax rolled forward in column, divided his squadrons, and wheeled in on the battery from two sides.[65] George Moffett of Company F recalled, "Lomax swept down upon the battery on a side swipe. This necessitated a shifting of the guns, in which the gunners lost their range, and the volley of grape and canister was not so effective."[66] Nonetheless, the volley still shredded the 11th's colors and ripped the flag-staff from the color-bearer's hands as the Virginians charged the guns. The covering squadron of sharpshooters tried to mount their horses as Lomax closed, only to be caught halfway in the saddle and quickly dispatched. Martin's remaining gunners suffered a similar fate but still spiked their guns as they fell. "Of the 36 men I took in to the engagement," wrote Martin, "6 came out safely."[67]

Lomax reformed his men and rolled on, pitching into Wyndham's milling squadrons at the depot and taking a stand of colors in a final push that cleared the ground and captured the depot.[68] Wyndham took a bullet through the calf in this final assault and had to leave the field for loss of blood.

The charges for Fleetwood came to a close. Gregg's division was played out, and many of the horses from Grumble Jones's brigade could barely stand.[69] Only Hampton's brigade stood ready for more, and they stood formed atop Fleetwood, ready to strike a crippling blow on the retiring Federals. Stuart, however, had been surprised twice in one day, and with enemy threats still at large, he refused to risk his only sizeable reserve still available.

7

STEVENSBURG AND YEW RIDGE

Farther south of Fleetwood Heights, Alfred Duffié's 2nd Division continued moving for Stevensburg. Duffié's orders called for him to first move
on Stevensburg and secure the intersection of the Old Carolina and Kirtley
Roads. Once he'd secured the intersection, Duffié would communicate
with Gregg for instructions and either press on for Brandy Station, turn for
Culpeper Courthouse, or fill whatever role needed.[1] Duffié put his 1st Brigade, comprising the 1st Rhode Island, 6th Ohio, and 1st Massachusetts, up
front. Colonel John Irving Gregg, a cousin of General David M. Gregg, led
Duffié's 2nd Brigade, composed of three Keystone regiments: the 3rd, 4th,
and 16th Pennsylvania Cavalry. Lieutenant Alexander Pennington's Battery
M, 2nd U.S. Artillery, marched between the two brigades, making for a
substantially sized column moving along the Kirtley Road.[2]

As Duffié approached Stevensburg, he ordered a battalion of the 6th
Ohio to fast march ahead, and they gained the small hamlet without incident. The Federal battalion had not been there long before Confederate
cavalry arrived from the north via the Old Carolina Road. Major Benjamin
Stanhope commanded the Federal battalion and sent word to Duffié in the
main column. Duffié directed Stanhope to hold if he could, but Stanhope
judged it better to fall back and instead withdrew down the Kirtley Road.[3]

The enemy Stanhope encountered were Colonel Matthew Butler's
troopers from the 2nd South Carolina Cavalry. Butler was a citizen soldier
and a good one. A lawyer before the war, he married Miss Maria Calhoun
Pickens, the daughter of South Carolina's sitting governor during the state's
withdrawal from the Union. Earlier that morning, Butler received orders
from Stuart to move south and seize the same vital crossroads in Stevensburg
Duffié meant to secure.[4] As Butler closed on Stevensburg, he sent forty men
ahead under Major Thomas Lipscomb, then an additional detachment under

Lieutenant Colonel Frank Hampton, the younger brother of General Wade Hampton. Hampton arrived just as the 6th Ohio withdrew from Stevensburg, and Lipscomb's forty men pursued the Federals until they came upon the head of Duffié's 1st Brigade, where a carbine skirmish ensued. Now outnumbered, Lipscomb and his men fell back for Stevensburg.[5]

While this occurred, Butler arrived with the balance of the 2nd South Carolina. He dismounted the majority beside the Kirtley Road along Hansborough Mount—a tree-lined ridge of high ground that offered good fields of fire covering the approach to Stevensburg. At the same time, Frank Hampton took command of a small mounted element of thirty-six men near the Salubria Plantation.[6] While Butler and Hampton took their positions, Captain William Farley galloped in with a message from General Stuart's headquarters. Farley, one of Stuart's favored scouts, told Butler reinforcements were on the way, courtesy of the 4th Virginia Cavalry, and a gun crew from Captain Moorman's horse battery.[7]

Duffié's Federals soon came in sight, and Farley left to escort the 4th Virginia into position by a shortcut that bypassed the Stevensburg crossroads. The Federals began dismounting sharpshooters, and the two sides traded volleys, with the Confederates enjoying a distinct advantage from the tree line atop Hansborough Mount.[8] Armed with muzzle-loading rifles, the South Carolinians had a longer range than the quicker loading breechloaders carried by Duffié's men.[9] "We were in an open field," recalled a Federal. "They had got a good range on us and our men and horses began to fall when our supporters came up in line of battle."[10] Provoked by this accurate fire, the 1st Massachusetts dropped the fence rails before them and pulled sabres. As the 1st Massachusetts made ready to charge, the 1st Rhode Island followed suit, along with a squadron from the 6th Ohio.[11]

Meanwhile, Colonel Williams Wickham and his 4th Virginia were arriving via Farley's shortcut, which brought the 4th Virginia to the Kirtley Road via a narrow sidetrack bound with heavy trees to either side. This put Wickham on the right of Butler's South Carolina sharpshooters, with the head of his Virginia column behind Colonel Hampton's mounted detachment at Salubria. However, the majority of the column stretched back for hundreds of yards and was hemmed in by trees bordering the sidetrack where they could do little good.[12] To clear themselves for action, the leading squadrons of the 4th Virginia turned out on the main road to Stevensburg and wheeled about in a column of fours. The Virginians should have posted a force to cover this maneuver; instead, this evolution put the 4th Virginia's backs to the enemy as the column first had to turn away from the Federals and travel down the road, and then thread their way back about

Figure 7.1. Colonel Alfred Duffié, Army of the Potomac. An adept drill instructor, Duffié failed as a field officer and should never have advanced beyond a battalion-grade commander. *Library of Congress.*

like a long snake caught in a pipe. The Federal troopers recognized the mistake immediately and pounced on the opportunity.[13]

Bugles pealed, and the combined Federals spurred forward. Frank Hampton recognized a disaster in the making and pitched his thirty-six men into the Federal's path to buy the Virginians time to come about.[14] It was a gallant act, but the greater weight of the Federals shredded his smaller detachment in short order. Slashed across the face and shot through the stomach, Hampton fell mortally wounded as the Federals bowled his men aside and crashed into the rear of the Virginians.[15] Colonel Wickham wrote his command "broke and fled in confusion" and failed to rally for more than a mile despite repeated calls for the veteran 4th Virginia to reform.[16]

The 2nd South Carolina still held the ridge north of the road, but with their right flank now open, Butler pulled his men back along the Carolina Road. Di Cesnola's brigade then turned after Butler, but the accurate fire of the South Carolina rifles curtailed the Federal pursuit and kept the Union brigade at a distance. Butler's men kept up a sustained fire as they retired north, negating di Cesnola's numbers and allowing the 2nd South Carolina to cross the narrow ford over Mountain Run, a steep, soft-banked creek, practically unpassable to horses and wagons outside the ford. After gaining the north bank, Butler's sharpshooters took positions overlooking the creek, and Moorman's gun quickly deployed, effectively corking Duffié from any direct pursuit to Brandy Station without risking significant casualties. Butler could hear sustained artillery fire coming from Brandy Station in his rear, where the fight for Fleetwood Heights raged full tilt. The battle noise prompted Butler to send a courier spurring for Stuart to inform him he'd lost Stevensburg but would attempt to hold at Mountain Run.[17]

After sending the courier, Butler and Farley were sitting on their mounts side by side, watching the Federals advancing in the distance, when a gun from Pennington's Battery M, 2nd U.S. Artillery, fired a round across the creek.[18] The solid bolt struck the ground before the two Confederates and ricocheted upward, smashing through Butler's right leg just above the ankle, and traveling through Butler's horse to hit Farley beyond and sever his leg at the knee. Butler endured a painful field amputation but lived to fight another day. Farley bled out and died within minutes of being hit.[19]

As stretcher-bearers carried the officers clear, Duffié began preparing an attack to batter his way across the narrow bridge spanning the ford when two sets of orders arrived from General Gregg. Both instructed Duffié to turn about and join Gregg back "on the road to Brandy Station."[20] Duffié chose not to question Gregg's orders despite the cannon fire he could clearly hear raging from Brandy Station. Duffié's division would have certainly aided Gregg at Fleetwood, and many have been quick to criticize Duffié for turning about; however, caution should be made when faulting an officer for following a direct order. Others will counter and say higher-caliber officers have the courage to interpret orders from their superiors and implement the correct solution to fulfill the intended result.

The responsibility might have weighed more with Gregg than Duffié. Gregg received multiple dispatches from Pleasonton that morning, and the second set of orders Gregg sent explicitly directed Duffié to return by his original route, collect his brigade along the way, and follow Gregg into Brandy Station. Gregg expected a hard fight in short order and wanted his "entire command in hand" to meet the enemy.[21] Duffié followed the orders, turned his division around, and returned to Gregg by the longer route. By the time he arrived, the fight for Fleetwood Heights had passed.

∾

Meanwhile, Brigadier General "Rooney" Lee, the second son of Robert E. Lee, sat with his brigade on the northern slope of Yew Ridge. The ridge ran a mile north of Brandy Station and actually linked back to the same ridge, which ended in Fleetwood Heights, where Stuart had placed his headquarters. During the early fighting that morning, Lee found an excellent position on the Greene family farm that sealed Stuart's left and joined elements from the 7th and 11th Virginia from Grumble Jones's brigade. Lee then placed sharpshooters from his 9th, 10th, and 13th Virginia behind the stacked rock walls of the Greene family farm across the base of Yew Ridge, and he held the final regiment of his brigade, the 2nd North Carolina, as a ready reserve. For artillery support, Lee placed Lieutenant Phillip Johnston's two smoothbores from Captain Breathed's horse battery atop Yew Ridge, where it overlooked the ground leading to the Hazel River below, now occupied by John Buford's 1st Division.

Buford had set his headquarters on the Cunningham farm across from the neighboring Greene family property. Using troops from both Devin's and Davis's brigades, Buford placed units between the Hazel River and the Beverly Ford Road, the 17th Pennsylvania, 6th New York, and 8th Illinois opposite Rooney Lee's men, and skirmishing soon commenced between the opposing sharpshooters. As the morning wore on, Buford shored up his position with artillery batteries under lieutenants Albert Vincent and Samuel Elder, who began firing round shot and time-fused shrapnel to cover the Federal approach. Carbine volleys crashed back and forth, and Buford sent in more sharpshooters from the 2nd U.S. Cavalry, as well as infantry from the 2nd Massachusetts and 3rd Wisconsin.[22] Lee countered by dismounting squadrons from his last regiment, the 2nd North Carolina Cavalry, and Lieutenant Johnston rained down case shot on the Federal artillery crews from his upper perch on the ridge.[23]

The firing escalated with the rising heat of the day. Well posted behind a set of stone walls, Lee's men were enjoying this superior position, and one of his troopers recalled, "Whenever a Yank would show himself someone would draw a bead and he would fall dead as a wedge."[24] Near 11:00 a.m., the sounds of artillery fire shifted in tone and direction as Gregg's division arrived at Brandy Station and pressed ahead for Fleetwood Heights.

Buford welcomed the new sounds of battle, but they had a different effect on Rooney Lee as Jones and then Hampton began pulling their people out of the line at St. James Church and moving for Fleetwood. This shift uncovered a road running from St. James to the back of Yew Ridge, and it forced Lee to withdraw up the face of the ridge to keep Buford from flanking his troopers and linking up with Gregg's division just

Figure 7.2.   Brigadier General W. H. F. Lee, Army of Northern Virginia. Rooney Lee attended Harvard prior to the war, where he served as class president and captain of the rowing team. *Library of Congress.*

a mile distant at Brandy Station.[25] The ground still worked in Lee's favor, however, and rolled downhill before his position with stone walls cutting through the pastures and woodlots ringing the side fields. At the top of the ridge, a saddle of sloping ground linked Yew Ridge to the long, northern face of Fleetwood Ridge, and Lee moved Johnston's smoothbores here as a stopgap, on the southern side of the saddle.[26]

Buford pressed forward when he saw Lee shift his men up the ridge to a fresh set of walls. Under covering fire from his batteries, Buford dismounted more troopers from the 5th U.S., who sprinted forward to capture a crucial section of the Southern-held walls. Confederates poured fire in return, but the stubborn Regulars held firm and returned a brisk fire until their ammunition ran low. Sharpshooters from the 2nd North Carolina then rushed the Regulars, killing some, taking eighteen prisoners, and regaining the contested section of walls.[27] Vincent's Union battery raked the wall with shrapnel, but the exploding shells had little effect on the Confederates tucked tight behind the wall.[28]

Buford soon grew tired of this new stalemate and rode over to his supporting infantry, the 2nd Massachusetts and 3rd Wisconsin Infantry. As with all armies, Federal infantrymen had little respect for Federal cavalrymen, even if they were division commanders. "Do you see those people there?" asked Buford. "They've got to be driven out." An officer reminded Buford that the enemy outnumbered his infantry two to one. Buford responded dryly, "Well, I didn't order you . . . but if you think you can flank them, go in, and drive them off."[29] One can imagine a standoff here as Buford sat on his horse, puffed on his pipe, and refused to blink. Buford wasn't the preening sort of cavalry officer despised by ground troops, and as the riflemen studied the rough, mud-spattered officer before them, a company got up from each regiment and shuffled forward.

The riflemen found a hidden approach that neither Buford nor his troopers had noticed. The infantrymen shucked their packs and began a slow belly crawl through the weeds and heavy brush to shield their approach. Once they'd closed on the Rebel flank, the Federals stood and unleashed a lethal rifle volley down the length of the wall that cut through Lee's men like a torrent. "The poor wretches were taken by surprise. Some crawled off on their hands and knees; others fell dead or writhed in wounds."[30] The riflemen charged forward, capturing twenty men and retaking the wall.[31]

Lee now started retiring farther up Yew Ridge behind a screen of sharpshooters, and Buford sent his 6th Pennsylvania in pursuit. Marking the coming horse charge, Johnston's smoothbores began raining down covering fire as Lee mounted his brigade. Despite the cannon fire, the 6th Pennsylvania gamely drove the last Rebel sharpshooters from the stone wall with their pistols. After expending their ammunition, the 6th Pennsylvania drew sabres and vaulted the wall in pursuit of the running enemy. "Out flew the sabers and most handsomely were they used," wrote Buford as his troopers galloped forward, slashing down at the Rebels.[32]

Lee called for a countercharge, and the 9th Virginia swept over the ridge and piled into the Pennsylvanians, "breaking them into confusion and forcing them back . . . not along their line of retreat, but directly back on the stone fence through which there was but a small opening."[33] The Virginians pinned the Yankees tight to the fence, the gate clogged in a press of horses, and a storm of pistol balls blasted through the scrambling ranks of the 6th Pennsylvania.[34]

The Federals finally broke clear with the 9th Virginia on their heels, chasing them down the ridge and losing their own order in the pursuit. Buford ordered a countercharge by the 2nd U.S. Cavalry, and the Regulars slammed into the scattered 9th Virginia, spinning the Rebels about like a top "and punishing them severely with the sabre and pistol."[35] Regulars captain Wesley Merritt gained special notice as he closed on Rooney Lee and cut a blow at the enemy brigade commander. Lee parried Merritt's attack and leveled a cut of his own that sent Merritt's hat spinning through the air and creased Merritt's scalp in the process.[36] A second cut opened a gash on Merritt's leg, and then the two combatants lost one another in the whirling chaos. The 9th Virginia retreated, and the Regulars gave chase, snapping at the Rebels' heels and clearing saddles along the way.[37]

Bugles split the air, and Lee's reserves pressed across the face of the ridge. The 10th Virginia charged first, then reined up and fired a volley in unison. The volley screened the approach of the 2nd North Carolina, who "right obliqued" past the 10th Virginia's flank and charged home with the sabre, their blades thudding down and splitting the Regulars wide open. "The Federals were [now] the fleers and the Confederates the pursuers."[38]

Yelling, "Hurrah for Hell, Wade In!" Private Massie Smith of the 10th Virginia spurred into the melee.[39] The Federals fled downhill with the 2nd North Carolina and 10th Virginia in close pursuit, "driving them back precipitately, killing many, chopping many over the head and taking some prisoners."[40]

As the Rebels pressed forward, a carbine ball struck Rooney Lee in the thigh. Bleeding profusely, Lee retreated to the rear, and Colonel Solomon Williams of the 2nd North Carolina took command and led the chase after the Regulars. Closing on Buford's reserves, Williams posted a guidon for his troopers to rally upon when a Union bullet struck him in the head and killed him instantly. The rapid losses of Lee and Williams robbed the Rebel brigade of their momentum, and Buford soon advanced a gun from Vincent's battery, enfilading the ground where Williams fell. The remains of Lee's brigade moved back up to the saddle, spanning the two ridges, and reformed before Johnston's Southern smoothbores.[41]

A lull descended over the field, and the Federals stabilized their line. Now lying on a stretcher in the rear, Rooney saw his father, who came to witness the mounting battle within a few miles of his headquarters. The elder Lee struggled at the sight of his son's suffering, and his concern grew at the amount of blood Rooney continued to lose. Rooney assured his father he would be fine, and the elder Lee made sure his son would soon have a good doctor at his side.

By now the firing had ceased on Fleetwood Heights, and Buford received orders from Pleasonton to retire. This occurred just as Colonel Thomas Munford finally arrived with most of Fitz Lee's brigade: the 1st, 2nd, and 3rd Virginia Cavalry. Rooney Lee's squadrons now lay scattered far and wide, and Colonel Lucien Davis of the 10th Virginia conceded command to Munford's arriving force. Posted seven miles away that morning, Munford arrived late after receiving two contradictory messages from Stuart's staff. Once he reached the field, Munford edged forward along the Hazel River with little knowledge of the ongoing fight. He brought forward a battery, sent in sharpshooters, and opened an attack on Buford's right flank; however, the moment to mount another sweeping charge had passed, and Buford fell back in a series of stiff skirmishes between Munford and the Federal brigades.[42] Gregg's and Duffié's divisions enjoyed far easier retreats on their way back to Kelly's Ford, where Robertson's brigade continued to spar at sharpshooter distance for most of the day.[43]

Charles McVicar, a horse gunner with Stuart's artillery, recalled in his diary how he and his fellow gunners were too tired for the jokes they typically enjoyed following an enemy retreat. As the battery made their way to camp, they came across a wounded Union trooper with a piece of shell embedded in his skull. At the wounded Federal's request, McVicar and a fellow gunner carefully extracted the metal from the trooper's head with a pair of horseshoe pinchers. "We sent this Yank to the hospital in Culpeper."[44]

Stuart's Confederates suffered 351 battle casualties and had 132 men captured. Pleasonton's numbers were near double that, with 484 men killed and wounded and 372 taken prisoner. Pleasonton's attack had neither dispersed nor destroyed the Confederate cavalry, nor had his men discovered the whereabouts of the Confederate infantry. But this didn't tell the whole story; Pleasonton's men had held the initiative for the greater part of the day and driven the Confederates back on their heels on multiple fronts. The early loss of Grimes Davis was a costly blow, and Alfred Duffié's late arrival at Kelly's Ford certainly disrupted the planned timing of the Federal attacks. Still, Pleasonton's new corps had surprised and almost defeated Stuart's vaunted veterans, and Stuart's adjutant, Henry McClellan, would later state the fight at Brandy Station "made" the Federal cavalry.[45]

8

INTO THE VALLEY

On June 11, two days following the fight at Brandy Station, Alfred Pleasonton inspected his troops in a formal review.[1] Reports from northern newspapers were better than he could have hoped for. The *Philadelphia Inquirer* headlined their article on the Battle of Brandy Station as "Stuart's Rebel Cavalry Defeated," and called the action "a very brilliant affair. . . . [T]he slaughter of the rebels was fearful. . . . Nearly all the fighting was done by the cavalry and it was of the bloodiest character."[2] Songs were sung, speeches were made, and everyone patted themselves on the back for a job well done. Pleasonton had indeed taken the fight to the Confederacy, and a hard fight was the result prompting him to write headquarters that "Stuart's cavalry was crippled. . . . [M]ine was not."[3]

Pleasonton also claimed to have captured intelligence that Stuart and his horsemen were gathering at Brandy Station to stage a raid across the Potomac. Found on the battlefield was a letter from someone named "Bill" who wrote a family member that Stuart had been planning a raid into the enemy's country.[4] This was hardly official intelligence, but a second letter from one of Stuart's horse gunners stated, "[W]e are going to make a grand raid toward the Potomac as soon as the valley is cleared."[5] The two letters seemed to confirm earlier reports that Stuart had formed in Culpeper to make a raid. Pleasonton even informed the press that the attack on Brandy Station had thwarted Stuart's impending raid from taking place. "By this sudden and brilliant dash of our cavalry into the enemy's lines their plans have been frustrated, and the intended raid of Stuart's Cavalry prevented."[6]

Pleasonton clearly thought he'd crippled Stuart's cavalry, and thus the great cavalry raid many Federals believed to be brewing lay dead on the vine. It only followed that Lee's offensive capabilities were curbed as well. "I am inclined to believe they [the Army of Northern Virginia] will not send off their cavalry or make a move until they are satisfied of ours. . . . [T]hey will play the defensive until we make a false step," wrote Pleasonton. "The most serious loss to the enemy has been horseflesh. We left very few with him. I am sending from Buford's brigade . . . some 250, that have nearly all been hit with bullets."[7]

The reference to Confederate horseflesh shows Pleasonton believed his men had crippled Stuart's force by killing or wounding a great number of Confederate horses. Just hours after the battle, Pleasonton penciled the following dispatch to Hooker: "I did what you wanted, crippled Stuart so he cannot go on a raid."[8] Had Pleasonton crippled Stuart's animals as he assumed, one could expect any plans Lee had for his main army were influenced in kind. Stuart's brigades had been stationary since the fight at Brandy Station; therefore, Stuart must be crippled and Lee hindered in turn without an effective cavalry to screen his movements.[9] On the surface this formula worked, given many of Lee's prior campaigns began with Stuart scouting the way. The truth differed drastically from the theory, however, and Pleasonton's attack on Brandy Station may have actually aided the Confederate cause as the events would play out.

On the morning of June 9, Stuart sat poised in Culpeper County to march north and begin screening the advance of Ewell's II Confederate Corps. Had Pleasonton not made his attack, Federal patrols watching Stuart, or Federal spies within Culpeper, would have likely noted Stuart's brigades moving north and reported the activity to headquarters. Hooker would have ordered increased scouts; Pleasonton's troopers would have focused more attention on Stuart and perhaps surmised Ewell's II Corps was moving north. Thus, Pleasonton's Federals may have discovered the opening moves of Lee's northbound invasion early on.

As it happened, Pleasonton attacked on June 9 and came away believing he'd greatly injured the Confederate cavalry, at once ruining Stuart's planned raid, and severely retarding Lee's ability to move his infantry. Lee, however, had been on the field at Brandy Station and knew Stuart was far from crippled. After Pleasonton retreated across the Rappahannock, Lee waited to see if the Federals would stay on the offensive. When no further actions threatened his plans, Lee put Ewell's corps in motion for the Shenandoah Valley—without Stuart's screen of cavalry—just one day behind schedule. Lee's goals remained unchanged—steal a march north and keep his movements hidden from Hooker. He judged the Federal cavalry would be scrambled and spent after the recent fight and, therefore, Lee broke convention and began moving his infantry while Stuart's cavalry remained in Culpeper serving as a static screen.[10] Lee gambled Federal attention would remain on Stuart following the battle, especially if he kept Stuart parked in plain sight at Culpeper. Meanwhile, Ewell's corps marched north for Chester's Gap, entered the valley, and effectively disappeared.[11] The Federals had no idea twenty thousand Confederates were slipping into the valley because Pleasonton saw no point in looking beyond Stuart's "crippled" forces in Culpeper.

Hooker, however, lacked Pleasonton's confidence and remained haunted by his defeat at Chancellorsville—a defeat greatly aided by Stuart's cavalry. "Look sharply to your right. By no means allow the enemy to turn it, though he may be crippled. . . . [H]e will use the more exertion to get you or us at a disadvantage."[12] Even after Hooker read the reports of Pleasonton's success at Brandy Station, he continued to worry about his right flank and had his chief of staff, Major General Daniel Butterfield, keep watch on Pleasonton.[13]

> Headquarters, Army of the Potomac
> *June 12, 1863, 7:45 p.m.*
>
> General Pleasonton:
>   The general desires to know how far beyond Sulphur Springs and in what portion of the Valley your scouts have penetrated; what reports and what you know positively regarding enemy's movements in that direction. This is of importance and information is desired as soon as possible.
>
> DAN'L BUTTERFIELD
> *Chief of Staff*

Pleasonton responded with a series of quick scouts and then hedged just how far west his patrols went.[14]

> Headquarters Cavalry Corps
> *June 12, 1863, 10 p.m.*
>
> General Butterfield
>   Dispatch of 7:45 p.m. received. My scouts have been beyond Waterloo. Saw no signs of the enemy. Have scouts out on the way to Luray and Chester Gaps. Will report as soon as I hear from them.
>
> A. PLEASONTON
> *Brigadier General*[15]

The best light one can put on this is that Pleasonton, having been at Brandy Station, probably felt he knew more about the state of Stuart's cavalry than anyone at headquarters, and Stuart's lingering presence in

Culpeper only affirmed Pleasonton's conviction that Stuart's cavalry lacked the horse power for large-scale maneuvering. Pleasonton's new corps had also just fought the largest cavalry battle of the war and suffered almost a thousand casualties, plus a similar number of horses. Therefore, most all of his own brigades needed refitting and supply.[16] This definitely affected Pleasonton's abilities, and he would certainly have preferred keeping his men close at hand to facilitate this refitting.[17] It might be that Pleasonton simply played the middle of the road: scouting for the enemy to appease requests from the War Department in Washington but all the while keeping a primary watch on Stuart's cavalry at Culpeper, which he considered the key to any Confederate campaign.[18] In the meantime, he went about shoring up his regiments rather than sending them out to fill every far-ranging request from headquarters. All general officers are effective politicians or they wouldn't wear the rank, and this certainly included Pleasonton.

Elsewhere, Hooker struggled in his steadily declining relationship with President Lincoln; Lincoln's secretary of war, Edwin Stanton; and Lincoln's general in chief, Henry Halleck. Secretary of War Stanton rose to prominence as a famous trial lawyer before the war and then served as an adviser to Lincoln's administration before Lincoln selected him for his cabinet. Another lawyer Lincoln respected was General in Chief Halleck, who held command over all Federal armies in the conflict. He graduated West Point in 1839 and made a name for himself as a military scholar before resigning and founding an extremely successful law firm. Upon his return to the military, the tightly wound lawyer proved to be a capable organizer—albeit a poor frontline performer. Nonetheless, Lincoln appointed Halleck general in chief. He clearly recognized the lawyer's administrative skills early on, and probably felt a bond through their shared legal backgrounds; however, the majority of Lincoln's generals didn't appreciate Halleck, including General Hooker, who never cared for the fretful attorney. To be fair, Halleck didn't care for "Fighting Joe" either. This resulted in a three-on-one wrestling match through the telegraphs where Halleck, Stanton, and Lincoln all pressed Hooker heavily for information. Hooker, in turn, pressed Pleasonton for actionable news on Stuart, and the location of Lee's three Confederate corps.[19]

This dysfunctional dynamic only worsened when Hooker decided to move the Army of the Potomac north on June 13. Despite Stuart's cavalry remaining static, mounting intelligence convinced Hooker the Confederate I Corps of James Longstreet was on the move, as was the Confederate II Corps under Richard Ewell.[20] Hooker directed Major General John Reynolds, the Union commander of the Federal I Corps, to take command of

Figure 8.1.   Camp of the 1st Massachusetts Cavalry. *Library of Congress.*

the right, or western, wing of the army, consisting of four Federal corps, and move north to keep between Lee and Washington, DC.[21] Hooker would command the Federal left wing of three corps and take a more eastern bearing, or interior, line back north to cover the capital city via Fairfax Courthouse.[22] General Reynolds promptly ordered Pleasonton to supply his right wing with three cavalry brigades—half of Pleasonton's corps. Pleasonton complied, and his primary role now became screening Reynolds's wing as they marched north for Manassas Junction with orders to secure Thoroughfare Gap in the Bull Run Mountains.[23]

These new demands would tax Pleasonton's cavalry to the limit. His regiments were still suffering from a basic shortage of horses dating back to Stoneman's raid on Richmond in May, and the losses incurred at Brandy Station only exacerbated the situation. "Everything quiet to the front and right to-night," wrote a frustrated Pleasonton on the evening of June 13. "I have now three brigades on picket. Presently we shall want cavalry, and we will have none."[24] The simplest solution to solving the problem would be to find more cavalry, and there happened to be a close source nearby—the cavalry defending the capital city in the Department of Washington.

The Department of Washington ringed the capital in a massive series of forts, entrenchments, and artillery batteries under the command of Major General Samuel Heintzelman, and within Heintzelman's command were some thirty-five hundred troopers assigned to Major General Julius Stahel. Stahel was a Hungarian immigrant who fought on the losing side of a revolution for Hungarian independence. He migrated to America and, in 1861, helped form a Federal regiment of German-speaking immigrants and gained the rank of lieutenant colonel. He rose to brigadier general, and then major general to command his own division of three cavalry brigades.[25]

Stahel's division defended the capital and the communication lines leading to and from Washington, DC. Though not frontline service, it was still hard duty, and it often pitted Stahel's troopers against Stuart's irregular scouts in brutal point-blank encounters—particularly John Mosby's Partisan Rangers and the Iron Scouts from Wade Hampton's 2nd South Carolina. Confederate Prioleau Henderson recalled one ambush launched upon Stahel's troopers riding below a steep bank in the road. On command, the Iron Scouts emptied their revolvers on the Federals below. "Men and horses down; those behind running or riding over those in their front; some trying to ride their horses up the steep slippery bank and never succeeding but falling back on those below." Fifteen Federals were killed and wounded.[26]

The firm support these irregular units enjoyed from local farmers and tradesmen made it hard for Stahel's troopers to defend against such actions, especially with men who frequently boarded with relatives in family homesteads between raids. To thwart this growing trend, Stahel's 5th Michigan Cavalry arrested a number of suspected civilians in Fauquier and Fairfax counties. "We are taking Secesh sympathizers and laying them away in the Old Capitol Prison so rapidly that we shall depopulate the country pretty soon."[27] Despite the arrests, the raids continued.

The success of the Rebel scouts did little to win Stahel a shining reputation. What did draw a rash of positive attention was the arrival of a thousand fresh remounts for Stahel's cavalry from Quartermaster Meigs.[28] In the past, Hooker used portions of Stahel's command to support the Army of the Potomac with good results, and Hooker now made overtures to Halleck back in Washington to again use Stahel's cavalry to fulfill the growing number of missions and requests Pleasonton received on a daily basis. The general in chief flatly refused: "There is no possibility of sending you more cavalry," wrote Halleck on June 12.[29] Halleck had his own concerns of Lee starting a major offensive, and rumors still lingered of a cavalry raid against Washington. All this combined to make Halleck feel far from secure inside

Figure 8.2.   Private Cecil Johnson, a member of Hampton's Iron Scouts. Johnson was killed on June 21, 1863. *Library of Congress.*

the capital city, and Halleck still wanted Stahel to concentrate on curbing the Rebel partisans in the surrounding District of Washington.[30]

The denial of Stahel's troopers went squarely against Hooker's real need to assess the situation in his front, and Hooker continued to think Lee, and Stuart's cavalry, posed an imminent threat to his right flank. Hooker wrote Halleck a reply stating, "General Pleasonton, without additional cavalry . . . will not be able to prevent the rebel cavalry from turning [our] right."[31] Hooker knew elements of Longstreet's corps were already in Culpeper, and he believed more of Lee's infantry would soon shift northwest.[32] To counter Lee's plans, Hooker thought he could move a large Federal force to the south, and attack the Confederate capital at Richmond once Lee moved north, clearing the way for Hooker to land a "mortal blow" against the Confederacy.[33] Hooker presented this idea in a rambling telegram to the president, and Lincoln swiftly turned it down: "Lee's army . . . not Richmond, is your sure objective."[34] Halleck agreed with Lincoln and ordered Hooker to stay in front of Lee or, at the very least, between Lee's army and Washington.[35]

This may have been somewhat shortsighted. Washington may have been the most fortified city in North America at that time, with a garrison of forty-six thousand men and an extensive series of fortifications guarding the perimeter. Had Hooker launched a coordinated attack at the Confederate capital, Lee would have been forced to respond and at least alter his plans. Lincoln and Halleck, however, were losing faith in Hooker's abilities, and as a result, the pair limited Hooker's options. Hooker, on the other hand, remained quite sure he knew more about the situation than anyone ensconced inside the perimeter guarding Washington City. Regardless of who was right or wrong, Hooker certainly felt little support from Washington.

As Hooker dealt with Washington, Pleasonton continued to screen for Reynolds's wing, watch for Stuart, search for remounts, field the requests coming his way, and make several adjustments to his command all at once. Displeased with Duffié's performance at Brandy Station, Pleasonton relegated Duffié back to the command of his original regiment, the 1st Rhode Island Cavalry. Next came Percy Wyndham's brigade. Wyndham fought his heart out at Fleetwood Heights to Pleasonton's fervent approval, but Wyndham's leg wound would keep him out of the saddle for some time. In his place, Pleasonton picked Colonel John McIntosh, the steady commander of the 3rd Pennsylvania Cavalry, to take over the brigade. Pleasonton also approved of Judson Kilpatrick's gutsy performance at Brandy Station and promoted him to brigadier general. Pleasonton wanted aggressive field officers, and he promoted Kilpatrick for the determination he'd shown on Fleetwood Heights. Likewise, John Buford received formal command of the 1st Division to include three brigades: the first under William Gamble, the second under Thomas Devin, and the Regulars Brigade under Major Samuel Starr, a long-serving Regular army cavalryman. Elements of Duffié's prior division were folded together with Gregg's division, and the command of both went to David M. Gregg. Like the 1st Division, Gregg's new 2nd Division would have three brigades: the first under Colonel John McIntosh, the second under Colonel J. Irvin Gregg, and the third under the newest brigadier general in Pleasonton's corps, Judson Kilpatrick.[36]

While Pleasonton made these changes, Jeb Stuart, the *Beau Sabre* of Virginia, endured an evisceration from the Southern press. "The more the circumstances of the late affair at Brandy Station are considered, the less pleasant they appear," wrote the *Richmond Examiner*. "If the war was a tournament, invented and supported for the pleasure of a few vain and weak headed officers, these disasters might be dismissed with compassion" and "this much-puffed cavalry of the Army of Northern Virginia has been . . . surprised."[37] Enraged and embarrassed, Stuart wrote to his wife, Flora, "The papers are in great error, as usual, about the whole transaction." Stuart was no stranger to the press and knew reporters often sought out the wives of general officers for information. He leaked his preferred version through Flora and her peers: "It was no surprise. The enemy's movement was known and he was defeated. We captured three pieces of Artillery. . . . I lost no paper—no nothing."[38] The first sentence was a lie. Pleasonton had definitely surprised Stuart at Brandy Station. The rest held true; Stuart recovered, captured three enemy guns, and lost no official documents.[39]

Regardless of Stuart's internal measures, the press continued to attack his recent performance. The *Richmond Daily Dispatch* wrote, "The Reports of the late fight in Culpeper County, are hardly more satisfactory than those which had previously reached us. That our forces were surprised there seems no longer any reason to doubt."[40] Being caught unaware came as a hard blow to any horse soldier, and Stuart's pride certainly suffered under these rebukes. Stuart knew the game, however, and countered with plenty of praise for his troops: "[T]wo divisions of the enemy's cavalry and artillery . . . 'tested your metal' and found it 'proof steel.'. . . Your sabre blows, have taught them again the weight of Southern vengeance."[41]

Stuart also knew the greater part of the story. His command may have been surprised, but while Pleasonton claimed he'd crippled the Southern cavalry, Ewell's corps was stealing a march on the Federal Army. Twenty

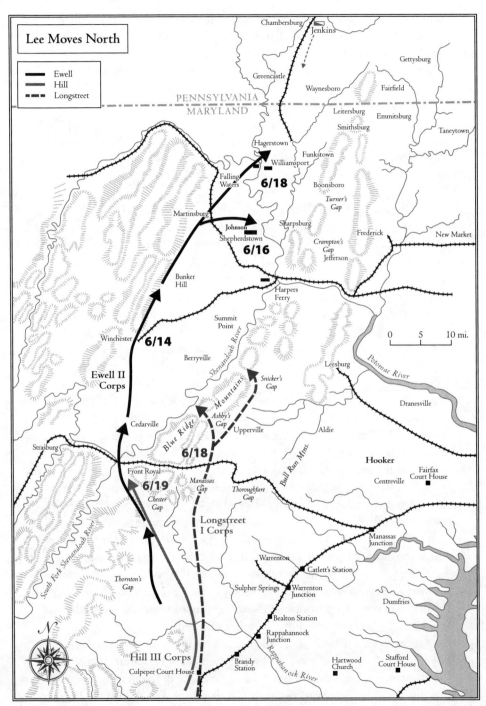

Map 4. Lee Moves North

thousand Confederates, complete with infantry and artillery, were sliding down the Shenandoah Valley, and regardless of what the papers said, Pleasonton remained oblivious to this fact, making for a far greater sin than suffering a surprise attack. Stuart bided his time by pacing about camp, fitting up his remounts, and following the progress of Lee's infantry.

After entering the Shenandoah Valley on June 12, Ewell's II Corps linked up with General Albert Jenkins's cavalry brigade.[42] A graduate of Harvard, Jenkins was a former congressional representative who enlisted in Confederate service and gained his own regiment of Virginia cavalry. Jenkins made a name for himself out on the western edges of the state, where one Southern general gave Jenkins's 17th Virginia the nickname "Wildcat Cavalry."[43] The moniker wasn't necessarily meant as a compliment, but the men of the 17th took it as one. The rest of the brigade included the 14th, 16th, 34th, and 36th Virginia and were considered closer to mounted infantry than true cavalry with many of the brigade's troopers carrying full-length muzzle-loading rifles. Still, Jenkins's troopers were well familiar with the Shenandoah Valley, and Lee selected the brigade early on to screen Ewell's advance down the valley as it approached the Federal garrison at Winchester.[44] Jenkins's troopers drove the Union cavalry from Berryville on June 13 and then threaded a path north toward the Federal garrison at Winchester.[45]

~

On the Federal side, the search continued at Hooker's direction. Union signal parties attempted to intercept Confederate signals, Pleasonton's troopers scouted the roads and kept watch on Stuart, and the Bureau of Military Intelligence pressed all their sources. All found pieces to the puzzle, and the combined evidence convinced Hooker the Confederates were moving north, prompting Hooker to shift his forces in kind.[46] On June 14, an escaped slave claimed to have seen Lee's entire army on the march and headed for Harper's Ferry at the confluence of the Shenandoah River and the Potomac.[47] That same day Pleasonton reported that a Confederate prisoner stated Lee's three Confederate corps—Longstreet's, Ewell's, and Hill's—were all in motion. "He thinks Ewell will be heard from before tomorrow night."[48]

That same evening, a dispatch at 7:15 p.m. reported gunfire "a long distance off, in the direction of Harper's Ferry."[49] At first glance this would seem trivial, but the report came from Federal troopers posted east of the Blue Ridge, on the far side of the mountains from Harper's Ferry. Musketry heard from that distance meant a battle was under way in the Shenandoah Valley.

A later telegram laid everything bare.

June 14, 1863. 12 Midnight

Major-General HOOKER,

Milroy is surrounded at Winchester, and so closely invested that no scout or other information has been had from him later than 11 o'clock. . . . Heavy firing was heard in that vicinity until 7 o'clock, and then ceased. . . . [T]elegraphic communication was broken at the same time. . . . Ewell's force is at Winchester.[50]

Several things were now clear: Longstreet's I Corps was staged in Culpeper, Ewell's 2nd Corps was attacking Winchester, and Hill's III Corps was moving north from Fredericksburg.

Robert E. Lee's grand raid was a reality, and well under way.

9

ALDIE

The Army of the Potomac now stood on high alert, and President Lincoln sent urgent requests to the governors of Northern states for an additional one hundred thousand troops.[1] Winchester and its Federal garrison fell on June 15, and the armory at Harper's Ferry expected a similar fate any day. Civilian sightings came in by the scores, and Confederates were reported everywhere from Front Royal, Virginia, to Chambersburg, Pennsylvania.[2] Hooker knew he was flanked and kept pulling troops from all fronts to stay between Lee's army and Washington per Lincoln's instructions.

The Federals knew Lee's forces were under way, but they still didn't know where they were going, or what they were planning. Frustrated with Pleasonton, the War Department sent out the following directive to their new cavalry corps commander:[3]

> Headquarters Army of the Potomac
> June 17, 1863
>
> Brigadier General Pleasonton, *Commanding Cavalry:*
> GENERAL: . . . Verbal orders have been sent you by Captain Dahlgren. . . .
> [P]ut the main body of your command in the vicinity of Aldie, and push
> out reconnaissances toward Winchester, Berryville, and Harpers Ferry.
>
> The commanding general relies upon you with your cavalry force to
> give him information of where the enemy is, his force, and his move-
> ments. You have a sufficient cavalry to do this. Drive in pickets, if nec-
> essary, and get us information. It is better that we should lose men than
> be without knowledge of the enemy, as we now seem to be.

This tone was a far cry from the earlier praises in the Northern papers, and while aimed squarely at Pleasonton, it may not have been entirely his fault. With Lee on the loose, Hooker remained even more determined to keep his cavalry close and avoid a repeat of Chancellorsville, and he met with Pleasonton on June 16 on the eastern side of the Bull Run Mountains. Exactly what they discussed went unrecorded, but Hooker appears to have directed Pleasonton to hold short of Aldie Gap, on the east side of the Bull Run Mountains. Hooker wanted intelligence on Lee's movements, but Hooker also wanted his cavalry close enough to negate any attacks on his flank from Lee's forces.[4]

Pleasonton advised a different course and recommended Hooker push west of Aldie Gap. If Lee was moving up the Shenandoah Valley for an offensive on Washington, then one of the better places for Lee to turn and strike Washington would be through the Loudon Valley, formed between the Blue Ridge Mountains and the smaller eastern chain of the Bull Run Mountains. By using Snicker's Gap and Ashby's Gap in the Blue Ridge, and Aldie Gap and Thoroughfare Gap in the Bull Run Mountains, Lee had multiple entrance and exit points to stage an attack toward Washington from the Shenandoah Valley, just as Lee had done before in the 2nd Manassas campaign.[5] There were also modern roads coursing east to west across the Loudoun Valley to facilitate moving troops, artillery, and ammunition wagons.[6]

Hooker relented, and on June 17, Pleasonton received orders to move his command through Aldie Gap.[7] The small township of Aldie lay just inside this pass of the Bull Run Mountains where two critical roads formed a junction, the Ashby's Gap Turnpike and the Snickersville Turnpike. The Ashby's Gap Turnpike ran east to west across the Loudoun Valley for twenty-six miles to the pass at Ashby's Gap in the Blue Ridge Mountains and then dropped into the Shenandoah Valley. Likewise, the Snickersville Turnpike ran northwest from Aldie to the Blue Ridge via a second pass through the Blue Ridge at Snicker's Gap.[8] Both turnpikes were commercial avenues with macadamized surfaces—a nineteenth-century technique that laid multiple layers of crushed limestone atop one another to facilitate drainage and allow easier travel for heavy wagons and wheeled vehicles.

Pleasonton left Manassas Junction by noon and sent Colonel Duffié ahead with the 1st Rhode Island Cavalry on a lengthy reconnaissance. Duffié would enter via the south-running Thoroughfare Gap, in the Bull Run chain, and loop back north to the town of Middleburg, the commercial center of Loudoun Valley. Pleasonton would follow with Gregg's 2nd Division on a direct course for Aldie Gap.[9] Kilpatrick would act as the advance element and push through Aldie Gap with his restructured brigade: the 2nd New York, 4th New York, 6th Ohio, and 1st Massachusetts.[10]

～

On June 15, General Lee released Stuart and his troopers to screen the advance of Longstreet's I Corps as they marched north along the eastern face of the Blue Ridge.[11] Once in Loudoun Valley, Longstreet would turn west via Ashby's Gap and Snicker's Gap, gain the Shenandoah Valley, and there turn for points north while hidden behind the Blue Ridge Mountains from Federal eyes.[12] Meanwhile, farther south, A. P. Hill's III Confederate Corps would complete its march up from Fredericksburg and enter the Shenandoah Valley via Chester's Gap, as Ewell had done following the fight at Brandy Station. Stuart's five brigades would act as the rear guard for both the I and III Corps as they moved behind the mountains.[13]

Stuart detailed Wade Hampton and Grumble Jones to remain south along the upper Rappahannock, cover Longstreet's rear, and wait for Hill's corps to come up. Rooney Lee's brigade, now led by Colonel John Chambliss, would move northeast and cover the southern pass in the Bull Run Mountains at Thoroughfare Gap. Fitz Lee's brigade, still under Munford's command, would move north by northeast and screen the upper flank of Longstreet's I Corps by securing Aldie, a small mill town perched on the northeast side of Loudoun Valley.[14]

Normally serving as commander of the 2nd Virginia Cavalry, Colonel Thomas Munford often served as a substitute for Fitz Lee when he fell out sick with bouts of arthritis. Brave on campaign and steady under fire, Munford graduated from the Virginia Military Institute in 1852. "I was not a West Pointer," wrote Munford after the war. "I graduated at the Virginia Military Institute, and had seventeen graduates of that school in my regiment. . . . I don't say this unkindly, but our army had to supply places for graduates of West Point. . . . [S]ome of them had better been at home."[15] Despite Stuart's distinctly divergent opinion on educational institutions, and Munford's tardy arrival at Brandy Station, Stuart still trusted Munford with leading Fitz Lee's brigade: the 1st, 2nd, 3rd, 4th, and 5th Virginia.[16]

The first Confederates to arrive at the crossroads of Aldie were men of the 5th Virginia under Colonel Thomas Rosser. Born in Virginia, Rosser attended West Point, where he became fast friends with one George Armstrong Custer, who went by the nickname "Fanny" at the academy.[17] Rosser chose not to graduate with his pal Custer and, instead, resigned from the academy two weeks before graduation when his home state seceded from the Union.[18] Rosser first served the Confederacy as a gunnery instructor and artillery officer, where he attracted Stuart's notice.[19] Rosser was just the sort of ever eager, always forward West Pointer Stuart liked, and he had the young officer transferred to his cavalry and soon promoted him to command the 5th Virginia.[20] Wounded at Kelly's Ford in March 1863, Rosser had only recently returned to duty when Munford directed him to move on Aldie via the Ashby's Gap Turnpike and pitch camp west of the township. With Rosser out front, Munford and men from the 2nd and 3rd Virginia took a slower advance for Aldie via the Snickersville Turnpike and foraged for needed horse grains along the way. A third detachment from Munford's brigade, the 1st Virginia, 4th Virginia, and Captain Breathed's horse battery, moved toward Aldie in the wake of Rosser's 5th Virginia.[21]

~

Kilpatrick's brigade approached Aldie from the east and soon spotted Confederate pickets ahead in the small township just east of the intersection of the Ashby's Gap and Snickersville Turnpikes. Troopers from the 2nd New York were in Kilpatrick's advance, and these New Yorkers were eager to redeem themselves after the drubbing they took on the railroad tracks below Fleetwood Heights at Brandy Station. Led by Lieutenant Daniel Whitaker, the Federals drew sabres and scattered the enemy in a quick flurry. Not to be outdone, Rosser's picket counterattacked and drove Whitaker back, and pursued their quarry until they came in range of Kilpatrick's main column. Unsupported, Rosser pulled up and sent riders spurring back to inform Munford he had found a sizeable enemy force. Rosser then retreated and posted men on a section of high ground wedged between the intersection of the two turnpikes.[22]

In the following lull, Kilpatrick came forward and placed the 2nd New York along the lower Ashby's Gap Turnpike with the 6th Ohio in support, and directed a two-gun section of Captain Alanson Randol's battery on high ground north of the turnpike junction.[23] As Randol laid his guns, Kilpatrick deployed his skirmishers, and General David Gregg moved up with his staff in tow, including an overly eager young captain named George Custer. Captain Custer had garnered some attention for joining in several horse charges at Brandy Station—including one where he fell from his horse.[24] He drew particular notice this morning when he spurred his horse up a steep creek bank, causing his horse to tumble back into the creek and dunk its rider, much to the amusement of everyone nearby. Now soaked head to toe; the road dust of the turnpike coated Custer's wet clothes in a thick layer of limestone chalk, and he soon resembled a piece of milk-battered chicken ready for the frying pan.[25]

On the other side of town, Colonel Wickham arrived with the 1st and 4th Virginia and conferred with Rosser. Both officers realized the importance of covering the two turnpikes and soon discovered the Cobb House Road, which ran a mile west of the junction and formed an interior

Figure 9.1.   Brigadier General H. Judson Kilpatrick, Army of the Potomac. At times an inspiring officer, Kilpatrick too often threw his men in harm's way for minor gains. *Library of Congress.*

line linking the two turnpikes. Wickham sent the 1st Virginia to cover Ashby's Gap Turnpike, and the 4th Virginia up to the higher-running Snickersville Turnpike. Wickham then placed two guns from Breathed's battery on high ground covering the lower Ashby's Gap Turnpike, and Rosser deployed a line of sharpshooters across a sloping pasture on William Adams's farm that covered the junction of the two turnpikes under Captain Rueben Boston. The rest of the 5th Virginia formed a mounted reserve in close support.[26]

The two sides began trading volleys, and the opposing batteries soon found the range. Kilpatrick, still grossly disappointed with the 2nd New York's prior performance, turned to his former unit and challenged the troopers to "drive everything before you."[27] Squadron commander Samuel McIrvin called for sabres, and led his men through a gap in the turnpike's stone fence. The Virginia sharpshooters opened fire, but the New Yorkers kept coming. They spurred over a knoll and down the reverse slope, where they encountered an unexpected ditch stretching before Boston's sharpshooters. Running purely on fear and adrenaline, some horses leaped the ditch, others refused, and the Virginia sharpshooters opened fire with a devastating volley at close range. Men tumbled from the saddle, but the loose horses now bolted ahead in a panic, stampeding their way through the Virginians among the haystacks. The darting horses broke the Southern line apart, and the remaining New Yorkers jumped from their saddles and started taking cover in the ditch, where they began firing their carbines at Captain Boston's scrambling sharpshooters.[28]

Now grounded and fearing a Confederate counterattack, the New Yorkers signaled for support, and Kilpatrick sent in the rest of the 2nd New York, along with the 6th Ohio.[29] Randol's Federal battery shifted their fire and soon found the range on Captain Boston's mounted reserves, driving them back from the action.[30] Randol's guns continued to rain down cover as the Federals charged forward with the 2nd New York slamming into Boston's left, and the 6th Ohio driving in on the right. Captain Boston and his sharpshooters had no choice but to surrender.[31] This marked the first time a company-sized element of Stuart's troopers had ever surrendered to the enemy.[32]

An elated Kilpatrick lifted his voice in salute and congratulated the 2nd New York leading the captured Virginians to the Federal rear.[33] Kilpatrick now judged any deeper push along the Ashby Gap Turnpike would be a dodgy proposition at best with the 1st Virginia and Breathed's battery still holding the high ground above the haystacks. Kilpatrick couldn't have known exactly what troops he was facing, but the high price he'd paid in

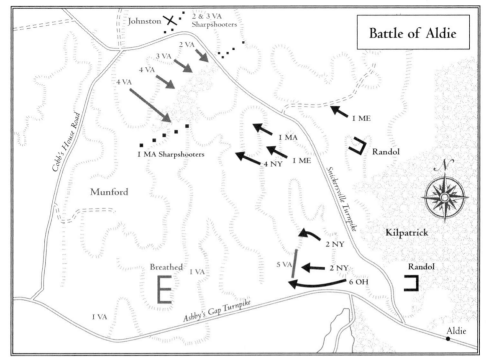

Map 5. Battle of Aldie

removing fifty sharpshooters certainly aided his decision to strike out to his right on the upper turnpike.

~

As the firing began on his right, Munford wisely moved to cover his left flank resting on the upper Snickersville Turnpike and dismounted his escort under Lieutenant William Walton of the 2nd Virginia. Walton soon arranged the sharpshooters behind a series of stone fences flanking a curved section of the roadway.[34] To support Walton's sharpshooters, Munford sent forward a twenty-man section of the 4th Virginia, and he directed a gun under Lieutenant Phillip Johnston to unlimber on the farm of Dallas Furr, where Johnston's gun would overlook the curve in the turnpike and enjoy a clear field of fire at any coming troops.[35]

The movement of these Confederate troops on the upper roadway soon drew the attention of the 1st Massachusetts Cavalry. Many members of the 1st Massachusetts came from a distinguished pedigree going back to the American Revolution, and they formed militia companies in the Boston area prior to the war with names like the "Springfield Horse Guards"

Figure 9.2.   Colonel Thomas Munford, Army of Northern Virginia. Munford was a proud graduate of the Virginia Military Institute, and far from a universal fan of West Point graduates. Munford once stated, "[S]ome of them had better been at home" (Bliss, *Personal Narratives of Events in the War of the Rebellion,* 40).

and the "Boston Lancers." These lofty militias were a popular attraction, and they held public drills where the officers gave fiery speeches and often received tokens from the crowd. Since arriving in Virginia, the 1st Massachusetts had been true to their word and performed particularly well at Stevensburg on June 9 when they routed the 4th Virginia. Today, the Bay Staters would find ample opportunities to continue their record as they moved forward to support a section of guns from Randol's battery posted alongside the Snickersville Turnpike.

Major Henry Higginson led two squadrons of the 1st Massachusetts; the first, under Captain Lucius Sargent, spotted Lieutenant Alexander Payne's 4th Virginia picket on the turnpike, and Sargent moved forward to intercept them. Sargent's larger squadron put Payne's twenty troopers to flight but overpursued, and Higginson galloped forward to rein in his troopers.[36] As Higginson pulled his men back on the road, Captain Sargent, trailing behind Higginson, pulled up and taunted Payne's men with a finger gesture. Having been bested at Stevensburg by the 1st Massachusetts, these 4th Virginians were in no mood for games. They closed on the Federals with a purpose and, in short order, shot down Captain Sargent, Major Higginson, and a lieutenant, and cut a sergeant from the saddle for good measure.[37]

Honor intact, Payne's men galloped back west toward Johnston's gun on Dallas Furr's farm, as the remains of Higginson's squadrons charged after them in earnest. Charges rolled back and forth along the upper turnpike, and both sides began staging additional sharpshooters flanking the roadbed.[38] Kilpatrick now came forward to sweep the Confederates clear with two additional squadrons of the 1st Massachusetts. Captain John Tewksbury commanded the first squadron, and Charles F. Adams, the great-grandson of President John Adams, commanded the second. Tewksbury would charge straight up the turnpike, while Adams's squadron would form south of the turnpike, on Tewksbury's left, and advance over a series of fields stretching between the turnpike and a heavy tree line. The 4th New York Cavalry would stand in reserve on the south side of the pike.

As the Federals made ready, the 2nd Virginia arrived under Lieutenant Colonel James Watts, along with two hundred troopers from the 3rd Virginia Cavalry under Colonel Thomas Owen.[39] Munford saw the Federal squadrons rolling forward and ordered Watts to meet Tewksbury's squadron charging up the turnpike. Watts pointed his men down the road in a column of fours, where the front ranks of Virginians engaged the leading Massachusetts ranks in the roadbed. Watts pushed his next squadron through a gap in the rails on the north side of the turnpike fence, and he directed his following squadron through a gap to the south, which prompted the 4th New York to charge forward from their reserve position. This opened a spreading melee, as the squadron Watts sent north of the turnpike dropped their sabres by the sword knots and opened a destructive flanking fire on the Federals, which routed Tewksbury's squadron in the road.[40]

South of the turnpike, the Federals gained an initial advantage until Watts's Virginians cleared the fence gap, broke the supporting Federal columns, and pressed them back at a gallop with help from elements of the 4th Virginia who also charged forward to join the growing melee.[41] Meanwhile, Captain Adams's squadron of the 1st Massachusetts attempted to make their own charge farther south of the turnpike along the edge of the pastures to flank the 2nd Virginia but were met instead with quick blasts of canister from Johnston's smoothbore posted above the curve in the turnpike. This lone gun kept switching between round shot, to trade counter battery fire with Randol's section at the far end of the turnpike, and close doses of canister to repel the Federal charges as needed. Johnston's gunners later recalled the unusually close nature of the day's combat: "That gun used more canister on that occasion than was ever used by the entire section in any previous engagement."[42] The canister fire caused Adams's Massachusetts squadron to stall before a wide ravine of steep ground in their front on the south side of the turnpike. Adams described the terrain before him as a ditch with a hill beyond, and the canister forced the Federals back from the ravine to take cover in the woods bordering the pastures.[43]

Kilpatrick was far from finished, however, and began rallying the 4th New York in the fields south of the turnpike. That morning, the 4th's commander, Colonel Louis di Cesnola, almost created a regimental-sized brawl when he marched his regiment through the middle of a Union infantry camp, creating a substantial ruckus. Pleasonton had ordered di Cesnola's arrest, and despite this situation, or perhaps because of it, the 4th New York gave out a shout when they saw their colonel duck his guard detail and ride forward to join the 4th New York in a second charge.[44]

Unarmed due to his arrest, di Cesnola formed his men and gamely led them back into the fray.[45] The rallied New Yorkers charged behind di Cesnola and quickly rolled over a company of the 2nd Virginia, spawning a confused jumble of quick charges and countercharges. Watts soon regained control of his men and responded by pulling his command back beyond Johnston's gun, which entailed crossing the ravine south of the turnpike. Now armed with a sabre, di Cesnola and the 4th New York pursued across the ravine and closed on the Cobb House Road.[46] A general melee followed as the Virginians quickly wheeled about—slashing, shooting,

Figure 9.3.   Artist Edwin Forbes drew this image following the Battle of Aldie.
Library of Congress.

and spurring their horses into the Federals. Di Cesnola suffered a hard cut from a sabre before his horse fell and forced his surrender.[47] The rest of the New Yorkers retreated in a disordered wave with the 2nd Virginia in close pursuit.[48]

Captain Adams of the 1st Massachusetts had just dismounted his squadron behind a fence when the 2nd Virginia boiled up out of the ravine on the heels of the New Yorkers. Colonel Watts marked the opportunity and turned for the New Englanders.[49] "Lieut. Col. Watts ran his horse at the fence, cleared it and landed among the enemy. I saw him standing in his stirrups and knock a Yankee off his horse with his sabre. My horse carried me forward, and that was the last time I saw Col. Watts."[50] Shot from his horse, Watts fell to the ground; the rest of the 2nd Virginia followed Watts over the fence and quickly chopped their way through the Massachusetts sharpshooters. "In a second the rebs were riding, yelling and slashing among us," wrote Captain Adams. "I had just dismounted my squadron and given it to the enemy."[51]

The Virginians sabered the Bay Staters back into the trees and then turned about to dress their ranks and ready themselves for the next round in the frantic combat boiling up and down the turnpike and surrounding fields. Kilpatrick did the same on his end and hurriedly called for reinforcements. He had only one squadron of the 1st Massachusetts left; the rest were strewn left and right from prior charges, with some attempting to reform in the rear near Randol's guns.

Luckily for Kilpatrick, a squadron of the 1st Maine came cantering in from Colonel John Gregg's brigade and swung south of the turnpike to wait on the rest of their regiment.[52] Kilpatrick rarely waited on anything, and when he recognized the Virginians were still loading and reforming from their last attack, he ordered Lieutenant Charles Davis and the last Massachusetts squadron to charge up the roadbed. Davis responded and spurred forward in a column of fours, the men standing tall in the irons and ready to clear all before them. They galloped straight up the turnpike, only to be met by a withering storm of canister, carbine, and revolver fire. Munford's men posted behind the fences could hardly miss as the Federals galloped past. "I was so close to these men as they charged by that I could see dust fly from their blue jackets as the bullets from our revolvers would strike them."[53]

Corporal John Weston of the 1st Massachusetts wrote, "[B]ullets rattled in amongst us, hitting scabbards and carbines [and] sounded like hail on a window."[54] Weston watched as a trooper went down in front of him, only to be dragged by his stirrup into the pile of bodies building in the road. "The road was narrow here . . . all blocked up with horses dead and wounded with their legs broken, kicking and floundering. . . . [I]f a wounded man fell amongst them there was not much chance for him." Weston got off a single round from his carbine, only to suffer a wave of return fire. Shot through his right arm, Weston turned his mount about and galloped for the rear, but his horse flipped head over heels from a gunshot. Weston rolled up, grabbed an available horse from a less fortunate comrade, and sprinted back in retreat. He later wrote his sister from a hospital: "Cavalry fighting against Cavalry is exciting I can tell you."[55]

The rest of Weston's squadron weren't as fortunate and milled wildly about between the fences. Now was the perfect time to launch a sabre charge, and Colonel Thomas Owen led his 3rd Virginia forward with blades aloft. The Virginians piled into the turnpike and drove everything before them with elements of the 2nd and 4th Virginia to their right, and the 5th Virginia to their left.[56]

Kilpatrick recognized the enemy barreling down with supporting troops on either side of the turnpike. The first squadron he had in line was Captain Andrew Spurling's of the 1st Maine, which charged forward and struck the 3rd Virginia head-on in a blaring crash of men, mounts, and steel. Sabres scraped, pistols snapped, and a pair of Federal standards fell to the Virginians as they bowled over the squadron from Maine and then rode through the remains of the 4th New York. The Rebels captured fifty men in this sweeping charge of supporting columns, including the fry-battered Custer, but the act of driving through the enemy scattered and disordered the Southern columns in kind. Colonel Owen tried to rally his men back to reform, but they continued on in a reckless bid to take Randol's Federal guns farther down along the turnpike.

Kilpatrick was on the verge of defeat when two additional squadrons from the 1st Maine arrived and charged into the fight along with a rallied battalion of the 4th New York. This combined force took the Rebel squadrons in flank and reversed the momentum in an instant; Custer and half the Federal prisoners bolted free, and Rosser's 5th Virginia quickly lost their standard to the 1st Maine Cavalry.[57]

The Confederates retreated by squads and sections as Colonel Calvin Douty of the 1st Maine arrived, took in the scene, and wisely halted his men. He reformed his ranks and prepared to make a proper charge with enough numbers to carry the position. The roadbed now lay clogged with dead and wounded, and Douty opted for a different course and launched his attack in two wings—one south of the turnpike, and the other to the north. Leading the northern wing, Douty swept everything in his path before rounding the back side of the Furr farm and galloping across the barnyard. Douty drove his men past the farmhouse and all the way up to the wall where Johnston's lone gun lay deployed. Rebel sharpshooters opened with a volley point-blank, and Douty fell dead, shot twice through the body.[58] The loss of Douty stalled the northern wing; however, the southern wing across the turnpike carried past and surged ahead for the Cobb House Road in a rolling melee back through the ravine beside the turnpike.

Meanwhile, Nathan Webb traded sabre blows with a galloping Confederate. "I saw a Reb with his sabre raised. . . . I threw up my bridle arm and received the blow partly there and partly on my head, at the same time giving him a left thrust. . . . My sabre went in between his ribs." Webb reined up and lost contact with his troop; "[T]he dust was so thick I might as well have been a half mile away." Webb turned down a bypath to rejoin his company. "I took this path hoping to get within our line. Just before coming to a turn, I heard horses. . . . They came around the corner three abreast and before I could think twice, one of them had run me down. The concussion grounded both of us. My horse fell on my right leg and before I could disentangle myself, two revolvers were at my head and I heard a voice say 'surrender, you Yankee whelp.' I surrendered."[59]

Far from its base and unsupported, the twin charges by the 1st Maine now ran out of momentum. With Colonel Douty killed, the Mainers rallied back for their lines, while the Virginians reformed around Johnston's smoothbore on the Furr farm. Both sides were redressing their ranks for the next blow when Munford received an urgent summons to fall back from General Stuart.[60]

While the charges surged at Aldie, the Federal cavalry had attacked Middleburg four miles west of Aldie on the Ashby's Gap Turnpike, prompting Stuart to send word for Munford to retreat immediately. Munford withdrew as ordered and turned about for Middleburg, and an unknown enemy in his rear. Kilpatrick didn't know the reason for Munford's retreat but chose not to pursue. The desperate charges coursing along the turnpikes came to a close, and the fighting ended as quickly as it had started. The Battle of Aldie remains one of the classic meeting engagements of the war.

10

MIDDLEBURG 1ST AND 2ND

While the fight at Aldie raged along the two turnpikes, a different scenario unfolded with Colonel Alfred Duffié and his 1st Rhode Island Cavalry. As mentioned before, Pleasonton ordered Duffié to take the 1st Rhode Island Cavalry and mount a reconnaissance through the center of Loudoun Valley. While Gregg's division pushed through Aldie Gap, Duffié would swing south through Thoroughfare Gap in the Bull Run Mountains. Once through, Duffié would turn northwest for Middleburg to occupy this key town on the Ashby's Gap Turnpike.[1]

Guarding the Thoroughfare Gap was Colonel John Chambliss, the former commander of the 13th Virginia, whom Stuart selected to lead Rooney Lee's brigade while Lee recuperated from the gunshot wound to his leg.[2] Stuart knew Chambliss from West Point, where the fellow Virginian graduated a year prior to Stuart. Well mannered and good looking, Chambliss had drawn considerable praise for his role in a sharp fight on the Rappahannock in April 1863.[3] Chambliss's father also happened to serve in the Confederate Congress.[4]

Today would be Chambliss's first real test as a brigadier, and he reached the narrow Thoroughfare Gap in the early afternoon, made a scout of the position, and saw no sign of the enemy. Chambliss ordered sentries set at the pass, and then he and a group of officers from the 9th Virginia retired from the afternoon heat to share an early meal. Not long after, pickets came galloping in to report the appearance of Federal cavalry.[5] The two sides exchanged fire, and the outnumbered Southern pickets fell back before the Union troopers. Shortly after the Federals passed, Chambliss arrived and sent couriers to warn Stuart. As the sun dropped into the tree line, Chambliss ordered the rest of the brigade to saddle up and pursue. Chambliss was not off to a good start as a brigade commander.[6]

Figure 10.1.   Alfred R. Waud's depiction of a cavalry scout. *Library of Congress.*

As Duffié "slid" past Chambliss, Jeb Stuart and his staff parked their horses in Middleburg, where Stuart could keep track of his brigades from a central location. No word had arrived from Chambliss yet, and Stuart and his entourage busied themselves by flirting with some local Virginia belles in the center of town. Around 4:00 p.m., Stuart received a dispatch that Munford had engaged the Federal cavalry at Aldie. Moments later, gunfire erupted on the outskirts of town, alerting all to the sudden arrival of Duffié and his 1st Rhode Island Cavalry.

Stuart and his staff hightailed it out of town without saying farewell to the girls, or in the words of Stuart's adjutant, they were "compelled to make a retreat more rapid than was consistent with dignity and comfort."[7] Two squadrons from the 4th Virginia skirmished with the Rhode Islanders while Stuart and staff rode west along the turnpike to Rector's Crossroads. Along the way, Stuart sent a courier for Munford with orders to retreat from Aldie immediately, and Stuart sent additional riders after Chambliss and Robertson with orders to converge on Middleburg and contest the Federal arrival.

After clearing the Middleburg streets, Duffié began erecting barricades while his men continued to skirmish with the 4th Virginia on the outskirts of the picturesque little town. Duffié guessed his only hope for holding

Middleburg would be through reinforcements from Aldie, and he sent couriers galloping for help. As darkness settled in, Duffié received reports of Stuart approaching with overwhelming numbers, and Duffié moved his horses to a fallback position on the south end of town. Here a stand of trees offered better cover on his flanks than the converging streets along the turnpike, and he erected a second, stouter series of barricades and prepared to meet the enemy.[8] The prudent course would have been to fall back out of town, but Duffié had orders to occupy the town, and after Pleasonton had rescinded his brigade, Duffié determined to follow all his orders to the letter. As stated before, worthy officers have the good sense and courage to know when to disobey an order. Duffié clearly did not.[9]

It wasn't only Pleasonton suffering discontent with his officers. Jeb Stuart had long found Beverly Robertson to be overly cautious, and following Robertson's tepid performance at Brandy Station, Stuart continued to feel his old rival lacked the proper zeal and drive to lead men in close combat. Therefore, when Robertson arrived with his brigade after dark, Stuart pointed Robertson into Middleburg, albeit with a little guidance from Major Heros von Borcke, the self-titled chief of staff of Stuart's military family.[10] von Borcke held a commission in the Prussian cavalry and willingly ran the Federal blockade to serve with the Confederacy. Heavy, and standing six feet four inches tall, von Borcke preferred riding a robust white mule named Katy to support his vast frame.[11] His boisterous personality matched his vanity and sense of humor, but the corpulent Prussian proved a willing scrapper and soon won a friendship with Stuart.[12] His presence beside Robertson was probably no accident, given Stuart wanted to assure Robertson's full participation in the assault on Duffié's troopers.

Robertson's men approached the town at a trot and charged the first barricade. von Borcke, who had been with Stuart earlier in the day when they fled at Duffié's approach, wrote, "As I felt rather ashamed at having been forced to run from the enemy under the very eyes of my fair friends, [I] was naturally anxious to afford them a spectacle of a totally different character." The fleshy Prussian "took his place of honor" at the head of the column and plunged through the first enemy barricade. "It lasted but a few seconds, for the main enemy, unable to withstand the shock of our charge broke and fled."[13] Robertson pursued those who fled to the east, and von Borcke turned south with several squadrons from the 5th North Carolina. The Tarheels bounded after the Federals, giving out the Rebel yell as they charged through the town in a column of fours.

Additional barricades lay ahead of the Tarheels, and the 1st Rhode Island knelt behind the makeshift structures, waiting in ambush. "On they came at a gallop with that peculiar battle yell," recalled a Federal.[14] "When I tell you that this occurred in the darkness of night, and that the enemy . . . were in such order that every carbine discharged was within six feet of a rebel soldier, you can form some estimate of the fatal effect."[15] The Federals opened fire, virtually punching the forward Confederates out of their saddles. Major James McNeill of the 5th North Carolina rode at the column's head when shot through the thigh by a Union carbine; the ball ranged up across his lower torso and exited his hip to drop McNeill in the road among the rest in a wicked pile of men and horses.[16] von Borcke, who apparently wasn't all the way forward at his "post of honor," recalled, "[W]e were engaged in a severe conflict. Bullets whizzed from either side—men and horses fell dead and wounded amidst unavoidable confusion."[17]

Colonel Duffié wrote, "The enemy surrounded the town and stormed the barricades, but were gallantly repulsed by my men with great slaughter. . . . They did not, however, desist, but, confident of success, again attacked."[18] The Tarheels made two determined attempts, and then Robertson arrived and flanked the barricade with additional troops; the Federals withdrew from town.[19] "I was compelled to retire on the road by which I came," continued Duffié, "the only one open to retreat."[20]

As Duffié left town, the North Carolinians captured many of his men, however, some two hundred Rhode Islanders formed on the outskirts of Middleburg and followed after Duffié in the dark. Duffié shook his pursuers after a few miles, and his exhausted men slipped silently from their saddles in a dark clearing where they pitched a silent camp with no fires. Without realizing it, Duffié had set his camp within a half mile of Chambliss's brigade, who had pursued the 1st Rhode Island until the moonless night forced his own command to dismount and rack out with no fires on the far side of this same expansive field.[21]

Gunfire broke the dawn as startled pickets exchanged volleys with the enemy. The 1st Rhode Island rushed to their horses and sprinted down the road, with the 9th Virginia hot on their heels. "Captain Tom Hayne's squadron . . . took the lead," recalled Lieutenant George Beale, "the remainder of the regiment moving after him at a gallop." Haynes's squadron dashed headlong through the morning mist, pressing the Federals so close they couldn't gain enough space to turn and form a proper defense. The Rhode Islanders attempted to come about and engage the Virginians, but at each point several were shot down, marking the failed attempts by the Federals.[22]

Rather than pool together and form for a last stand, Colonel Duffié told his men to scatter and run for the hills. The resulting chase resembled a fox hunt and concluded in less than an hour. All told the 1st Rhode Island lost 225 men killed, wounded, and captured, and only a handful of survivors made it back to the Federal lines with Duffié.[23] This essentially wiped out the 1st Rhode Island Cavalry and cleared Chambliss of his fragile performance the day before. Duffié requested an immediate audience with General Hooker upon his return. It's hard to generate much pity for Duffié. He lied about his past, lied his way into an officer's commission, left his men in the field, and likely lied about that when he met with Hooker. Remarkably, he had won a promotion to brigadier general for his positive actions back in March at Kelly's Ford, and he received this promotion during his meeting with Hooker. In the same meeting, Hooker ordered the new brigadier general out of the Army of the Potomac and sent him to train recruits in West Virginia.[24] Duffié would never again serve in the Army of the Potomac.

John Singleton Mosby was a rare individual among Confederate officers. He didn't come from a particularly wealthy family, grew up in the Catholic Church, and as a young man served a term in jail for shooting a fellow student in a questionable case of self-defense. There was always an edge to Mosby. He often sought controversy, and an acquaintance once described him as a "disturbing companion."[25] While serving his jail sentence for assault, Mosby read law with his prosecuting attorney and following his release became one of Virginia's newest lawyers. At the start of the war, he enlisted as a private in the 1st Virginia Cavalry, where he served in Captain William "Grumble" Jones's company. Captain Jones quickly recognized Mosby's bravery and uncanny ability to slip through Federal lines without notice. He rewarded Mosby with a lieutenant's commission and all the reconnaissance work the young lawyer could handle.

Stuart also recognized Mosby's abilities and soon had the officer attached to his staff. Mosby then scouted the route around McClellan's army that won Stuart a major general's stars.[26] In return, Stuart had Mosby awarded his own command of Partisan Rangers, fully commissioned and sanctioned by the Confederacy, and created to operate behind Federal lines. On June 17, as Robertson's troopers were battling with Duffié in and around Middleburg, Mosby and his Rangers caught and kidnapped a pair of Federal officers carrying dispatches from Hooker to Pleasonton.[27] Mosby recognized the value of the information right away, calling it "the open sesame to all Hooker's plans," and sent the dispatches on to Stuart.[28]

Figure 10.2.   Colonel John S. Mosby, Army of Northern Virginia, circa 1865. By 1863, Mosby had gained the trust of both Jeb Stuart and R. E. Lee. *Library of Congress.*

Stuart read the material and realized he was significantly outnumbered and now faced Pleasonton's new corps, plus an enemy infantry division poised to push west across the Loudoun Valley. In addition, a separate force of Stahel's Federal cavalry from the Washington defense forces would push south via Warrenton in search of A. P. Hill's III Corps.[29] Stuart would have to adopt a purely defensive posture to keep Lee's infantry from being discovered—in particular Longstreet's I Corps—now passing through the Loudoun Valley on its way over the Blue Ridge to gain the west side of the mountains.[30] Stuart passed this intelligence on to General Lee and ordered Wade Hampton to intercept Stahel's Federal probe driving southwest for Warrenton.[31]

~

Meanwhile, behind Federal lines, Hooker and his staff knew Ewell's II Corps had taken Winchester, and elements linked with Ewell had crossed the Potomac; however, that only represented a third of Robert E. Lee's forces. Hooker needed to find the rest of Lee's army and determine Lee's intent for the rest, some fifty thousand Confederates that, for all practical purposes, had gone missing somewhere in Virginia.

Lincoln and general in chief Halleck continued to press Hooker for information, and Hooker responded to Halleck on June 17: "All my cavalry are out, and I have deemed it prudent to suspend any farther advance of the infantry until I have information that the enemy are in force in the Shenandoah Valley."[32] Hooker then turned to Pleasonton for the latest news, and Pleasonton responded following the fight at Aldie: "I have driven Fitzhugh Lee's cavalry from this place . . . their [number in] killed and wounded is very large. . . . The fact of Fitz Lee's cavalry being here does not speak well for Stuart's raid."[33]

Pleasonton's dispatch showed the idea of a raid by Stuart still lingered in the Federal mind-set, and the fighting at Aldie failed to answer the larger questions of what Lee's greater plans were. Pleasonton's dispatch also illustrated the fact that Pleasonton had yet to clear the Loudoun Valley. Worse still, Pleasonton had to amend his first glowing report on the fight at Aldie as Union casualties continued to mount in the surgeon's logs from the sharp contest; 19 Union officers were killed, wounded, and captured, along with 286 enlisted men.[34] In Hooker's mind, this only underscored the continued need for more cavalry, which Halleck had flatly rejected. "We can never discover the whereabouts of the enemy," wrote Hooker, "or divine his intentions so long as [the enemy] fills the country with a cloud of cavalry. We must break through that to find him."[35]

Hooker also advocated for an attempt to divide Lee's forces, if Lincoln would simply direct Halleck to allow Hooker the leeway to do so: "It may be possible now to move to prevent a junction of A. P. Hill's corps with those of Ewell and Longstreet. If so, please let instructions to that effect be given me."[36]

Lincoln, however, had already picked his dog in this fight. He continued to support Halleck over Hooker, and the president informed Hooker he had been placed "in the strictest military relation to General Halleck," meaning Hooker wore the shortest command leash possible.[37] Hooker rankled at the insult and felt his ability to perform in the field had been cut to the quick.

As Hooker sparred with Halleck, Pleasonton continued to comb the Loudoun Valley for intelligence. The day after Aldie, he sent the following dispatch: "Some [escaped slaves] report that they heard Lee's forces were returning toward Culpeper. Should this prove to be the case, it seems to me this entire movement of Lee has been with the object of getting off re-enforcements from his army to Vicksburg."[38] Pleasonton went on to ask for infantry support, stating, "I will push my entire command through, and compel the enemy to show his hand."[39]

~

Pleasonton's forces departed Middleburg the morning of June 19 and headed west along the Ashby's Gap Turnpike. Sparkling creeks, spreading oaks, and giant chestnuts dotted a landscape rich in pastures, grain plots, and orchards. Stone fences and walls were everywhere, with shorter, three-foot-high stone walls between pastures often topped with staked wooden rails, while taller, five-foot stone fences framed the main roads, carriage-ways, and turnpikes. A Federal described the country west of Middleburg as "a succession of ridge and valley, of field, meadow and wood. . . . A prominent feature of the landscape, as viewed from the ridges, were the stone fences. They intersected each other in every direction and at all angles."[40]

The Federal advance under Colonel John Irvin Gregg had only gone a mile past Middleburg when they came under Confederate artillery fire from an enemy gun posted behind one of the many stone walls. On the brow of the hill stood a single Confederate gun, and to either side of the pike were several more scattered across the high ground. Stacked stone walls flanked either side of the crest, with a taller stone fence on the north side of the pike extending down the roadbed to sweep any advance coming up the pike. Back top the hill sat a blacksmith's shop south of the turnpike, and along the crest the stone fences bristled with the silhouettes of hat brims and carbine barrels.[41]

Figure 10.3.   Colonel John Irvin Gregg, Army of the Potomac.
Gregg led an impressive attack on a strong Confederate position outside Middleburg, Virginia. *NARA.*

The Rebel shelling continued, and Colonel Gregg dismounted and edged closer to the enemy line with his field glasses. Determined in action, John Gregg never hurried about half-cocked; his men called him Long John for his six-foot, four-inch frame, and he sported a drooping cavalier mustache any one of Napoleon's Hussars would have been proud to wear.[42] After glassing the enemy guns, Gregg judged a mounted attack would never take the position alone, and he began dismounting his troopers to prepare for a ground assault. Horse holders collected their comrades' mounts and headed for the rear as Gregg anchored the left of his line with the 4th Pennsylvania, followed by the 16th Pennsylvania and then the 10th New York. Two squadrons of New Yorkers remained mounted to serve as the reserve along with the entire 1st Maine, now commanded by Lieutenant Colonel Charles Smith in place of the fallen Colonel Douty.[43]

As the minutes ticked by, and Gregg continued to study the enemy ahead, General David Gregg, John's elder cousin and division commander, grew restless and sent a staff officer forward to ask why the attack was taking so long to begin. Cousin John didactically explained that he faced significant opposition ahead; enemy batteries were well posted, and dismounted troopers sat perched and waiting behind solid cover. If the attack was to succeed, the colonel recommended additional troops deploy from outside his brigade to flank the north side of the Confederate line and "get those fellows started [for the rear] behind that wall."[44]

General Gregg weighed his cousin's reply and sent the 2nd New York and 6th Ohio, all that remained of Kilpatrick's brigade, to boost Colonel Gregg's forces. A delay ensued as these troops shuffled forward and took positions on the north side of the pike. This all took a considerable amount of time, and it was an hour or more before Colonel Gregg's assault stood ready to advance.

The assault started to the south, as the 4th and 16th Pennsylvania sharpshooters advanced across open fields. As they closed on a family cemetery, they came under fire from sharpshooters with the 4th and 5th North Carolina, tucked in behind a stone wall bordering the old graveyard. The wall and attending headstones gave excellent cover, and the Tarheels were dealing lethal volleys into the coming Federals until they were driven in by a sprinting foot charge made by the 4th Pennsylvania, which gained the Tarheel flank. As the Tarheels fell back, Gregg's men stormed into a stone-built house beside the cemetery but soon received fire from Southern gunners, who whistled a few rounds of solid shot into the home, and the Pennsylvanians quickly fled from the stone splinters flying through the dwelling. Elsewhere, the Tarheels continued to fall back for the cover of some woods, and the Federals pursued, bringing on a point-blank firefight as the two sides scrambled for cover from tree to tree.[45]

Gregg now ordered a charge from his mounted reserves by Captain George Brown's squadron of the 1st Maine, and Brown's men spurred across the open field. Surprised by the sudden dash, the Rebel gunners and the sharpshooters scrambled to turn back the charge. Brown regrouped, charged twice more, and caught the Rebels falling back to another position. Dodging trees and ducking branches, the North woodsmen opened a running stream of revolver and carbine fire that turned the flank of Robertson's line and, again, forced the Tarheels back for the rear. Brown's troopers and the dismounted Pennsylvanians closed quickly, capturing Lieutenant Colonel Edward Cantwell and taking numerous prisoners from the 4th North

Carolina.[46] Gregg later praised Brown's mounted squadron for "capturing more prisoners than they had men in their command."[47]

At the same time, Federal dismounts from the 10th New York swept forward for the high ground along the turnpike, with the 2nd New York and 6th Ohio making concurrent foot charges in the fields farther out on the Federal right. These attacks suffered stiff artillery fire from Stuart's gunners and endured a series of rolling carbine volleys from sharpshooters of the 13th Virginia deployed behind the stone walls flanking the turnpike. Luckily for these Confederates, the Federal horse gunners were more intent on counter battery fire, and poured round shot on McGregor's battery, deployed beside a fence on the crest of the hill. "We being near a stone fence made it more dangerous for us, as the stones would fly in every direction when struck by the enemy's shells."[48]

Gregg's attack now grew in pace, and he sent two squadrons of the 1st Maine galloping straight up the turnpike. Rebel carbines opened on the 1st Maine, but covering support from Gregg's sharpshooters forced many Rebels to keep their heads down behind the walls; as the Mainers closed the distance, the lone Rebel gun in the roadbed couldn't fire canister for want of hitting their own sharpshooters. This allowed the two Federal squadrons to bull forward, gain the hillcrest, and boil over the Confederate gun in a wave of slashing sabres.

Waiting in reserve on the far side of the crest, Colonel Richard Beale of the 9th Virginia pressed forward in a well-ordered charge by platoons. The 1st Maine saw the Virginians coming and wheeled into the attack as Beale's men struck their flank, shooting, slashing, and unhorsing the 1st Maine's commander, Lieutenant Colonel Smith, and killing Captain George Kimball.[49] With their command structure wavering, the Federals steamed back down the pike until they approached the Federal skirmish line, where a volley halted the 9th Virginia's pursuit. A second melee broke out here, and an officer in the Pennsylvania infantry witnessed the clash from a distance. "The two lines intermingled in . . . inextricable confusion. Sabers flashed, men yelled, horses reared. There was cutting, slashing, cheering; rider-less horses dashed madly to the rear, or ran aimlessly up and down the line."[50]

Lieutenant George Beale of the 9th Virginia recalled an unhorsed Federal who, "having fired his last cartridge," began furiously throwing rocks at his assailants until he was shot down and killed. Beale then hurried a prisoner back at the point of his sabre as bugles sounded the recall, and the Federals began forming for a counterattack.[51] As the 9th Virginia retired through their lines, they passed General Stuart at the crest of the hill with his attendant staff in tow. Stuart sensed the time had come to start staging a withdrawal and now ordered his guns to the rear.[52]

As the Southern gunners limbered for the rear, Gregg sent the 10th New York Cavalry charging up the turnpike, but Rebel carbine fire turned them back in short order. However, Gregg's left-hand Federals, the sharpshooters of the 4th and 16th Pennsylvania, had reformed and came charging forward through Robertson's riddled right flank, and these Union sharpshooters effectively flanked Stuart's position on the crest of the hill. John Gregg's coordinated attacks were succeeding, and Stuart ordered Chambliss's sharpshooters to retire. The 13th Virginia fired a volley and withdrew north of the pike, and the 2nd New York raced forward to gain the abandoned wall and use the same to fire on the retreating Rebels.[53]

Meanwhile, Stuart, his staff, and Heros von Borcke were directing the fire of the 2nd North Carolina, still holding the line near the blacksmith's forge on the crest of the hill south of the turnpike. The 2nd North Carolina were good troops, and many carried quick-firing, revolving cylinder carbines—essentially side hammer revolvers fitted with long barrels, deep cylinders, and shoulder stocks—and these Colt carbines came in handy as the Tarheels began exchanging fire on multiple fronts to buy time for their horse gunners and drivers to retire.[54] Federal carbines tore across the crest in reply, splattering through the forge and ricocheting up off the roadbed. The Federals "commenced pouring a galling fire into our ranks," recalled a member of Stuart's staff. "[T]he line fell back across the open field with a steadiness . . . halting and returning fire with all the promptness and regularity of an everyday drill."[55]

Stuart and his staff were now the only mounted Confederates near the crest, and the Federals soon directed their fire at the moving cluster of horses behind the Tarheels. "Just then I heard a thump," recalled Captain Blackford, "like someone had struck a barrel a violent blow with a stick. I knew well enough what it meant. I looked around to see which of the group would fall. My first glance was towards General Stuart, but he sat firm as a rock in the saddle. I then saw von Borcke who was riding close by my side drop his bridle hand and become limp, his horse bounding forward as the rein relaxed."[56] Blackford and the others grabbed von Borcke and gained control of his panicking mount by sharply twisting the animal's ear to settle it down. They led the horse and rider from the field and straight for a surgeon as bullets continued to pepper the ground about them.

The Tarheels continued firing and falling back, slowly surrendering the crest to Gregg's Federals before joining the rest of Stuart's gunners and troopers at a second line of stone walls and fences a half mile down the

Copyright 1914
E. B. Higgins

Figure 10.4. Major Heros von Borcke. A Prussian-trained cavalry officer, von Borcke joined the Confederate service and became fast friends with Jeb Stuart. *Library of Congress.*

turnpike.[57] Unbeknownst to the Federals, Stuart had picked this fallback position earlier that morning in the event his first line failed.

Colonel Gregg rode to the hard-won crest followed by his cousin, David, along with General Pleasonton. As Colonel Gregg collected his brigade, the two general officers studied Stuart's second position. This second line appeared as formidable as the first, and Pleasonton halted to wait on Buford's two brigades operating north of the turnpike to arrive before pressing any farther. This proved a mistake as Buford was actively skirmishing with Grumble Jones's and Fitz Lee's brigades near the hamlets of Pothouse and Union, and they didn't join Gregg's division until early evening, in effect halting the Federal advance where it stood while Pleasonton waited.[58] Ever composed, Pleasonton seemed content to hold and rest on John Gregg's laurels as reporters from the *New York Times* scurried forward over the captured ground.[59]

The Federals began to bury the dead, and many bodies received shallow graves where they fell. General Gregg was riding about the field after the battle when he came across a Welshman of the 10th New York, sitting beside an empty grave and near a Confederate body lying on the ground. The Welshman appeared to be in a daze as he stared into the distance.

"What's stopping you?" asked Gregg.

The Welshman looked up at Gregg and motioned to the fallen Confederate. "I jus' waiting fer 'im to die."[60]

Middleburg had seen a marked improvement in Federal tactics. Under John Gregg's leadership, the Federals executed a brilliant attack combining artillery, sharpshooters, and well-timed horse charges. Tactically, the Federals won a clear victory, strategically perhaps not.

11

BATTLE ON THE TURNPIKE

June 20 delivered a torrent of rain that flooded the local creeks and rivers and completely curbed all operations in both the Federal and Confederate camps. While waiting for the weather to clear, Pleasonton received new intelligence from David Gregg: "A rebel infantry soldier . . . states that the [Confederate] infantry force which was on this side of the Blue Ridge, passed through Ashby's Gap yesterday into the Shenandoah Valley and that only Stuart's force is this side of the Blue Ridge."[1]

This information fell in line with earlier reports and convinced Pleasonton he only faced Stuart's cavalry in the Loudoun Valley and that Lee's infantry had all passed west of the Blue Ridge. This meant Pleasonton could now engage Stuart's troopers without the worry of facing Rebel infantry, and he quickly moved to take advantage of the opportunity. "I . . . respectfully request that the general commanding permit me to take my whole corps tomorrow morning, and throw it at once upon Stuart's whole force."[2]

Pleasonton also asked Hooker for a sizeable force of Federal infantry to bolster his attack against Stuart and batter the unsupported enemy cavalry. "I should like to have a couple of large brigades, or a division of infantry . . . so that they can get in position without being seen by the enemy, and engage the sharpshooters with Stuart while [my] cavalry attacks and puts to flight their horses."[3] Pleasonton's plan was simple— he'd clear the way through Ashby's Gap, breach the Shenandoah Valley to determine Lee's plans, and perhaps cripple Stuart's cavalry along the way. Hooker approved the request, and Pleasonton began issuing orders for the coming assault. Gregg's 2nd Division would again drive straight up the Ashby Gap Turnpike, while Buford's 1st Division advanced along secondary roads to the north of the turnpike.[4]

Unfortunately for Buford's troopers, many missed drawing rations the night before and had to make do with a short fare of hardtack and water. Private Daniel Pulis of the 8th New York Cavalry wrote his parents: "I have heard you tell how hard it must be to fight on 1 [hard]tack a day but I [don't] think it is. I eat 1 for my supper the night before the fight and did not eat any more till the night after."[5] It's doubtful many of Trooper Pulis's comrades would have proclaimed the same glowing outlook as they saddled up and swung aboard, all intent on breaching the Blue Ridge.

~

For the first time since Brandy Station, Stuart had all five of his brigades collected in one place, along with all five of Major Beckham's horse batteries. To keep Lee's intentions hidden, Stuart set his brigades in a rough line running north to south, in effect bridging the Ashby's Gap Turnpike on his south flank and the Snickersville Turnpike on his north.[6] Thomas Munford would take the far left across the Snickersville Turnpike, Grumble Jones's brigade would cover the hamlets of Union and Pot House, and John Chambliss's brigade would hold at the Welbourne Plantation. Next in line, between Pantherskin Creek and the Ashby's Gap Turnpike, he placed Beverly Robertson's weakened brigade of North Carolinians, and finally, anchoring the far right across Ashby's Gap Turnpike sat Wade Hampton's brigade, having had just returned from a successful mission to the south against Stahel's Washington District cavalry.[7]

With his brigades effectively standing shoulder to shoulder and no poised reserves, Stuart wasn't setting a trap; instead, his plan meant to cover a broad front more than five miles wide and trade ground for time.[8] Stuart expected the major push to come along the Ashby's Gap Turnpike in an attack much like the Middleburg assault two days prior, and he directed his brigades to the north to fall back with the sound of the guns, honoring—or, in effect, tracking—Stuart's line as they maneuvered through the day.[9] As added insurance, infantry from Longstreet's I Corps would hold picket at Ashby's Gap and act as a stopgap to ensure the pass remained in Southern hands.[10]

~

Lieutenant William Fuller, Battery C, 3rd U.S. Artillery, opened the fight on June 21 by firing on Hampton's Confederates on the Ashby Gap Turnpike about halfway between Rector's Crossroads and Middleburg. Captain James Hart's horse battery returned the fire. Hart's four guns straddled the turnpike and spread south, well covered by sharpshooters from Hampton's 1st North Carolina and the Jeff Davis Legion.[11] "Hotly at it they went" with sharpshooters and infantrymen firing at one another while the horse

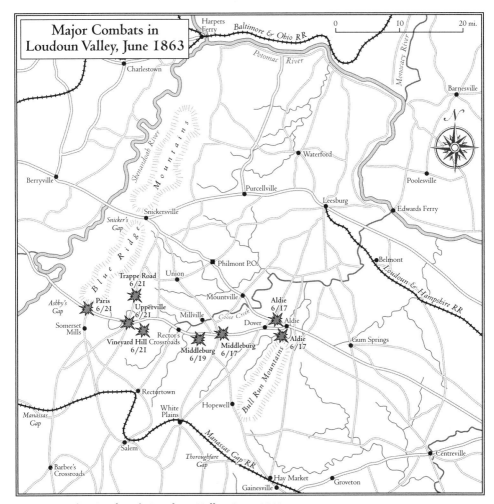

Map 6.   Major Combats in Loudoun Valley, June 1863

gunners dueled at long range until one of Hart's guns splintered its axle—
likely caused by the wheels being mired in the mud from recent rains—that
forced the carriage to absorb more recoil.[12] The gun remained mounted but
had to be pulled out of line as the rest of Hart's battery continued to fire
at the enemy. As the artillery duel continued, a similar fate befell a second
gun in Hart's battery, and he ordered it led away as well.[13]

In the meantime, Pleasonton directed Vincent's infantry to come up
and flank the right of Hampton's position. Vincent sent companies from
the 16th Michigan to make the assault with dismounts from Kilpatrick's
2nd New York Cavalry. Bullets whistled back and forth as the Federals

tried pressing ahead but made little initial headway against Hampton's sharpshooters, and Pleasonton responded by ordering the rest of Vincent's infantry into the fray. The added firepower of the additional infantry soon compelled Hampton's troopers to retreat.[14] Captain Hart also began retiring when a Federal round from Fuller's battery struck the gun's limber chest and triggered a series of explosions, which flipped the gun, disabled some of the crew, and killed several horses in their traces.[15]

The Federal infantry surged forward after the cannon, followed by a sprinting knot of horsemen. The infantry now grew angry at what they thought were Kilpatrick's cavaliers coming to claim the capsized cannon for their own, as the infantry felt they should have the honor of claiming the piece by being the first to arrive.[16] In reality, the honor should go to Fuller's battery, and whatever gun commander sighted the round that struck the Confederate ammunition chest! As it turned out, the "cavalry" claiming the piece was actually the horse gunners from Fuller's battery, and they dashed back to their battery after claiming their prize.[17]

All honors aside, Pleasonton was driving Stuart down the turnpike and making good time for Ashby's Gap.

∽

Elsewhere, Buford and his 1st Division were doing their best to press west between the two turnpikes. Colonel William Gamble's brigade led the advance, composed of the 8th Illinois, 12th Illinois, 3rd Indiana, and 8th New York. A forty-five-year-old native of Ireland, Gamble talked with a lilting brogue and wore a wiry pair of muttonchop side-whiskers that epitomized the look of a veteran. The look came well earned. Gamble had served a prior stint in the British dragoons before immigrating to the United States in 1838, when he joined the U.S. 1st Dragoons. He rose to the rank of sergeant major, fought in the Seminole Wars, and left the army in 1843. In 1861, he received a lieutenant colonel's commission in the 8th Illinois Cavalry. The following year, he took a bullet through the chest while leading a charge against Southern pickets and had only recently returned to action.[18] This morning Gamble's Irish was up, and he started the day hell-bent on making up for lost time.

Gamble's 3rd Indiana made contact with Grumble Jones's brigade that morning, and suffered a stinging fire from sharpshooters with the 11th and 12th Virginia, under the command of Colonel Lunsford Lomax. Heavily wooded and broken, the terrain between the turnpikes was cut through with steep-banked creeks, brush-choked hollows, and large brambles of thorn-ridden blackberries. Farm lanes switched back and forth through the tight woods, and every pasture approached stood flanked by stone fences, stone walls, timber rails, or combinations of all three. It was a sharpshooter's paradise, and Lomax's rear guard wreaked havoc on Gamble's column, repeatedly forcing the Federals to halt, dismount, shake out a line, send in additional troopers, and even bring up guns from Captain Graham's Battery K, 1st U.S. Artillery, to hammer a way through.[19]

Buford soon grew impatient and attempted to bypass Lomax's stubborn sharpshooters, but the recent rain had turned the banks of the local creeks into quagmires. Horses would sink to their knees at places and would only cross with the greatest exertions. It was one thing for a single trooper and his mount to cross, but pulling the cannons and caissons over the flooded creeks proved extremely difficult. At one point, Buford heard firing to his left between Stuart and Pleasonton on the turnpike and attempted to push cross-country, only to find the course blocked at every turn by more creeks, the unrelenting stone fences, and vine-strewn brushwood. Falling behind, Buford sent Major Samuel Starr to take his Regulars Brigade on ahead to join Pleasonton via the Millville Road, while Buford and Gamble turned west only to lag farther and farther behind with his artillery.

Out on the turnpike, Hart's whittled battery continued to deploy, fire, and withdraw again, under the cover of Hampton's troopers. Stuart was hard pressed by Pleasonton's coordinated use of infantry, artillery, and cavalry on the turnpike, and when he heard about Buford pressing Jones's brigade on his left, he sent orders for Jones and Chambliss to move ahead and "effect a junction at Upperville" where they could join Stuart and "make a more determined stand" with combined numbers.[20]

Watching the Rebels withdraw, Pleasonton believed his first brush with Stuart had gone quite well, and he remained intent on sweeping Stuart's cavalry aside.[21] Pleasonton continued to drive forward from wall to wall along the turnpike until they came to the bridge at Cromwell's Run, a steep-banked creek where Stuart placed the remains of Hart's battery with sharpshooters in support. Pleasonton deployed Calef's and Fuller's batteries in kind, and the Federal horse gunners soon found the range, suppressing the fire of not only Hart's lone gun but the newly arrived batteries of captains William McGregor and Marcellus Moorman as well.[22] The rapid and accurate fire of the Federal batteries allowed Pleasonton's skirmishers to push on to the creek, climb down the banks, and swarm across the narrow stone bridge.

Stuart again withdrew to the next major obstacle on the turnpike, the bridge at Goose Creek. To screen the retreat, Hampton's 1st South Carolina Cavalry came up to cover the retiring Confederate gunners. Like many

Figure 11.1. Brigadier General Wade Hampton, Army of Northern Virginia. Hampton was an excellent brigade commander who proved his worth on multiple occasions. *Library of Congress.*

of Stuart's regiments, not all of Colonel John Black's 1st South Carolina squadrons were flush with shoulder arms, and as Black dismounted a contingent of sharpshooters under Captain Angus Brown, he soon saw they were outnumbered by Federal infantry bearing down the turnpike and firing as they came on.[23]

Black's sharpshooters opened in reply, but the swarming Federal infantry were expert in this work and kept up a continual fire that pressed the South Carolinians rearward. Colonel Black ordered mounted squadrons forward, and the troopers drew sabres and presented on the road to stall the Federal infantry with the threat of poised squadrons ready to charge. Pleasonton saw the Rebels's display and brought up Fuller's battery, which unleashed a severe shelling on the enemy. The fire swept over the 1st South Carolina and Moorman's guns. Captain Brown went down with several of his troopers, and the South Carolinians retired back across the bridge.[24]

Despite the heavy price, the time bought by Moorman and the 1st South Carolina allowed Stuart's remaining gunners to find a position on a western bluff overlooking the bridge at Goose Creek.[25] The contest again reverted to an artillery duel as the two sides arced shells across the lengthy bridge, and new guns arrived from batteries E and G of the 1st U.S. Artillery, giving the Federals twelve guns to open on the Confederates.[26] The terrain here strongly favored the Union troops, as the creek bed below the bridge ran sharp and steep on the Federal side and lay flat and broad on the Confederate end, offering little close cover for Southern sharpshooters to sweep the bridge. This meant Hampton's dismounts would have little effect on any Federals charging the bridge or the creek, and the Confederate batteries would have to shoulder the burden with little support.[27]

The twelve Federal guns soon gained the upper hand and swept the Confederate position with a maelstrom of shell and case, killing artillery horses and troopers alike, and driving the Southern gunners to shelter. Pleasonton ordered a charge and Kilpatrick turned to his 4th New York Cavalry, but the charge fell apart when Stuart's gunners jumped back to man their pieces and turned the New Yorkers about. Unfazed, Pleasonton sent for Vincent's infantry while Fuller's guns continued to pound the Southern batteries and dismounted the last gun in Captain Hart's battery. Stuart knew the time had come and began pulling his people as Vincent's infantry forded the creek. Not to be outdone by the infantry, Kilpatrick sent a squadron from the 2nd New York Cavalry charging across the bridge, and the Federals took the position with few additional casualties.

Trading ground for time is what Stuart had expected. What he hadn't expected were the losses accrued in his horse batteries, nor the surprising drive the Federals were showing today—the same recent drive they'd shown at Brandy Station, Aldie, and Middleburg.

~

Pleasonton also suffered his share of casualties, including Vincent's infantry brigade, which could no longer keep pace with the cavalry. Vincent's men had been marching since before dawn and were now worn out by the midday heat and hard fighting. Dripping with sweat, they fell out beside the road and left the rest of the fighting to the cavalry. Pleasonton regretted their loss, but he still had plenty of cavalry on hand as he approached Upperville with Kilpatrick's brigade in the lead. The brigade topped a rise in the turnpike to reveal a large section of open ground and a carriage drive for Oakley Plantation, which bore sharp to the left at the top of the rise. Sloping down, the turnpike sank to a low spot of ground straight ahead, and then lifted again to the high ground of Vineyard Hill on the south side of the turnpike. A mile past Vineyard Hill lay the town of Upperville, and looming behind the town rose the Blue Ridge Mountains with the telltale notch of Ashby's Gap now just five miles away.

With their goal now in plain sight, the Federals pushed their mounts into a canter. At this same moment, back across Pantherskin Creek on the Federal right, Kilpatrick's troopers saw Buford's men accelerating into an advance from a half mile out. Kilpatrick's men lifted a cheer at the sight of Buford's squadrons, even as they started their own separate advance along the pike. Kilpatrick described the moment: "I pushed forward . . . throwing the 6th Ohio into three columns with Squadron front on the right of the road, the 2nd N.Y. in the road, and the 4th N.Y. on the left and in columns of Squadrons. At this moment a shout was heard far on our right—it came from Buford's people charging the enemy—it was a most beautiful sight— my men caught the spirit . . . and with one wild hurrah: they echoed back the shout and rushed upon the foe."[28]

Awaiting this charge were the brigades of Beverly Robertson and Wade Hampton. Robertson's 4th and 5th North Carolina sat north of the turnpike, where they deployed as sharpshooters behind yet another set of Loudoun County stone fences. Kilpatrick's columns had just crested the turnpike when the Tarheels saw Buford's squadrons advancing in the distance on their flank. The 4th and 5th North Carolina had lost many field officers in the recent fights around Middleburg, and the sight of Buford barreling down on their left, and Kilpatrick charging their front, caused many troopers to break for the rear. Some remained to fire a few scattered volleys, but eventually all abandoned their position.

What the North Carolinians didn't realize was the nature of the ground Buford would have to cross to reach their line. What appeared to be open ground actually lay crisscrossed with a maze of steep ditches and fences that halted Buford's advance before he ever reached Pantherskin Creek.[29] Robertson's North Carolinians, however, were already streaming to the rear, and to Kilpatrick's troopers this was a miracle in the making. The Federals brought back their spurs, eased out the reins, and came on at the charge.

Stuart rode forward as the Tarheels broke. He knew the brigades of Chambliss and Jones were heading for the Trappe Road, which joined the turnpike behind him in Upperville proper. If Stuart couldn't hold the Federals here at Vineyard Hill, Chambliss and Jones could be cut off, and their trains and artillery captured or destroyed. The last brigade Stuart had on hand was Hampton's, now falling back upon Vineyard Hill south of the pike to keep their own flank from being turned by the sudden retreat of Robertson's brigade.[30]

Fortunately for Hampton, Kilpatrick had allowed his charge to lift into a sprint from entirely too far away and he hadn't noted the low, flooded ground beside the turnpike from yesterday's rains. This resulted in his horses flagging as they strained through flooded bar ditches beside the road, and his ranks were spreading badly when they closed on Hampton's rear regiment, the Jeff Davis Legion of Mississippi on the south side of the turnpike. Fumbling and sliding, Kilpatrick still managed to spur forward at the head of the 4th New York and roll into Hampton's rear, but in a decidedly push me–pull me fashion. Sergeant Creekmore of the Davis Legion recalled, "When [Hampton] saw them charging us he ordered us to right about wheel and meet them, but we had no time to execute the wheel. . . . We did not wait to form but dashed [right] at them."[31]

The Mississippi troopers bowled into the left front of the 4th New York, cutting, slashing, and driving into the Federal ranks. The charging Rebels boiled past Kilpatrick without notice and, instead, focused on Captain Nehemiah Mann, actively leading his New Yorkers forward in the midst of the melee. Mann received a sabre stroke across the face, cutting him from cheek to jaw, and he fell to the deck, where a second Rebel shot him in the back below the shoulder blade.[32] Seeing their captain fall, the New Yorkers boldly rushed to his defense and, joined by rear ranks still arriving, surged into the Rebels and rescued the still unnoticed Kilpatrick.[33] At the same time, gunfire ripped through the Davis Legion from Union cavalry on the turnpike when the 2nd New York, blocked in the roadbed

Figure 11.2.   Edwin Forbes's sketch of the fighting along the turnpike at Vineyard Hill. *Library of Congress.*

by the bordering stone fences, fired across the barrier at the Mississippi troopers.[34] The gunfire peppered the Mississippi ranks and forced some to turn and engage in a running gunfight fired over the stone fence lining the pike.

The Davis Legion had no sooner faced this threat when Major Samuel Starr's Regulars charged in on the south side of the turnpike.[35] Starr's command had been on the north side of the road when ordered in, and the 1st and 6th U.S. bolted across the pike above Kilpatrick's route, dropped into single file, and squeezed through what gaps they could find in the fence and turned after Hampton's brigade. "Our Regt. was ordered to charge & wheeling had to pass a narrow defile in a stonewall," wrote Lieutenant Tattnall Paulding of the 6th U.S. Regulars. "[W]ithout waiting to form we were ordered to charge."[36] Captain George Cram led the 6th Regulars in their wild rush to reach the enemy, while the more disciplined 1st U.S. under Captain Robert Lord reformed after passing the

wall, kept their order, and wheeled in on the Davis Legion's right flank. The Federals pierced the Mississippi ranks and drove through; a surging sabre brawl spread across the ground below Vineyard Hill, prompting a captain of the 1st Regulars to claim this attack was "the finest sabre charge of the war. . . . We completely overthrew the Jeff Davis Legion and captured many prisoners."[37]

Wade Hampton countered the Federal onslaught by drawing his sabre and leading a battalion of the 1st North Carolina straight into the mix.[38] Bugles pealed and the 1st North Carolina charged "in echelon to its right."[39] Squadrons charged, reformed, and charged again in a rolling melee that saw men hacking one another to the ground and firing point-blank, their pistols popping and cracking like a wildfire in a cane break. "By this time our ranks were so confused that it was almost impossible to rally them correctly," recalled Sergeant Creekmore.[40] The Southern ranks were slipping, and Stuart spurred into the middle of the melee to rally his men to the moment. Recognized by Federal officers of the former frontier 1st Dragoons, Stuart became the target of a torrent of pistol fire as he threaded his way through the surging lines: "[A] fierce hand to hand fight took place and Stuart fought with the men like a common soldier. I never witnessed a greater jumble of gray and blue uniforms."[41]

Lieutenant Colonel William Delony of the Cobb Georgia Legion recognized the rapidly deteriorating situation as Federals swarmed through the Confederate ranks. Without orders, Delony charged in with his Georgians and delivered the needed weight to drive the Federals back across the field.[42] Yet even this blow didn't end the fight, and the contest raged on as Captain Lord's 1st Regulars bent but refused to break.

"My squadron lost 26 men in a few minutes," recalled Captain Isaac Dunkelberger of the 1st Regulars. Now falling back, the captain spotted Confederates "charging us in the rear with drawn sabres. . . . I gave the order left about wheel. Private Casey wheeled about, he and a Confederate brought their sabres in [at] tierce point and ran each other through the chest."[43] Both men fell to the deck and later died. Watching from the balcony of her home, Ida Dulany viewed the action spellbound as Hampton's men pressed the Federals back across her front lawn in a whirlwind of sabre cuts and surging horses: "[T]he shouts of the men, the cries of the wounded, and the flash of the [guns], made a scene terrible to me, and every now and then a horse with an empty saddle ran terrified by the house, telling the sad tale of his rider's fall. Once my blood turned cold at seeing one gallop by dragging a dead man under him."[44]

Attrition began to tell as Hampton's troopers drove the Federals back up to their line of sharpshooters posted along the Oakley estate's carriage drive.[45] "I had gained ground to the right and front of more than half a mile," wrote Hampton, but his left flank along the turnpike still lay wide open. "At this moment the 2nd South Carolina was brought up . . . and under its protection I reformed my command."[46]

From this new position, Hampton noticed more enemy cavalry in his front and even more Federal dismounts deploying behind the turnpike's stone fences. The Federal fire increased, and men began to drop in the 2nd South Carolina soon after they deployed, with the first man shot in the head and the second having half his face torn off by a Union shell.[47] After facing Federal infantry earlier that morning, Hampton mistakenly judged the growing number of carbine barrels peering over the fences as full-length muskets belonging to Federal infantry.[48] At this point, Stuart received word Jones's and Chambliss's brigades were in range of the turnpike, and Beverly Robertson's Tarheels had reformed in Upperville. The need to hold a firm line at Vineyard Hill had passed, and Stuart called for a withdrawal.

Hampton's brigade rode out at their own pace with eighty prisoners in tow, bypassed the town, and left the field to Pleasonton and his troopers. Hampton's men might have ridden out at their leisure, but it had been no easy day for the brigade. The Davis Legion lost thirty-two men in the fight, and George Saussy, a veteran of the fight on Fleetwood Heights, recalled seeing more "gory sabres on exhibition" in the ranks here than ever before.[49]

Pleasonton watched the Confederates go. He hadn't exactly driven Stuart from Vineyard Hill, but he had forced him to retire. The Federal corps commander now turned toward Upperville and began forming his last brigade for the push through Ashby's Gap.

12

TRAPPE ROAD AND UPPERVILLE

John Buford pulled his columns to a halt and watched the Federal charge roll down the Ashby Gap Turnpike for Vineyard Hill. Once again, Buford found his column barred from reaching the fight by the terrain in his front, this time by a series of steep ditches and intertwined walls on the high ground north of Kinchloe's Mill.[1] Blocked yet again, Buford now pushed west where his scouts were closing on the Trappe Road, which linked the Millville Road to the Ashby's Gap Turnpike below. Buford guessed Chambliss's and Jones's wagons would turn from Millville Road onto Trappe Road and drive south to join Stuart's Confederates at Upperville. Buford knew he couldn't reach the turnpike to join Pleasonton, but he might gain an inside leg on the Confederate column as it turned south on Trappe Road, and offer his men a chance to cut the enemy column and capture the Confederate train and artillery.[2]

The 2nd North Carolina Cavalry rode at the head of the Confederate train. Following the death of Solomon Williams at Brandy Station, Jeb Stuart selected Colonel William Payne of the 4th Virginia to command the 2nd North Carolina. Today Payne's new Carolinians were serving as the advance element of Chambliss's brigade, with the 9th and 10th Virginia, and Lieutenant John Shoemaker's two-gun section from Moorman's horse battery forming the front half of the train. The second half began with Captain Roger Chew's horse battery followed by Jones' brigade; the 6th, 7th, 11th, and 12th Virginia, all trailing after Chew.[3] The Rebel train turned south on the Trappe Road and began making good time when Federal Minié balls started whining through the air and ricocheting off the stone fences lining the road.

The column came under fire as they passed the Thomas family farm, a large sprawling set of fields east of the Trappe Road, divided by stone walls topped with stake and rider rails to separate the family pastures, stock pens, orchard, and barnyard. Ranging out front, the 2nd North Carolina spotted Federal sharpshooters posted behind a corner in the stone walls near the Thomas farmhouse, with the Trappe Road passing just two hundred yards from this corner.[4] Composed primarily of Gamble's 12th Illinois, these troops had just arrived from above Kinchloe's Mill and quickly took up sharpshooter positions in range of the road until more help could arrive.[5]

Colonel Payne ordered the 2nd North Carolina to charge forward and clear the enemy from the walls, and allow the Confederate wagons and artillery to reach Stuart on the turnpike in Upperville. The Tarheels quickly formed platoons and spurred ahead. "We had to charge in a line across an old field some ½ mile exposed," recalled George Bryan of the 2nd North Carolina.[6] Bryan and his fellow troopers closed on the far wall at a gallop, and a bullet swept Bryan from his saddle just as he reached the wall. More Federal volleys followed, and the 2nd North Carolina turned about, enduring the Federal fire coming and going.

Federal brigade commander William Gamble arrived at this moment and looked out over the open pastures of the Thomas farm to see enemy cavalry on the run. Colonel Gamble had suffered a hard morning of crumble-banked creeks, thick woods, and hidden fire from Lomax's rear guard. When he saw Rebel troopers galloping back over open ground, he quickly formed his men for a charge.[7]

While Gamble rushed to form his men, Chambliss kept moving down the Trappe Road with the rest of his brigade.[8] The narrow roadbed sat flanked with combinations of stone fences, shorter stone walls, and rail fencing, and Chambliss easily recognized the threat building in the Thomas family pastures. In response, he directed Shoemaker's section to form on high ground west of the road on the elevated Gibson property, and the gunners "rushed at the stone fence, partly pulling and partly pushing the stone[s] down."[9] After tearing a gap in the wall, Shoemaker's men pulled their guns off the road and went into battery across the road from Gamble's Federals. While the gunners made ready, Chambliss ordered the 9th Virginia to support Shoemaker and, next, directed the remaining wagons to turn on the Llangollen Road, running west for the mountains.

Luckily for Chambliss, Captain Roger Chew's battery now came trotting down the Trappe Road. Though only twenty years old, Captain Chew had studied artillery tactics at the Virginia Military Institute under Stonewall Jackson and, later, served extensively as a battery commander in Jackson's Valley campaign of 1862.[10] The young captain could see Shoemaker's guns west of the Trappe Road with the 9th Virginia, as well

Figure 12.1. Colonel William Gamble, Army of the Potomac. An intrepid horse soldier, Gamble is shown seated center, with his staff, following the campaign. *Library of Congress.*

as the rest of Chambliss's wagons milling about in the roadbed.[11] Chew knew time was crucial—Gamble's sharpshooters were within two hundred yards of the road, and he could see the 2nd North Carolina falling back in disorder across the fields in the Thomas pastures on his left.[12] Chew made the snap decision to deploy his battery by sections, one east of the Trappe Road, and the other to the west, to support the 2nd North Carolina, and keep the Federals from charging forward and cutting the Confederate column in half.[13] The fence east of the road had already been let down, and Chew directed one section through this gap on the east side of the road.[14] "The first section ran through the gap in that little field."[15] Chew then deployed his second gun section west of the Trappe Road, to act in tandem with the first.[16]

Chew's gunners unlimbered as Gamble's men came charging forward to engage the 2nd North Carolina, but when the Federals spied Chew's first section on the near side of the road without close support, they rushed forward to capture this section.[17] Chew's gunners were quick to respond and opened in a fury. "We unlimbered and gave them 10 rounds," recalled gunner Charles McVicar from Chew's battery. "We are firing faster than I ever saw artillery fire."[18] Canister burst through Gamble's men and shattered the Union attack, "pitching the colonel headlong to the ground,"

Figure 12.2.   Light artillery going to the front. *Library of Congress.*

wounding Lieutenant Colonel David Clendenin's mount, and killing others as troopers instinctively hunkered down tight over their saddles as horses dropped in heaps before the guns.[19] "The guns were served with deadly effect," said Chew after the war, and later witnesses counted dozens of dead horses piled in one section of the Thomas pasture.[20]

The Federals scattered before this killing fire until Major William Medill of the 8th Illinois pressed forward, waving squadrons into the flanks of the maelstrom.[21] Troopers spurred back in and delivered a volley with their carbines, driving Chew's gunners to the deck behind "two impassable stone fences" that prevented the guns from being overrun.[22] Bullets rattled off the smoking cannon, and things were looking poorly for Chew's gunners when the rallied 2nd North Carolina hit the Illinois troopers in the flank.[23]

"At it we went," recalled an Illinois trooper, "chiefly relying upon our revolvers, and the rebels upon their swords."[24] The lines mixed, and the battling troopers closed in tight. "Sabers flashed all around. . . . [T]he fire of small arms was raging all over the field."[25] Troopers grappled for control as Chew's gunners retook their posts and opened on targets of opportunity. The surrounding fences and stone walls served as a blessing and a curse, providing havens for Federal sharpshooters and Confederate gunners alike, but curbing any quick support from mounted squadrons outside the partitions. The Federals easily had the numbers, but the close support of Chew's battery firing from both sides of the road balanced the odds.

This combination of canister and Carolinians proved too much for the Federals; Gamble's men fell back, unmasking Chew's guns from the Federals still posted behind the Thomas stone walls, and the Union sharpshooters again opened on the Southern gunners. In addition, Shoemaker's section had used up the last of their ammunition and now limbered up and took out cross-country for Ashby's Gap, leaving Chew with dwindling support.[26] In response, Grumble Jones sent the 12th Virginia forward with colors flying.[27]

Gunners Charles McVicar and John W. Henry were ordered to let down a fence beside the guns for the cavalry. Henry was shot through the head and fell dead on McVicar just as they completed the task. McVicar dragged his friend's body aside, and the 12th Virginia stormed through the gap and rushed at the distant fence shielding the Federal sharpshooters. "Major Charles O'Farrell [*sic*] used our gap and with sabre drawn led a squad to charge the fence."[28] The Virginians were met with a wave of carbine fire, O'Ferrall was shot through the chest, and his color-bearer fell beside him.[29] W. H. Redman of the 12th Illinois later wrote his parents that he fired his carbine twenty times from behind the Thomas stone walls. "I should hate to say now that I did not hit a Reb. . . . We can whip [them] any time."[30] The 12th Virginia fell back from the deadly stream of fire, and Gamble's Federals swept forward yet again. Squadrons of the 8th Illinois, 3rd Indiana, and 12th Illinois now cantered across the stone-ringed field, determined to take the ground once and for all and seize Chew's forward guns.

Grumble Jones replied with a second charge, this time from the 11th Virginia.[31] Led by Lieutenant Colonel Oliver Funsten, the 11th burst into the field and turned for the coming Federal horse soldiers.[32] The two sides met in a spinning crash as the 2nd North Carolina and a squadron of the 10th Virginia spurred in to join the fray. "[T]he fight became general all over the field. . . . [M]en on both sides were charging in every direction."[33] The sprawling melee gave Captain Chew the cover he needed, and his drivers galloped forward, "in horse artillery style," limbered the guns, and took out at a gallop.[34] Gaining the road, the drivers whipped the guns between the fences, crossed to the west side of the road beyond Chew's other section, and slung the cannons back about. Gunners dropped the trails in seconds and reopened in earnest.[35]

As the Virginians and North Carolinians traded blows with the Illinois and Indiana troopers, Grumble Jones sent still more support from Company D of the 7th Virginia. The Company D troopers sprinted down the face of the Thomas walls, emptying their revolvers down at Gamble's sharpshooters as they spurred past.[36] The novel tactic failed to dislodge the sharpshooters but managed to screen their fire long enough to aid Jones's and Chambliss's men in their swirling fight with Gamble's men in the field. Chambliss now looked for fresh troops to feed in and soon realized the 9th Virginia had retired with Shoemaker's battery when the gunners had

Figure 12.3. Captain Roger Preston Chew, Army of Northern Virginia. An outstanding horse gunner, Chew studied artillery tactics under Stonewall Jackson at the Virginia Military Institute. *Wiki Commons VMI Digital Collection Original Author, Heywood, Charles Town VA photographer.*

expended their ammunition, and riders galloped after the 9th Virginia with orders to return to the fight immediately.[37]

This proved a wise decision, as Devin's Federal brigade now arrived to lend their weight in the contest. Devin formed the 17th Pennsylvania Cavalry for an attack and rapidly deployed a two-gun section under Lieutenant Theophilus von Michalowski for support.[38] The Pennsylvanians entered the fight just as Jones's men were retiring and the 9th Virginia was returning, with the 9th taking the field in clumps of ones and twos as they filed through narrow gaps in the stone walls bordering the road. "We charged . . . not in well ordered ranks, but rather each man for himself, and drove the mounted men before us, but soon found ourselves exposed to the fire of [their] carbineers . . . and were forced to retire with heavy loss."[39] Still, the combined Confederate elements of Chambliss, Jones, and Chew effectively stalled the Federals on all fronts. "The enemy frequently charged up to the stone fence," wrote Chew, "but it was easy to make the gap so hot with canister that they would not venture across."[40] After a quarter hour of nonstop combat, the Southerners were quick to take advantage of the lull and retreat for Ashby's Gap.[41]

One of the last to leave was Corporal Stephen Terry of the 2nd North Carolina, whose battle-whittled squadron endured the entire fight. He covered his remaining troopers with a few parting shots from his Colt revolving rifle and slipped through a gap in the wall on the Trappe Road.[42] In their wake, Devin's men stormed across the field, only to be shelled and scattered by Chew's battery as the Rebel guns fell back by stages, firing, limbering, and redeploying, with one section leapfrogging the other on a course for Ashby's Gap. "This is undoubtably the hardest place the battery has ever been in," recorded diarist Charles McVicar from Chew's battery. "We are cooling our guns and filling our ammunition chests on the move at a gallop. We fought them hard for about fifteen minutes and were compelled to fall back through fields and across high ridges at an awful rate."[43]

Buford had come within a stone's throw of cutting the Confederate column to pieces; however, the prize now slipped between his fingers, as the Confederate train rode on for the Blue Ridge, albeit in a decidedly piecemeal fashion.

≈

Hugh Judson Kilpatrick had never been long on self-examination. There stood a very good chance he'd already forgotten his botched charge at Vineyard Hill as he sat his horse on the turnpike and studied the hamlet of Upperville and the looming mountains behind. Clearing Ashby's Gap remained the Federal objective, and Upperville clearly had to be taken if

Pleasonton wanted to cross the mountain pass. A New York newspaper described the township as "a beautiful little village laying at the foot of the Blue Ridge and but a few miles from Ashby's Gap. For many miles around the village the plantations are all large and the mansions generally in a good state of repair. Nearly every family has a representative in the Rebel army. All are Rebels, and not an open door or a cheerful countenance is seen."[44]

Kilpatrick looked over his shoulder to see John Gregg's brigade coming up beside Pleasonton with the 1st Maine in the lead. Kilpatrick still held a strong appreciation for these New Englanders after Brandy Station and Aldie, and he turned to Pleasonton and nodded at Upperville. "If I had the First Maine, they would go through."[45] This came as a direct slight to John Gregg, the 1st Maine's brigade commander, but Pleasonton liked aggressive commanders with "the proper dash" and gave his permission, no doubt pleased his chief gutter brawler still wanted to push ahead.[46]

A squadron of the 1st Maine soon went galloping down the turnpike with the rest of the regiment following and Kilpatrick trailing in their wake. A scattering of Rebel troopers and a single Confederate gun lay in wait as the Federals steamed forward. Fortunately for the sons of Maine, the gun commander fired high and late, and the spreading cone of grapeshot sailed over the heads of the charging troopers. With the Federals now upon them, the gunners abandoned their cannon and turned west. Galloping after their quarry, the 1st Maine spied enemy cavalry on a hill to their right above the turnpike. These were elements of Robertson's North Carolina Brigade who, after fleeing earlier, had rallied on their officers among some stone walls covering the turnpike.[47]

The Tarheels let fly with a volley that swept the roadbed and checked Captain George Brown's squadron, but Brown's Federals rallied and turned down a crossroad to return fire.[48] Brown passed a gate, switched from column to line, and spurred up a hill as the rest of the 1st Maine pressed ahead on the turnpike. Now flanked, the North Carolinians fell back with Brown's squadron in pursuit, turned back onto the turnpike, and closed on the intersection with the Trappe Road, where tall stone fences constricted the road on either side. Waiting here were squadrons from the 5th North Carolina staged in columns of four, who let their fellow Tarheels past, before charging straight ahead at the coming Yanks. The Federals fired a parting volley and did their best to turn about in the roadbed, with the Carolina squadrons closing fast. Things were looking dim for Brown's squadron, when other squadrons of the 1st Maine dismounted in the field north of the pike, braced their carbines along the stone fences, and opened fire.[49]

Figure 12.4.   A sketch of the 1st Maine engaging the enemy dismounted.
Library of Congress.

Bullets whined off the walls and horses tumbled, but the 5th North Carolina closed ranks and kept coming when fortune again smiled on the Federals. John Gregg had not simply abandoned his men to Kilpatrick; instead, he'd posted his 4th and 16th Pennsylvania as a ready reserve, and when the 1st Maine came fleeing down the turnpike, the reserve fired a volley square into the teeth of the pursuing Tarheels. Saddles emptied, but the 5th North Carolina again closed up and rushed in. The fight turned hand to hand, with men slashing, clubbing, dragging, and wrestling one another between, over, and across the stone fences bordering the pike. Colonel Peter Evans of the 5th North Carolina charged past the bodies littering the lane and made straight for the enemy, cutting down the first Yankee he reached and spurring past, only to be shot from the saddle and fall in the turnpike with a mortal wound.[50] A handful of Tarheels charged after their colonel and suffered similar fates. The rest realized the numbers were hopelessly unequal and turned in retreat. Beverly Robertson watched the last of the 5th North Carolina filter back, and he pulled up stakes, effectively surrendering the township to the Federals.

Charles Gardner of the 1st Maine later wrote, "[T]hrough all this, I seemed to lead a charmed life and had not been hit, but many times had been badly scared. However, I kept the ranks O.K. and shot all I could. Whether I hit anyone or not, I do not know, and do not want to know."[51]

The remains of Robertson's brigade continued west for Ashby's Gap and soon gained the hamlet of Paris, Virginia, on the eastern slope of the mountains. The hamlet offered an excellent view back out over Loudoun Valley, and Captain Chew's battery now sat astride the turnpike, covering the approach to Ashby's Gap.[52] Trailing Federals soon appeared, and Chew opened fire, sending shells arcing down on Pleasonton's troopers, who scattered rapidly below. After thirty rounds, Captain Chew ceased firing, certain the Federals weren't coming up the turnpike that evening.[53] Pleasonton had driven Stuart all day and come a scant half mile from taking Ashby's Gap. Nonetheless, he'd determined Lee's infantry was clear of the Loudoun Valley and now turned back about for Middleburg, writing, "Stuart has the gap covered with heavy Blakelys and 10-pounder parrots."[54]

After five days of combat, Stuart's screen had held but only by the thinnest of margins. Both sides performed exceptionally well, and for perhaps the first time in the war, the opposing cavalries rode evenly matched, with the Federals holding the edge in resources and the Confederates still a shade out front in experience.

As the sun set that Sunday evening, Daniel Pulis and his fellow "hard tack" troopers from the 8th New York gained a glimpse into the Shenandoah Valley. Ordered to scout west by Buford after the fight on the Trappe Road, the lone company of troopers avoided the heavily guarded pass at Ashby's Gap and, instead, climbed the crest to peer down into the valley.[55] Lying below were the evening cook fires of a Confederate camp that stretched for miles in either direction—proof positive Robert E. Lee was not heading for Vicksburg.[56]

13

CROSSING THE POTOMAC

The following points define the tactical situation of General Lee's campaign as it stood on the evening of June 21, 1863:

- Stuart moves his cavalry into Culpeper County in late May.
- June 4: Longstreet's I Corps marches north from Fredericksburg.
- June 4: Ewell's II Corps marches north from Fredericksburg.
- June 7: Longstreet's I Corps joins Stuart at Culpeper.
- June 9: Pleasonton attacks Brandy Station.
- June 11: Lee orders Ewell to move ahead without Stuart.
- June 13: Hooker marches his infantry north from Fredericksburg.
- June 14: Ewell attacks the Federal garrison at Winchester.
- June 15: Stuart screens Longstreet's I Corps north from Culpeper.
- June 17: Pleasonton enters Loudoun Valley; engagement at Aldie.
- June 18: Ewell's II Corps crosses the Potomac. Longstreet's I Corps enters Shenandoah Valley.
- June 19: Hill's III Corps enters Shenandoah Valley.
- June 21: Pleasonton takes Upperville; fails to clear Ashby's Gap.

On the evening of June 21, about the time Captain Chew's gunners were firing the last rounds at Pleasonton's troopers, Stuart met with generals Lee and Longstreet on the east slope of the Blue Ridge. It had been a long day for Stuart, but he still took time to meet with Lee and broach the subject of how he would cross his cavalry over the Potomac.[1] Stuart's five brigades had screened Longstreet's corps since June 15, while Ewell's corps struck the advance, toppled Winchester, and crossed the Potomac with Jenkins's cavalry. This put Ewell several days ahead not only of Hill and

Longstreet but also Stuart, and Lee now wanted Stuart at the head of his army as it moved through Pennsylvania.[2] As a former frontier cavalryman, Lee knew this would be no easy task, and much consideration went into how it could be achieved.

The most obvious route would have Stuart cross to the west side of the Blue Ridge and follow the army down the Shenandoah Valley to the Potomac. This would entail navigating roads snarled with Rebel infantry, artillery trains, and miles and miles of sustenance and supply wagons.[3] Passing them would jam the roads, slowing the wagons, the infantry, the artillery, and Stuart's troopers from reaching their destinations.[4] Longstreet also thought if Stuart took this western course, his movements would draw Pleasonton's attention and increase the existing threat to Lee's line of march.[5] An alternate route, with Stuart moving north along the eastern face of the Blue Ridge, no longer remained an option as Hooker's infantry was now moving north to cover Washington, and thousands of Federal eyes were watching the eastern slope of the Blue Ridge.[6]

According to Charles Marshall, General Lee's aide-de-camp, Stuart proposed a third option. "Stuart suggested that he could move down with his cavalry near Hooker, and annoy him if he attempted to cross the river, and when he found that he was crossing he could rejoin the army in good time." Marshall did not witness this meeting; he heard all this secondhand from Lee, and he claimed Lee further stated "that General Longstreet thought well of the suggestion and had assented." Marshall said Lee, "in reflecting on the subject," thought it might be possible for Stuart to cross the Potomac "east of the Blue Ridge and above General Hooker, thus avoiding the delay of returning through Snicker's or Ashby's Gap and crossing [the Potomac] above Harpers Ferry."[7] Stuart could then rejoin the army north of the Potomac.

This option held advantages and disadvantages. [O]n the positive, it kept Stuart away from Lee's columns and therefore limited Lee's exposure to Federal cavalry patrols. It also gave Stuart the opportunity to harass and range the Federals as they moved north, and it would sever Hooker's line of communications with Washington, DC. An eastern route also held the potential of scrambling large amounts of Federal forces to deal with a perceived raid on Washington—an attack the Federals had long been expecting—and any diversion of Federal attention onto Stuart would drain Federal forces away from Lee and give the Confederate infantry a greater head start on their march to Pennsylvania. On the negative, it would entail a separation between Stuart and Lee, and Stuart risked being cut off and defeated by overwhelming Federal numbers.

It is extremely unlikely Stuart divined this idea out of thin air on the evening of June 21, and far more likely Stuart adapted a prior plan to current conditions.

Pleasonton's attack on Brandy Station delayed Stuart's advance by six days, and the original plan for Stuart's movements are unknown; however, Stuart's interactions with scouts Frank Stringfellow and John Mosby reveal several clues.

In early June, Stuart sent Frank Stringfellow from the 4th Virginia Cavalry to examine the fords of the Potomac on the east side of the Blue Ridge.[8] Stuart also sent Confederate partisan John Mosby to Rowser's Ford, another crossing point east of the Blue Ridge, to attack the Federal outpost guarding Rowser's Ford.[9] Mosby crossed the Potomac and made the assault at dawn on June 10.[10] His rangers killed seven Federals, captured seventeen, and scattered the rest. Mosby had found, tested, and confirmed a crossing point for Stuart east of the Blue Ridge—just twenty-four hours after Stuart had originally planned to screen Ewell's march north. Lee never intended crossing his infantry east of the Blue Ridge, so the actions of Stringfellow and Mosby appear to be for Stuart's benefit and show Stuart was seeking a path across the Potomac separate of Lee's course—before Pleasonton launched his attack on Brandy Station.[11] It's highly unlikely Stuart kept Lee in the dark regarding these operations.

As events played out, Stuart now sat with General Lee at Ashby's Gap on the evening of June 21, discussing the option of crossing the Potomac east of the Blue Ridge to gain Ewell's right flank in Pennsylvania. The following morning, Lee wrote the orders below for Stuart, which first passed through General Longstreet.

HEADQUARTERS

Millwood, June 22, 1863, 7 p.m.

Maj. Gen. J. E. B. Stuart *Commanding Cavalry:*

GENERAL: General Lee has enclosed to me this letter for you, to be forwarded to you, provided you can be spared from my front, and provided I think that you can move across the Potomac without disclosing our plans. He speaks of you leaving via Hopewell Gap, and passing by the rear of the enemy. If you can get through by that route, I think you will be less likely to indicate what our plans are than if you should cross by passing our rear.

Please advise me of the condition of affairs before you leave, and order General Hampton—whom I suppose you will leave here in command—to report to me at Millwood, either by letter or in person, as may be most agreeable to him.

Most Respectfully,

JAMES LONGSTREET, *Lieutenant-General*

N.B.—I think that your passage of the Potomac by our rear at the present moment will, in a measure, disclose our plans. You had better not leave us, therefore, unless you can take the proposed route in rear of the enemy.[12]

General Lee's orders followed:

HEADQUARTERS,
22nd June, 1863

Major General J. E. B. Stuart, *Commanding Cavalry*

GENERAL: I have just received your note of 7:45 this morning to General Longstreet. I judge the efforts of the enemy yesterday were to arrest our progress and ascertain our whereabouts. Perhaps he is satisfied. Do you know where he is and what he is doing? I fear he will steal a march on us and get across the Potomac before we are aware. If you find that he is moving northward, and that two brigades can guard the Blue Ridge and take care of your rear, you can move with the other three into Maryland and take position on General Ewell's right, place yourself in communication with him, guard his flank and keep him informed of the enemy's movements, and collect all the supplies you can for the use of the army. One column of General Ewell's army will probably move towards the Susquehanna by the Emmitsburg route, another by Chambersburg. Accounts from him last night state there was no enemy west of Fredericktown. A cavalry force (about one hundred strong) guarded the Monocacy Bridge, which was barricaded. You will of course take charge of Jenkins' brigade and give him necessary instructions. All supplies taken in Maryland must be by authorized staff officers for their respective departments, by no one else. They will be paid for or receipts will be sent to the owners. I will send you a general order on this subject, which I wish you to see is strictly complied with.

I am, very respectfully, your obedient servant.

R. E. LEE, General[13]

These two letters show Lee and Longstreet agreed Stuart might be best advancing on an eastern course, and both officers agreed there were several disadvantages to Stuart crossing the river west of the Blue Ridge Mountains via the Shenandoah Valley. One was time. Lee states, "General Ewell's army will probably move towards the Susquehanna by the Emmitsburg route, another by Chambersburg." Lee's letter shows he planned to divide Ewell's corps and move both elements against the Pennsylvania capital at Harrisburg on the Susquehanna River. One part of Ewell's corps planned to move via Chambersburg, Pennsylvania, while the second part planned to move farther south via Emmitsburg, Maryland.[14] The Chambersburg route would pass west of the mountains to reach Harrisburg; the Emmitsburg route required crossing back over to the east side of the mountains, and then a move through York, Pennsylvania, to screen any Federals coming north from Washington, before again turning north for a drive on Harrisburg. Lee wanted Stuart to join Ewell's southern column somewhere near York, Pennsylvania.[15]

Stuart currently sat east of the mountains at Rector's Crossroads in the Loudoun Valley. If Stuart were to cross the Potomac west of the mountains, he would first have to double back and cross over the mountains in Virginia, and then recross the mountains a second time in Maryland or Pennsylvania to gain Ewell's flank at York, Pennsylvania. The western course would be inefficient, longer, and harder on Stuart's horses. If Stuart stayed east of the mountains, he would have a more direct track to York, on what promised to be a much faster route.

Lee was clearly concerned about time, and the possibility of Hooker stealing a march ahead of him. "I fear he will steal a march on us and get across the Potomac before we are aware." Lee adds, "If you find that [Hooker] is moving northward . . . you can move . . . into Maryland and take position on General Ewell's right." Lee knew the clock was ticking, and he wrote a set of orders to General Ewell the same day informing him that Stuart might cross the Potomac east of the mountains, separate from the main army.

HEADQUARTERS,
June 22nd, 1863, 3:30 p.m.

Lieut. Gen. R. S. Ewell, *Commanding, &c.:*

GENERAL: I have just received your letter of this morning from opposite Shepherdstown; mine of to-day authorizing you to move towards Susquehanna has reached you ere this. After dispatching my letter, learning that the enemy had not renewed his attempt of yesterday to break through the Blue Ridge, I directed R. H. Anderson's division to commence its march towards Shepherdstown; it will reach there tomorrow. I also directed General Stuart, should the enemy so far have retired from his front as to permit the departure of a portion of the cavalry, to march with three brigades across the Potomac and place himself on your right and in communication with you, keep you advised of the movements of the enemy and assist in collecting supplies for the army. I have not heard from him since; I also directed Imboden, if the opportunity occurred to cross the Potomac and perform the same offices on your left. I am, most respectfully.

R. E. LEE, General[16]

Circumstances permitting, Lee appears to have already decided on sending Stuart east of the mountains.

Stuart next met with Mosby at Rector's Crossroads; Mosby reported a route to Rowser's Ford remained open. Encouraged by this news, Stuart left to meet with Lee on June 23 to discuss the details of his route.[17] After meeting with Stuart, General Lee issued a second set of orders for Stuart.

HEADQUARTERS,

Maj. Gen. J. E. B. Stuart, *Commanding Cavalry,*

GENERAL: Your notes of 9 and 10:30 a.m. to-day have just been received. . . .

If General Hooker's army remains inactive, you can leave two brigades to watch him, and withdraw with the three others, but should he not appear to be moving northward, I think you had better withdraw this side of the mountain to-morrow night, cross at Shepherdstown [west of the mountains] next day, and move over to Fredericktown.

You will, however, be able to judge whether you can pass around their army without hinderance [*sic*], doing them all the damage you can, and cross the river east of the mountains. In either case, after crossing the river, you must move on and feel the right of Ewell's troops, collecting information, provisions &c.

Give instructions to the commander of the brigades left behind, to watch the flank and rear of the army, and—in the event of the enemy leaving their front—retire from the mountains west of the Shenandoah, leaving sufficient pickets to guard the passes, and bringing everything clean along the Valley, closing upon the rear of the army.

As regards the movements of the two brigades of the enemy moving toward Warrenton [Stahel's cavalry] the commander of the brigades left in the mountains must do what he can to counteract them, but I think the sooner you cross into Maryland after tomorrow, the better.

The movements of Ewell's corps are stated in my letter. Hill's first division will reach the Potomac to-day, and Longstreet will follow to-morrow . . .

R. E. LEE,
General[18]

This second set of orders has been parsed over for years by students, enthusiasts, and historians, and certain elements can easily be confused. However, the crux of Lee's second set of orders lies in the words, "If General Hooker's army remains inactive . . ."—meaning if Hooker continues to wait and watch Lee on the banks of the Potomac or follow Lee north across the river (which Lee expected), then Lee directs Stuart to pass around the Federal army, cross the Potomac east of the mountains, and join Ewell's southern column near York, Pennsylvania. If Hooker holds south of the river, with an apparent purpose, "should he not appear to be moving northward," Lee wants Stuart to move into the Shenandoah Valley and fall in beside Lee on the west side of the mountains.[19]

This shows Lee is concerned about two contingencies. If Hooker ceases to follow Lee, it's Lee's first concern that Hooker will push west over the Blue Ridge into Lee's rear in the Shenandoah Valley, and why Lee has ordered Stuart to place two brigades of cavalry to cover Ashby's and Snicker's Gap and scout Hooker's movements. The second contingency arises because Hooker's army now sat between Lee and the Confederate capital at Richmond, and both Lee and Jefferson Davis still thought Hooker might pivot on impulse and drive on the Confederate capital.[20] In both cases, Lee wanted Stuart close at hand to deal with Hooker.

These were just contingencies. Lee expected Hooker to follow him across the river, and Lee assumed the Federals would cross the river near Leesburg. If Hooker did as Lee expected, Stuart could cross the river east of the mountains. Lee, a former field officer in the 2nd U.S. Cavalry, fully understood Stuart would then be on the far side of the enemy and beyond communication. Still, the potential benefit of Stuart taking the eastern course, and the intelligence Stuart could gain passing the Federal army, might provide a windfall much like Stuart gained a year prior on his ride around McClellan outside Richmond.[21] Beyond that, if Stuart went east, and severed Hooker's line of communications, he would maintain the illusion his cavalry, and potentially Lee's army, were attacking Washington. This could panic Federal forces in Washington, drain troops from Hooker's front, and aid Lee's march north. Lee had tremendous confidence in Stuart, and he left the decision to Stuart to interpret the best course of action: "You will, however, be able to judge whether you can pass around their army without hinderance [*sic*], doing them all the damage you can, and cross the river east of the mountains."

Given this context, Stuart's orders are clear: If Hooker's army continues to shadow Lee's movements and assemble to move north, Stuart should cross the river at his discretion and move to find Ewell north of the river near York, Pennsylvania. If Hooker threatens Richmond, or makes a push west over the mountains, Stuart should move into the Shenandoah Valley and join Lee. And finally, "the sooner you cross into Maryland after tomorrow, the better." Whichever path Stuart decided, Lee wanted Stuart moving soon, before Hooker stole a march north.

Stuart now had two decisions to make. Whether he went east or west, he first had to decide which brigades to leave behind to man the Blue Ridge passes in Lee's rear, and Stuart chose Beverly Robertson and Grumble Jones to remain. Because of his date of commission, Robertson would command the rear guard over Lee's supply line, and this might provide Robertson's troops a brief moment to refit after their losses at Middleburg and Upperville. Stuart left detailed instructions to ensure Robertson would hold Ashby's and Snicker's Gaps and keep the Federal cavalry from "pouring in Lee's rear."[22] Robertson would also keep a sharp watch on the Federals to his front and stay in contact with General Lee while reporting the Federal movements.[23] Robertson had shown some improvement in the night attack at Middleburg, and the irascible but hard-hitting Jones would remain alongside Robertson's Tarheels, hopefully as a guiding influence to help protect Lee's only route of resupply and supplemental artillery ammunition via the Shenandoah Valley.[24] This decision also allowed Stuart to keep his three most trusted brigade commanders: Fitz Lee, now back at the head of his brigade; Wade Hampton; and John Chambliss. Stuart knew there would be hard work ahead requiring a willing, unified force, and he didn't want personalities flaring as he pushed north, regardless of the route.[25]

As to crossing the river east or west of the mountains, the choice remained Stuart's, and an eastern route still looked to be the best course. This came primarily from Major Mosby, who reported on June 24 that the route to Rowser's Ford still lay open.[26] Mosby suggested Stuart move not behind but through the mostly static enemy infantry corps. He explained Hooker's army sat waiting on information regarding Lee's army, and there were significant gaps of ten miles or more between each Federal corps for their supply, sustenance, medical, and ordnance wagons.[27] Mosby regularly used such intervals for slipping through the Union lines, and Mosby believed these same gaps would allow Stuart the space to pass between the Federal corps.[28] The quickest route would push over the lesser Bull Run range, slip through the Federal infantry, cross the river at Rowser's Ford, continue up through Maryland, and join Ewell's southern column outside York.[29] "The distance was not more than twenty miles to the Potomac from the point where he would enter Hooker's lines," said Mosby, and he further claimed

Stuart "intended to march in three parallel columns" to increase speed and maneuverability and lessen the exposure of his command.[30]

An often-overlooked factor governing Stuart's decision was the state of his horses. The Confederate commissary continued to struggle with providing adequate rations for Stuart's mounts. This troubling lack of grain on the march north prompted Lee to mention to Jefferson Davis, in a letter written on June 23, that "[f]orage [grain for the horses] is very scarce, and we have mainly to rely on grass for the animals."[31] A case in point was Private John W. Peake, a courier sent by Stuart with a dispatch for General Lee. Worried over the condition of his horse, Peake asked General Lee if his mount could have any grain. Lee apologized and said he simply had none to give. Lee then invited the young trooper to climb down and graze his mount on some nearby grass.[32]

The problem was nearing critical proportions in Stuart's ranks. "There was but little grain for horse fed in this section," recalled a captain from Stuart's ranks, and the horses instead made do on clover and orchard grass in the Loudoun Valley.[33] Without sufficient grain, the recent combat and constant maneuvering had taxed Stuart's mounts considerably.[34] In addition, many of Stuart's horses were unshod, and Loudoun's macadamized turnpikes were degrading the hooves on Stuart's mounts. Stuart cautioned his men to march beside the macadamized surface of the roads whenever they could, and be extremely diligent over the care of their horses. "Particular attention will be paid to shoeing horses, and to marching off of the turnpike."[35] Obviously, the horses' condition was paramount. It made no sense for Stuart to ride north if he arrived on crippled mounts with no feed.[36]

If Stuart went west, his horses would suffer a difficult trip as they threaded their way past macadamized roads already clogged with Lee's main army.[37] Stuart's mounts would first have to travel back across Loudoun Valley, cross the Blue Ridge, travel more macadamized roads down the Shenandoah Valley, then cross the Potomac and climb back up over the mountains in a second traverse to reach Ewell at York on the east side of the mountains. Given this string of impediments, and the continuing reports from Mosby confirming the eastern route remained open—a faster route promising to deliver his horses in far better condition—Stuart did what any good horse soldier would. He went east.

❧

Three days' rations were cooked, and on the night of June 24, the brigades of Chambliss, Hampton, and Lee headed for the Potomac via Glasscock's Gap in the Bull Run chain, with six guns from Stuart's horse artillery.[38] Stuart planned to link with Mosby in the morning, where Mosby would take command of the advance and guide Stuart's command through the Federal lines.[39] According to Mosby, Stuart "could pass the Bull Run Mountain early in the morning and cross the Potomac early in the evening; in passing through the [Federal] army he would sever communication between Hooker and Pleasonton." Mosby added Pleasonton would then "be sent in pursuit of Stuart; that was the very thing Lee wanted him to do. It would relieve [Lee's] army from the [Federal] cavalry pressure and Stuart would be so far ahead Pleasonton could never overtake him."[40]

However, Mosby's recent actions had drawn the ire of the Federals; they increased their patrols and laid an ambush that prevented Mosby from joining Stuart on the morning of June 25.[41] Now moving without Mosby, Stuart marched east for Haymarket only to find an entire enemy corps moving down the road along Stuart's proposed path, and Stuart found Federal infantry "well distributed" through the gaps in the attending trains.[42] The Federals were no longer static. The ample gaps Mosby predicted were now filled with Federals marching amid the wagons. Mosby's intelligence had gone stale in just twenty-four hours; it was no longer possible to get through by Mosby's route.[43]

Stuart responded with a blunt reconnaissance by fire from his artillery.[44] Amid the ensuing confusion, Stuart captured some Federal prisoners and determined he'd found Hancock's II Corps, marching north for the Potomac. In fact, they received orders to march that very morning after the Federal Signal Corps witnessed Confederate infantry crossing the Potomac at Shepherdstown on June 24.[45] This triggered the Federal army to start across the Potomac, and Stuart at once sent a dispatch informing General Lee of the Federal movements.[46] Stuart then fell back to Buckland, to throw the Federals off track. He laid low there and grazed his horses until nightfall.[47] There is no record of Stuart's dispatch ever reaching General Lee.

With his course blocked, Stuart now had to consider his options. He could turn around, but the surrounding roads were crawling with Federals. If he turned back west, he faced a potential swarm of enemy troops before reaching the Bull Run chain, plus the lengthy macadamized turnpikes of both the Loudoun and Shenandoah valleys. In short, there was a significant risk of strong enemy contact, plus a hard march for his already depleted horses over a route known to be short on forage and grain. The earliest Stuart and his artillery could reach Shepherdstown, the closest ford west of the mountains, was the evening of June 27.[48] Moreover, Stuart now knew Hooker was moving north to cross the Potomac, and this meant Hooker would almost certainly move to block the mountain passes above the

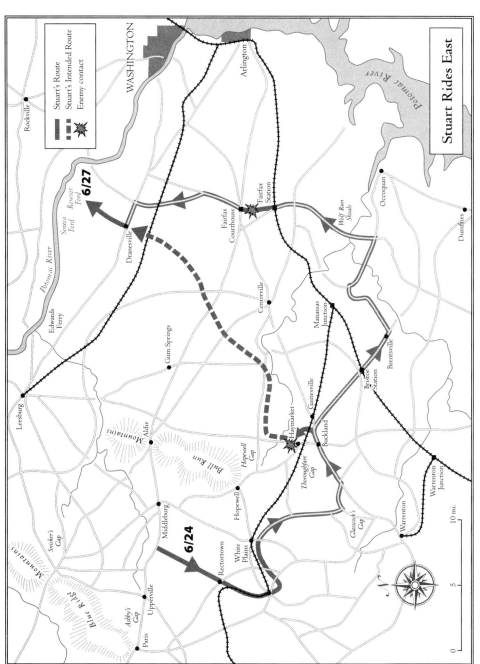

Map 7. Stuart Rides East

Potomac in Maryland. If Stuart now turned about and crossed the Potomac west of the mountains, he could only assume he would have to fight his way back through Federal forces guarding the passes of South Mountain in Maryland on his return traverse.[49] South Mountain now loomed as a hurdle to be avoided.[50]

In addition, Stuart's horses continued to suffer from a lack of grain. "We . . . had to halt again in order to graze our horses, which [after] hard marching without grain [were] fast breaking down."[51] With flagging horses, time and distance became the overriding concerns. Hooker was on the move, and Stuart had orders to gain Ewell's flank as quickly as possible.[52] Stuart kept on for Rowser's Ford, the closer option that negated a double traverse of the mountains and their potential hazards.

The enemy presence surrounding Stuart now forced him to adjust his route for Rowser's Ford, and Stuart had to jig farther east through Fairfax Courthouse to slip past the moving enemy columns.[53] On Stuart's approach, the head of his advance received a sudden charge by a single squadron of the 11th New York Cavalry. The game Federals thought they were attacking a small party of Mosby's Rangers rather than Stuart's front-line troopers, and with sabres drawn, the New Yorkers piled into the lead squadron of the 1st North Carolina. The surprise attack spun the Tarheels about, but Hampton's veterans soon launched a countercharge, and chased the New Yorkers from the field.[54] Losses were high in the 11th New York: they entered the fray with eighty-two men and suffered four killed, twenty wounded, and fifty-seven captured. Still the New Yorkers left their mark, killing Major John Whitaker of the 1st North Carolina in the initial melee and wounding an additional ten Confederates.[55]

Once in town, the Confederates found a supply of grain left behind and promptly fed it to their mounts.[56] For some, it came too late, and many Confederate horses collapsed along the road. The mounts of Chambliss's brigade were particularly affected, and a "considerable squad" of troopers from the 2nd North Carolina had to turn back for lack of a serviceable mount. The 9th Virginia also furloughed several officers and troopers for the same reason.[57] This illustrates the tenuous state of Stuart's horses following the Loudoun Valley fights and supports Stuart's repeated decisions to keep on the eastern route. Grass alone wouldn't keep his horses going, and as the ride progressed, they continued to drop weight dramatically. By this point, the horses had consumed their natural fat reserves and needed to replace whatever daily calories they spent or risk muscle atrophy. The grain discovered at Fairfax surely saved many of his mounts from breaking down and allowed them to continue.

While at Fairfax Courthouse, Stuart sent the following dispatch to General Lee and the War Department, informing both of his status and reporting that Hooker's Federals were indeed heading north:

> HEADQUARTERS Cavalry Division
> *June 27, 1863*
>
> General—I took possession of Fairfax C.H. this morning at 9 o'clock. The main body of Hooker's army has gone toward Leesburg, except the garrison of Alexandria and Washington, which had retreated within the fortifications.
>
> Very respectfully, Your obedient servant,
> J. E. B. Stuart, Major-General[58]

A copy of this dispatch reached the Confederate War Department in Richmond, but no copy would reach General Lee until after the campaign.[59] Stuart continued north, through Hunter's Mill and on to Dranesville, where he skirted the Federal VI Corps and finally closed on Rowser's Ford after sunset. The advance crossed over to find the ford unguarded but running high and flowing a half mile wide with the water coming up to a horse's withers. The horses could cross, but the ammunition stored in the caissons would get wet when the river washed over the axles. The ammunition would have to be unloaded on the Virginia bank and carried over one shell at a time by the troopers atop their horses, with the cannons and empty limbers following partially submerged in the current behind their teams.

The process began under a moonless sky.[60] By 3:00 a.m. all men and mounts were across without a hitch—a testament to the horsemanship of the gunners, drivers, and troopers, many of whom crossed the strong current with one hand holding the reins, while the second lifted an artillery shell overhead. A necessary halt occurred on the far bank to graze the mounts and rest the artillery horses after their hard pull of the submerged guns across the river.[61] Stuart now stood on the north bank of the Potomac—three and a half days after leaving Rector's Crossroads.[62]

14

THE PURSUIT

Meanwhile, in the Army of the Potomac, all things were in flux. Hooker continued to shield Washington from Lee's army and quarrel with Halleck and Lincoln as he moved north for the Federal depot at Frederick, Maryland. On the night of June 25, Federal pickets from Hancock's corps reported seeing "a body of several thousand cavalry" at Gainesville, Virginia. Pleasonton, whose men were already north of the reported activity on a line from Aldie to Leesburg, dismissed the report, stating, "My dispositions cover that."[1] This report clearly referred to Stuart's brigades passing the Federal army, and it seems extraordinary that Pleasonton would disregard the report. However, Pleasonton's men were now spread from the Loudoun Valley to Edward's Ferry to screen Hooker's army crossing the Potomac—the clear priority at that time. Given the task at hand, the limited number of healthy horses available, and the blizzard of complaints, requests, and reports Pleasonton received from Hooker, Halleck, and Lincoln, plus the various corps commanders of the Army of the Potomac—Reynolds, Hancock, Sickles, Meade, Sedgwick, Howard, and Slocum—it becomes increasingly more fathomable to understand this shortcoming. Pleasonton also had his eyes on the cavalry from the Department of Washington under Major General Julius Stahel.

Since leaving his usual grounds guarding the capital and its approaches, Major General Julius Stahel and his division of thirty-six hundred Federal troopers had been bounced about at the combined whims of Hooker, Howard, Hancock, Reynolds, and Pleasonton. Stahel had first been directed to the upper Rappahannock to track down A. P. Hill's III Confederate Corps.[2] Upon his arrival outside Warrenton, yet before he determined the actual location of Hill's corps, Stahel was ordered back north, first to pursue Mosby, and then redirected over the Potomac to join Major

General John Reynolds in guarding the Maryland passes through South Mountain. Reynolds had orders to seize Crampton's Pass and Turner's Gap, and to do this quickly, and Hooker wanted cavalry to first secure the passes and hold them for the infantry.[3]

Reynolds first looked to Pleasonton for cavalry, but the combination of his ongoing screen, multiple combats, sustained marches, and the macadamized turnpikes in the Loudoun Valley had worn Pleasonton's horses to a nub.[4] His mounts required a mandatory rest and refit to maintain their health, and this put the mission on Stahel's relatively fresh mounts from the Department of Washington and explains why Stahel was turned about and redirected for Maryland. Stahel's troopers had been on the verge of making contact with Hill's III Corps when Stahel received orders to turn about, and had Stahel continued with his mission, he may have done serious damage to Lee's line of communications and perhaps altered the course of the campaign.[5]

Instead, Stahel turned north and reached Edward's Ferry on June 25. He arrived riding a spring seat wagon, drawn by four ornery white mules, which promptly created a traffic jam at the ford. This drew the attention of XI Corps commander Oliver Howard, who was less than impressed by the eccentric Stahel and his four white mules.[6] After some heated conversations, Stahel crossed the Potomac and sent a brigade ahead for South Mountain, where he found both passes clear of the enemy and secured them on June 26.[7] Tensions continued to grow between Reynolds and Stahel, which led to poor communications between the two commands, and Reynolds wrote, "The cavalry sent out by Stahel does nothing. They go into camp behind the infantry and send out small squads from them."[8]

This was not a fair assessment, and part of this judgment came from the fact that Hooker, Howard, Hancock, and Pleasonton were all American born, all from West Point, and all assigned to the Army of the Potomac. Stahel was born in Hungary, trained in the Austrian army, and was stationed not on the front lines with the Army of the Potomac but inside the Washington perimeter with the Washington Defense Force. Stahel also received a promotion to major general largely for the sake of politics, chiefly by Lincoln's need to show his appreciation for the flood of German-speaking immigrants who volunteered to serve the Federal cause. This promotion never sat well with the hard-line West Pointers in the Army of the Potomac, and Pleasonton felt Stahel's foreign birth should exclude him from such a command. "I have no faith in foreigners serving our government or country. Stahel has not shown himself a cavalry man and it is ruining cavalry to place it under him."[9] Whether Stahel knew it or not, he was swimming in a pool of West Point sharks and about to be pulled under.

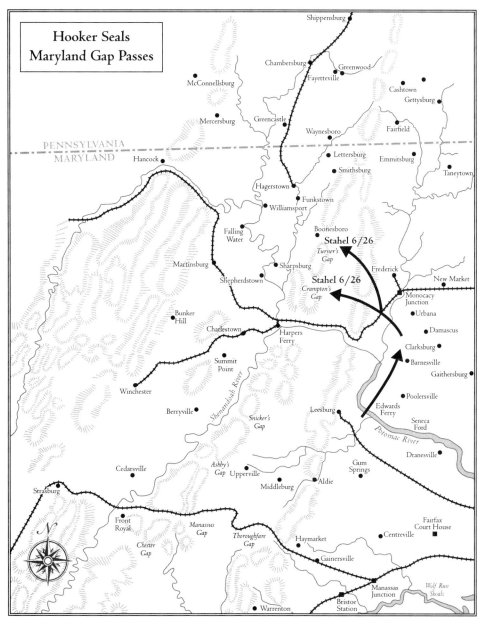

Map 8.   Hooker Seals Maryland Gap Passes

Congress had recommended Pleasonton for promotion to major general on June 18, but nothing was ever certain in Congress, and Pleasonton wanted to ensure his next step to major general.[10] Until he held the same rank as Stahel, Pleasonton felt his own command might be placed under the foreign general. "I will not fight under the orders of a Dutchman," declared Pleasonton. Acquiring Stahel's troops would not only remove this potential threat but also give Pleasonton a third division and justify his promotion to major general. Pleasonton did, genuinely, need more cavalry to fulfill the flood of requests pouring in from Hooker and his seven corps commanders, and Pleasonton felt consolidating the cavalry into a single force would make it capable of delivering more "heavy blows" upon the enemy "rather than be frittered away on trifling objects."[11]

The day after the fight at Upperville, Pleasonton wrote to the assistant adjutant general of the Army of the Potomac that he "would most respectfully and earnestly request that my force . . . be augmented by . . . regiments drawn from other commands."[12] The following day, June 23, Pleasonton sent a letter to Congressman John Farnsworth, a former cavalry officer and the uncle of Captain Elon J. Farnsworth, a young staff officer Pleasonton had recently noted for distinctive service at Brandy Station.[13] Pleasonton's letter to the congressman stated his nephew "has done splendidly" and hinted, "I have serious thoughts of having him made a brigadier general." Pleasonton added another line for good measure. "Do assist us until we can get ahead of the Rebs."[14] An accompanying letter to the congressman came from young Captain Farnsworth, who wrote his uncle the same day. "Trains passing Fairfax C.H. are burned by Bushwhackers and dispatches intercepted, and yet Stahel does nothing. Now, if you [were] to get the cavalry consolidated and Stahel left out, for God's sake do it."[15]

The letter campaign worked. On June 26, the sharks closed in and relieved Stahel of his command. The Army of the Potomac absorbed most all of Stahel's men from the Department of Washington and placed them in Pleasonton's corps.[16] Pleasonton quickly split his windfall into two brigades: the 5th New York, 18th Pennsylvania, 1st Vermont, and 1st West Virginia in one, and the 1st, 5th, 6th, and 7th Michigan in the second.[17] Judson Kilpatrick would command the new 3rd Cavalry Division. Captain Farnsworth won a promotion to brigadier general and would command Kilpatrick's 1st Brigade. Captain George Custer also received a promotion to brigadier general and the command of Kilpatrick's 2nd Brigade.[18]

Pleasonton's furtive grab of an entire division of cavalry from the capital defense was not, however, the most sweeping news to hit the ever-evolving soap opera then known as the Army of the Potomac.

On the evening of June 27, Joseph Hooker once again found himself at odds with General in Chief Halleck. In this latest scrum, Hooker wanted to absorb the ten thousand men Halleck had posted to cover Harper's Ferry. Daniel Butterfield, Hooker's chief of staff, claimed Hooker wanted to use these troops to support an attack on Lee's line of communications and retard the Confederate advance.[19] Whatever the purpose, Halleck refused to release the troops, and Hooker offered his resignation upon Halleck's refusal. Halleck forwarded the resignation to Lincoln, and Lincoln quickly accepted the offer.[20]

Major General George Meade became the fourth commander of the Army of the Potomac in eight months. Meade came from a wealthy Philadelphia family and graduated in the top third of his class at West Point. Awkward, deliberate, and excruciatingly reserved, Meade wore thick glasses that gave him the appearance of a bug-eyed klutz, and he struggled awkwardly in most social affairs. This prompted the secretary of the navy, Gideon Welles, to describe Meade as more of a "smooth bore" than a rifle.[21] Yet despite Meade's bungling manner, there lurked a surprising temper boiling behind his spectacles, and one of his aides described Meade as "a firework always going bang at someone, and nobody ever knows who is going to catch it next." Others compared Meade to an old snapping turtle.[22]

But appearances are not always accurate. Under fire Meade was measured, intelligent, and remarkably steady. He would often stand motionless while ranging the enemy, peering fearlessly through his field glasses even as swarms of bullets whizzed by like bees. During one scout, Meade slowly lowered his glasses as his staff ducked and dodged left and right and prayed for the fire to die down. "This is pretty hot," remarked Meade flatly before lifting his glasses back up to the task.[23] Meade served in the Seven Days Battles and 2nd Manassas, and at the Battle of Fredericksburg, he performed exceedingly well, and even penetrated the Confederate lines before falling back with the rest of the Federal army.

On campaign Meade proved a competent and careful commander, and in camp held little interest in regimental intrigues or national politics. He had, however, criticized prior commanders for acting overly cautious before Robert E. Lee. "So, you see I am among the *fire-eaters*," penned Meade. "I am tired of this playing war without risks. We must encounter risks if we fight, and we cannot carry on war without fighting."[24] This combination made him an attractive choice for Lincoln, who wanted a steady, eager commander at the helm with no underlying agendas.[25] There were many rumors in the army that, after Chancellorsville, Lincoln met with General John Reynolds and offered him command of the Army of the Potomac. Reynolds purportedly turned the promotion down because he felt the powers in Washington wouldn't allow him the freedom and independence needed to successfully command the army.[26] In contrast, George Meade discovered his promotion when shaken awake in his tent at 3:00 a.m. Still half asleep, Meade reportedly declined what he thought was an offer to take command of the army. Meade then learned he had orders to take the position from the president. Meade acquiesced.[27]

HEADQUARTERS ARMY OF THE POTOMAC
Washington D.C. June 27, 1863

Maj. Gen. George G. Meade

GENERAL: You will receive with this the order of the President placing you in command of the Army of the Potomac. Considering the circumstances, no one ever received a more important command. . . . You will not be hampered by any minute instructions from these headquarters. You will, however, keep in view the important fact that the Army of the Potomac is the covering army of Washington as well as the army of operation against the invading forces of the rebels. You will, therefore, maneuver and fight in such a manner as to cover the capitol and also Baltimore, as far as circumstances will admit. Should General Lee move upon either of these places, it is expected that you will either anticipate him or arrive with him so as to give him battle. . . .

I shall always be ready to advise and assist you to the utmost of my ability.

Very respectfully, your obedient servant,

H. W. HALLECK
General-in Chief[28]

By accepting command, Meade inherited a strategic nightmare. Lee's army now coursed across Maryland and southern Pennsylvania, Washington was on high alert, and Jeb Stuart's cavalry appeared to have vanished somewhere near Fairfax Courthouse.

In the last days of Hooker's command, he set the Army of the Potomac on a northern track. Thus, the army was already in motion when Meade took command, and Meade wisely kept it on the same path. He also kept Hooker's chief of staff, General Daniel Butterfield, as he tried to get a solid grasp of the situation both logistically and strategically. Lee's army was purported to be moving north, on the west side of the Blue Ridge in Virginia and South Mountain in Maryland, and thought to be heading for the Susquehanna River in Pennsylvania.[29] One of the first things Meade asked

Figure 14.1.   Major General George Meade, Army of the Potomac. Meade received orders to take command of the Army of the Potomac in the dead of night. *Library of Congress.*

for were the ten thousand troops stationed at Harper's Ferry, which Halleck had just denied Hooker. Halleck promptly awarded them to Meade.[30] General Meade also met with Alfred Pleasonton to discuss the particulars of his cavalry. Much like General Lee a week past, Meade found his cavalry covering the rear of his army along the Potomac, when they were needed farther north in his front.

On June 29, Major General Pleasonton issued the following orders. Buford's 1st Division would take Devin's and Gamble's brigades and ride for Emmitsburg, Maryland; from there Buford would march on to Gettysburg, Pennsylvania, some ten miles east of South Mountain to cover the front of the army. The two brigades at Gettysburg were to "communicate all information of the enemy rapidly and surely."[31] At Pleasonton's request, the War Department also promoted Captain Wesley Merritt to brigadier general, and Pleasonton gave Merritt command of the Regulars Brigade in Buford's 1st Division. General Merritt's first assignment would be to picket the Maryland passes through South Mountain: Crampton's Gap, Turner's Gap, and Fox's Gap.[32] David Gregg's 2nd Division would cover the left flank of the army and march for Littlestown, Pennsylvania. Kilpatrick's 3rd

Division would divide by brigades, with Custer taking an eastern route, and Farnsworth a western route, both to protect the rear of the army from Stuart's Confederate cavalry, thought to be ranging somewhere west of Baltimore and north of Washington City. Gregg and Kilpatrick would then unite at Littlestown, Pennsylvania, and seek further orders.[33]

Meade differed from Hooker. He didn't share the ghosts of Chancellorsville and wasn't overly concerned about a raid on Washington while Lee's army was in his front.[34] He also wanted Pleasonton to stay at his side and act more as a staff officer than a free-ranging corps commander. Meade's conservative view effectively removed Pleasonton from the saddle and changed the role Pleasonton had played along the turnpikes of Loudoun Valley. It also meant Pleasonton would have to shepherd his new set of handpicked general officers—Custer, Farnsworth, and Merritt—from a distance.

All three of Pleasonton's picks came from the rank of captain. Of the three, Custer appeared uniquely unqualified for brigade command after graduating dead last in his class at West Point. He had since shown a propensity for staff work, and a strong willingness to join in mounted charges against the enemy; he also revealed a troubling knack for falling out of the saddle at inappropriate times—at Brandy Station, and again on the turnpike at Aldie, where he wasn't even being shot at. On the other hand, Farnsworth had shown a legitimate aptitude for command in several engagements and had an uncle who served in Congress. The third pick, Wesley Merritt, may have appeared the most predictable choice following his steady performance with the 2nd Regulars at Brandy Station, but commanding a brigade would still be a big step even for Merritt. There were, however, several traits Pleasonton recognized in each of his new brigadiers: they were all confident and ambitious, and each had shown the proper dash Pleasonton wanted to see in his general officers.

∾

After crossing the Potomac, Stuart's brigades closed on the outskirts of Washington and cut miles of telegraph wire along the way. As they continued ahead, Chambliss's 2nd North Carolina and 9th Virginia ranged out front in the advance and soon spotted a massive train of government wagons lumbering down a turnpike north of the capital. Stuart's men gave chase and swept down on the wagons with revolvers drawn. The teamsters at the head of the column fled as fast as they could, whipping the mules into a gallop, and a race unfolded until the head of the column struck a bend in the road and the column crashed to a halt. As the Confederates pored over the wagons, they found them loaded down with oats, hardtack, bacon, hams, whiskey, and tobacco: basically everything a column of horse soldiers would want.[35] The windfall of these 120 wagons, their contents, and the mule teams alone were worth millions in period currency. Moreover, the wagons' primary contents were horse grains, a godsend for Stuart's horses. In the words of an officer watching his horse consume the captured grains, "[I]t did one's heart good to see the way the poor brutes got on the outside of those oats."[36]

As Stuart's men marshaled the wagons, they caught brief glimpses of the capitol dome, and the jutting church spires across the city now sounded the alarm. Guards removed planks from bridges, and citizens braced for whatever came next. All troops in Washington were placed on high alert and issued "100 rounds of ammunition, forty in their boxes, the rest in their haversacks," and everyone in Washington wondered if Stuart was screening a Confederate assault on the capital city.[37] With only five thousand men and six guns, Stuart could only play a decoy, and he soon turned north, riding beyond the ringing bells of the densely fortified city.

Stuart passed Rockville, Maryland, and met with no major incidents as they wrecked tracks on the Baltimore and Ohio Railroad, burned a bridge at Sykesville, and continued to slash telegraph wires on his way north.[38] The column moved day and night, stopping for short rests at midmorning and before midnight. Captain W. A. Graham of the 2nd North Carolina also began searching for fresh mounts for the men in his company. Officially forbidden from seizing horses in Maryland, Graham looked at it differently: "I confess to disobedience of this order. When a man's horse gave out it was simply a question of whether he should be abandoned in enemy territory, or offered a means of escape." Graham remembered waiting until nightfall to send his troopers looking. On at least one occasion, the owner of a missing horse appeared in camp and reported the theft to Stuart, and Stuart had the mount returned.[39]

At Westminster, Fitz Lee's men fought a sharp skirmish with the 1st Delaware Cavalry. The results were again lopsided. Two lieutenants from the 4th Virginia were killed, while the Federals suffered sixty-seven men killed, wounded, or captured in a brief series of charges that swept the Union cavalry aside. Once in town, "[W]e found abundant supplies for man and beast," recalled a Rebel. "After a hearty feed for both," the remains were loaded in the captured wagons.[40]

The column crossed the Pennsylvania state line on June 30, and Captain Graham quickly captured twenty horses along with a Lieutenant Shields from the 18th Pennsylvania Cavalry.[41] By midmorning, Stuart's men were approaching Hanover, Pennsylvania, and Stuart was now looking for any sign of Ewell's southern-bearing column from the II Corps.[42] Unbeknownst to Stuart, Judson Kilpatrick and his new division were actively searching for Ewell's Confederates as well. In fact, that very morning, Custer's brigade passed through Hanover at approximately 8:00 and stopped in the town square, where local citizens were handing out food to the passing Federals.[43]

The next Federal force to reach Hanover was Farnsworth's brigade, with the 1st Vermont in the lead, followed by the 1st West Virginia, the 5th New York, and last in line, the 18th Pennsylvania.[44] The 18th Pennsylvania were relatively green troops and, being native to the state, were enjoying an especially fervent welcome from the citizens crowded around the town square. Men and women cheered from the balconies and passed cigars about, and schoolgirls crowded the curbs, singing patriotic songs.[45]

At the same time, Chambliss's Confederate brigade was working north from Union Mills, with the 13th Virginia up front, followed by two squadrons from the 9th Virginia, then the 2nd North Carolina, and the 10th Virginia in reserve. Behind Chambliss's brigade came a section of McGregor's battery and the captured wagons taken outside Washington, with Hampton's brigade bringing up the rear along with Breathed's battery. Farther west, Fitz Lee's brigade ranged Stuart's left to cover this flank from any approaching Federals.[46] As the Confederates gained the edges of Hanover, they spotted the rear guard of the 18th Pennsylvania and quickly formed for a charge.[47]

Troopers from the 9th and 13th Virginia came bolting up in columns of four, funneling forward between the fences and hedgerows in the town streets as they closed on the unsuspecting Federals. This was the first close-quarters combat the troopers of the 18th Pennsylvania had encountered, and Lieutenant Henry Potter recalled the moment the Rebels piled into his ranks at a gallop, with the lines mixing so close Potter compared it to a fistfight.[48] The Virginians surged over the Union rear guard, and the Federals began to flee.[49] Stuart saw Federals falling away and waved in more troops to create a rout as Rebel gunners deployed on high ground beside the Westminster Road and opened in support.[50] With shells screaming overhead, Lieutenant Colonel William Payne led the 2nd North Carolina for the town center but on a street parallel with the advancing Virginians to avoid a snarl.[51] "Each cross street gave us a glimpse into . . . town," wrote Lieutenant Colonel Payne. "[W]e saw it packed with masses of cavalry." Payne's North Carolinians soon turned in, striking the Federal flank beyond the Virginians, and breaking through the Federal ranks in a flurry of sabre strokes and pistol shots. A panic ensued as the Tarheels poured through the town streets like a stampede of cattle. Teamsters from the Federal columns lost control of their wagons, and the panicked mounts bolted out of control. Sergeant Bradley Alexander of the 5th New York led his detail into the enemy, only to be slashed over the head and trampled beneath the stampeding wagons.[52]

The Federals scattered, and the streets were soon filled with loose horses as the celebration flipped from joy to confusion. Despite the artillery fire, many civilians didn't realize an attack was under way; one woman passing out food mistook the first charging Confederate she saw as just another Federal trooper until he opened fire with a revolver and toppled an officer clad in Union blue.[53] Payne's troopers kept coming, slashing through the 18th Pennsylvania and inflicting heavy losses as the Pennsylvanians scattered north of the town square, with many running into the rear of Farnsworth's main column.[54]

The remains of the 18th Pennsylvania rallied here on the veteran 1st Vermont and 5th New York; at the same time, the Virginian and North Carolinian attacks now spider-webbed outward on the streets above the square, diffusing the momentum of the horses barreling down the converging streets leading to the square. Two-day general Elon Farnsworth saw the enemy stretching and directed a squadron from the 1st Vermont into the fight. "[T]he Rebel column had come some distance and was pretty well scattered," wrote Horace Ide of the 1st Vermont, and the Federals soon began mounting a series of countercharges.[55]

Major John Hammond of the 5th New York had pulled his men off Frederick Street and waited on a hidden side street as the Confederates charged ahead. As the Rebels boiled past, Hammond launched his men into the passing enemy flank. Lieutenant Colonel Payne of the 2nd North Carolina recalled how Federals "poured out from every street. My command was cut in two." Combatants slashed one another from the saddle and shot down those who refused to surrender. "I remember nothing but firing pistols, clouds of dust, an occasional thump with a sabre."[56] Payne's horse tumbled beneath him, and the colonel regained his feet only to be knocked down by a speeding horse in the swirling mix. Payne crawled free of the fight and sprinted for a nearby tanning house in the confusion. As he cleared the street, a Union trooper laid a sabre blow across his back, and Payne toppled into a tanning vat of toxic, urine-scented stew. Retching, Payne exited the vat and stumbled into a pile of hair removed from the hides. As he struggled to his feet, Federal officers took him prisoner, asking, "What ----- sort of Santa Claus are you?"[57] Outflanked, outnumbered, and now taking fire from civilians in upper balconies, the rest of the 2nd North

Figure 14.2. Brigadier General Elon Farnsworth, Army of the Potomac. Though Farnsworth gained his promotion with the help of his uncle, he soon proved he could lead light cavalry. *Library of Congress.*

Carolina spilled back down Frederick Street in a running gunfight with the 5th New York coursing after them.[58] Payne later wrote of his regiment, "156 entered the town . . . 23 . . . got out."[59]

Meanwhile, Farnsworth rallied elements of the 18th Pennsylvania and led them back into the fight with orders "not to shoot until they could see the color of the Rebels' eyes."[60] In his element, Farnsworth kept his men pressing after the enemy and personally led a charge down the narrow streets.[61] Elsewhere, the 9th Virginia saw the coming tide of Federals and rushed to form a line along the Westminster Road. They fired a stiff volley into the New Yorkers and cleared a number of saddles as the Virginians broke down a fence and mounted a countercharge.[62]

This effort halted the Federals, but the buildings in the town fractured the lines of sight and isolated the combats from one another, allowing a victory on one block to be overturned by a reverse on the next. Farnsworth again proved equal to the task and ordered different sections forward in independent actions. These short, sprinting charges, many less than a hundred yards long, drove the Rebels back through town in a series of hammer-like blows. In one reencounter, privates Thomas Burke and William Herrick of the 5th New York spurred forward and opened fire on the 13th Virginia's Color Guard. Herrick was shot and turned out, but Burke bore forward, returned fire, wounded the color-bearer, and snatched the enemy banner. Burke later received the Medal of Honor for his heroic efforts.[63]

The 1st West Virginia now joined Farnsworth and charged down Baltimore Street. As they advanced Hampton's 1st South Carolina arrived, moved past Mount Olive Cemetery, and took advantage of a side street to flank the 1st West Virginia and take almost nineteen prisoners.[64] The rest of the West Virginians dismounted and advanced with their carbines from house to house as the fighting now swirled south and east through the town along Baltimore and Frederick Streets and the alleys between. This fresh advance forced Chambliss to fall back to the open-pasture lots and gardens south of town and Stuart now advanced with elements of his staff to rally Chambliss. Captain Blackford of Stuart's staff recalled, "[A] hot skirmish fire" had opened on Stuart's men, directed by the citizens of the town who had been firing "from the windows on the street," and this forced the troopers back in "utter confusion."[65] Stuart and staff turned about with their men and promptly exited the town. A deep gully, and continued resistance by pockets of North Carolinians and Virginians, allowed the rest of Chambliss's brigade to retire to the fields south of town near the Jacob Forney farm.[66]

Smelling blood, Farnsworth's troopers rode out of town like a cloud of angry blue bees and began spurring after the Southern horsemen until Breathed's gunners opened fire. The Rebel shells burst over the Yankee column, bringing a quick halt to the Federal pursuit.[67] This firm reverse bought enough time for Chambliss to rally his men and place sharpshooters on the high ground south of town.[68] Federal guns answered from the north, and shells soon arced back and forth over Hanover in a growing standoff.[69]

Kilpatrick arrived during the continuing standoff, having forced his horse to make a two-hour hand gallop. Lathered in sweat, and shaking uncontrollably, his mount sank to his knees and died. Apparently unfazed, "Little Kill" stepped clear, grabbed a flag, and gave a rousing speech to his troopers. Custer's Michigan brigade then came up after Kilpatrick, counted out sharpshooters, and went into position.[70]

Farther east, the Cobb Legion Cavalry took positions along the Baltimore Road to engage Farnsworth's sharpshooters, and the remaining Southern guns deployed behind the Georgians. Fitz Lee appeared shortly after and deployed on Chambliss's left to complete Stuart's line. The 6th Michigan then attempted to flank the Rebel artillery, but a volley by the Southern gunners and a series of counterattacks by the 1st and 10th Virginia put an end to the effort.[71] The carbine fire petered out, and the affair turned into a slow-paced artillery duel for the rest of the afternoon.

In the end, the fight at Hanover cost Stuart a day he simply couldn't afford.[72] What's especially baffling about the engagement is that Major General Jubal Early—who led the southern column from Ewell's II Corps, which Stuart had been sent to join—sat eating lunch just ten miles away and clearly heard the artillery fire coming from Hanover. Yet Early sent no couriers, nor made any attempts to investigate the source of the artillery, despite knowing that Stuart was projected to be in the area with orders to join Ewell's flank. Early later ascribed the battle sounds as nothing more than a small militia skirmish—just who the Pennsylvania militia may have been in an artillery skirmish with apparently held no military value in Early's mind.[73] Had just one scout investigated the reverberating fire they may have discovered Stuart's brigades and effected a juncture between Stuart and Ewell's corps as per General Lee's orders.

Besides losing their commander, the 2nd North Carolina suffered significant casualties. The regiment entered the fight already undermanned with just 150 troopers mounted. By day's end, it could only muster 30 men fit and ready.[74] On the Union side, the 18th Pennsylvania suffered the brunt of the Confederate attack, and several companies endured a severe mauling. Farnsworth then recovered from the surprise assault, rallied, and directed a series of close-range counterattacks to drive the Confederates out of town. Kilpatrick had little opportunity to improve the situation, and by late afternoon, he sat static as Stuart moved his wagons east with Fitz Lee's brigade.

Kilpatrick didn't pursue. His orders from Pleasonton were to screen the Federal infantry, and that strategic concern outweighed a meeting engagement with the Confederate cavalry, even if that cavalry happened to be Stuart's brigades.[75]

~

Despite ducking Kilpatrick, Stuart felt far from secure.[76] It had now been six days since he started his march. After crossing into Pennsylvania, he'd expected to locate Ewell's corps, and he'd sent scouts coursing the countryside; however, all attempts failed to make contact, and Stuart's men were now exhausted to the point of confusion. Simple tasks became chores, and his horses were in a similar state after six hard days of riding, scouting, and skirmishing.[77] Not only that, the macadamized roads north of the Potomac were rapidly reducing the serviceable mounts remaining in Stuart's columns, and many of Stuart's troopers were soon walking beside limping horses and stopping at the nearest farm to "enlist" a remount.[78]

The captured Federal wagons were now proving to be a double-edged sword. They were worth a small fortune and extremely valuable to any army on the march. In addition, the grain captured within had replenished Stuart's horses when they needed it most. They were also useful for collecting additional grain gathered along the way and even served as a mobile paddock where captured horses could be tied behind on the march rather than hand drawn from the saddle. Yet, despite their attributes, they slowed Stuart's column significantly. One officer wrote, "[A]t first they were considered a great prize, they soon became a great burden."[79] Stuart later admitted the captured wagons and the ever-growing number of prisoners his men took along the way slowed him considerably, and their combination had grown into a "serious embarrassment." At this point, his men's mounts could handle little more than a steady walk regardless, and Stuart felt he must be in close range of Lee's army. Therefore, he kept the wagons.[80]

Stuart reached Dover, Pennsylvania, on the morning of July 1, but again could find no sign of either Lee or Ewell. The most his scouts could determine was that Jubal Early's division had recently passed northward in the direction of Shippensburg and Carlisle, and that might indicate a concentration of Lee's forces in that area.[81] Stuart pushed on for Carlisle,

Figure 14.3.   Recruits training at the U.S. Cavalry barracks in Carlisle, Pennsylvania, April 1861. Jeb Stuart shelled these barracks on July 1, 1863. *Dickinson College.*

with Fitz Lee's brigade leading the column as it closed in range of the U.S. Cavalry barracks located at Carlisle. Upon arrival, Fitz Lee demanded the garrison's surrender. The garrison refused, and Stuart's gunners began shelling the barracks. Later that night, as artillery shells trailed over Carlisle, a dispatch arrived from Robert E. Lee. The dispatch stated Lee was thirty miles to the south and had been heavily engaged with the Federal army that same day. Stuart was to move for Gettysburg with all practical haste.[82]

15

GETTYSBURG

On the early evening of June 28, Robert E. Lee sat at his headquarters near Chambersburg, Pennsylvania. Lee's army had largely kept pace with his expectations, and he continued to hold the initiative. Captured supplies were accumulating at a rapid pace, and the advance of Ewell's II Corps ranged in two directions. The main force, with two divisions and Jenkins's cavalry, continued north, closing on the state capital at Harrisburg. A second force consisting of General Jubal Early's division drove east and crossed the mountains on June 26 with White's 35th Virginia Cavalry Battalion and Colonel William French's 17th Virginia Cavalry.[1]

Early's forces swept through Gettysburg and then York, and found only Union militia and no sign of any troops from the Army of the Potomac. Early also reported no signs of Stuart's cavalry, and Lee had received no word from Stuart since June 24. In addition, Lee had received no word from his rear guard under Beverly Robertson that Hooker had crossed the Potomac, and this dovetailed with the reports from colonels French and White riding with General Early.[2]

Elsewhere, A. P. Hill's III Corps had marched up the Cumberland Valley, followed by Longstreet's I Corps, and both encamped near Chambersburg, Pennsylvania. On Lee's left, General Imboden's cavalry cleared out Federal forces guarding the Baltimore and Ohio Railroad and continued working with Lee's quartermasters in securing a steadily growing mass of supplies west of South Mountain near McConnellsburg.[3] Lee's plan had worked near perfectly to date. He managed to shift his army from Fredericksburg, Virginia, to Chambersburg, Pennsylvania, in under a month's time, and maintain the initiative throughout. Aside from Stuart's absence, Lee must have been pleased to date.

As the evening grew toward dusk, word arrived that Hooker's army had in fact already crossed the Potomac River, and three Federal corps were reportedly driving northwest across Maryland for South Mountain.[4] This information did not come from a courier attached to Beverly Robertson, and not from the three cavalry brigades with Stuart, nor did it come from the two cavalry regiments attached to Early's division ranging through York, Pennsylvania, or Mosby's Rangers, or any scouts with the Army of Northern Virginia. Instead, the information came from a civilian spy named Henry Harrison, a man Longstreet knew and eagerly vouched for. Lee interviewed Harrison, found him credible, and believed what he said.[5]

Lee knew Hooker's Federals had been massing at Edward's Ferry to cross the Potomac, but Lee expected Stuart or Robertson to send word when Hooker crossed the river. Thus, Lee had to assume his supply line was at least threatened, if not cut altogether.[6] This perceived threat, coupled with Harrison's report of three Federal corps moving rapidly across Maryland, prompted Lee to abandon Ewell's northern thrust on the state capital at Harrisburg.[7] Instead, Lee needed to protect his supply line with Virginia—his only source of additional artillery ammunition—and move to protect the immense train of supplies his quartermasters had already accumulated.[8] "As our communications with the Potomac were thus menaced, it was resolved to prevent [the enemy's] further progress in that direction by concentrating our army on the east side of the mountains."[9]

Lee ordered Ewell to turn back from Harrisburg and, along with Early's division, assemble near Cashtown or Gettysburg. Hill's III Corps, currently west of South Mountain, would march east on the Chambersburg Turnpike and cross South Mountain via the Cashtown Gap. Lee's building supply train would follow after Hill, and Longstreet would follow the supply train, where all would concentrate on the east side of South Mountain. It's also likely that Longstreet's spy, Henry Harrison, informed General Lee that Lincoln had removed Hooker and given George Meade command of the Army of the Potomac.[10] Lee must have seen the advantage in his enemy switching commanding officers in midcampaign; however, Lee knew Meade, knew his diligence, and knew Meade was not an opponent to make a mistake before.[11]

∾

A. P. Hill's III Confederate Corps crossed South Mountain on June 30, led by Major General Henry Heth's Infantry Division. Heth came from good "Old Dominion" stock. He graduated last in his West Point class of 1847 but served as a capable frontier infantry officer before the war. Popular with many fellow officers, Heth had been promoted to major general following

Figure 15.1.　Chambersburg Road to the west of Gettysburg. *Dickinson College.*

the Battle of Chancellorsville.[12] As his division closed on Gettysburg, Heth sent Brigadier General James Johnston Pettigrew's brigade in search of provisions. Educated at the University of North Carolina, Pettigrew excelled at mathematics, liberal arts, and foreign languages, and as a young man he was prepped for a key slot at the U.S. Naval Observatory.[13] As Pettigrew departed for Gettysburg, Heth warned him local militia might guard the town, and he should have little trouble driving them off. If, however, Pettigrew encountered Federal troops from the Army of the Potomac, Pettigrew's orders were to withdraw and not precipitate an attack.[14]

As Pettigrew's men approached Gettysburg, they encountered a large force of Federal cavalry, suspected the presence of more troops nearby, and reportedly heard infantry drums in the distance.[15] The Federals advanced from the town, and Pettigrew and his officers determined the troopers' "movements were undoubtedly those of well-trained troops and not those of the home guard."[16] Pettigrew promptly ordered a withdrawal per his orders and reported making enemy contact with regular Federal troops when he returned to camp. Henry Heth and A. P. Hill each interviewed Pettigrew, and neither trusted Pettigrew's report of finding regular Federal troops in Gettysburg. There had been no prior sightings of regular Federal troops this far northwest, and Pettigrew had only recently transferred to A. P. Hill's command. Hill then interviewed Lieutenant Louis Young, a junior officer on Pettigrew's staff, whom Hill knew from prior campaigns.

Young fully supported Pettigrew's statement and said the troops they encountered outside Gettysburg were proper Federal cavalry and definitely not militia.[17]

General Heth then pressed A. P. Hill for permission to make his own reconnaissance. "If there is no objection, I will take my division tomorrow and go to Gettysburg."

"None in the world," replied Hill.[18]

Years later, Heth would state that he stumbled like a blind man on his march to Gettysburg, even though he wrote in his own after-action account that a large force of enemy cavalry supported by infantry was reported outside Gettysburg on June 30. And a large force of Federal cavalry, supported by infantry, is exactly what Heth would encounter at Gettysburg the following morning.

~

The cavalry Pettigrew spotted west of Gettysburg belonged to John Buford's 1st Division. Since crossing the Potomac on June 27, Buford and his men had moved through Maryland and into Pennsylvania by a series of hard marches in the sweltering summer heat, arriving at Gettysburg in the late morning of June 30.[19] Citizens welcomed the dusty troopers riding down Washington Street, and schoolchildren sang songs for the troopers, while their parents handed ladles of cool well water to the passing troopers. Lieutenant John Calef of the 2nd U.S. Artillery received a bouquet of flowers from a young girl as he passed through Gettysburg to pitch camp west of town.[20]

Buford opted for a room at the Eagle Hotel and promptly sent dispatches to both Reynolds and Pleasonton. "I can't do much. . . . My men and horses are fagged out. I have not been able to get any grain yet." Buford also complained that "[f]acilities for shoeing are nothing" and prior Confederate raids had "seized every shoe and nail they could find," and Buford went on to report large numbers of Confederates closing on Gettysburg. "A. P. Hill's corps is massed . . . about 9 miles from this place. . . . [T]he enemy's pickets are within 4 miles." Buford believed Longstreet's corps was behind A. P. Hill's, and Buford reported Ewell's corps was moving down from Carlisle, some twenty miles to the north.[21]

Buford met briefly with Reynolds earlier that day when Buford's two mounted brigades passed through the Federal I Corps on their march north. One of Reynolds's staff officers then accompanied Buford to Gettysburg and hand carried Buford's findings back to Reynolds that evening. Up to this point, Meade wanted to create a defensive position along Pipe Creek near Emmitsburg, Maryland, but after reading Buford's report, Meade changed his mind and ordered the I Corps to move for Gettysburg. The Federal XI Corps would range in support, and the Federal III Corps would move to Emmitsburg.[22]

That evening, Buford convened with Gamble and Devin commanding his 1st and 2nd brigades. With Rebel pickets within five miles, Buford expected the Confederates would be back in the morning with plenty of friends. "They will attack you in the morning," warned Buford. "[T]hey will come booming—skirmishers three deep. You will have to fight like the devil to hold your own until our supports arrive."[23] After scouting the ground west of town, Buford wanted to delay the expected enemy advance long enough for Reynolds and the Federal I Corps to come up from Moritz Tavern and secure Gettysburg and its important hub of roads. Buford's two brigades had no chance of halting an entire Confederate corps, but his troopers' breech-loading carbines would give his men a higher rate of fire than the Confederate infantry's muzzleloaders.[24] This, coupled with the rolling series of ridges west of town and the natural cover they provided, persuaded Buford his two thousand veterans could at least blunt the Confederate attack. Devin's brigade would cover the Federal right, while Gamble's brigade held the left.[25]

≈

Shortly after dawn, the first contact on the Chambersburg Pike occurred when Confederate infantry from Henry Heth's division came marching down the pike through the morning mist. Waiting for the Confederate column were Gamble's forward pickets. The troopers rested their carbines on fence rails and fired at the distant enemy. Private Thomas Day of Company E, 3rd Indiana Cavalry recalled watering his horse from a farmer's trough beside the Chambersburg Pike. The sun had just crested the horizon when Private Day heard three shots; he looked up and saw "a few straggling Johnnies cresting the hill." Day mounted and spurred back to camp to spread the alarm. "Our company being the first to form, we rushed [back] over the bridge and down to the house where I had watered my horse. . . . [W]e were deployed and skirmished with the Johnnies as we could."[26]

Gunfire escalated as Company E of the 3rd Indiana opened with their Gallagher carbines and were soon joined by others.[27] The crisp volume of fire convinced the Rebels they were not facing militia after all, prompting Heth to halt, reform, and call up a battery of artillery for support.[28] Rebel shells flew through the air, shrapnel burst over the Federal sharpshooters, and gray-clad infantry again pushed forward as the 8th Illinois and 3rd Indiana fired from behind fence rails, tree trunks, creek banks, and whatever cover they could find.

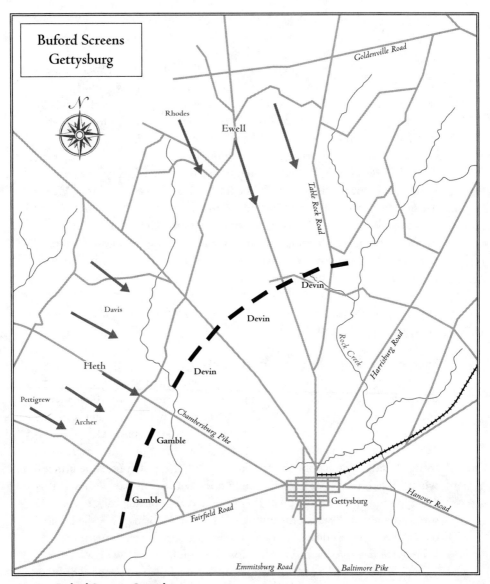

Map 9. Buford Screens Gettysburg

Now hard pressed, Private Day and his fellow troopers fell back over Herr Ridge to take new positions along Willoughby Run. "One of our boys was shot and we put him on [a milk white] horse to take him back," recalled Day. "[T]he blood gushed over him so that it nearly turned the horse red." General James Archer's Tennessee Brigade drove Gamble's men back up McPherson's Ridge and then halted to reform on the edge of the woods for the next push. In this lull, Private Day and his fellow skirmishers crossed through Buford's next line, now supported by Lieutenant John Calef's horse battery. "When we came back across the bridge, we found the artillery and the men dismounted all in one line, lying down. . . . I remember well the set look on the faces of those boys as they lay in that line, knowing the crash was now coming on them."[29]

Lieutenant Calef described the Confederates exiting the woods before him as "a double line of battle in gray. . . . [T]heir battle-flags looked redder and bloodier in the strong July sun than I had ever seen before." Calef's gunners aimed for the Rebel flags and quickly threw the enemy lines into disorder, but the Confederates reformed and kept coming, spilling into the fields, stretching across McPherson's Ridge, and driving full bore on Buford's line. Gamble's troopers continued firing, but the scales were rapidly tipping in the Confederates' favor.[30]

North of Gamble's fight, Devin's men endured a separate battle of their own. Posted to the right of the Chambersburg Pike, Devin's troopers fanned out across the Mummasburg Road, and up to Oak Hill for a front more than a mile long. Confederate infantry from Mississippi and North Carolina advanced in the morning light and soon ran into Devin's waiting troopers. Armed with Sharps carbines, the 6th and 9th New York Cavalry "responded with a rapid carbine fire from behind trees, rocks and stonewalls . . . giving the enemy the impression that he had infantry before him."[31]

Rebel skirmishers crept forward into rolling fields of oats and wheat, and Devin's New Yorkers opened a stream of fire on the first skirmishers and forced them to withdraw. The New Yorkers regrouped behind a stone wall, and still more Confederates swept forward at the double quick and advanced through the fields. Skirmishing continued, and the New Yorkers displaced to another set of walls as Colonel John M. Stone's 2nd Mississippi pressed down the Mummasburg Road, "a lane with a post and rail fence on both sides of the road."[32]

Troopers from the 6th and 9th New York Cavalry waited on the Rebel infantry to come in range and then swept the funneling road with a flood of carbine fire. The fire came in waves as the Federals remained prone, took careful aim, and the hammers tripped down the line from end to end like a stick run down a picket fence. Caught between the fence rails, the heavy stream of fire quickly brought the Rebels to a halt. Colonel Stone came forward to rally his men, and Devin's troopers shot him down. John Marshall Stone was the first regimental commander to fall at Gettysburg, and his loss caused yet another halt in the Confederate advance.[33]

Legend holds that as Buford stood glassing the enemy advance from the cupola of the Lutheran Seminary General John Reynolds rode up and called out, "What's the matter, John?"

"The Devil's to pay!" said Buford, climbing down the ladder.

"Let's ride out and see all about it," replied Reynolds.

The pair, arguably the best two general officers in the Union army, rode ahead side by side to scout the Confederate infantry driving east down the Chambersburg Pike. Buford's troopers were doing their best to hold on, but this wasn't a fair fight, particularly north of the Chambersburg Pike, where Devin fought outnumbered two to one.[34]

Luckily, the Federal I Corps came up and started deploying under Reynolds's direction. Reynolds fired off a rapid string of orders and sent General James Wadsworth's division north of the pike to aid Devin's brigade, and then Reynolds waved the 2nd Wisconsin from the Federal Iron Brigade into the fight south of the pike. The veteran 2nd Wisconsin engaged Archer's Confederates, and Reynolds spurred his horse forward as a stiff firefight developed. Reynolds was pointing the next regiment forward when a bullet tore through his head, killing him instantly.[35] Minutes later, the rest of the Iron Brigade arrived, and volleys lashed across the lines as fresh Federal troops poured forward and blunted Heth's advance.[36]

A lull descended over the field, and the battle could have ended here, inconclusively with both sides licking their wounds. Instead, the battle again escalated as Heth doubled down, recommitted Archer's brigade, then threw both Johnston Pettigrew's and John Brockenbrough's brigades into the mix. Volley after volley ripped through the Federals below the pike, and the Federal left streamed back in retreat.[37]

Richard S. Ewell graduated from West Point, served in the frontier dragoons, and earned a reputation as a notoriously brash and eccentric individual fond of cursing, drinking, and leading from the front. Ewell also earned a reputation for making sound decisions in deadly environments and became Stonewall Jackson's most trusted subordinate. Badly wounded at 2nd Manassas, Ewell lost a leg and entered an eight-month period of recuperation and soul searching where he married, shunned alcohol and foul language, and joined the Christian Church. These changes caused some officers to question if Ewell still held his former zeal to engage the enemy. Robert E. Lee never questioned Ewell, and he picked Ewell not only to take over Stonewall Jackson's former corps but also lead Lee's invasion into Pennsylvania.[38] To date, Ewell had performed exceptionally well.

On the morning of July 1, Ewell was en route to Gettysburg and under orders not to bring on a general engagement until Lee merged all his forces.[39] Approaching the town, Ewell unexpectedly found A. P. Hill's corps heavily engaged with a large force of Federals. Seeking to aid Hill's men, and honor Lee's orders, Ewell ordered an artillery battalion forward to open on the Federal right flank. Just then, a dispatch arrived from General Lee asking Ewell to contact Jeb Stuart, and again avoid a general engagement until the Confederate army had fully joined. Moments later, Major Andrew Venable from Jeb Stuart's staff rode up in a cloud of dust on a lathered horse. Greatly relieved, Ewell advised the officer to send back for Stuart with great haste, and directed the officer on to General Lee.[40]

As Ewell looked out over the field, he saw Federal troops reacting to his artillery fire and maneuvering to contest his closest division. Ewell later wrote, "It was too late to avoid an engagement without abandoning the position already taken up. . . . I determined to push the attack vigorously."[41] Ewell pitched a single division into the fight, only to have it soundly rejected. Unfazed, Ewell launched a second division, which landed like a hurricane, and sent the Federals streaming back for town.[42]

With Hill's rallied III Corps driving from the west, and Ewell's II Corps sweeping from the north, the Confederates drove the Northern ranks back on their heels. Buford and his men did their best to help, extending the Federal line and engaging the Confederates with their carbines in disparate attempts to slow the Confederate juggernaut. One of the more unique moments occurred in the afternoon near the seminary, when Pettigrew's brigade advanced in a broad front of three regiments, and threatened to overlap and engulf the 121st Pennsylvania Infantry. To counter the threat, Gamble's 8th Illinois Cavalry charged forward in a column of squadrons at the regiment on Pettigrew's flank, the 52nd North Carolina Infantry. Led by Major William Medill, the Yankee troopers bore down on the right flank of the 52nd, which promptly came to a halt and formed a square in a throwback to the Napoleonic Wars of Europe! The North Carolinians fired a hurried volley that sailed high, and the 8th responded with a mounted volley before galloping out of range. By then, the 121st Pennsylvania had redressed and retired at their own speed.[43]

As the Confederate assault developed against Seminary Ridge, Pender's Confederate Division swept forward for Shultz's Woods, where Private Day and his 3rd Indiana Cavalry now formed behind a stone wall. The Hoosiers held their fire until the Confederates approached and exposed their right flank at close range. "[T]hey were not 50 steps from the wall when we opened into them. . . . [H]aving them in flank they dropped frightfully fast."[44] Immediately left of the 3rd Indiana stood the 8th New York Cavalry: "We went to popping at them," recalled Daniel Pulis. "[T]hey fell like rain. . . . The ground soon got covered with them. The front column broke and started to run but their rear column pressed on."[45] Taken in flank the Confederates wheeled into the fire and advanced for the section of wall shielding Private Day and the 3rd Indiana: "[T]hey came for the wall three lines deep. . . . [W]e fired into them as fast as we could. . . . [T]hen we had to go." As the Federal line broke, the Confederates opened on the retreating troopers, and Day testified to the Confederate fire, "[H]ere we lost more men than in all the rest of the day."[46]

Elsewhere, Ewell's II Corps swept into Gettysburg proper and Devin's men skirmished with the Confederates in the town streets, but there was no stopping the Rebel tide as it rolled through the town.[47] The Federals soon abandoned Gettysburg and withdrew to the range of hills south of town still held by Federal artillery.[48]

∾

Lee knew nothing of the battle until he heard the distant rumble of artillery while on the march from Cashtown Pass. He picked up the pace and rode to the sound of the guns, no doubt wondering what set of events could have caused an engagement of this scale when he had issued orders to the contrary: Stuart remained absent, Lee's supply line might be cut, and Longstreet's I Corps had yet to cross over South Mountain.[49] In short, Lee wasn't ready for a pitched fight and, certainly, not a rushed engagement against an enemy of unknown strength before he halted and reconsolidated his position. However, as Lee gained the field, he found his troops attacking and not only winning but pressing forward on two fronts, and driving the Federals back through town. Word then reached Lee that contact had been made with Stuart, and his brigades were marching for Gettysburg.[50]

Lee studied the ground again, taking in the terrain and the course of the battle. The conditions were far from perfect. The careful alchemy Lee built in prior victories with Jackson, Stuart, and Longstreet was lacking here. But Lee knew the challenges of maneuvering an army in enemy territory; he knew the endless pitfalls and complexities of coming to grips with an enemy on campaign. The Federals were here in force and clearly broken; their dead littered the field marking their retreat, a retreat brought on by Lee's brigades on Union ground. Now was the moment; a final push would sweep the Federal guns from the high ground south of town and secure a major victory. Lee sent orders for Ewell to press the attack.[51]

Lee's order arrived, but Ewell hesitated. His men were tiring, there were no quick reinforcements close at hand, and his last fresh division was miles away.[52] Ewell's gunners were also struggling to find a good position for the Southern artillery to support an attack against the Federal guns on Cemetery Hill.[53] Ewell decided to hold where he was, allow his hard-fought men to rest, and wait for his last division to come up. Darkness fell before he could marshal his forces for an assault; his attack would have to wait until tomorrow.

The Federals still held the best ground—not the ground west of town Buford selected, but a second, much stronger position formed around Cemetery Hill. No one influenced the day's outcome more than Buford. His troopers had not held their ground against the tides of enemy infantry—that wasn't the role of light cavalry. Instead they bought the time needed for Federal infantry to arrive and contain the enemy attack; by day's end, the Army of the Potomac held the superior position on the field. The price had been high, with the Federals suffering almost nine thousand casualties, but without Buford's scouting reports on June 30, Henry Heth's march on Gettysburg would have been the supply lark Heth intended, and the major contest of the campaign would have likely occurred at another time and place.[54]

Buford acted with vision and bravery, and the men of the 1st Cavalry Division followed him straight into the storm.

16

HUNTERSTOWN AND
BRINKERHOFF RIDGE

General Meade arrived at Gettysburg's Evergreen Cemetery just before midnight. He found several officers waiting for him at the gatehouse to the graveyard, and Meade dismounted and exchanged greetings with Oliver Howard, Daniel Sickles, Henry Slocum, and a number more. Everyone present assured him his army sat on good ground after the day-long fight, and Meade felt confident. So confident, he planned to not only offer battle here but also to attack Lee's Confederates: "It seems to me we have so concentrated that a battle at Gettysburg is now forced upon us, if we get up all our people, and attack with our whole force to-morrow, we ought to defeat the force the enemy has."[1]

Meade walked to Cemetery Hill where the batteries sat, the guns still laid as they'd been placed that afternoon. The moonlight offered little detail of the surrounding ground, but Meade could see a vast array of cook fires flickering in the distance. Lee's men were clearly here in force, and not leaving soon. Meade had met Lee's army in the battles of the Seven Days, at 2nd Manassas, at Sharpsburg, and at Fredericksburg, and knew the fires portended another bloodbath. He called for a scout and rode south along the ridge with a small group of officers including his artillery commander, Henry J. Hunt; his XI Corps commander, Oliver Howard; and Captain William Paine, a captain of engineers Meade brought to make a map of their reconnaissance.[2]

The party rode through dawn, examining Culp's Hill on the far Union right, guarding his only supply line via the Baltimore Pike. From there the line hooked back west and coursed south along Cemetery Ridge, and the low ground stretching beyond before the ground rose again to the pair of round-topped hills on the far Union left. After riding the ground, Meade agreed with his officers: his army held an excellent position with high ground on either flank, commanding terrain for their artillery, and short interior lines to shuffle men and ordnance as needed. This, plus one look at the field of Confederate cook fires, told Meade it was too late to maneuver his army for an attack. He would hold tight on the better ground and invite an enemy assault instead.

As Meade squared his position through the morning, his staff convened and made moves to guard the Federal rear and protect the Federal supply line. One crucial area of concern was the railhead at Westminster, Maryland; Meade needed a solid, trustworthy force to cover these important stores in case a retreat became necessary. Pleasonton selected Buford's two hard-fought brigades, but by late morning, Pleasonton's orders found Devin's and Gamble's troopers already in position, and Devin's brigade actively engaged in heavy skirmishing with Confederate infantry west of the Emmitsburg Road.[3] Buford's division had suffered relatively few casualties the day before, but his troopers were running low on all supplies and his horses badly needed shoeing after traveling up from the Potomac and crossing through Maryland.[4] Worse, his horses had been subsisting on grass alone for several days over this march and were now played out. In an arm where combat performance was directly dependent upon healthy mounts, Buford's horses needed to be rotated out and fed up or he'd risk losing them as casualties.

Pleasonton ordered Buford's two brigades to the rear, but somehow his staff failed to issue orders for a similar force to come forward and replace them. Instead, the 4th Pennsylvania Cavalry from John Gregg's brigade came forward but were "stationed in rear of a battery in the center of our line by a captain on General Pleasonton's staff."[5] Buford's men had essentially screened the left of Meade's battle line, and the three-hundred-odd troopers of the 4th Pennsylvania couldn't have replaced even one of Buford's brigades, let alone two. Advancing Confederates would no longer have to deal with a large cavalry screen before launching an attack on this portion of the field, a fact correctly identified by III Corps commander Daniel Sickles and staff.[6]

Since George Meade assumed command, he had held Pleasonton on a short leash at headquarters, where Pleasonton examined dispatches, directed the movements of his distant brigades, and advised Meade on a constant basis. He likely chaffed under Meade's close authority as opposed to Hooker's more fluid style of command, but Alfred Pleasonton had to be proud of his recent gains. Over the past two weeks, he'd gained a third division, secured a major general's star, and maneuvered his new corps from Virginia to Pennsylvania in a taxing, but largely successful, shift of operations.

Figure 16.1. General Meade made his headquarters at the Leister farmhouse. The small farm would suffer heavy damage from sustained artillery fire during the battle. *Library of Congress.*

For the second day of battle, Judson Kilpatrick's 3rd Division would move down from Heidlersburg to cover the northern approaches to Gettysburg. David Gregg's 2nd Division would leave one brigade in Maryland, then march through Hanover and place his remaining two brigades under McIntosh and Gregg on the far right of the Federal line. Wesley Merritt, now commanding the Regulars Brigade, would move north from Emmitsburg, Maryland. Things were still very much in flux. A second day of battle loomed, and mistakes were being made; however, a plan now stood to hold at Gettysburg, and Pleasonton's troopers were attempting to fulfill the plan as it evolved.[7]

~

On the morning of July 2, Robert E. Lee's headquarters sat on the western slope of Seminary Ridge, a mile to the west of Cemetery Hill. Rising before dawn, Lee ate in the dark, glassed the enemy lines at first light, and found to his dismay that the Federals had improved their position overnight. Worse still, Lee's trains of captured supplies, the primary reason for his invasion, were now a hindrance. Some three thousand head of cattle, sheep, and hogs, plus hundreds of wagons bearing horse grains, forage, and food stores of all sorts, were now parked east of South Mountain. Lee had not expected a battle yesterday and, therefore, ordered the wagons across South Mountain to join the concentration of his army east of the mountains.[8] Now the miles of wagons and livestock were clogging the rear of his lines and hindering Longstreet's corps from making their way forward.[9] The mountains and vital supplies now snared Lee's ability to move in any direction except forward, straight into the Army of the Potomac.[10] With Meade's army at such close range, Lee had little option but to attack. "A battle thus became, in a measure, unavoidable."[11]

That morning Lee ordered three patrols to examine the ground on his right flank. He also sent a staff officer to meet with Ewell on his left. Shortly after dawn, generals Longstreet and Hill arrived, and Longstreet began advocating that his I Corps move far to the right, out beyond the Federal flank to draw the Federals from their current position. Lee disagreed. Yesterday, victory had briefly been in Southern hands. Lee's army broke the enemy line, invested the town, and captured some five thousand prisoners. Lee still believed he had the best army on the field, and though the Federals had the better position, Lee knew he still held the initiative. A proper concert of action aptly coordinated between his three corps commanders could still yield the victory Lee wanted and the Confederacy urgently needed. "The enemy is here," declared Lee. "[I]f we do not whip him, he will whip us."[12]

Lee issued orders for Longstreet's I Corps to make the primary attack against the Federal left, while Ewell's II Corps would make a simultaneous demonstration on the Federal right, one that could develop into a full assault if the opportunity developed. Hill's III Corps would demonstrate against the Federal center and supply a fresh division to attack in league with Longstreet's primary assault.[13] The key to Southern success would be early, coordinated assaults from multiple fronts.[14] It was now roughly 9:00 a.m., and Lee rode to the far left of his line to meet with Ewell and ensure he supported Longstreet's attack on the opposite flank.[15] Lee returned to his headquarters roughly two hours later, surprised to find Longstreet's corps still in the same place as when Lee left. Longstreet then asked Lee for permission to wait for one of his brigades to arrive and Lee assented, though he must have been losing patience with every passing hour.[16]

Jeb Stuart arrived at Lee's headquarters early that afternoon. According to author John Thomason, Lee greeted his chief of cavalry by saying, "Well, General Stuart, you are here at last."[17] Whether Lee offered this as a relieved greeting for a long-lost comrade or as an angry rebuke for a wayward subordinate is debatable; however, there were few, if any, witnesses in actual hearing range of the event.[18] Stuart's detractors have long blamed him for leaving General Lee without any cavalry to guide him into Pennsylvania, allegedly hamstringing Lee by not informing him of the enemy's movements, and forcing him to stumble about in the dark before the enemy. If such a charge were true, Lee would have arrested Stuart on the spot. Yet Lee did not arrest Stuart, and the reality is that Stuart's detractors are mistaken of the facts.

At the beginning of the campaign, Stuart had seven brigades of cavalry under his overall command: Fitz Lee's, Wade Hampton's, John Chambliss's, Grumble Jones's, Beverly Robertson's, Albert Jenkins's, and John Imboden's. Stuart took three brigades with him as he moved to pass around the Federal army. Enemy forces interrupted Stuart's course, and Stuart sent word to Lee that the Federals were moving to cross the Potomac on June 27.[19] Stuart then crossed the Potomac, gathered supplies, and marched for York, Pennsylvania, to link with Ewell's II Corps—exactly as described in Lee's orders.[20]

When Stuart departed from Lee with three brigades, he left two brigades of cavalry behind under the command of Beverly Robertson. These brigades were ordered to harass the enemy and keep a sharp watch on the Federal army perched below the Potomac.[21] Robertson did neither, and Lee had no word of Hooker's crossing the Potomac until a spy informed

Lee of the event on June 28. The enemy had not deterred Robertson; Robertson had simply failed to fulfill his orders.[22] The final two brigades, those of Albert Jenkins and John Imboden, would travel west of the mountains and into Pennsylvania along with White's 35th Virginia Battalion. Jenkins and White traveled north with Ewell's corps in advance of Lee, and Lee was aware of their actions. Lee was also in communication with Imboden, operating on Lee's left flank near McConnellsburg, Pennsylvania, on July 1.[23] Why was Imboden's cavalry brigade sixty miles to the west of Gettysburg on the first day of the battle? Because Lee had not expected to fight an engagement on July 1.

Much of the criticism leveled at Stuart came from General Lee's aide-de-camp and military secretary, Colonel Charles Marshall. After Lee's death in 1870, Marshall claimed they should have shot Stuart for disobeying orders and arriving late to the Battle of Gettysburg.[24] Stuart clearly acted *within* the orders he received from Lee when he passed round the Federal army and pushed north for the Potomac.[25] Marshall, however, is entirely correct in one regard: it is true that Stuart arrived late for the Battle of Gettysburg, but Stuart was not alone in this. Also late for the Battle of Gettysburg was Robert E. Lee, commanding the Army of Northern Virginia; James Longstreet, commanding the Confederate I Corps; Richard Ewell, commanding the Confederate II Corps. Even Lee's self-venerated secretary, Colonel Charles Marshall, was late to the Battle of Gettysburg because Lee had made no plans to fight a battle on July 1! The only Confederates on time to the Battle of Gettysburg were from Henry Heth's division, when they brought on a general engagement the rest of the army was not expecting, not prepared for, and, thus, not on time for.

To blame Stuart for being late to an unplanned collision defies simple logic, and to suggest he should have been shot for doing so is patently ridiculous. If Lee did snap when Stuart arrived on July 2, it may well have been over Lee's frustration with the delayed advances of his three corps commanders—not Stuart's timing. Irrefutable is the fact that Lee did not censure Stuart and did not have him shot. Instead, General Lee sent his best horse soldier out to scout his army's left flank.[26]

～

Stuart's three brigades began arriving near Gettysburg by midday, with Fitz Lee's and John Chambliss's brigades taking post beyond Hunterstown, Pennsylvania, five miles northeast of Gettysburg. Last came Hampton's brigade, and the rear guard fell to the Cobb Legion Cavalry under Colonel Pierce Young. Like all of Stuart's men, the Georgians were exhausted and their horses worn to nubs. The past week had been a stress-filled hardship of skirmishing and endless riding on dust-choked roads during the hottest part of the year. "The utmost verge of endurance by men and horse had been reached."[27] Young's troopers were undoubtably looking forward to a night's rest and a chance to sit down and cook some rations. In the meantime, they perched their carbines on their saddles and fought to stay awake in the baking heat as the captured wagons lumbered through the tiny hamlet, kicking up clouds of dust as the sounds of artillery played in the distance from the fields south of Gettysburg.

Farther northeast, in the hamlet of Berlin, Judson Kilpatrick and his men slept until dawn, when they received orders to move south. Kilpatrick's troopers were soon up and moving, with Custer's brigade taking the lead down the Gettysburg Pike. When awarded his command, Custer inherited the 5th, 6th, and 7th Michigan, led by colonels Russell Alger, George Gray, and William Mann, respectively. Before the war, Alger had been in the lumber business, Gray had been an engineer, and Mann, the youngest at just twenty-three, had been a practicing attorney from Detroit.[28] It was a good brigade, with the 5th, and some squadrons of the 6th, fitted with Spencer repeating rifles and the balance issued breech-loading Sharps and Burnside carbines.[29] Known as the "Wolverines," this brigade had seen its share of campaigning around the capital but only gained limited results in chasing after John Mosby's Rangers and Wade Hampton's Iron Scouts.

Custer also asked to have the more senior 1st Michigan Cavalry assigned to his brigade. The veterans of the 1st Michigan had seen service in the Shenandoah Valley, and the 2nd Manassas campaign. Colonel Charles Town, a machinist before the war, received five wounds during the fight at Lewis Ford while under John Buford's command and clearly earned the right to lead the regiment.[30] Unfortunately, Town was also battling the middle stages of tuberculosis and often wracked with intense pain.[31] Despite this fatal sentence hanging overhead, Town fought through the daily torment of his chronic condition and kept to the saddle, perhaps half hoping to die at the front rather than a sanitarium.[32]

By midafternoon, Custer and his new brigade were closing on Gettysburg when they received reports from scouts of the 18th Pennsylvania Cavalry. Roughly handled at Hanover, these Pennsylvanians were eager to reverse this performance and diligently coursed ahead of Custer's brigade to discover Pierce Young's Georgia troopers posting guard on the fringes of Hunterstown. A shot rang out on the York Pike, and Young soon saw what was coming. He grabbed his hat in his rein hand to keep from losing it and spurred his horse into a dead sprint for Hunterstown.[33]

Figure 16.2. Brigadier General George A. Custer, Army of the Potomac. Custer was very image conscious and poses here in a uniform of his own design. *Library of Congress.*

A young boy standing nearby saw the Federals draw sabres and charge after Young. "Down the street they came, hard as they could go, waving their sabres and yelling."[34] Young alerted his men and formed them as the Federals rolled down the pike, reversing the roles from the opening charge of Hanover two days prior. Carbines split the air, and the two sides met head-on. Pistols cracked and sabres rang as the larger Federal column drove the Georgians back through the town square and then south down the Gettysburg Road.[35] Hearing gunfire, Custer quickened the pace and invested Hunterstown with his new brigade. Dressed in a childlike sailor suit of blue velvet worn over a Federal naval blouse and collar, Custer appeared eager to prove his worth in his spanking new duds. Across the way watched Pierce Young, a former classmate of Custer's from West Point. Custer had long wanted a crack at Young, who once needled Custer near the end of their term, saying, "[W]ho knows . . . we may move against each other during the war."[36]

Custer moved his brigade through the town square and set his men along the Gettysburg Road, leading south from Hunterstown. The new general placed a rear guard, and next set the 1st and 7th Michigan east of the Gettysburg Road, with the 5th and 6th in and around a two-story barn west of the road. A battery of rifled guns under Lieutenant Alexander Pennington, of the 2nd U.S. Artillery, came hustling forward in support.

General Wade Hampton began making similar preparations farther down the Gettysburg Road. Turning at the sound of the opening skirmish, Hampton moved back north along the road and halted at a ridged tree line that looked back over a basin of wheat where the road dipped and rose again to a ridge before Hunterstown. Young rallied here in the road at this southern ridge beside Hampton, and the pair soon saw glimpses of Federal cavalry moving down from Hunterstown. Tasked by Stuart with holding this flank, Hampton staged sharpshooters from the Cobb Legion, Phillips Legion, and the 2nd South Carolina Cavalry across the Gettysburg Road. In addition, Hampton sent men edging forward through the wheat to a bend in the road, while keeping Young's mounted squadron as a ready reserve.[37]

Back at Hunterstown, Kilpatrick established his headquarters at the Grass Hotel, which looked out over the basin below. Kilpatrick soon gave Custer the go-ahead to launch an attack, and Company A of the 6th Michigan promptly formed for a charge down the lane. The stout fences bordering the lane meant the column wouldn't be able to deploy wider than a column of fours, meaning hard work lay ahead and everyone seemed very aware of the fact. As they prepared to advance, Custer bravely moved to the front and called over his shoulder, "I'll lead you this time, boys. Come on!"[38]

This was Custer's first charge as a general officer, and he led his men down the narrow lane at a gallop, gaining in speed and spurring on until they reached the first bend in the road, where Southern gunfire erupted from the fences.[39] Men and mounts tumbled to the dust in pain and panic. Custer's mount went down, and the roadbed was instantly strewn with wounded men, jettisoned equipment, and thrashing horses.[40] Custer kicked his way clear and swung up behind the saddle of his orderly, Private Norvill Churchill, who spurred Custer back to safety on the rear of his horse.[41]

In retrospect, the Georgians should have simply held their position after turning the Federal charge. Instead, Colonel Pierce Young of the Cobb Legion called for sabres and gave chase with two squadrons, spurring after the remnants of Custer's broken charge and cutting down all they caught. Pennington's battery then opened, slowing the Georgians as they reached the large barn, where they came under a blistering crossfire from the crops on the right and the barn loft on the left. The Spencers opened from their elevated position in the loft of the barn and shattered the Georgians in a rapid stream of repeating fire that downed men, horses, and anything that moved in the road. Young's mount pitched face forward, and the colonel tumbled down hard in the narrow lane. Dazed and dizzy he regained his feet, grabbed a fallen comrade's horse, and rode clear of the repeating enemy fire. Federals now galloped forward in a counterattack of their own, slashing down at the scattered survivors in the road, including Lieutenant Colonel Delony of the Georgia Legion. Slashed, bleeding, and unhorsed, Delony refused to surrender and, instead, planted a knee and fended off a series of sabre cuts. Henry Jackson of the legion rushed forward, buried his blade in the side of a Federal, and bore Delony back to Hampton's lines in a similar fashion to Custer's earlier rescue by his orderly.[42]

William Baird of the 6th Michigan Cavalry recalled a handful of Georgians who kept coming, riding all the way to Pennington's battery: "[A] few Rebels rode right over us and up to the guns of the battery and it was then [a] hand to hand encounter with the sabre." The fight boiled over the battery, and half the Georgians were cut down or shot from their saddles. A final swirl of sabres rang out, and the remaining Rebels cut their way clear.[43]

The Cobb Legion suffered heavily and had six officers killed in the contest.[44] Company A of the 6th Michigan suffered two killed and twenty-five wounded, including the company commander, Captain Henry E. Thompson.[45] After Young's failed charge, Hampton ordered up a pair of guns, and they traded random shots with Pennington's battery until the sun went down. Later that evening, Kilpatrick received new orders and moved south for Two Taverns on the far-left flank of Meade's line.[46]

～

Brigadier General Albert Jenkins's two thousand Confederate troopers had maneuvered with Ewell's II Corps since June 12 in preparation of the assault on Winchester. The brigade had since skirmished repeatedly with Federal forces; crossed the Potomac; wrecked enemy railroad tracks; helped gather thousands of dollars' worth of food, animals, and supplies for Lee's quartermasters; and provided countless screening and scouting missions for the Confederate II Corps. Today would be no exception, with the brigade slated to cover Ewell's left flank during his attack on Culp's Hill. Jenkins had only recently received these orders when he was struck by a piece of shell from a Union artillery round and knocked out of action.[47] After Jenkins, the next senior officer in the brigade was Colonel Milton Ferguson of the 16th Virginia Cavalry.[48] For some reason, Ferguson failed to carry out the brigade's orders, and the brigade never arrived beyond Culp's Hill to cover Ewell's flank.[49]

This absence meant infantry would have to cover this vital position, and the task fell to Brigadier General James Walker, the commander of the renowned Stonewall Brigade, which formed the left flank of Ewell's II Corps. Beginning that morning, Walker and his veterans had skirmished with Federal skirmishers until ordered forward, where they spied a large force of Federal cavalry moving east of Brinkerhoff's Ridge. Walker promptly wheeled out of line to face the new threat: "[O]ur line was advanced . . . and took position immediately on the north side of Hanover Road."[50] Walker sent the 2nd Virginia Infantry under Colonel John Quincy Adams Nadenbousch to engage the enemy and "ascertain, if possible, what force the enemy had at that point."[51]

The troopers Walker saw belonged to David Gregg's 2nd Division—specifically, the brigades of J. Irvin Gregg and John B. McIntosh, with Gregg deployed north of the Hanover Road and McIntosh to the south. These two brigades had only recently arrived at Gettysburg, "having been in the saddle day and night almost continuously for three weeks," recalled one of McIntosh's officers. "We were much reduced by short rations and exhaustion, and mounted on horses whose bones were plainly visible to the naked eye."[52] As was the case for many troopers North and South, the last month had been a near constant strain of hard marching, pitched fights, and meeting engagements that left their horses in sad shape. This afternoon looked to be little different as the men from the 10th New York Cavalry dismounted, checked the loads on their carbines, and walked across Cress Run to form a line near the Howard farm.

The New Yorkers didn't have long to wait before the 2nd Virginia Infantry crossed over Brinkerhoff's Ridge and the Federals opened fire on

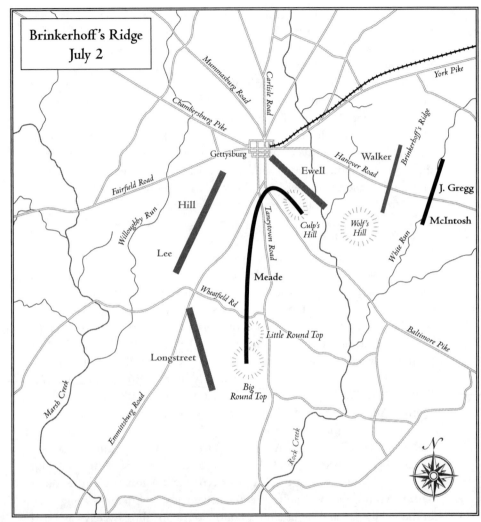

Map 10. Brinkerhoff's Ridge, July 2

the advancing gray line. The Virginians absorbed the fire and kept coming in earnest. "Our line was broken by an attack from the Rebel infantry," recalled a New Yorker, and several troopers were captured as they fell back along the Hanover Road.[53]

Jeb Stuart and his escort watched the Rebel foot soldiers push forward. Stuart had been out studying this far flank when the firing began. Glassing the enemy troopers, Stuart quickly recognized the colors of Gregg's 2nd Division. He studied the surrounding ground, taking special note of Cress

Ridge, Brinkerhoff Ridge, and the Hanover Road beyond.[54] Stuart continued glassing the surrounding fields and how the terrain lay until he received a dispatch and moved north to link with Fitz Lee's brigade.[55]

As Stuart rode off, Gregg's troopers mounted a brief counterattack, stunning the Confederate veterans and driving them prone, but this check soon passed as the Federals burned through their ammunition and the Virginians rallied and charged forward, this time coming on with a Rebel yell. "With their celebrated 'Ki-yi,' they charged on," recalled one of Gregg's officers; "all our carbine ammunition was gone, so I ordered the boys to give them the contents of their revolvers and fall back." The Federals ran downhill, firing their revolvers, darting under the Confederate fire, and taking shelter along the banks of Cress Run.[56]

At this point, Colonel McIntosh waved his 3rd Pennsylvania forward and sent elements of the 1st New Jersey and the Purnell Legion Cavalry racing for a stone wall south of the Hanover Road, flanking the Confederate approach. Federal gunners from Captain William Rank's Battery H, Pennsylvania Artillery, opened in support, and McIntosh's troopers arrived in time to knock holes through the wall and steady their aim as the 2nd Virginia again pressed forward.[57] Carbines blazed down the line, stunning the Virginians and driving them to cover. Nadenbousch attempted to flank the wall, but the 1st New Jersey rushed forward in support and the fighting stalled. As the sun dropped on the horizon, Nadenbousch left a covering force to watch the Federals and retreated to join Walker's brigade.

To the west, all could hear Ewell's II Corps making their attack on Culp's Hill, but the presence of Gregg's and McIntosh's brigades kept Walker's Virginians out on this flank. Without Walker, Ewell's flank would have hung wide open. "I deemed it prudent to hold my position until after dark, which I did," explained Walker.[58] This meant the most celebrated infantry brigade in the Army of Northern Virginia, fourteen hundred veterans of Stonewall Jackson's vaunted foot cavalry, didn't join Ewell's diminished II Corps in their attack on Culp's Hill and, instead, guarded Ewell's flank in a skirmish with Federal cavalry.

17

THE FIGHT FOR RUMMEL FARM

Late morning July 3 saw Stuart and his men up and mounted. One night's rest was hardly enough for his horses, or his men, after the exhausting trek of hard marches and combats the command had suffered since leaving Rector's Crossroads. Yet, Stuart still remained eager to pitch in. Lee had nearly shattered the Federal line the day before, and today Lee planned a massed effort on the Federal center, an assault of twelve thousand men against Meade's center with one hundred Confederate guns in support.[1] Stuart's cavalry would have little to do with this operation, and Lee left no written orders for his cavalry chief, perhaps preferring Stuart keep a light watch on his far flank and mostly rest his men and mounts.[2] Despite a lack of orders, Stuart rode out on the left flank of the Confederate line, in the same vicinity of his scout the day before along Brinkerhoff's Ridge.[3] Should a breakthrough occur, Stuart had apparently come up with a plan to "effect a surprise on the enemy" and exploit a break in the Federal line if one occurred.[4]

Stuart set out with four brigades, including Chambliss, Hampton, and Lee, along with Jenkins's command—the 14th, 16th, 17th, 34th, and 36th Virginia Cavalry—today led by Colonel Milton Ferguson. On paper, Stuart's brigades counted five thousand sabres. The reality proved far different, especially in Chambliss's command. One month earlier, the brigade numbered more than fifteen hundred troopers, but by July 3, just three hundred men rode in the brigade's ranks with the 2nd North Carolina Cavalry suffering especially heavy casualties in both men and horses. The 2nd counted three hundred sabres at Brandy Station; just thirty-five Tarheels were ready and mounted on the morning of July 3.[5] Wade Hampton also found his regiments in dire condition. The Cobb Legion had been hard pressed at Hunterstown, and the 1st South Carolina had but one battalion with him, led by Lieutenant Colonel William Walker, the other battalion being sent to scout for Longstreet's I Corps under Colonel John Black.[6]

Stuart's horse artillery was also depleted. Captain James Hart's battery was detached on separate duty, and captains Breathed and McGregor now struggled to draw ammunition from the ordnance train, partly because of the massive bombardment scheduled for the Confederate assault on the Federal center. This drew an animated reaction from Captain Breathed toward the ordnance officers, but despite all his efforts, his gunners sat waiting for ammunition and missed Stuart's departure.[7] Instead of his usual gunners, Stuart would only have Captain Thomas E. Jackson's Charlottesville Battery, currently attached to Ferguson's brigade, to accompany him at the outset.

Stuart led Ferguson and Chambliss southward, using the woods along Cress Ridge to screen his approach from the enemy. After scouting these same fields the previous afternoon, he had a route in mind as he gained a high point on the ridge. Stretching before him were the farms of John Rummel and then Jacob Lott, drifting to the junction of the Low Dutch and Hanover Roads. West of the Lott farm lay a series of open fields intersected by Little's Run, a small, tree-lined creek emanating from separate head springs on the Rummel and Lott properties. Through his field glasses Stuart could see elements of blue-clad cavalry moving about Lott's farm—a debilitating hurdle in Stuart's hopes to "effect a surprise on the enemy."[8] Stuart responded by sending forward a pair of guns from Jackson's battery and had them fire four rounds in different directions.

Exactly why Stuart did this remains a mystery. He could have been performing a reconnaissance by fire, to make any near Federals return fire and mark their positions, or perhaps he meant to needle captains Breathed and McGregor to hurry along with their guns.[9] Most likely Stuart hoped to draw the attention of whatever Federal troops lurked nearby, and coax them into a fixed fight around the Rummel farm with elements of Ferguson's brigade.[10] Chambliss's brigade might then aid Ferguson as a mounted reserve and help pin the Federals in place. With a little luck, Stuart could use the high ground along Cress Ridge as a terrain screen for sneaking Hampton's and Lee's brigades around the Federal flank. "My plan was to employ the enemy in front with sharpshooters, and move a command of cavalry upon their left flank," whereby Stuart hoped to separate the Federal cavalry from Meade's main force.[11] Stuart's cannon fire drew no obvious response from the Federals, but Stuart saw more and more flashes of Federal blue moving in the distance, marking more than just scattered pickets. With few cards left to play, Stuart dismounted sharpshooters from Ferguson's brigade and sent them striding for the Rummel farm.[12]

~

The Federals Stuart saw belonged to Colonel John McIntosh's 1st Brigade, from Gregg's 2nd Division. McIntosh had been born in the Florida Territory, where his father, a native Georgian, served as a U.S. Army officer. In 1861, McIntosh received a commission in the 5th U.S. Cavalry and served in the Seven Days and at Sharpsburg before taking command of the 3rd Pennsylvania Cavalry. McIntosh appeared quieter than most field officers, and though not a firebrand, he'd shown himself to be a solid field tactician, with a calm head and good judgment.[13] He'd done well leading his brigade at the Battle of Kelly's Ford in March and had held the brigade ever since.[14] Described as a "born fighter, a strict disciplinarian, and a polished gentleman," McIntosh commanded the 1st Maryland, 1st New Jersey, 3rd Pennsylvania, and Purnell Legion cavalries.[15]

Federal command of this sector went to Brigadier General David M. Gregg, commanding the 2nd Division of Pleasonton's cavalry corps. This morning Gregg received orders from headquarters to relieve Custer's brigade and cover the approaches to the Union rear. "On the morning of July 3, I was ordered to take a position on the right of our line . . . about three-fourths of a mile nearer the Baltimore and Gettysburg Turnpike [than held the day before]."[16] Gregg and McIntosh knew the importance of protecting the Baltimore Turnpike—the turnpike not only served as Meade's only remaining supply line but also led straight into the rear of Meade's army and would form the primary escape route if needed. Near noon, General Gregg received a dispatch from General Howard; Federal lookouts had spotted a large force of enemy cavalry moving toward Gregg's position.[17]

Howard's report, coupled with the recent appearance of enemy cavalry on Cress Ridge, convinced Gregg he would soon see action: "[A] strong line of skirmishers displayed by the enemy was evidence that the enemy's cavalry had gained our right, and were about to attack, with the view of gaining the rear of our line."[18] Gregg found himself in a precarious spot. A large enemy force had arrived and looked to be deploying for a fight. Gregg's orders were to relieve Custer and allow the Wolverine Brigade to rejoin Kilpatrick's division, but Gregg, McIntosh, and Custer all agreed a heavy clash was brewing here along the Hanover Road. Gregg countermanded the order; Custer would stay with Gregg's 2nd Division. Custer's presence gave David Gregg a total of three brigades: McIntosh's—already deploying on the field with thirteen hundred men—and two ready reserves, his cousin John Gregg's twelve hundred men, and George Custer's sixteen hundred troopers.[19]

McIntosh dismounted sharpshooters on his left from the 1st New Jersey behind a stout wooden fence of mortised posts and tightly fixed rails running between the Rummel and Lott farms.[20] As the Jerseys moved forward, McIntosh also shored up his right flank across the field spreading to the east. "I placed the 3rd Pennsylvania Cavalry, in a woods to our [far] right, and had that part of the woods mostly dismounted."[21] McIntosh next sent Lieutenant James Chester, Battery E, 1st U.S. Artillery to deploy near an orchard on the Lott farm and engage Captain Jackson's southern guns along Cress Ridge. Farther back he deployed Lieutenant Pennington's Battery M, 2nd U.S. Artillery with six three-inch rifles near the intersection of the Hanover and Low Dutch Roads.

~

Back along Cress Ridge, the 34th Virginia under Lieutenant Colonel Vincent Witcher moved forward. Vincent "Clawhammer" Witcher hailed from the mountains of southwestern Virginia, where he made his living as a country lawyer, and there earned his nickname for wearing the long, spike-tailed dress coats popular two decades prior. Witcher and his men had acquired an effective but brutal reputation along the Kentucky-Virginia border early in the war. Observers described the regiment as "a company of mounted gunmen" and found them a "rather rough bunch . . . fierce and hard bitten," and not the sort of individuals Stuart typically sought to fill his ranks.[22] Despite the rumors, Stuart fully approved of the full-length Enfield rifles the 34th carried, and he sent Witcher's men down to the Rummel farm to act as sharpshooters.

As Witcher stepped off, Captain Jackson's battery opened on the distant blue columns. Moments later, Jackson's guns came under the combined fire of Chester's section on the Lott farm, and Pennington's battery beyond.[23] The Federal gunners quickly found the range, killing half the battery horses and wounding several of Jackson's gunners. Jackson promptly withdrew his guns behind the ridge. "I fired 23 rounds at the opposing [Federal] Battery but not a shot took effect. . . . I am confident that had our men remained ten minutes longer all our guns would have been dismounted & many of the men killed."[24]

Gaining Mr. Rummel's barn, Witcher's sharpshooters spread out in skirmish order and kept moving. They passed a stone wall and headed for a second a hundred yards farther on that anchored on a springhouse.[25] Hidden from Witcher's view lay a third wall held by McIntosh's 1st New Jersey. As Witcher's men came in range, the third wall exploded with carbine fire, killing several of Witcher's men and driving the rest to cover. A firefight erupted as both sides went to it with each side hunkered down behind their respective walls. The Confederates had the advantage in range and stopping power with their Enfields, and the Federals in rate of fire with their breechloaders. As the volleys increased, McIntosh fed in more skirmishers from the 3rd Pennsylvania and gained the Virginians' flank. Casualties mounted, Witcher's adjutant fell in the crossfire, and Witcher pulled the 34th back to the first wall near Rummel's two-story barn.[26] Several Virginians took sniper positions in the loft of the barn and soon opened on McIntosh's troopers. Moments later, Lieutenant Chester opened fire on the barn, forcing the Virginians to vacate the premises.[27]

Stuart appeared to be facing a strong opponent with superior artillery. Yet Stuart still felt he might busy the Federals to his front with Ferguson's men and use the high wooded ground along Cress Ridge to screen the brigades of Hampton and Fitz Lee.[28] He sent orders to this effect, and as the temperature soared, the brigades of Hampton, and then Lee, mistakenly blundered out onto the open fields east of Cress Ridge.[29] This lapse may have been due to a mix-up of orders, or simple fatigue given the prior weeks' events, but fatigue or not, the sight of two Rebel brigades tipped Stuart's plans to the Federals; there would be no surprise move on the Federal flank.[30]

Now vexed, Stuart ordered Hampton and Lee to come and discuss the changing situation with him in person.[31] Hampton and Lee each received the order to report but decided it would be imprudent for both to leave their commands at the same time; instead, they would take turns with Hampton going first, and the South Carolinian set off in search of Stuart.[32]

～

Meanwhile, the fighting continued to flare across the stone walls on the Rummel farm. Additional sharpshooters from the 14th and 16th Virginia joined the fight on Witcher's right, along with a dismounted squadron from Chambliss's 9th Virginia.[33] At this point, Stuart had still not heard from gunners Breathed or McGregor, and Stuart sent the borrowed half battery of Captain Charles Green, Louisiana Guard Artillery, to support Witcher on the Rummel property.[34] Though new to cavalry service, Captain Green was an experienced gunner and knew his two Parrot rifles were badly outnumbered by enemy batteries on the far side; Green countered by repeatedly shifting his guns to keep the Federal batteries from gaining a hard fix on his position.[35]

As Green deployed his guns, Fitz Lee sent sharpshooters forward on the far left of Stuart's line. Lee's men formed along a "high stake and rider fence" running east to west on the north boundary of the Lott farm near where it intersected with the Stallsmith farm lane.[36] Once Lee's Virginians

Figure 17.1.   Colonel John R. Chambliss, Army of Northern Virginia. Chambliss's brigade made a key charge, which is sometimes overlooked during the fight at the Rummel farm. *Wiki Commons. Public domain. Unknown original author.*

gained the fence, they came under the combined fire of sharpshooters from the 1st New Jersey Cavalry and Chester's two guns posted on the Lott farm.[37]

The firing now escalated across the field, sweeping from the east side of the lines along the Stallsmith lane to the west end at the Rummel farm. Vincent Witcher, now reinforced before Rummel's barn by Green's battery, pushed John McIntosh's 1st New Jersey and 3rd Pennsylvania back over the stone walls on the Rummel farm, and Custer countered by sending the 5th Michigan forward with their Spencer rifles. "I ordered the 5th Michigan Cavalry to a more advanced position, with orders to maintain their ground at all hazards."[38] Witcher's advance stalled when they encountered the 5th Michigan. The rapid-firing repeaters brought the Rebels to a dead stop, and the well-heeled Wolverines quickly counterattacked. Witcher again retreated back before the Rummel barn, and Lieutenant William Gaines of the 14th Virginia rushed to help a wounded comrade lying on the ploughed ground: "[D]amn you, go into the fight," cursed the wounded trooper. "I will die in a few minutes," regardless.[39]

Seeing Witcher's line in danger, and Federal cavalry starting to move forward farther out on his left, Stuart ordered Chambliss to make a mounted charge with his waiting brigade.[40] As Chambliss formed for the charge, the 5th Michigan was burning through their ammunition with their quick-firing repeaters. Their fire slacked, and Witcher's men leveled a pair of lethal volleys into the Federals and "swept them down by scores."[41] Witcher's men rushed in, capturing the 5th Michigan's colors and killing their battalion commander, Major Noah Ferry. Witcher later praised the Wolverines' nerve: "They . . . simply close[d] their ranks, returned our fire with the pistol and stubbornly held their ground until charged in flank and rear by our cavalry."[42]

Chambliss now came storming up at the head of his brigade, gained the Rummel lane, and drove past the Rummel springhouse. This forced the remaining Federal sharpshooters back across the Rummel property, and they began climbing over the rails of the fence. Chambliss's men hit the fence at a corner in the farm lane, dismounted, and tried to toss the rails aside. The fixed rails, however, proved harder to remove than the common stake-and-rider fences in Virginia. Chambliss ordered more men to dismantle the fence, while others struck up a covering volley with their carbines.[43]

～

Simultaneous with these actions, on the far Confederate left, Fitz Lee's sharpshooters from the 1st and 2nd Virginia had grown tired of the harassing fire from Federal sharpshooters posted in the Lott family woods. Mounted squadrons from each regiment came up, and the sharpshooters battered a gap through the fences bordering the Stallsmith farm lane.[44] The mounted squadrons poured through, and the sharpshooters followed to engage the Union dismounts along the woodlot. Major William A. Morgan commanded the sharpshooters of companies D and K, 1st Virginia. "We were confronted by a line of dismounted Federal cavalrymen equal to my own . . . who opened [on] us with a volley at close range. My men instantly returned the fire. . . . I ordered an advance on their position at the double quick, doing good execution with our carbines."[45] The combined Virginians drove the Union sharpshooters back into the woodlot and then turned for Chester's guns with the mounted squadrons leading the way and the sharpshooters hustling up behind.[46]

At this point a staff officer of General Gregg's rode forward yelling to Lieutenant Chester that the general wished his guns to limber up and withdraw to safety. "Tell the General to go to hell!" shouted Chester, and his men continued loading.[47] Chester felt the charging Confederates were too close to limber his guns, and he judged the best course was to keep firing and wait for his designated support from the 1st Maryland Cavalry to come to his aid. Chester, however, couldn't see that his support was elsewhere on a different mission. Chester switched to canister, and then double canister, and when no support arrived, he dashed to the rear as the 2nd Virginia, and then 1st Virginia, closed the final yards at a gallop, only to be stalled at another stout rail fence.[48] Chester later admitted to fleeing so fast he left canister rounds piled before his guns.[49]

When General Gregg saw the mounted charge coming across the Lott farm, he turned to Custer and the 7th Michigan.[50] "During the skirmish of the dismounted men, the enemy brought upon the field a [mounted] column for a charge," wrote Gregg. "The charge of this column was met by the Seventh Michigan Cavalry."[51] Sabres hissed from scabbards, and Colonel William Mann led his 7th Michigan out at the trot.[52] Unseen by the enemy, the Wolverines rose to a canter and struck the Virginians' flank near the Lott fence. Trading blows, the Virginians wheeled back to protect their flank, and at the same moment, Fitz Lee sent orders for the Virginians to retire.[53] Now flanked and forced about by the Wolverines, the Virginians quickly gave ground and fell back behind their sharpshooters in a leap-frog-style retreat.[54]

Smelling blood, Mann's 7th Michigan spurred forward, pressing after the fleeing Rebels. One sharpshooter squadron of the 2nd Virginia ducked into a string of woods and opened on the pursuing Federals. "We made it rather too warm in there for them," remembered James Biggs of the 2nd Virginia.[55] The Wolverines veered away from this makeshift redoubt and, instead, pursued Morgan's 1st Virginia sharpshooters who topped a rise of ground, and turned about to deliver a volley that emptied several saddles, again checking the 7th Michigan's advance.[56] Morgan's foot squadron then sprinted for the high stake-and-rider fence along the Stallsmith lane, as Custer came up with the 7th's reserves, squared the ranks, and waved them forward, screaming the legendary entreaty, "Come on, you Wolverines!"[57]

Major Luther Trowbridge watched the 7th Michigan charge from a distance: "To our astonishment and distress we saw that regiment, apparently without any attempt to change directions, dash itself upon a high stake and rider fence, squadron after squadron breaking upon the struggling masses in front, like the waves of the sea upon a rocky shore, until all were mixed in one confused and tangled mass."[58] The 7th Michigan slammed straight into the fence. The front horses crashed into the barrier, and the rear ranks piled against the rest, as Virginians on the far side of the rails opened at point-blank range, their bullets tearing through men and horses with abandon.[59] Lieutenant Colonel Allyne Litchfield had his horse killed beneath him as the 7th Michigan collapsed in a pile: "[I]n the charge my horse was killed and it was with difficulty I extricated myself."[60]

A frantic melee developed as the two sides blazed away, thrusting carbines, revolvers, and sabres alike through the wooden rails amid a mass of dying horses. The resulting chaos and confusion prevented either side from making a proper volley, and probably saved many lives. This finer point seemed unobserved by Lieutenant Colonel Litchfield of the 7th Michigan, who later wrote a tongue-in-cheek letter to his wife describing General Custer as brave but "rather rash."[61] Some of the Wolverines attempted to let down the fence, with mixed results, and a few game troopers made it across the barrier, only to be shot down by the Virginians. The 7th Michigan looked back for support, only to find they were now being flanked by a second Confederate force and wisely gave ground.[62]

This second threat came from Chambliss's brigade, which Stuart ordered forward in a charge against the dismounted Federals at the Rummel farm.[63] Stuart ordered Chambliss to charge at roughly the same time Custer led his Wolverines forward, and once Chambliss opened a gap in the stubborn Rummel fence, he turned left and zeroed in on Custer's retreating Federals. Revolvers cracked in rapid succession, and the Rebels stormed through the fractured Wolverines. They shot down the 7th's color-bearer, Sergeant Benjamin Church, and then Lieutenant James Birney grabbed the Michigan colors and emptied his revolver into Chambliss's ranks until felled by a sabre cut. The Rebels captured Birney and the colors, and the rest of the 7th Michigan fled back in disorder with Chambliss's men tight on their heels.[64] Watching from their wooded redoubt, James Biggs and his fellow 2nd Virginia sharpshooters took this opportunity to sprint back for their lines. "I tell you we did some good running across that field back to our horses."[65]

Meanwhile, Captain Walter Newhall of McIntosh's staff saw Chambliss's Confederates pursuing Custer's people across his front. Quickly mounting an ad hoc collection of four officers and sixteen men from the 3rd Pennsylvania Cavalry, Newhall led the men forward against Chambliss's flank.[66] Sergeant William Harrison, the 13th Virginia's color sergeant, carried his standard on a "John Brown style pike," and as Newhall spurred in range, Harrison dipped the colors and lanced Newhall through the mouth, gaffing the captain like a fish and hooking him out of the saddle.[67] Harrison then lanced Newhall's orderly through the abdomen as the rest of the Virginia color party swarmed forward to protect their flag. Eventually, every officer in Newhall's forlorn hope fell wounded, and the rest scattered in earnest.[68]

Though unsuccessful, Newhall's bold attack still disordered Chambliss's ranks, and Russell Alger's 5th Michigan now charged forward with Major Luther Trowbridge in the lead.[69] Lieutenant Beale, of the 9th Virginia, turned out with a section to stem Trowbridge's charge, but Beale lacked the numbers to stem the assault. Trowbridge cut his way through Beale's men and continued on, striking the rest of Chambliss's brigade as the balance of the 5th Michigan remounted and charged forward in Trowbridge's wake.[70] Chambliss now turned for safer ground, and the Federals chased him back through the gap in the fence and into the Rummel wheat field, where a sprawling sabre fight broke out among Alger's 5th Michigan; Chambliss's men; and Company G of the 17th Virginia, sent to cover Captain Green's guns.[71]

～

Since being summoned, Wade Hampton had failed to find Stuart, and he returned to his command, only to find Fitz Lee had sent orders for Hampton's brigade to advance and support Chambliss. This was extremely unorthodox, and Hampton instantly countermanded the order.[72] Seconds later, another courier arrived from Chambliss seeking support in the Rummel wheat field, and this time Hampton ordered the 1st North Carolina and the Jeff Davis Legion to charge forward. As the two regiments swept forward, Alger and his remounted 5th Michigan turned on their heels, debauched through the gap in the Rummel fence, and headed for the cover of their artillery. Instead of coming back about, Colonel Baker and his 1st North Carolina turned in pursuit of Alger. This forced Hampton to spur after Baker, and Waring's Davis Legion, to end their pursuit of the Federals.

Hampton swept past the 9th Virginia with a Confederate flag in hand, attempting to rally the 1st North Carolina and Davis Legion and turn them back around.[73] Hampton's adjutant, Captain Theodore Barker, misunderstood Hampton's forward sprint with the colors as a signal for the entire brigade to advance, and Barker mistakenly ordered the rest of the brigade ahead. The 2nd South Carolina, the Phillips Georgia Legion, one battalion of the 1st South Carolina, and the remains of the Cobb Legion now moved forward in formation, and Hampton looked back to see the rest of his brigade following his course.[74] Hampton had not ordered his brigade to charge, but he also saw Fitz Lee's reserve squadrons shifting behind the Stallsmith lane, and Hampton may have witnessed Jeb Stuart actively rallying Fitz Lee's troopers at this same time.[75] Hampton never shared his exact thoughts of this moment, but given his failure to link with Stuart, and the fact he had no defined battle plan, he may have thought Stuart ordered a general advance.[76] Whatever the cause, his brigade was moving forward, and Hampton waved his men at the Federal lines.

Across the fence, the sudden appearance of Hampton's men struck the Federals with admiration: "They were formed in close column of squadrons. . . . They marched with well-aligned fronts and steady reins; their polished sabre-blades dazzling in the piercing rays of a bright summer's sun."[77] This Federal admiration soon turned deadly, as the Union batteries opened with shrapnel on the Southern troopers. Captain Miller of the 3rd Pennsylvania witnessed the carnage: "Shell after shell met the advancing column and tore through their ranks . . . and horse after horse staggered

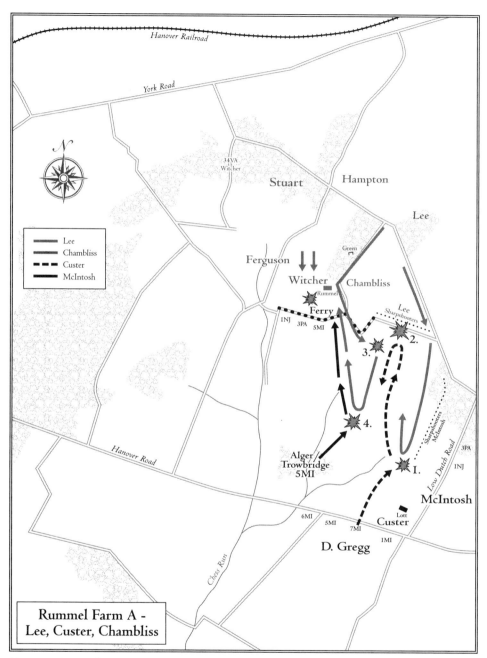

Map 11. Rummel Farm A—Lee, Custer, Chambliss

and fell."[78] A total of ten Federal guns were now firing on Hampton's columns, and General David Gregg wrote there was never "a more accurate and effective fire delivered by the artillery."[79]

Posted on the high ground along the Hanover Road, lieutenants Frank Hamilton and Carle Woodruff each commanded a section of guns with clear fields of fire: "[W]e could pour our fire into the Confederate cavalry until they were almost face to face."[80] Woodruff began firing with an elevation of five degrees and kept dropping his muzzles as the enemy rolled forward until his guns were firing flat to the horizon.[81]

George Saussy, a veteran of the Jeff Davis Legion, attested to the heavy fire the regiment endured. Saussy watched the Mississippi colors fall three times "either by hit of the color bearer or his mount" each time "the flag was grasped by another" and carried forward.[82] As the Southerners closed on the fence, the narrow gap forced them to break gait and pare down from a broad column of squadrons to a slender column of fours to clear the opening. Such a maneuver was difficult to perform on a parade field, and to perform it now, at a gallop while blasted by artillery, made it nearly impossible. Staggered and frayed, the Confederates absorbed the fire and slipped through the gap in ragged clumps of darting horses running on their most basic instinct to keep with the herd.

Colonel Charles Town and his 1st Michigan Cavalry were sitting in reserve just south of the Hanover Road when Custer waved them forward. "Upon receiving the order to charge, Colonel Town, placing himself at the head of his command, ordered the 'trot' and sabers to be drawn." Town's Wolverines rolled forward in steady ranks, and Captain Amasa Matthews, leading Town's forward squadron, remembered Lieutenant Chester's section of guns firing from the Lott orchard as they closed on the Confederate column. "The first wavering at the head of the [enemy] column signaled a forlorn hope, the entire column which, not by order or detachment . . . turned back."[83] Unable to handle artillery and a sabre charge at the same moment, the lead element of the 1st North Carolina started to spread, then opened fire with their revolvers and turned in the shadow of the Wolverines.[84] Federal gunners ceased fire for fear of hitting their own men, and Town drove the 1st Michigan straight into the enemy ranks, "sabering all who came in reach," and driving the rest about.[85]

Matthews rode at the head of the Union column. "Our men kept to the sabre, kept their organization perfect: while the enemy dashed backward and forward, shooting in our faces."[86] The Wolverines drove through the Confederates, cutting and thrusting, driving the enemy in all directions. Matthews recalled but two casualties in his squadron from this initial contact: one man shot in the chest, and another in the wrist, as the Wolverines spurred after their quarry. "We followed them, until they struck the gap that caused the 'jam' and here the melee occurred."[87]

The "melee" occurred as the second half of Hampton's brigade—the 1st South Carolina, 2nd South Carolina, and Phillips Legion—pared down and drove through the gap in the fence. These rearward units hadn't suffered as much from the Federal artillery and maintained their momentum as they filed down to fours and breached the gap at a gallop. Closing on the enemy, Captain Matthews of the 1st Michigan noted the edges of the column squeezing in as the horses began converging on instinct. "I nerved myself to the utmost."[88]

Seconds later, the two columns struck with the sound of falling timber.[89] Horses collided and then rose skyward, borne upward by the pressure of those behind.[90] Sabres thrust home, carbines landed like mallets, and revolvers triggered tight to flesh. "[We] met the enemy at a small opening in a fence," recalled P. J. Malone, 1st South Carolina. "We were soon at the sabre point and fighting desperately."[91] The tide now shifted as the weight of Hampton's column struck like a wedge and split the 1st Michigan apart, with Southern troopers bowling through the gap and slamming into the Wolverines.[92] Stephens Calhoun Smith of the 2nd South Carolina wrote, "I was completely surrounded, I discharged every barrel of my pistol and then went to work with my sabre, I brought it out bathed in blood."[93]

At this point, Captain Matthews opted out of the fight. His squadron had scattered, and as he described it, "[P]rudence and discretion dictated a hasty retreat."[94] As the captain cut his way clear, his horse was shot, and Matthews rode back to the rear, where he found Custer already sitting in the saddle at the Lott farm and continuing to gather up Federal stragglers.[95] The 1st Michigan had blunted Hampton's brigade, but the attack would cost Colonel Town six officers and eighty men by day's end. As Confederates continued pouring through the gap, the Federal gunners again began blasting case and shell at the gray columns, preventing the Confederates from squaring up and sweeping the field clear.[96] "The guns made it so lively they [the Rebels] did not get any shape," and these salvos allowed several bands of Federals to ride forward and join the fight.[97]

Captain James Hart of the 1st New Jersey led one of the first. Galloping into the mix with two squadrons, Hart's men crashed into the Confederate ranks, aimed straight for a stand of Confederate colors, and drove Wade Hampton back against the fence rails. Hampton received a hard cut across the head and a pistol shot between his ribs as troopers Jordan More and John Dunlap of the Davis Legion rushed to his aid. Seconds later, both

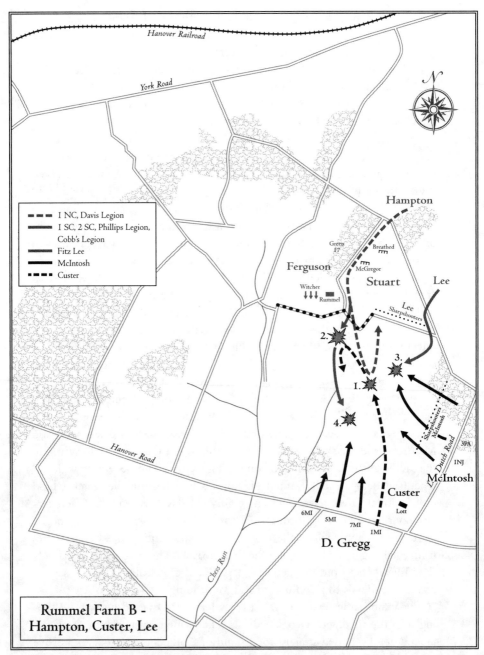

Map 12. Rummel Farm B—Hampton, Custer, Lee

Dunlap and More were cut down by Federals closing on Hampton. Fighting on, Hampton raised his sword and cleft a Yankee skull from top to teeth. Private Jackson of the Cobb Legion came to Hampton's aid, along with Sergeant Nat Price of the 1st North Carolina, who spurred in and shot down a Union trooper to open a way clear.[98] The trio jumped their horses across the fence, and Hampton, bleeding badly from his wounds, was borne to the rear.

Elsewhere Lieutenant Daniel Littlefield of the 7th Michigan gathered his squadron and charged forward, setting off a series of trip hammer blows as elements of Fitz Lee's brigade galloped through the Stallsmith gap and entered the melee.[99] Trooper Samuel Murrill of the 2nd Virginia quickly engaged three Federals, shooting the first with his carbine and driving the others back with his revolver.[100] At the same time, men from the 5th Michigan spurred forward, and Allyne Litchfield's troopers from the 7th Michigan rallied and reentered the fight.[101] Fitz Lee exchanged a round of running sabre blows with a Federal soldier until Lee's adjutant, Major James Ferguson, drove in and shot the Federal down.[102] "Every man was in up to the hilt," recalled William Morgan of the 1st Virginia. "[T]he fighting became hand to hand, blow for blow, cut for cut, and oath for oath."[103]

Acting without orders, Captain William Miller of the 3rd Pennsylvania mounted two squadrons and "sailed in" against the Confederates. His men struck a fissure in the enemy ranks and rode all the way across, "gallantly and successfully" peeling a path through the Southern files and driving the Confederates apart. Miller's force eventually scattered from contact, but Miller pushed on with a few rankers and pressed through the gap in the Rummel fence, only to be taken under fire by Witcher's tenacious 34th Virginia.[104] Shot through the arm, Miller turned back and rejoined his lines.[105]

Lieutenant William Brooke-Rawle led a similar charge on Captain Miller's flank, piercing the Confederates in a "very handsome charge" until his command ran out of steam and were forced about by the Rebels.[106] Meanwhile, Colonel McIntosh cast about for fresh squadrons and, finding none, gathered every straggler he could find, fitted them to his headquarters company, and led them into the mix, hewing left and right.[107] Together these impromptu attacks, some led by colonels and some by corporals, whittled and harried the Confederates amid the fences, forcing them back through the gaps in tangled clumps and files.[108]

Stuart quickly rallied his returning troopers as captains James Breathed and William McGregor—whose batteries arrived just as Hampton rolled forward—opened a blistering fire on the Federals.[109] Despite defective

Figure 17.2. Colonel John B. McIntosh, Army of the Potomac. McIntosh did a masterful job of directing his brigade through the fighting at Rummel farm. *Library of Congress.*

ammunition, the two batteries' abrupt appearance and rapid fire distracted the Union gunners from shredding the retiring Confederate cavalry. "Shell was fired as fast as men could load," wrote a Southern gunner, and the sudden salvoes dampened the chances of Gregg ordering a Union counter-charge to clear Cress Ridge.[110] The combat quickly wound down with the Federals holding their original positions around the Lott farm and Little's Run, and the Confederates holding the Rummel barnyard and Cress Ridge.[111]

David Gregg later claimed Stuart was "defeated at every point," and Custer added, the 1st Michigan had "the proud satisfaction of seeing the much-vaunted 'chivalry' led by their favorite commander, seek safety in headlong flight."[112] Stuart countered with, "[T]he enemy's masses vanished before [us] like grain before the scythe."[113] The truth lay in the middle, and Victorian platitudes aside, the troopers and company officers from both sides fought brilliantly, at times covering one another without orders, and often performing far better than their commanders deserved. Custer was still learning his craft and did not perform well. Despite the legend built in later years, he nearly lost the 7th Michigan in his first charge of the day, and were it not for the Federal horse gunners and a series of ad hoc squadrons coming to his support, he may have lost the 1st Michigan in his second. McIntosh turned in a solid performance, albeit in a more reserved role than Custer, and pitched into the thick of the fight at the end of the battle. Gregg did well in directing the overall action, and the Federal gunners were outstanding all day.

On the other side, Stuart's outrageously poor communication with his brigade commanders caused him to lose control of the action, and the charge of Hampton's brigade was an unauthorized mistake, awkwardly formed in sight of the enemy and delivered through a funneling fence gap straight into the teeth of ten enemy guns. It could well have ended in total failure, yet Stuart's troopers somehow managed to cut their way clear in the surging series of charges. Later Federal claims that this engagement stopped an attack aimed at the Federal rear via the Baltimore Pike, and therefore saved Meade's army from a potential retreat-bearing blow, ring hollow when one examines the actual numbers, the state of the commands, and the distances involved.[114]

Stuart did hope to pass by the Federals on the Hanover Road, but Gregg's early warning of Stuart's presence limited his options, and any remaining possibility of slipping by Gregg vanished when Hampton's and Lee's brigades blundered out on open ground. The rest of the day spiraled into a series of escalating charges until both sides returned to their respective sides with depleted ranks and winded horses. Stuart did manage to occupy the Federal cavalry in his front and thereby guard Lee's left flank, but this was a poor showing for the Virginia cavalier. He still tried to put the best bow on this as possible: "During this day's operations, I held such a position as not only to render Ewell's left entirely secure . . . but commanded a view of the routes leading to the enemy's rear. Had the enemy's main body been dislodged, as was confidently hoped and expected, I was in precisely the right position to discover it and improve the opportunity."[115]

In the end, Gregg held his army's flank and blocked Stuart from gaining a potential opportunity that never matured on Cemetery Hill. Thus, Gregg can claim a victory by curbing Stuart's plans.

Officers typically overstated their deeds in after-action reports, and some used the reports to advance their reputations, but the following simple summary comes from a frontline sergeant with nothing to prove: "There were more men killed and wounded in this fight than I ever saw on any field where the fighting was done mounted. I shall not attempt to say who got the better of this engagement as they seemed to mutually agree to quit. One party afraid to advance, and the other glad of it."[116]

18

FAIRFIELD AND FARNSWORTH

On the morning of July 3, a civilian farmer found General Wesley Merritt's brigade in their camp and reported seeing a Confederate wagon train. The farmer said the enemy train sat parked on his farm near the hamlet of Fairfield, some seven miles behind Confederate lines. The man insisted the Confederates were "all over at the big fight," leaving the wagons lightly guarded and offering a prime opportunity for "you'ns to capture it."[1] Merritt had orders to march for Gettysburg that morning, but he found the civilian credible and sent Major Samuel Starr of the 6th U.S. Cavalry to take the Rebel train and perhaps threaten the Confederate supply line.[2]

Born in 1810, Samuel Starr started his military career in the antebellum army, serving in the infantry, the artillery, and finally the cavalry. Once there, he rose from the ranks and won an officer's commission in the frontier dragoons.[3] At the outbreak of the war, Starr gained a colonelcy in the volunteer 5th New Jersey Infantry, but the degrading punishments Starr learned in the prewar army met with considerable resistance from his Garden State volunteers. One particular penalty remained from the eighteenth century, where the offender's hands were bound behind his back. Next, the offender had to sit astride a sharp-cornered fence rail with his feet tied below and weighted down with a bag of grain. This arrangement quickly cut the flow of blood into the legs and caused substantial pain. As a bonus, Starr had a feedbag placed over the offender's head like a giant hood, which soon earned Starr the sobriquet of "Old Nose Bag," or "Nosey."[4] Already unpopular with his troops, Starr next clubbed a dozing sentry over the head with the flat of his sword. Compelled to resign his commission, the regiment banished Starr to a recruiting post. He languished behind the lines until his reinstatement in April 1863 as a major in the 6th U.S. Cavalry.[5]

The 6th U.S. Cavalry differed from other regiments, having been formed as a Regular unit of the U.S. Cavalry, but from a pool of mostly recent Pennsylvania volunteers. The unit fought heartily at Brandy Station, and again at Upperville in the charges across Vineyard Hill, where they were badly handled. Much of the blame fell on Major Starr for his poor judgment, and to be fair, Starr had little help from his chief subordinate, Captain George C. Cram. Before the war, Cram served as a lawyer for his father's law offices at the prestigious but awkwardly named firm of Cram & Cram, in New York City.[6] Friends of Cram felt him poorly suited for cavalry service, and to Cram's lingering embarrassment, Mosby's Rangers had already captured him in May 1863. Cram received a quick exchange from his captors and arrived back in the ranks of the 6th Cavalry by mid-June.[7]

And so, on the morning of July 3, the rankers of the 6th Cavalry expected an easy ride and a quick chance for plunder as they turned out for Fairfield behind Major Starr and Captain Cram. The ride progressed over pleasant country roads, with farmers' families plying the passing troopers with food and young girls smiling and wishing the troopers well. South of Fairfield, they crossed a railroad cut, and Starr dispatched Captain Cram with a squadron to sweep north along the cut to scout for Confederate stragglers. The main column soon reached the hamlet of Fairfield, where a party of civilians told the Regulars the enemy wagons had just left and were heading north along the Cashtown Road. Starr sent Lieutenant Christian Balder forward in pursuit, and the lieutenant departed with a single squadron in a column of fours.[8]

The Confederate wagons had indeed just cleared Fairfield and turned for Cashtown, but unbeknownst to either Starr or Balder, Grumble Jones's Confederate brigade now occupied the same road. Jones's men, recently part of Beverly Robertson's wayward rear guard covering the mountain gaps in Virginia, had departed the Old Dominion on June 29 and arrived at Cashtown, Pennsylvania, on July 3, where Jones received orders to protect the Rebel train.[9] Jones marched with the 7th Virginia Cavalry up front, followed by the 6th Virginia, 11th Virginia, and finally Chew's horse battery in support.[10] "About 2 miles from Fairfield, we encountered the Sixth U.S. Regular Cavalry, en route to capture our cavalry division train. . . . [M]any wagons in quest of forage were already within a few hundred yards of the enemy."[11]

Lieutenant Balder's forward Federal squadron first spotted a detached Rebel platoon in advance of the wagons, and Balder formed his squadron in columns to either side of the road, and pushed after the smaller Rebel force. As Balder pursued, he soon spotted a much larger section of Jones's brigade, and Balder wheeled about for Fairfield as the train continued north. The tables turned, and the Virginians now pursued the Regulars down the country lane bordered by tall "post and rail fences."[12] Major Starr soon realized the Confederates were coming on in force and formed accordingly.

The major picked a narrow section of the road that enjoyed a slight rise, with an apple orchard to the east of the road. Starr dismounted half his command atop a ridge and formed a carbine line on either side of the road, with an apple orchard on the west end of his line, and a wheat field to the east. The second half of his regiment remained mounted as a reserve, and he kept them in the road, just behind the orchard. Had Starr pressed a reconnaissance forward and better identified his adversary and attending artillery, he may well have responded differently.

On the opposite side, Grumble Jones studied the Federals barring the road, and the position taken. The terrain sat level overall, with the surrounding ground sectioned into small fields partitioned by fences. The best route to reach the enemy was straight down the lane. Confident of success over a single regiment, Jones decided to press a quick attack while his enemy stood still. Lieutenant Colonel Thomas Marshall's 7th Virginia deployed for the charge in the road, drew sabres, and quickly spurred forward. The veterans gave a collective shout and advanced in a column of fours at a military gallop, then a sprint in the final fifty yards.

Major Starr gave the order to fire, and Federal carbines lashed across the 7th's right flank, causing the Virginians to first weave, and then "accordion" in the road between the fences. Troopers fell, and others balked, letting their sabres hang from the wrist as they returned fire with revolvers and carbines. Still others failed to rally altogether and rode clear of the enemy fire, even as their officers called on them to reform.[13] This failure to rally sent the mercurial Jones into one of his high-pitched tirades: "Shall one damned regiment of Yankees whip my entire brigade?"[14]

Never short on passing judgments, Jones later wrote that the 7th Virginia's "failure to rally promptly and renew the fight is a blemish in the bright history of this regiment."[15] He may have been correct, but if the veteran 7th Virginia turned back, it's hard to name a unit that would have gone through the same deadly fire dished out that day by the 6th U.S. Cavalry.

Jones decided to aid his next attempt at the Federal line with more of the resources he held at hand, particularly the guns of Captain Chew's horse battery, and the help of the 11th Virginia.[16] As the 6th Virginia deployed in the road to take their turn, Chew's guns unlimbered in a field east of the lane and sent shells streaking ahead at the Federal position. Meanwhile, Major Starr, after successfully repulsing the Confederate charge, decided to order his own charge up the lane in the wake of the 7th Virginia's repulse—even as the Confederate guns opened and a second regiment of enemy troopers stepped forward. "I saw the enemy in great numbers forming beyond us," recalled Lieutenant Tattnall Paulding, who commanded the section of Starr's sharpshooters east of the road, "& very soon rec'd an order from Maj. Starr to withdraw my men as he was about to charge."[17]

Starr must have figured he could beat the Confederates to the punch and strike before the Virginians got under way, allowing him to disengage from the enemy. Whatever the cause, this would soon prove a severe mistake, as Starr depleted his sharpshooters by half. Farther down the lane, Jones continued to hurl auditory fireballs as the 6th Virginia stepped off, or, as Major Flournoy reported, "[A]t the intimation from the commanding general, [I] gave the order to charge."[18] The 6th Virginia went forward with a yell, sabres aloft and guidons flapping in the warm summer air. The Federal sharpshooters again opened fire, but Starr's charge, Chew's guns, and the reduction of Union carbines reduced the effect.

The Virginians weathered the coming fire, and the two columns sprinted for one another between the fences. Virginian John Opie described the encounter: "[T]he boys rode sabre in hand, right into the 6th Regulars." The Virginians spurred through the Regulars, cutting, stabbing, and hurling them back down the lane. Major Starr fell in the dirt, shot through the arm and flayed by a sabre across his skull.[19] In the following pursuit, Lieutenant Duncan of Company B, 6th Virginia sabered several Regulars between the fences, "running his sabre entirely through one, [and] twisting him from his horse."[20] Outside the lane, rallied elements of the 7th Virginia pulled down the fence bordering the lane and drove into the orchard, cutting down at the Federal sharpshooters and chasing them back for their mounts, while the 11th Virginia opened with their carbines from west of the lane.[21]

The Regulars, however, were far from done and continued fighting in small pockets of resistance. A Federal color-bearer went down with his horse beneath a flurry of shots, and both sides raced for the prize. James McDowell of the 6th U.S. Cavalry charged in and watched fellow Regular George Platt grab the Regulars' colors and, despite suffering cuts to his head, made off with the talisman at a gallop down the fence line. McDowell bravely spurred in to cover Platt's escape and intercepted the chasing Virginians, only to be cut from his horse as Platt spurred clear. Platt later received the Medal of Honor for his actions; Jones's Virginians captured the equally brave McDowell.[22]

As Platt rode for Fairfield, Captain Cram arrived on the field with Company I. Cram gamely pitched into the fight, but his mount fell beneath him, and the former lawyer once again fell captive to the Confederacy. The fight wound down, and the Regulars began to surrender. Many had lost their mounts and now hid in the head-high wheat of the near fields. "A great many were knocked from their horses with the sabre," recalled a Southern trooper, "but succeeded in escaping through the wheat."[23] Lieutenant John Connell remembered one gravely wounded Regular they came across: "[a] beardless youth that particularly attracted my sympathy. He was badly wounded. . . . We gave him water and placed him in as comfortable a position as possible. He had an honest face, a brave heart."[24]

Jones pursued the fleeing Federal troopers to Fairfield and then returned, satisfied that the threat to the wagons had passed. Jones's casualties totaled 58 killed, wounded, and missing, with all losses coming from the 6th and 7th Virginia. Major Starr's 6th U.S. Cavalry suffered 232 men killed, wounded, or captured, and only 3 officers were present for duty at the next morning's roll call.[25]

As Jones's men made their way back from Fairfield, they looked north, where they could hear the terrible crash and roar of the distant struggle at Gettysburg. "The artillery fire at one time was so heavy that the hills shook and the air trembled," recalled gunner George Neese. "[W]e had a distant view of the battlefield and saw nothing but a vast bank of thick battle smoke with thousands of shells exploding above the surface."[26]

In the midst of these exploding shells sat a white board farmhouse belonging to Mrs. Lydia Leister, a widow with six children. The widow and her children had wisely vacated the premises prior to the Confederate bombardment, and the house now served as General George Meade's military headquarters. Located just east of a tall copse of trees on Cemetery Hill, the house suffered wave after wave of shell fire and round shot. One round screamed through an open door, and another wrecked the attic and shattered the porch supports.[27] Meade's staff pleaded with him to leave, but Meade insisted he needed to stay close to the action, where his generals could find him.[28] He went outside and joked about the level of fire the Confederates were throwing, while his aides continued to recommend Meade leave runners here at the house and retire to a safer place. A shell then hit a member of his staff, and Meade finally agreed, mounting one of the few surviving horses left in his string.[29]

Meade rode back from the crest to the Taneytown Road and halted in a field as the Confederate guns continued to hammer away at the Federal line. Even here shells shrieked through the air, plowed the ground, capsized guns, killed artillery horses, and rained down shards of whistling iron on the ducking Union gunners. Eventually the barrage lifted—a temporary silence replaced by the rattle of muskets and the Rebel yell.[30] Union gunners stood, moved forward, and opened on the charging Confederate infantry. Federal batteries poured round after round of case and canister into the coming enemy ranks. Union infantry stood behind stone walls and laid down volley after volley on the Rebel tide until powder smoke covered the ridge in a thick blue shroud. The fire slacked, then died. Meade rode up the ridge, cresting the top, and tried to peer through the lingering cloud of musket smoke. "Have they turned?" wondered Meade.[31]

Cheers rose from the ranks, the smoke cleared, and Meade could finally see it. Confederate dead littered the ground like a carpet. The rest now streamed for the rear in shattered columns of drifting wounded. The Federal line remained; Lee's infantry had turned.

Ever the soldier, Meade ordered his troops to hold their positions, in case Lee launched another attack.[32] Others were quick to advise differently; generals Warren, Wadsworth, and Pleasonton all called for a counterattack.[33] Even the vaunted Hancock, wounded in this very assault, wrote a message from the ambulance bearing him from the field. If Meade would launch his reserves now, "he would win a great victory."[34]

Meade disagreed. After three days of combat, his lines were in total disarray. His men were exhausted and would soon run short on ammunition. Meade could see he'd just won a victory, but to what degree? Had he truly broken Lee, or had he simply rebuffed a division? If he had won a victory, should he counterattack? Might that risk a defeat? Certainly, Lee's artillery was still in position and capable of repulsing a Union assault. Meade continued to ruminate on the issue as the Confederates limped to the rear.

◇

Judson Kilpatrick listened to the distant fighting in the Federal center from his post on the far-left flank of the Federal line, just west of the rock-strewn round tops. This was difficult ground for cavalry, patched through with stands of scrub oaks and strewn with boulders, stone walls, and rail fences. To Kilpatrick's right stood the larger of the two hills, a steep granite eminence crowned in elder and oaks that would come to be known as Big Round Top, and beyond that a smaller, sparser outcropping later called Little Round Top. Yesterday, this ground had seen horrific fighting. Confederate infantry rolled forward in waves, carrying assaults on a den of boulders and up the side of the smaller, rock-crowned round top, only to be blasted back by Federal infantry and artillery. These Confederates still

Figure 18.1. Brigadier General Wesley Merritt, Army of the Potomac. Merritt proved to be a steady and stable light cavalry commander. *Library of Congress.*

remained on the field, refusing to part with the ground they won and holding tight among the fallen bodies from both sides.

Kilpatrick received orders in the morning of July 3 to attack the enemy on the left flank of the Federal line, and lacking Custer's brigade, Kilpatrick advanced with only Farnsworth's command—the 1st Vermont, 1st West Virginia, 5th New York, and 18th Pennsylvania—and moved east of the Emmitsburg Road in a dismounted front. Joining in this advance were Merritt's Regulars, who arrived on the west side of the Emmitsburg Road and pressed forward against a lone battalion of advancing enemy cavalry in their front.[35] "By 11 a.m. we became heavily engaged with the enemy," recalled a captain in Merritt's 1st Regulars, "and struck the enemy west of [the] round top."[36]

This enemy battalion came from Colonel John Black's 1st South Carolina, who drove forward on foot, supported by Captain Hart's battery, from Stuart's horse artillery.[37] Major General Evander Law of Longstreet's I Corps had directed Black to secure his right flank, and Black duly moved past the Kern House on the Emmitsburg Road and engaged Merritt's sharpshooters. The firing increased, and Merritt extended his line, flanking the Rebels' advance, and forcing Black's troopers and Hart's guns to retire almost a mile to a new position.[38] This caused Law to shift several regiments of Georgia infantry around to his right to aid the cavalry and halt Merritt's Regulars.[39] Farnsworth's troopers also advanced, driving a skirmish line of enemy infantry onto a ridge crisscrossed with stone walls before the farms of Reverend Michael Bushman and John Slyder. This shift allowed Kilpatrick to deploy Lieutenant Elder's Battery E, 4th U.S. Artillery, and Graham's Battery K, 1st U.S. Artillery, atop Bushman's Hill in the shadow of Big Round Top.[40] General Law responded by sending a skirmish line of the hard-fought 1st Texas Infantry forward to a set of stone fences some two hundred yards across Kilpatrick's front, and the length of the position forced the Texas skirmishers to stretch out some fifteen feet between files to man the line.

Kilpatrick studied the ground before him and sent out scouts to determine the viability of a horse charge, but the broken ground in their front looked unsatisfactory. Undaunted, Kilpatrick sent more scouts, and all found the ground ill-suited for a mounted attack. Hours passed in the heat of the day, and the massed Confederate assault on the center of Meade's line rose to its peak and repulse.

Kilpatrick continued to study the ground in his front and determined a recent shift in the Rebel infantry had uncovered a pair of Rebel batteries off to his left near the Bushman property.[41] Immediately before Kilpatrick lay an open plateau, but beside the plateau, a stand of thick trees ran near a deep ravine that would shelter any assault against the enemy, who were now more focused on Merritt's Regulars, threatening their far flank. Kilpatrick felt the depth of the ravine would screen the Rebel guns from reaching any cavalry charging down the ravine's center, and once through the ravine, the skirmish line of the 1st Texas was just fifty yards away—close enough to catch the Texans unaware if distracted elsewhere.[42]

Near this same time, an order arrived from Pleasonton, now beside General Meade and watching the Confederate infantry stream back in defeat from their assault on Cemetery Ridge. "I went immediately to the extreme left of my line," recalled Meade, "with the determination of advancing my left and making an assault upon the enemy's lines."[43] Pleasonton dutifully sent an order for Kilpatrick to make a diversion to support an advance by Meade's infantry, and Kilpatrick in turn ordered Farnsworth to make the charge up the ravine.[44]

Fifty years later, Captain Henry Parsons of the 1st Vermont claimed Farnsworth challenged the order: "General, do you mean it?" Kilpatrick pressed again, and Farnsworth countered with concern for his men: "They are too good men to kill."[45]

Allegedly, Kilpatrick replied that if Farnsworth refused the order, then he, Kilpatrick, would lead the charge. Farnsworth purportedly demanded Kilpatrick, "Take that back." Kilpatrick then lowered his tone, saying softly, "I did not mean it; forget it." According to Parsons, the two officers stewed in silence until Farnsworth offered to lead the charge if Kilpatrick would bear "the awful responsibility" for the action.[46]

A second witness—Lieutenant Eli Holden, also of the 1st Vermont—claimed to see no overwrought exchange, or disagreement whatever: "[T]here was no quarrel between Gen. Kilpatrick and Gen. Farnsworth." They spoke "amicably and courteously" for some time before Farnsworth turned to lead the charge.[47] Heated or not, Farnsworth accepted the orders given and prepared to lead his men against the enemy. Farnsworth's first test as a brigadier came just days before at Hanover. Before this he'd served as a staff officer and squadron commander in the 8th Illinois Cavalry, where Pleasonton noted him in dispatches for leading a charge that resulted in the capture of an enemy standard.[48] Farnsworth came from a wealthy family and had an uncle serving in Congress, which clearly influenced Farnsworth's career, but Farnsworth proved to all he could lead cavalry with his recent performance at Hanover. Given Farnsworth's record and experience, it's unlikely the dramatic scene described by Captain Parsons played out in the way he portrayed it, more than fifty years after the fact.

The complex attack would occur in two stages, and three assaults. The first stage would charge up through the ravine, make a quarter wheel left, vault the Rebel skirmish line at the staggered stone walls, then wheel left again, and close on the enemy guns perched atop the ridge beyond. Farnsworth would lead this first stage, composed of Nathaniel Richmond's 1st West Virginia, the most experienced regiment in the brigade, and followed closely by the 2nd Battalion/1st Vermont under Major William Wells.

The second stage, under Captain Henry Parsons, would make a near simultaneous charge to the immediate right, beyond the first stone wall of the enemy skirmish line with the 1st Battalion/1st Vermont.[49]

The 18th Pennsylvania would post to the left of Kilpatrick's line and make a third charge to support the ravine attack.

Captain Andrew Grover would command the 3rd Battalion / 1st Vermont, posted as sharpshooters on the skirmish line for support.[50]

These three attacks would also have support from the batteries of Elder and Graham. Elder's battery moved to the crest on Bushman's Hill and would engage the enemy infantry posted on the slope of Big Round Top if they turned to attack the Federal push on the guns. Graham's battery would engage the enemy artillery with covering fire throughout the attack.[51]

❧

Richmond's West Virginians formed in the ravine and gathered their reins. With little fanfare, they drew sabres and spurred forward in a column of fours, dodging brush and boulders in the ravine. On the opposite side, the skirmish line of the 1st Texas Infantry unleashed a scattering fire on the coming column and then bolted for the first stone fence in their rear. The 1st West Virginia cleared the ravine, swung left, and continued to rumble forward with bugles pealing out the charge. The West Virginians rode through the Texas skirmishers, cutting down with their sabres and driving dead ahead for the stone wall topped with staked rails and backed by the rest of the 1st Texas Infantry.

Colonel Richmond's squadrons were closing on the wall when the Texans delivered a formed volley. Minié balls ripped through the Union troopers, tumbling men and mounts at the head of the column and wrecking the momentum of all behind. Farnsworth continued on and vaulted the wall only to have his horse shot down on the far side. Others reached the wall and cut down at the Texans, and a few more vaulted the wall after Farnsworth. "They were the bravest set of men I ever saw," recalled one Texan. "After their line was broken and all was disorder and confusion and many of their men shot, they would [still] advance singly, brandishing their swords."[52]

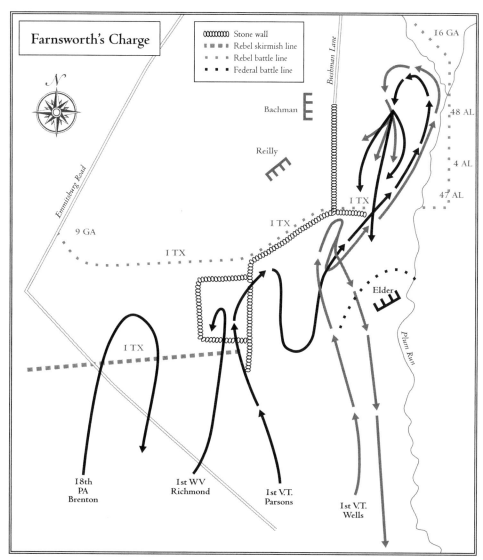

Map 13. Farnsworth's Charge

Those who lost their mounts picked up carbines, or rushed forward and attempted to let down the rails along the top of the wall for others to leap the barrier while the Texans reloaded. "I ran up the line to the regiment," said Private Berryman of the 1st Texas. "I soon found them all mixed up with Yankee cavalry, cutting and slashing in every direction. All the boys had fired their pieces and the Yankees would not give them time to reload, so the boys were using the butts of their guns. Newt managed to load. There was a Yank cutting one of the boys over the head with his sabre when Newt ran up and blew his brains out."[53]

Few troopers carried past the Texans. One of the few was Farnsworth, who, gaining his feet beside his fallen horse, received a second mount from a near trooper. Farnsworth swung aboard and made for another wall some thirty yards past the first. He took this second wall at a gallop, and then a volley cut him down on the far side. Farnsworth was hit five times: once in each leg, in his abdomen, through his shoulder, and square in the chest just above his heart.[54] In the confusion of the moment, no Federals realized Farnsworth had fallen.

Storming forward at the same time as the 1st West Virginia, Captain Parsons's 1st Battalion/1st Vermont advanced up the Bushman-Beamer farm lane, hoping to enfilade the Texas line. Instead, they found more Texans waiting behind a barricade they had erected across the farm lane, and the Rebels unleashed a withering volley. Minié balls streamed in from multiple flanks and wrecked the battalion. Captain Parsons took a ball through his ribs, and the rest of the battalion broke in separate directions, "some going to the right, others to the left. . . . [The remains] filed along a fence running perpendicular to our rear," recalled a Texan.[55]

This left Major Wells's 2nd Battalion/1st Vermont, which, after seeing the West Virginians crash against the Texans, wheeled right, seeking a better course. They passed the remains of Parsons's scattering rankers, and two companies under Captain Oliver Cushman joined up on the fly with Wells's 2nd Battalion. Together these three hundred New Englanders spurred on for Plum Run and, as they came to the creek, wheeled left by sections and charged the Texans deployed between the creek and the east side of Bushman Hill. Spurring forward, Wells called for the bugle, and the horses surged forward, the troopers bending over the withers and breaking through the Texas line where it lacked any stone walls for cover.[56] Major Wells later earned a Medal of Honor for his actions in this charge.

Meanwhile, down below, Kilpatrick began screaming at the 18th Pennsylvania, who continued to stand still and not move up in support. With no appropriate answer, the commander of the 18th, Colonel William

P. Benton, led his men forward and suffered a similar result as the West Virginians.[57] Benton's mount fell beneath him, and the 1st Texas shot down twenty of his men before the others turned about and fled across the field to form a skirmish line in the brush.[58] The charge of the Pennsylvanians at least allowed the remains of Richmond's West Virginians to cut their way clear and retire in kind. Charging alongside Benton's Pennsylvanians came Lieutenant Colonel Preston and Captain Grover's 3rd Battalion/1st Vermont, who veered right on the same course as Major Wells's battalion had before, and bypassed the Texas line.

General Evander Law watched this transpire and moved to counter the galloping Federals as they rode along Plum Run, beneath Big Round Top. The Confederate infantry closed fast. Men from the 4th and 15th Alabama turned about and rushed down to fire on the Union troopers. Volleys swept through the Federal ranks, retarding the charge until the middle horses surged past, their instincts driving them forward in a rush to gain the front of the herd. A Vermont bugler recalled the effects of the enemy fire with chilling detail: "Every time a man near me was hit, I could hear the pat of the bullet."[59] An Alabama soldier recalled one trooper who hit the ground when his horse fell and soon rolled up to return fire with his carbine. The Confederates took aim, and a "puff of dust flew out from his blouse. . . . [H]e fell, meeting the same fate as his horse."[60]

Wells now wheeled his column left only to come under fire from Captain William Bachman's battery and the 9th Georgia Infantry, who'd just arrived from the fight with Merritt's Regulars. The combined fire lashed through the running horses, and the Federals scrambled left again, this time swinging south and heading for a secondary stone wall in the rear of the 1st Texas.[61] Now losing their bearings, the New Englanders kept moving to try to find a way out while suffering a gauntlet of ringing fire from Texas, Alabama, and Georgia rifles.[62]

Wells's and Cushman's men charged back down the defile below Big Round Top and hit the Alabama infantry in the rear while these Confederates were facing Kilpatrick's main line. The Rebels turned and fired as the Federal horsemen surged by to regain their lines, and witnesses later claimed they saw an unhorsed Federal officer shoot himself here in the head.[63] In later years many claimed this officer was Farnsworth, but Farnsworth was already dead. Recent scholarship suggests this to have been Captain Cushman of the 1st Vermont instead.[64] The bullet traveled up through the roof of Cushman's mouth, which is consistent with a self-inflicted wound, but an infantryman could have shot Cushman as he rode by on his horse.[65] Federal stretcher-bearers found Cushman lying unconscious the following day, and though he survived the gunshot wound to his mouth, he never elaborated on how he received the wound.

Kilpatrick watched as his men galloped back to his lines in clumps of loose and scattered files, and the action wound to an end on their return. "Our cavalry broke, rallied, and broke again before that formidable barrier, but the First Vermont and First West Virginia, led by the gallant Farnsworth, cleared the fence, sabred the Rebels in the rear, and were only stopped by another fence and a third line of infantry and artillery."[66] Kilpatrick didn't know the exact fate of Farnsworth for some time.

Today some believe Farnsworth was a victim, that Kilpatrick ordered him to an unnecessary death. For three days running, Federals and Confederates alike made attacks against hard-to-take positions, and most failed when the odds were long. Farnsworth did his duty, as did many others, and all deserve full credit for their actions.

Kilpatrick learned after the charge that Meade decided against launching an infantry counterattack, and therefore the charge had been for naught. However, Kilpatrick had delivered on Pleasonton's request, and had Meade's infantry launched an assault on the Confederate right, Kilpatrick had created a sizable diversion that forced the Confederates to shift their forces and weaken their front. It's possible a well-timed infantry assault may have cracked the Confederate line if launched at the same time Farnsworth's troopers made their attacks.

Many of the veterans of this action understandably had trouble recalling their movements in the plunging charges beneath the round tops, and the different accounts of the veterans are often difficult to reconcile. Some veterans were pressed for greater details after the war regarding the course and flow of these desperate charges and the exact route they had taken. One veteran answered, "I was fighting, not looking."[67] Another former ranker stated, "If you rode a cyclone, how would you describe the scenery?"[68]

19

LEE RETREATS

Robert E. Lee sat his horse Traveller and watched his infantry retreat through the smoke over Cemetery Ridge. His men had endured massive casualties the first two days of the battle, and the fractured state of his returning ranks signaled worse news still. Reports soon confirmed Lee's suspicions: his infantry had suffered another defeat and again endured high casualties, particularly among his officers. Lee knew there was only one option to save his army: he had to get back across the Potomac—and quickly. He summoned corps commanders and selected routes, and a plan formed as his surgeons worked to save the legions of wounded.

Step one called for Lee to get his army and trains back across South Mountain. Longstreet's corps moved first, pulling back from the Round Tops to form the right of Lee's new line. Hill's corps went next, sliding back after midnight to form a bridge between Longstreet and Ewell.[1] The Army of Northern Virginia would march by two routes. The first ran fifty miles, coursing southwest through Fairfield and then over South Mountain via the Monterey Pass. From Monterey, the route pushed through Hagerstown, Maryland, and then down to one of two preprepared crossing points on the Potomac: Williamsport, an established commercial ford, and Falling Waters, where Lee had ordered a pontoon bridge constructed. The second, longer route, started at Gettysburg and moved due west, back through the Cashtown Pass and across South Mountain, and then turning south on a course through Greencastle, Pennsylvania, and on to Williamsport.

Lee sent the massive quartermaster train containing the lion's share of the supplies, silage, and livestock along the shorter route through Monterey Pass. Lee placed so much importance on these supplies that he gave his quartermaster train a fifteen-hour head start on the rest of his army. The ambulance train, some seventeen miles long, and containing thousands of Confederate wounded, would take the longer western route through Cashtown Pass to Williamsport.[2]

Finally, Lee's three infantry corps would fall back in stages to repel whatever attack the Federals might launch. If none came, they would march back for Virginia via the shorter Fairfield-Monterey-Hagerstown track. Hill's III Corps would go first, followed by Longstreet's I Corps in the center, which would also escort four thousand Federal prisoners. Ewell's II Corps would form the rear guard. Lee exhorted each of his corps commanders to see that "every officer exerts the utmost vigilance, steadiness and boldness during the whole march."[3]

To screen the retreat, Lee would rely heavily on Stuart.[4] This would be no easy task. Screening a retreat before a larger enemy was one of the most difficult maneuvers in mounted warfare, and the current state of Stuart's drained brigades would only complicate the matter. Lee met with Stuart, and the former student and teacher quickly went over the maps. Stuart would take the brigades of Chambliss, Ferguson, Jones, and Robertson, and cover the shorter route of the main army down through Hagerstown. Jones and Robertson, currently located near Fairfield, would secure the roads leading through the first set of mountain passes at Fairfield, and then Monterey. Stuart sent a staff officer to personally deliver instructions to Robertson and stress the importance of the passes—they had to be held until the main body of infantry came up and managed the task on their own.[5] Once across the mountains, Lee planned to use the looming crests and ridges of South Mountain to guard his retreating left flank on the way to the Potomac. To protect this course, Stuart would take the brigades of Chambliss and Ferguson; secure two additional passes that emerged farther south at Smithsburg, Maryland, on the west side of South Mountain; and block any pursuit coming up from the Federal supply depot at Frederick, Maryland.[6]

A separate mission—leading the ambulance train of wounded to Williamsport—remained for Imboden's brigade. General John Daniel Imboden hailed from Staunton, Virginia, and graduated from Washington College in Lexington, Virginia. Before the war, he practiced law in his hometown and served in the state legislature. He enlisted early, raised an artillery battery, and commanded it through 1st Manassas. Later, he took advantage of the Confederate Partisan Ranger Act and gained command of the 62nd Virginia Mounted Infantry. By 1863, he held a general's commission and command of his own cavalry brigade raised in the Shenandoah Valley and the western counties of Virginia.

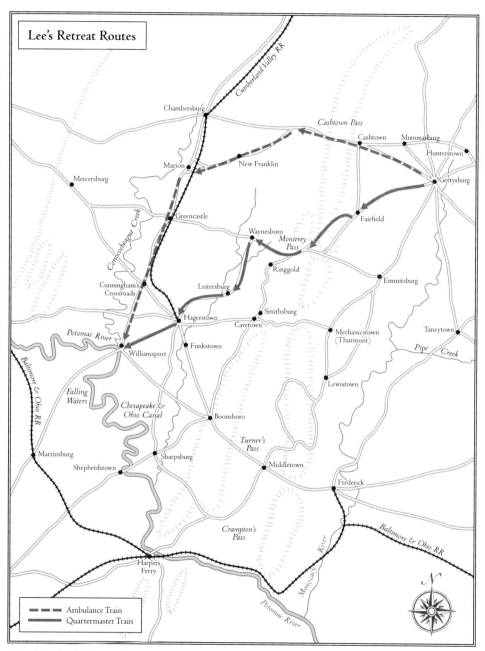

Map 14. Lee's Retreat Routes

Imboden found Lee outside his headquarters tent and recalled Lee "wore an expression of sadness I had never before seen." On the verge of exhaustion, Lee still invited Imboden into his tent. "[The] care of the wounded will be entrusted to you," began Lee as he sketched the course of the ambulance train. "You will cross the mountain by the Chambersburg Road, and then proceed to Williamsport . . . without a halt until you reach the river. Rest there to feed your animals; then ford the river and do not halt again till you reach Winchester."[7] General Lee asked how many men Imboden commanded, and Imboden replied he had two thousand troopers on relatively fresh horses, plus a battery of six guns. Lee warned Imboden that Federal cavalry would certainly attack him and added, "I can spare you as much artillery as you require."[8] In addition, Hampton's ravaged brigade, and Fitz Lee's relatively healthy brigade, would form a moving rear guard trailing the ambulance train and its flanks on the course for Williamsport. General Lee wanted his wounded brought home and insisted Imboden keep the ambulance train moving for the river at all costs.

Imboden rose to leave, and Lee told Imboden he would send a staff officer to him with "a sealed package for President Davis which you will retain in your possession till you are across the Potomac." Once across the river, Imboden would select a reliable officer to carry the package to Richmond and deliver it to President Davis. The selected officer would place the package in Davis's own hands. "[W]hatever happens, this package must not fall into the hands of the enemy. If, unfortunately you should be captured, destroy it at the first opportunity."[9]

The quartermaster train began moving at 3:00 a.m., pressing down the Fairfield Road in the early morning darkness for the passes ahead. Teamsters cursed, mules brayed, and horses snorted as the legions of hogs, cattle, and sheep shuffled around the creaking wheels; the supply train was now so long that once under way, it would take ten hours to pass a single point.[10] As the sun broke over the horizon, Grumble Jones's brigade could see the train from their camp. Seeing the wagons heading south, one of Jones's veterans sagely remarked, "That looks like a mouse," meaning such a movement never followed a success.[11]

～

On the afternoon of July 3, as Confederate cannon bombarded Meade's line atop Cemetery Hill, a hand-picked force of three hundred Federal horse soldiers rode out of Frederick, Maryland, and turned for the Potomac River. Composed of multiple detachments, these ad hoc troopers rode under the command of Major Shadrack Foley of the 14th Pennsylvania, and headed for the Confederate pontoon bridge spotted at Falling Waters.[12] A report claimed the floating bridge operated under a light guard, and every evening the bridge lay disconnected and moored on the southern bank until sunrise, when a camp of Confederate engineers rigged the pontoons and reopened for business with the Maryland shore. If that proved true, the bridge might be destroyed in a swift night attack. General William French, the commanding Federal officer at Frederick, swiftly approved Foley's mission, and the major drew troopers from the 1st New York, 6th Michigan, and the 14th Pennsylvania.

Foley's men approached the river in the dark of night and cut across the towpath for the Chesapeake and Ohio Canal. They dismounted to avoid alerting any lurking Confederates, and Foley waited as scouts crept forward to the river. They soon returned and confirmed the bridge lay dismantled on the far bank of the river, with no enemy guards in sight. Three men crept forward and swam the river. Bugler John Hetz of the 6th Michigan cut loose three pontoons, and the troopers swam them back across.[13] Forty sharpshooters then climbed into the boats, recrossed the river, crept forward, and suddenly opened fire on the Confederate camp. The Rebels bolted awake and sprinted for the woods in the face of the sudden attack. The Federals then pulled the disassembled pontoons and planks to the Maryland bank, and the troopers set about breaking the pieces apart and casting them into the current to float downstream.[14]

Foley soon recognized this would be a lengthy process to complete. To buy time and secure the mission, he guided a detachment upstream for Williamsport, engaged the enemy picket there, secured his prisoners, and returned to find the pontoons and planks either sinking or drifting in the current.[15] His men were back in the saddle before dawn and riding east for Frederick on the Fourth of July. The raid went off with commando precision. Foley's horse soldiers removed one of Lee's two crossing points over the Potomac and didn't lose a single man in the process.

As Foley rode back for Frederick, Meade's Federals woke from a fitful night's rest on the fields of Gettysburg. Camp smoke hung thick at dawn, but everyone in Federal blue knew they had defeated the Confederates the day before. As the sun rose, a Union signal station overlooking the battlefield sent the following message to General Meade's headquarters: "Wagon trains of the enemy are moving."[16] This meant the Rebels were in retreat, and now was the moment for the Army of the Potomac to surge forward and destroy the Army of Northern Virginia. The logistic realities of the situation, however, soon became apparent.

Despite winning a clear victory, Meade's army had suffered casualties of nearly 30 percent; thousands were dead, even more lay wounded, and his commands were scattered all across the battlefield.[17] In addition, some fifteen hundred Federal artillery horses had been killed along with nearly four hundred mules. Those that survived had eaten only grass through a week of hard service and were badly depleted.[18] Not only that, much of Meade's supplies were stranded twenty-five miles away at Westminster, owing to Rebel cavalry attached to Ewell's corps having cut several key railroad bridges prior to the battle.[19] This resulted in an unusually long Federal supply line, requiring even more cavalry to protect the road-bound supplies, and Pleasonton's divisions were already calling for two thousand remounts after chasing and fighting Stuart's troopers for a month straight.[20]

Between the losses in artillery horses, mules for pulling supply wagons, and remounts needed for his cavalry, Meade simply lacked the horsepower to launch an all-out pursuit of Lee's army. Before Meade could move any appreciable distance, he needed railways repaired so he could restock his ranks with food, horse grains, ammunition, and fresh horses at a bare minimum—and this only covered the logistics side of the equation. Strategically, Meade needed to determine if Lee meant to retreat across the Potomac, or shift to a secondary position and offer another battle in Pennsylvania.[21]

This posed an additional dilemma: If Lee was offering battle nearby, Meade should stockpile his resources at Westminster. If Lee was retreating for Virginia, Meade should stage his resources farther south at Frederick to pursue his enemy. A misjudgment between Westminster and Frederick could take a week or more to correct and sharply hinder Meade's chances of catching Lee's army.[22] Meade needed his cavalry to divine Lee's intentions and quickly determine Meade's proper course forward. In response, Pleasonton sent Buford's 1st Division from Westminster to Frederick, Gregg's 2nd Division over to Cashtown Pass, and Kilpatrick's 3rd Division would pursue the train of Confederate wagons purported to be heading for Monterey Pass.[23] "Gain his rear and line of communication," instructed Pleasonton. "[H]arass and annoy him as much as possible in his retreat."[24]

～

Kilpatrick's 3rd Division rose on July 4 feeling a mixture of loss and triumph. Yesterday the army had secured a great victory over Lee's Confederates, but the cost came at a high price and the ranks were decidedly thinner as the morning roll was read aloud—especially in Farnsworth's brigade, where their former commander remained missing while many others were known to be dead or wounded.[25] The following sets of cheers raised for the nation's birthday were certainly diminished in many throats that morning.

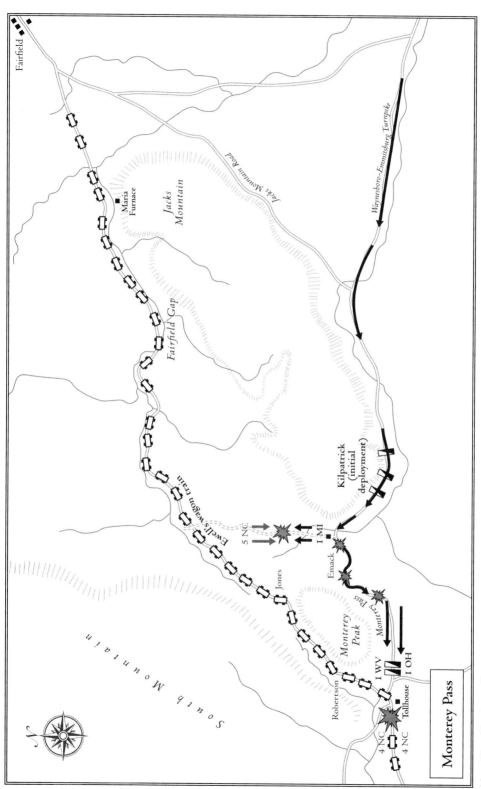

Map 15. Monterey Pass

Kilpatrick followed the celebration with a speech; he was good at speeches, and his words eulogized the fallen and praised the survivors still standing before him. They had the enemy on the run, and Kilpatrick promised to keep after the enemy while he could, and avenge the losses the division had suffered. He ordered three days' rations be drawn and the men to prepare for a "protracted absence from the army."[26]

As the troopers prepared for their march, the rain began to fall in sheets.[27] Captain James Kidd of the 6th Michigan wrote, "All set their faces to the weather and rode, if not cheerfully, at least patiently forward. . . . [T]he swollen and muddy streams that ran along and across our pathway fretted and frothed. . . . [T]heir banks couldn't hold them."[28] The rain continued to fall as Kilpatrick gained the Emmitsburg/Waynesboro Turnpike and turned west for Monterey Pass, where he hoped to cut the Confederate wagon trains bound for Maryland. The Rebel trains were reportedly following the Maria Furnace Road, which tracked north around Jacks Mountain before linking with the turnpike on the west side of Jacks Mountain. From here the turnpike continued west before dropping sharply down the mountain for Waynesboro.

As Kilpatrick moved west along the turnpike, he passed through the hamlet of Fountain Dale below Jacks Mountain, where a young girl named Hetty Zellinger reported seeing Confederate troops guarding a farm lane above Kilpatrick's right flank. Hoping to secure this flank, Kilpatrick sent Lieutenant Colonel Peter Stagg with two squadrons of the 1st Michigan climbing up the steep lane, with Miss Zellinger guiding the way in the evening light. As Colonel Stagg pushed forward in the light rain, he soon encountered sharpshooters from the 11th Virginia cavalry who opened on his advance and then withdrew. Pressing ahead, the Federals next came under fire from Moorman's battery of Stuart's horse artillery.[29] Stagg dismounted Captain Daniel Well's squadron in reply, and began pushing up the road while keeping to the inside of a turn in the road to avoid the fire of the battery. Captain Well's squadron eventually drove the Virginia sharpshooters up to a narrow crest in the road, and Colonel Stagg formed the second squadron for a charge. The Wolverines pulled sabres and spurred up the mountain, where they were suddenly met with a "galling fire" and a quick countercharge from the 5th North Carolina Cavalry.[30]

Now led by Lieutenant Colonel James B. Gordon, the 5th North Carolina had revamped their ranks since their tenacious defeat amid the stone fences at Upperville. A native of Wilkes County, North Carolina, Gordon was a natural leader, and following the death of Colonel Evans,

Stuart gave Gordon command of the 5th North Carolina. Gordon's new Tarheels gave out a Rebel yell as they charged over the crest and bowled into the Wolverines with chips on their shoulders and revolvers in hand.[31]

The 1st Michigan recoiled on the slippery road, but a small contingent surged back about, briefly cutting through the enemy until hit in turn by a second wave of Tarheels that came rushing forward through the rain. Lieutenant Colonel Stagg boldly charged back into the melee. "Their officer in command rallied a small body [and] calling on the others to follow . . . succeeded in dashing by." Stagg again pierced the Tarheel ranks before his horse fell in a heap, injuring Stagg in the fall.[32] Captain William Elliot and Lieutenant James McElhenny were killed, Stagg surrendered, and another sixteen Union troopers fell in a final point-blank exchange of sabres and revolvers.[33] "The [Federals] made several bold dashes to carry the position but were successfully repulsed in every attempt, leaving the pass strewn with dead and wounded."[34] The remaining Wolverines retired down the lane and threw up a barricade near the junction of the turnpike to secure Kilpatrick's right flank. The Tarheels and Moorman's battery continued to hold the upper farm lane, and the fighting stalled above Fountain Dale.[35]

Back on the turnpike, a farmer's son by the name of T. C. Buhrman heard the gunfire as the sun descended and made his way to Kilpatrick's column. The young man informed Kilpatrick the Confederate wagons were passing around the far side of Jacks Mountain, on the Maria Furnace Road. After attempting the farm lane and quickly losing twenty men, Kilpatrick switched tacks and kept to the turnpike, which would soon intersect the wagon train at a toll booth ahead. The 6th Michigan now came forward and struck the advance in the continuing rain.[36]

Ahead of the Federals waited Captain George Emack with a single company of the 1st Maryland Confederate Cavalry—and a lone cannon with less than a dozen rounds. Emack had placed the gun on the Emmitsburg Turnpike, roughly two miles forward of the junction with the Maria Furnace Road, where Confederate wagons were turning onto the turnpike at the toll booth. The sun had now set, and the last soggy glow of daylight still clung to the horizon as Emack spotted the Federal cavalry coming up the turnpike. Emack rode down the hill with one of his troopers at his side, both wearing gum ponchos over their uniforms as a disguise. Approaching the head of the Federal column, they calmly turned about as if they were Federal scouts, without "making any demonstration . . . and retreated before them at a walk, shielding the gun [ahead] as much as possible." As soon as Emack cleared the muzzle, the gun blasted out a dose of canister, blinding the Federals below as the cannon flashed bright as a bolt

Figure 19.1.   Extant drawing of a retreating supply train. *Library of Congress.*

of lightning. Emack and a handful of Marylanders then charged forward in the evening haze, driving the Wolverines down the mountain in a temporary panic.[37]

As the Federals rallied and regained their vision, Emack dismounted his men on the side of the road and had them crouch in the trees along the road's edge, their black gum ponchos serving as perfect camouflage in the dark leaves and wet branches. It was full night before the Wolverines reformed, reloaded, and pressed back up the road to halt below the hill where the cannon fired. James Kidd of the 6th Michigan Cavalry recalled the state of affairs: "It was too dark to distinguish objects at any distance, the enemy was across [our] front and no one could determine how large a force it might be."[38]

Kilpatrick and Custer rode forward and decided this was no place for horses. Troopers dismounted and counted fours, and stepped forward, one slow foot at a time. "The force in front did not appear to be formidable in number, but had the advantage of position, and was on the defensive in a narrow mountain pass where numbers were of little avail. We had a large force but it was strung out in a long column for miles back, and it was possible to bring only a few men into actual contact with the enemy." This nerve-wracking duty slowed the advance to a crawl as troopers inched up the road in the dark while the rain continued nonstop. Slow but steady, the Wolverines kept pressing, edging forward in the darkness until Emack's men opened fire. Muzzles flashed in the night; troopers marked the flashes and returned fire at the source. "Soon we encountered the Confederate skirmishers, but could locate them only by the flashes of their guns. The darkness was intense. . . . [M]ore than once a trailing vine tripped me up and I fell headlong. . . . [H]ad it not been for the noise and the flashing of the enemy's fire, we should have wandered away in the darkness."[39] Though delivered at a snail's pace, this pressure eventually forced Emack back up the road, where he redeployed his men on either side of the track. Once again, the Federals inched forward, forcing Emack's band to retreat with the help of farmer Buhrman's son, who guided the Federals past the Confederates on a game trail and forced Emack's troopers to give ground in a sudden spatter of pistol fire.[40]

~

Back on the far side of Jacks Mountain, Grumble Jones heard reports of Federal cavalry moving to cut General Lee's train at Monterey Pass. Jones led two regiments forward—his own 6th Virginia and Robertson's 4th North Carolina—plus Chew's horse battery up the road for the pass.[41] The constant rain had already made a mess of the road, gullies overflowed in small rapids, and it became a struggle just navigating the troopers' horses through the train's wagons. Pulling Chew's heavy guns up the roadbed proved to be a battle in its own right. Wheels sank to their hubs in the cloying mud, requiring frequent stops to pull the heavy cannons and limbers free of the mire.[42] To make matters worse, Captain Emack had ordered the wagons to halt up ahead, fearing the enemy would break through and seize the entire train.[43] Jones countermanded this order and had the teamsters move forward. With the wagons back under way, Jones heard gunfire ahead and rode to the sound with his staff, eventually making contact with Emack on the turnpike.[44]

Jones assured Emack help was on the way, and Jones ordered his own staff to dismount and fall in with Emack's 1st Maryland while Jones rode back to the furnace road for more help. After Jones departed, Emack and the rest fanned out, lying on the ground while lightning began to flash overhead, offering split-second views of Federals hunched over and stalking forward in the rain. The Confederates held their fire until a Union trooper stepped on the prostrate form of Confederate Richard Key. Key pulled the trigger, and the Federal dropped on the spot.[45] Gunfire now erupted along the road on either flank, bringing the Wolverines to yet another halt on the pitch-black mountain. Between the 1st Michigan's earlier pasting, and an unknown enemy in the dark, the Wolverines were spooked and quickly losing their willingness to engage. So far, Emack's band of fifty Marylanders and one cannon had stalled Custer's brigade for nearly four hours.

As the two sides separated and the fighting waned, Emack backed over the summit of the mountain and dropped down the far side to reform above the intersection of the furnace road and the turnpike, where wagons were again rumbling by on their way down the mountain. Emack's cannon crew were now out of ammunition, and the rest of his men were down to just their sabres and a few scattered loads for their revolvers when Jones returned with reinforcements from the 4th North Carolina and 6th Virginia. Dismounting a section of the 6th Virginia, Jones sent them up the mountain to form a forward skirmish line. Jones then rode down to the intersection of the two roads and posted the 4th North Carolina behind a barricade near the turnpike tollhouse.[46]

Atop the summit, Lieutenant Pennington's Battery M, 2nd U.S., deployed beside the Monterey Inn, a large yellow hotel perched beside the turnpike at the top of the pass. Kilpatrick kept the gunners lobbing shells down the mountain, hoping to wreck one of the distant Rebel wagons he could plainly hear rolling by below in the depths of the pass.[47] Kilpatrick still remained unaware of the immense size of the enemy train stretching back toward Gettysburg, and falsely assumed the prize would slip through his fingers if he didn't act quickly and cut the moving wagons. After four hours of creeping forward to gain the summit, Custer's men appeared rattled and no longer seemed up to the task, prompting Kilpatrick to call up the 1st West Virginia from Farnsworth's former brigade.[48]

As he waited on the West Virginians, lightning ripped across the mountain, and Kilpatrick's sharper personality was on display for all as he began eviscerating Custer over the time it had taken his brigade to make the summit. Still fuming after humiliating Custer, Kilpatrick turned his ire on his escort, Company A of the 1st Ohio Cavalry, under the command of Captain Noah Jones, and Kilpatrick now demanded to know if his escort had retreated in the latest exchange. Lieutenant Pennington, a rail-thin but stalwart gunner, had finally heard enough and spoke up in defense of Jones and his Ohioans, claiming the escort company held their ground and covered Pennington's battery in the last pitch-black encounter. Kilpatrick continued to fume in anger at any target available when a trooper from the 1st Ohio boldly spoke up from the dark, "Give us a chance, General, and we will show you whether we are cowards or not."[49]

Kilpatrick replied with a quick oath, and then added he would soon give them the chance.

Figure 19.2. 1st Lieutenant Alexander Pennington, seen here on the far right. Pennington went on to command his own regiment of cavalry in 1864. *Library of Congress.*

Major Charles Capehart now arrived, leading one hundred men from the 1st West Virginia. Capehart formed a column of fours in the road as Captain Jones and his forty Ohioans fell in at the head of the West Virginians. The combined force threaded fingers through sword knots, pulled sabres, and advanced at a walk, passing Custer and his Wolverines, and continuing on to a small wooden bridge spanning a creek on the turnpike, where they paused momentarily.[50] No one could see more than six paces ahead between lightning strikes, and the rain was still falling heavily.[51] The only way a charge could even occur in such rain came from the macadamized surface of the turnpike, which allowed a modicum of traction for the horses' shod hooves.

No doubt these Ohio and West Virginia rankers began to wonder if they would survive the coming orders. Sprinting down a hill on horseback is one of the more dangerous things a rider can do. All the rider's weight is forward over the horse's front feet, retarding the animal's balance, and any misstep or slip of the horse's feet—a loose stone, pothole, or patch of clay—could trip and cartwheel horse and rider, subjecting both to a brutal crash and the slashing hooves of all coming on from behind. To sprint downhill in the rain on a moonless night with one hand clutching the reins and the other a sabre or revolver bordered on suicide. To combine all those elements and attempt it during a lightning storm with a loaded enemy waiting your approach defies a printable description and explains why this charge still ranks as one of the most valiant ever attempted in the war.

Ever short on fanfare, Captain Noah Jones stood in his stirrups and called out, "Forward! Charge!"[52] The column burst across the bridge, the hollow sound of the wooden planks quickly giving way to the crunching of hooves on crushed rock as the horses came to the gallop and launched down the mountain. The bugle sounded the charge, and into the darkness the horses and riders plunged.[53] Once under way there was nothing for it but to give each horse his head, grab a handful of mane, and hang on as the column rushed ahead; one giant herd hurtling forward, eyes wide and nostrils flaring.

The Rebels heard the coming charge, then saw sparks flying in the night from the horses' iron shoes striking the rocks beneath.[54] Jones's men opened fire on command, but the horses plowed through the scattering fire, drove over the Rebels crouching in the road, and made for the toll-house below.[55] Captain Emack charged into the Federal stampede, only to be shot through both arms and struck with a sabre as his horse tumbled to the road.[56]

As Emack fell, Captain Jones and Colonel Capehart sprinted past, smashing into the barricade at the tollhouse and mixing with the enemy beyond. Federal horses rammed Emack's men aside and scattered the 4th North Carolina Cavalry in kind as the Federals galloped past the tollhouse and began shooting teamsters from their wagons. Pennington's battery continued lobbing shrapnel from the summit, and the combination of bursting rounds, flashing lightning, and cracking gunfire panicked the horses and mules pulling the Confederate wagons. The teams hurtled down the mountain, crashing into trees, colliding with each other, and tumbling off the sheer side of the turnpike to land on the boulders below.[57]

Grumble Jones read the tea leaves. Hoping to remain anonymous, he told his men to call him "Bill" as Federal troopers swarmed the turnpike, capturing Rebel teamsters and troopers alike, and sweeping up scores of prisoners.[58] Disguised in his black slicker, "Bill" pulled his hat down, eased out of sight, and took to the woods to avoid capture.[59]

As the pandemonium settled, Kilpatrick rode down from the summit, shook Captain Jones's hand at the tollbooth, and, according to Company A lore, said, "I knew you would go through."[60]

Captain Jones's reply went unrecorded.

Kilpatrick now moved to collect his spoils. He directed Pennington to put a section of guns up across the Maria Furnace Road to block any enemy advance from Gettysburg while Kilpatrick's troopers secured his prisoners and the captured wagons below. Pennington went into position and rebuffed whatever scattering of volunteers Beverly Robertson could collect from the wagon escort, and the scant remains of his 4th North Carolina Cavalry.[61] Due to these minor attacks, Kilpatrick still felt he was operating on borrowed time, and never pressed up the furnace road to discover the incredible cache of enemy supplies sitting lightly guarded and just waiting for him to leave.

In Kilpatrick's defense, he expected Confederate infantry and artillery to be arriving any minute, plus he had about all he could handle down on the turnpike as his men rounded up three hundred wagons and some thirteen hundred combined prisoners from the 4th North Carolina, Ewell's II Corps, and the teamsters manning the wagons.[62] It had been a good night's work, and Kilpatrick secured his spoils and beat a quick retreat down the mountain for Smithsburg, Maryland.[63]

20

GREENCASTLE AND SMITHSBURG

The rains cleared long before the sun rose on July 5, revealing a long mass of riding troopers, captured wagons, and walking prisoners. As Kilpatrick looked over his spoils, he had to be proud, but his horses, unaware of history, honor, and the laurels that go with it, lagged badly after carrying their riders for twenty-four hours straight. Now west of South Mountain, it became clear to Kilpatrick he'd landed in an area the Confederate army could soon sweep, and Kilpatrick's closest support now sat miles away on the far, east side of South Mountain.[1] Suddenly, the wagons he'd seized were looking more like a burden than a treasure, and he decided to pull his newfound train aside and set it on fire. His troopers rifled through the wagons and reported all manner of goods the Rebels had appropriated: petticoats, sewing machines, coffee, tea, ladies' shoes, men's clothing—most everything a country store would have on its shelves.[2] After gleaning through the better items, they burned the remainder.[3]

By midmorning, Kilpatrick reached Smithsburg, Maryland, a picturesque farming town nestled against the western face of South Mountain where it sat beside Raven Rock Gap, one of two passes across the twin ranges of South Mountain and Catoctin Mountain. The second pass, Eyler's Gap, ran due east from Smithsburg, and Kilpatrick quickly recognized the strategic value of this small town. Basing at Smithsburg, he could threaten Hagerstown and the major roads leading south to the Potomac, and withdraw back east over the mountains if needed. As an added bonus, the townsfolk of Smithsburg happily welcomed his blue-clad troopers as saviors, and they came out of their homes to cheer the arrival of his men and ply them with leftover food from yesterday's rain-soaked Independence Day celebrations. Kilpatrick set pickets about the town and placed three artillery batteries in an arc across the north and east side of the town to cover the mountain passes, and he began marching his prisoners under guard for Boonsboro. Finally, he gave his remaining men and horses a much-needed rest on the cloudless summer day. The troopers dropped saddles and butchered some cattle, and the rest napped in the morning sun or visited with civilians.[4]

~

John Imboden's ambulance train closed on Greencastle, Pennsylvania, in the early morning, and Imboden could still hear the ceaseless cries of the wounded emanating from the wagons. Once under way the ambulances rolled without stopping, bouncing the wounded over the rocky roads, and "from almost every wagon . . . issued heart rending wails of agony." The wretched cries made for a wheeled terror, bouncing down flooded roads with pelting rain, flashes of lightning, and cracking thunder. The constant jolting in the springless wagons proved excruciating for men with broken limbs and gunshot wounds. Hundreds begged to be taken from the wagons and left to die, but there could be no halting; all the wagons must continue rolling if any were to make the Potomac.[5]

The column had all the elements of a ghost story, and the train of ambulances stretched on for seventeen miles. One local farmer who witnessed the chilling procession wrote, "Their wagon train was about 56 hours passing and nearly all hauling wounded, some would groan at every jerk the wagon made. . . . I saw some walking that were shot in the arms, some [in the] shoulders, some in the face. . . . It looked awful as their wounds were not dressed yet [and] looked all black and blue." Civilians tried to help, but they could do little but fill the canteens with fresh water as the wagons passed. "Some were moaning; some were praying, and others uttering the most fearful oaths and execrations that despair and agony could wring from them," remembered Imboden. "For four hours I hurried forward on my way to the front [of the train] and in all that time I was never out of hearing the groans and cries of the wounded and dying."[6]

Imboden's column lacked adequate food but had one item in spades: artillery. General Lee had insisted the column get through and delivered plenty of fire support, including eight twelve-pound Napoleons with the famed Washington Artillery of New Orleans, Captain McClannahan's Staunton Battery of six ordnance rifles, a four-gun Virginia battery under Captain Tanner, and finally Captain Hart's battery from the Stuart Horse Artillery. The 18th Virginia Cavalry led the advance, commanded by Imboden's brother, Colonel George Imboden, and interspersed within the body of the train were the McNeill Partisan Rangers and the 62nd Virginia Mounted Infantry from Imboden's brigade. Hampton's brigade formed a close rear guard, temporarily commanded by Colonel Young of the Cobb Legion, as Wade Hampton rode in one ambulance, still recuperating from the wounds he received at Rummel farm.[7] Fitz Lee's brigade followed the ambulance train at a distance of several miles to keep a trailing eye out for any Federals pushing through Cashtown Pass.[8]

As Imboden's train passed through Greencastle, thirty or forty civilians rushed the ambulances with axes and, ignoring the wounded shrieking within, began hacking at the wagon spokes of the ambulances in a crazed attempt to chop the wagon beds down to the ground one wheel at a time. Imboden quickly arrested the axe-swinging civilians, but he'd no sooner squelched this attack when Federal cavalry swarmed over the column in the fields outside of the town, striking the unguarded sections of the train. Captain McClannahan drove fifty men off with two doses of canister from the Staunton guns, but the enemy soon returned and nearly captured Imboden but for the timely arrival of the 18th Virginia Cavalry.[9] Through it all, Imboden kept the train largely in motion per his orders, and his men captured some of the enemy troopers. "On, on, we must move on," became the order of the day, and Imboden's teamsters kept the wagons rolling for Williamsport in one of the more macabre, demoralizing, and crucial assignments in a war filled with macabre, demoralizing, and crucial assignments.[10]

～

Jeb Stuart arrived outside Emmitsburg, Maryland, at dawn on July 5, still soaked to the bone after riding through the driving rain the night before. In his advance rode Vincent "Clawhammer" Witcher, and his 34th Virginia, who quickly entered into a sharp skirmish with elements of Colonel Pennock Huey's Federal cavalry brigade near a local hotel.[11] Seventy men were taken prisoner, and as Stuart interviewed the prisoners and studied some local maps, he learned Kilpatrick's division had passed through Emmitsburg the prior afternoon on their way to Monterey Pass. Stuart's troopers collected a number of local horses, and some even purchased items from civilian stores with Confederate script. Orders came for the men to feed and water their horses, and while Ferguson's brigade were seeing to their mounts, several citizens approached and asked who won the recent fight at Gettysburg; Ferguson's men stated the South had won the battle.[12]

Leaving Emmitsburg, Stuart traveled south on the Frederick Road. To fulfill his orders, Stuart needed to move west, across the Catoctin and South Mountain ranges via Eyler's Gap, which linked Mechanicstown to Smithsburg, and clear the west face of these mountain passes of Union cavalry. This would greatly help secure Lee's eastward flank and allow Lee's trains and following army to reach Hagerstown on their march south from Monterey Pass. Unfortunately for Stuart, he needed to avoid Mechanics-town, sitting on the eastern entrance to Eyler's Gap, as it was currently held by enemy cavalry.[13] To avoid contact, Stuart turned short at Creagerstown and took a byroad to Franklinville at the base of the mountain. Before making the crossing, Stuart again halted and fed his horses at a local mill, where grain for two thousand horses was procured and poured out beside the road.[14]

After a needed rest, Stuart turned for the hamlet of Graceham, crossed Catoctin Mountain, and divided his forces near a country church, sending Ferguson's brigade on the direct route for Smithsburg while Stuart, Cham-bliss's brigade, and Captain Griffin's Maryland Battery turned right on a steep course over South Mountain that descended the mountain north of Smithsburg via Raven Rock Gap.[15] As Ferguson headed east, Chambliss's column dropped into a narrow ravine and soon came under fire from Kil-patrick's pickets, who unloaded on the head of the Confederate column, sending carbine rounds ricocheting down the granite walls of the defile. Chambliss called for a halt as Company H of the 9th Virginia dismounted, counted files, and pressed forward on foot.[16] The sharpshooters spread to the high sides of the ravine, fighting "from crag to crag" and dislodging the Federal picket in a sharp skirmish that allowed Stuart to continue on for Smithsburg.[17]

Alerted by his retiring picket, Kilpatrick went about deploying his troops, with Custer's brigade on the Federal left, north of Smithsburg; Pen-nock Huey's brigade on Gardenour Hill near the town center; and Colonel Nathaniel Richmond, now leading Farnsworth's brigade, on high ground covering the Federal right, or east approach via Eyler's Gap at the foot of South Mountain. Chambliss's men soon appeared on the high ground north of town at Raven Rock, and Fuller's battery quickly opened fire.[18] Cannon fire echoed off the mountain, blasting shrapnel and solid shot at the Confederate approach while Chambliss pressed forward with Griffin's battery close behind. "Climbing up the mountain side on our right, and using some cavalry horses to aid those of the artillery, several of our guns were drawn to the summit."[19] From this superior ground, Griffin's gunners opened on the Federal guns below. Southern shells soon plowed down Water Street near Smithsburg's town center, forcing Fuller's battery to retire from their position on Gardenour Hill. Farther south, a different story unfolded, as Kilpatrick's line held the advantage with Elder's battery, and this battery's fire effectively bottlenecked Ferguson's men in the eastern pass and kept them from advancing.[20]

Seeing this, Stuart ordered Ferguson to backtrack and take his northern route. Chambliss then extended his line of sharpshooters to the right above town, flanking Kilpatrick's northern line and forcing Custer to deploy the 6th Michigan in support of Pennington's battery.[21] As Stuart readied for another push, Kilpatrick suddenly pulled back, leaving the town to Stuart and setting out for Boonsboro. The move came so abruptly that one troop of Wolverines didn't get the order to retire and finally took it upon themselves to retreat when they saw the Confederates enter the town.[22] Kilpatrick later claimed that he left when "Stuart was in full retreat down the mountain side."[23] This sounds extraordinary, and Kilpatrick seems to be parsing his words and describing Ferguson's shift to join Stuart, and not an actual retreat. "I did not pursue," explained Kilpatrick as he justified his own retreat. "To save my prisoners, my animals and wagons, I returned to Boonsboro."[24] Kilpatrick simply didn't want to continue a fight with an unknown enemy on the wrong side of the mountains and potentially lose all he had gained.

Once in Smithsburg, Stuart sent couriers to Monterey Pass to inform Lee of the latest developments, and his own progress. He also predicted Kilpatrick was headed south for Boonsboro, ten miles south of Smithsburg.[25] Stuart then turned northwest for Leitersburg to better cover Lee's quartermaster train, now once again moving down from Monterey Pass en route to Hagerstown. Stuart's force reached Leitersburg after dark, and there linked up with Grumble Jones's and Beverly Robertson's brigades.[26] It had been a very long, but extremely successful day for Stuart. Lee's trains were again flowing south all the way to the river, the South Mountain passes through Smithsburg were clear, and the I and III Corps of Longstreet and Hill now flanked either side of Jacks Mountain above Monterey Pass. [27]

That was the good news. The bad news came from the Potomac River, where the pontoon bridge at Falling Waters had been cut by enemy cavalry. Worse still, the river now stood at flood stage from the recent deluge of rain, stopping all traffic from crossing over, and Lee's wagons were stacking up by the hundreds in Williamsport. Despite all of today's gains, a flooded river now blocked Lee's retreat cold, and Stuart and his troopers must have felt their backs were up against the wall.

⌒

Elsewhere, General Meade continued to grow increasingly frustrated. On July 4, Meade's army lay fractured and still short on horses, ammunition, and feed. By July 5, it remained in poor shape, and Federal signal stations at Gettysburg reported the enemy "batteries have disappeared from the hills near the seminary," confirming Lee's army was in full retreat.[28] Additional reports sighted Confederate cavalry moving through the Emmitsburg Gap, and Meade began making plans to bring Lee's army to heel.[29] Most everyone in the Army of the Potomac felt they should pursue the Confederates, and Meade agreed; only the devil lay in the details, and Meade first wanted to determine Lee's intentions before bringing on another engagement. The new commander wanted to avoid a costly fight in the mountain passes, where Lee could dig in on high ground and force a battle where the Confederates held every advantage. Instead, Meade hoped Lee would retire west of the mountains and drop into the Cumberland Valley, allowing Meade to take a parallel course east of the mountains toward his supply base at Frederick. Meade could then resupply and hopefully cross one of the many passes over South Mountain to close in on Lee's rear while Union cavalry harried the flanks of the enemy and slowed the Southern army.[30] Unbeknownst to Meade, Lee was making plans to do exactly what Meade hoped for, as Lee maneuvered his three corps down through Monterey Pass for the Cumberland Valley. Unfortunately, Meade had no way of knowing this and ordered Major General John Sedgwick's VI Corps to lead a foot reconnaissance in force from Gettysburg.[31]

Sedgwick's men pressed forward over the battlefield, wading through rows of dead bodies, expired horses, dismounted cannons, and shredded carriages. In one place, a caisson had exploded mid-action to leave all the horses dead in their traces "and sixteen bodies of cannoneers" at their stations.[32] Cast-off clothing and dropped equipment littered the fields, and recent rains had turned the fields into a quagmire that sucked at soldiers' boots and pried nailed shoes from horses' feet. A group of Sedgwick's infantry passed the burial parties stacking dead Confederates in open pits like cordwood.

> I noticed a young Confederate, who had been hit just over the eye. The ball or piece of shell had torn away a piece of the skull about two inches square, laying bare the brain over the eye back to the temple. He lay there motionless; but was he dead? The brain pulsated regularly, as though with every beat of the heart. The boys wouldn't put him in the trench. I thought, "What if he be conscious, and hears what we say?" The thought was agony, and all were glad when we left the burial party and resumed our march.[33]

Around noon, Sedgwick's advance approached Fairfield, crossed a creek, and deployed for battle. Out in front, the 15th New Jersey Infantry moved carefully over fields of waving grain, which they quickly trampled flat. A farmer bowed formally at the waist as they passed, his sarcasm directed at the soldiers for wrecking his crop. The Federals plodded along for another three miles, wreaking havoc like a herd of locusts, and bracing for contact with every step. They eventually reached the Confederate line, posted on a broad plain ringed in wooded hills that marked the entrance to Fairfield Pass. A member of the Jersey infantry recalled, "a few shots were exchanged, and stepping through the woods . . . we soon met the enemy's skirmishers."[34]

Alerted to the Federal presence by White's 35th battalion, Jubal Early sent skirmishers forward in hopes of slowing the Union advance.[35] An artillery duel broke out, and shells soon screamed across the plain as the infantry advanced and traded volleys over the open ground. The Federal effort seemed unexceptional and almost chaste in vigor, as the Confederates withdrew into the mountain pass. "There was considerable firing, but our casualties were not numerous," wrote a member of the 15th New Jersey. "One man from the Third Regiment was killed and two were wounded."[36]

Sedgwick wrote to Meade and described the Fairfield Pass as a formidable piece of terrain with high ground to either side, "in which a small force of the enemy could hold in check and delay for a considerable time any pursuing force."[37] Meade welcomed Sedgwick's report as the Confederates appeared to be retreating, and not holding for a battle. A perplexed member of Sedgwick's VI Corps watched the Confederates slowly retreat behind White's cavalry screen and pondered the current state of affairs: "I wonder, whether we really whipped the Rebs so very bad after all. . . . I wonder if Napoleon, or even Robt. Lee, were our commander this evening, would THEY pursue a defeated army in this cautious, courteous way?"[38]

21

HAGERSTOWN AND WILLIAMSPORT

Reveille sounded at 3:00 a.m. for John Buford's 1st Division on July 6. With their horses now rested and reshod, the troopers rolled out of their blankets and began grooming their mounts for an early departure. After four days of rest, Buford felt eager to get back to the front, and some of his impatience may have stemmed from a recent incident the day before when a civilian named Richardson was brought before Buford for distributing religious pamphlets and acting suspiciously. His captors found letters on the man from Confederate generals recommending his character, as well as a series of passes for traveling behind both Union and Confederate lines.[1] Sitting on a log and smoking his pipe, Buford questioned the man and then ordered him hanged for a spy. They hanged the man from a tree, and the body still dangled beside the road when the 1st Division rode out for Williamsport before dawn.[2]

Crossing South Mountain, Buford soon reached Boonsboro, Maryland, and there linked with Kilpatrick's 3rd Division. The two commanders talked and decided Buford would push west with his rested 1st Division, and strike the mass of Confederate wagons staged at Williamsport with all three of his brigades—Devin's, Gamble's, and Merritt's. Kilpatrick would screen Buford's right flank on the march with his 3rd Division and veer north for Hagerstown, a well-sized market town sitting on a busy hub of commercial roads. With Hagerstown secure, Kilpatrick could block any Confederate troops, or their trains, traveling down from Monterey Pass.[3] Kilpatrick's 1st Brigade, under Colonel Nathaniel Richmond, would push into Hagerstown.[4] His 2nd Brigade, under Custer, would hold on Richmond's left, securing the Hagerstown-Williamsport Turnpike, and be ready to support either Richmond or Buford as needed.[5]

≈

A courier woke Jeb Stuart at dawn on July 6 with a note from General Lee. The general reported his infantry and trains continued to move down through Monterey Pass with little trouble from the enemy. In response, Stuart directed Chambliss's brigade to rise early and march on a direct path to Hagerstown, as Stuart wanted to secure this key point in the Confederate route to the Potomac as soon as possible.[6] Stuart next sent Robertson's depleted brigade on to Hagerstown after Chambliss, and ordered Grumble Jones's brigade to head south of Hagerstown to the next hamlet of Funkstown, with orders to hold there and cover the southeastern approach via the National Road and Boonsboro. Stuart then joined Ferguson's brigade on their march for Hagerstown and had gone several miles when he received a dispatch that Federal forces were already approaching Hagerstown.[7]

Unbeknown to Stuart, Kilpatrick had passed south of Funkstown and turned north on the Sharpsburg Road, thus running west of Jones's position at Funkstown, and reaching Hagerstown without Jones's knowledge.[8] The news of Federals approaching Hagerstown alarmed Stuart, and he ordered Ferguson's men to take up a gallop. Luck is sometimes defined as the residue of good planning, and fortunately for Stuart, he'd ordered Chambliss and Robertson to march separately for Hagerstown that morning.

Chambliss had arrived in Hagerstown to see Lee's wagons rolling through the center of the township and then turning down for Williamsport. All seemed well until reports arrived of a large force of Federal cavalry closing fast on the town from the south. Chambliss placed pickets from the 9th Virginia and ordered Colonel Davis and his 10th Virginia to barricade South Potomac Street below the intersection of Franklin Street, or the National Road, as it was known throughout the state. Supporting Davis were the 9th Virginia pickets and Captain Frank Bond of the 1st Maryland Battalion with forty-odd troopers. Farther back, above the National Road on North Potomac Street, Chambliss and Robertson placed the 13th Virginia and 5th North Carolina Cavalry as a reserve line at the Zion Reformed Church.[9] In the meantime, Lee's wagons would halt north of town until the Federals were turned and all roads secured.[10]

Colonel Nathaniel Richmond led the Federal advance on Hagerstown, having taken command of the brigade after Farnsworth's demise. The twenty-nine-year-old Richmond grew up in Indiana and left college for health reasons to travel out west. His health improved, and for four years he worked odd jobs, exploring Wyoming, Idaho, and California before returning home and passing his bar exams. Richmond had no military experience before the war but still gained a commission as lieutenant colonel of the 1st West Virginia Cavalry in 1861 and proved a quick study.

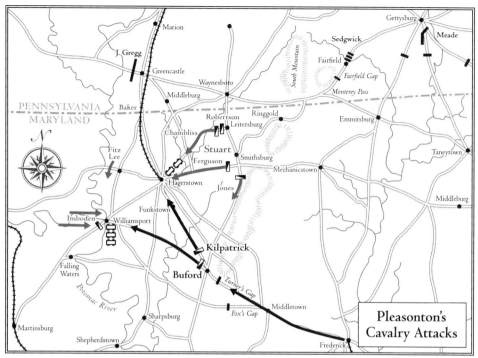

Map 16. Pleasonton's Cavalry Attacks

In heavy skirmishing prior to the Battle of 2nd Manassas, he led a plunging sabre charge against Confederate infantry. "The rebels retreated, and we were ordered to fall back. . . . Colonel Richmond was covered with blood from head to foot. Two noble fellows who were at his side had been shot and their life's blood was still warm on his clothes." Richmond's successful charge drew considerable praise from his commanders and likewise earned the respect of his men.[11]

As Richmond's Federal brigade entered Hagerstown from the south, Ferguson's Confederate brigade appeared from the east with Stuart galloping out front. Turning to meet this threat, Richmond deployed Lieutenant Samuel Elder's battery near the Female Seminary on the south end of town.[12] The Federal fire forced a halt in Ferguson's column, but Grumble Jones's brigade, having doubled back from Funkstown, now arrived, and Captain Chew's battery soon came into play as both batteries opened upon the other in the town streets.[13] "The artillery fire was severe," recalled a Southern gunner. "[T]he range was short and their ten pound shrapnel whizzed fearfully and exploded all around us."[14] Ferguson dismounted his sharpshooters and sent them forward to open on Elder's guns with their

Enfield rifles, forcing Elder and his supporting sharpshooters to shift their position.[15] Elder called for more support, and additional sharpshooters from the 1st West Virginia came up and supported the battery as it shifted and opened yet again, creating a rough stalemate in this eastern section of the town between the opposing batteries and their supports.[16]

As Richmond turned his attention to the Confederate barricade on South Potomac Street, Captain Ulrich Dahlgren arrived and volunteered to join the attack. Ulrich, the son of Federal Rear Admiral John Dahlgren, had attached himself to General Pleasonton's headquarters, where he served as another eager carpet knight from Pleasonton's revolving entourage of young staff officers. To date the twenty-one-year-old had been ranging across the countryside with a handpicked group of troopers, raiding wagons, seizing couriers, and wreaking havoc behind enemy lines like a Federal version of John Mosby. With hard work ahead, Richmond readily accepted Dahlgren's offer.

Dahlgren joined his command with two squadrons from the 18th Pennsylvania, and one from the 1st West Virginia. They formed columns and made for the Confederate barricade at a trot.[17] As the Federals increased their pace, pickets from the 9th Virginia rushed back for the barricade and unwittingly masked their comrades' fire. The lead Federals overtook the Virginia pickets, and all arrived at the same instant to crash through the Rebel barrier.[18] Unwilling to retreat, Confederate colonel Davis stubbornly ordered a counticharge. The Federals shot his horse out from under him, and the fifty-year-old West Pointer fell captive as Dahlgren and the rest boiled over the barricade and rushed up the street on the heels of the Rebel survivors.

Giving way before this onslaught, Captain Bond turned his Marylanders onto a side street and quickly wheeled his men about by section, with each section of fours spinning about independently to quickly reverse the column's direction. As the Federals swept by, Bond launched his forty men back onto the street, and drove into Dahlgren's flank, where Bond shot down a Federal sergeant.[19] Mounted reserves from the 5th North Carolina and 13th Virginia then charged the head of the Federals, and the fighting turned hand to hand as adversaries charged through the town streets. Bond recalled Sergeant Hammond Dorsey of the 1st Maryland hewing left and right and cutting down several men. "[T]he last of them was a bugler, by this time in full flight," and as he leaned over his horse's neck, the brass bugle shielded him; "repeated blows were necessary" to bring him down.[20]

Dahlgren and the rest of the Federals fell back through the town square, and Richmond fed in Company D, 18th Pennsylvania. These troopers rushed forward on foot, their carbines at right shoulder shift and

Figure 21.1.   West Franklin Street, Hagerstown, Maryland, circa 1870. This street saw heavy fighting on July 6. *Library of Congress.*

moving at the quick step, until Dahlgren halted them at the town square. The Confederates charged forward, and the Pennsylvanians opened fire, clearing saddles and rushing forward through their own powder smoke as the Rebels withdrew. Chambliss rallied his men on the high ground at Zion Reformed Church as Moorman's horse battery arrived and unlimbered.[21] As the gunners loaded, Chambliss dismounted many of his troopers who had carbines and placed them in the church cemetery, down the alleyways, and on either side of the street, where their concentric fire turned the Federal sharpshooters back down the hill. Mounted Confederates next worked their way south, supported by the sharpshooters at the church, and as Dahlgren moved to cut them off, he received a bullet through his foot in a sharp exchange of fire.[22] Rapidly losing blood, Dahlgren was moved to the rear, where surgeons amputated his lower leg and saved his life.

With Dahlgren out of the picture, the Federal effort stalled until Richmond marshalled another squadron of the 18th Pennsylvania, plus troops from the 1st Vermont, and sent them charging back for Chambliss's men up by the church. Quick in reply, Chambliss ordered a counterattack, and troopers from North Carolina, Virginia, and Maryland spurred forward with a yell. Civilian W. W. Jacobs watched the chaos from the rooftop of the Eagle Hotel, where he had a bird's-eye view of the combat: "The cutting and slashing was beyond description . . . the steel blades circling, waving, parrying, thrusting and cutting, some reflecting the bright sunlight, others crimsoned in gore. . . . The contending forces were so intermingled that sometimes two or more men were cutting at one."[23]

Captain Charles Snyder of the 1st Michigan struck down three Confederates, then took a gunshot to the abdomen and a cut across his head that dropped him in the street as more Rebels surged forward. Three officers from the 18th Pennsylvania soon joined Snyder on the cobblestones; Captain Henry Potter, Lieutenant William Lawes, and Captain Pennypacker all fell along the town square in the desperate fighting.[24]

Colonel Richmond responded by sending forward more sharpshooters. Horace Ide of the 1st Vermont Cavalry recalled moving up through the Hagerstown streets: "We deployed down the cross streets as skirmishers, hiding behind the houses and firing around corners. I saw a squad of them and resting beside a telegraph pole fired [m]y carbine. I didn't know as I hit them, but they dodged mightily sudden. At one time we came on quite a lot of them, three to one, and saved ourselves by running back through [a] house."[25]

Richmond's two-tiered assaults of mounted charges and dismounted sharpshooters eventually swept the town square clear of the enemy. Hagerstown's civilians also pitched into this fight. "After we passed the square," recalled a member of the 18th Pennsylvania, "an old citizen came out of a house with a musket in his hand and fell in with our boys, loading and firing after the rebels. He was shot down before he crossed the second block."[26] Not all the inhabitants supported the Federal cause; Colonel Rodenbough of the 18th Pennsylvania later wrote that "Sergeant Joseph Brown of Company B" was shot down by a woman who fired from inside a window into the street.[27]

The Confederates fell back to their line at Zion Reformed Church, where they reloaded, let their horses have a blow, and wiped their sabres clean before sheathing. Despite Rebel forces perched north and east, Richmond's lone brigade still held the center of town, while Elder's battery kept the Federal flank secure and continued trading rounds with Chew's gunners. A standoff developed in the center of Hagerstown as Lee's wagons sat parked on the turnpike with no route open to Williamsport. That changed with the arrival of General Albert Iverson's North Carolina infantry.

As the wagons of Iverson's brigade sat motionless, his men soon came forward at the double step and deployed as skirmishers.[28] These veterans of Ewell's II Corps suffered massed casualties on the first day at Gettysburg, and the survivors were eager for revenge as they pushed into the fight and began firing from house to house. The channeling buildings and streets were a hindrance to the cavalry, but these same obstacles were welcome havens to experienced infantry. Using cover and firing from stairsteps, porches, and corners, Iverson's men moved steadily downhill from the Zion Reformed Church and advanced block by block, alley by alley, and began placing men on rooftops as they went.

"We found ourselves being gradually forced back," recalled a New England trooper. "When we found the bullets coming down the side-streets we would fall back another street and so continue." One group of fourteen New Englanders held out too long and found themselves surrounded. Seeking an escape, they snuck into a Union-friendly house, where the owner hid them as the fighting continued and steadily rose in pitch. The Rebel infantry's rifled muskets were proving too much for the Federal's breech-loading carbines. "When we got there, the Yankees had possession of the town," bragged a Tarheel infantryman, "but we . . . soon had the town and the Yankees before us running."[29]

Richmond ordered a retreat. Ambulances rolled forward to collect the wounded, and the Federal cavalry pulled back to the edge of town to link with Custer and Kilpatrick.[30] Despite surrendering the town, all was not lost. Kilpatrick and the Wolverine Brigade still held the turnpike between Hagerstown and Williamsport, and Lee's wagons still sat trapped above Hagerstown. As the battle noise died out in Hagerstown, cannon fire erupted six miles away at Williamsport.

As Colonel Richmond drove on Hagerstown, Buford passed below Kilpatrick and pushed on for Williamsport. Moving on the Boonsboro-Williamsport Road, Buford struck the Confederate picket line posted outside of Williamsport near the College of St. James. Any thin hopes Buford may have had for surprising the enemy and razing Lee's trains quickly vanished before the peppering fire of the Rebel pickets. Undeterred, Buford set to work. He placed Merritt's brigade to the right of the Boonsboro Road with Lieutenant Graham's battery in support. Gamble's brigade moved to the left of the road along with Lieutenant Calef's battery. Devin's brigade would act as the reserve.

John Imboden saw the return of his pickets and knew he would soon have a fight on his hands. Though heavily outnumbered in cavalry, Imboden had twenty-six Confederate guns and two reduced regiments of infantry—the 54th North Carolina and 58th Virginia—plus Company F of the 21st Virginia. Imboden had the resources to offer a fight but struggled with the broad expanse of open terrain in his front. East of Williamsport there ran a long range of low hills that offered excellent high ground and dominated an otherwise flat plateau and the approach to town. This high ground needed to be secured and kept from the enemy, and Imboden quickly set his guns along the ridge; however, the length of this ridge stretched beyond the capacity of his available infantry and cavalry to cover the breadth of the position. This forced Imboden to take advantage of a rarely used resource: the men on detached duties, troopers waiting for remounts, and commissary soldiers commonly known as members of Company Q in the nineteenth-century military. These men, plus every army's "trumpery" of essential noncombatants: the clerks, cooks, farriers, saddlers, and armorers of every brigade. Williamsport teemed with noncombatants, all stranded by the flooded Potomac, and Imboden began forming them into hundred-man companies and armed them from available weapons stored in the wagons.[31]

But Imboden still needed officers to lead these ad hoc Q companies. This issue solved itself as wounded officers volunteered from the ambulances. Colonel John Logan Black, commander of the 1st South Carolina Cavalry, left his ambulance wracked with typhoid and took charge of one such troop. Next came Lieutenant Colonel William Delony from the

Figure 21.2. Brigadier General John D. Imboden, Army of Northern Virginia. Imboden mounted a creative defense at Williamsport with limited resources. *Library of Congress.*

Cobb Legion Cavalry. His head still bandaged from the fight at Hunters-town, Delony mounted his horse and started forming a troop of walking wounded, many of them from Hampton's brigade.[32] Other volunteers included infantry officers Major Reuben Reynolds of the 11th Mississippi, and Colonel William Aylet of the 53rd Virginia.[33] These men and others left their ambulances in response to the call for help, and Imboden's perimeter now took shape in a long arcing line transected by four roads: the Cumberland Valley Turnpike running due north, the Hagerstown Turnpike to the northeast, the Boonsboro Road to the southeast, and finally the Downsville Road running almost due south.[34]

By late afternoon, Buford's forces began to advance on either side of the Boonsboro Road. A Rebel captain described the Federal approach as the Union horse gunners "wheeled into line . . . unlimbered, and in an instant opened" on Imboden's position.[35] Skirmishers from Gamble's brigade then advanced, with a mounted section of 3rd Indiana following in support. These Hoosiers soon spotted a Confederate train of seven forage wagons moving up the Downsville Road and charged forward, sweeping over the target.[36] The Yanks caught the wagons and set fire to the hay in the wagon beds. Rebels soon saw the mule teams sprinting straight across the fields in a panic, the flaming wagons blazing and bouncing behind.[37]

Captain William Pegram's company of 21st Virginia Infantry, and a battalion of Colonel Aylet's walking wounded, pushed forward in the wake of the banshee attack to engage Gamble's men at Rose Hill Manor, a sweeping five-hundred-acre antebellum plantation. Pegram and Aylet took positions along the plantation's fence line and outbuildings and quickly drew the attention of Calef's Federal battery. Lanyards ripped and round shot blew holes through the outbuildings, driving shards of timber and brick through the air with lethal force as shrapnel burst left and right, shredding crops and knocking fence posts to pieces. Pegram and Aylet hunkered down and held their position despite the artillery fire, as Major William Medill of the 8th Illinois Cavalry brought forward four troops of sharpshooters to dislodge the Confederates. It was Major Medill who gamely rallied Gamble's men along the Trappe Road at Upperville, and he rode bravely here as well, guiding his men straight into the teeth of the firefight. The only mounted officer in this segment of the field, Medill brought his skirmishers on through a cornfield and began firing down at the Confederates with his revolver. Pegram's 21st Virginia returned the fire with their rifles and killed the daring major.[38]

The fight raged on as Pegram and Aylet continued to hold out in the face of the growing Federal assaults. Imboden sent a half battery racing in support, which drew a hailstorm of Federal fire from sharpshooters and gunners alike. Rebel driver Mike Keegan delivered the accompanying limber but had two horses killed in his team in the process. Remarkably, Keegan had two horses shot from his team at Gettysburg, and survived both experiences.[39] Captain Pegram of the 21st Virginia wasn't as fortunate. He fell here from a Union bullet and died almost instantly. Three of his men fell immediately beside him.[40]

Farther north, Merritt's Regulars encountered the same stiff resistance. Imboden anchored his line here on the high ground between the Hagerstown and Boonsboro Pikes, with half the Washington Artillery center right under Captain Charles Squires, and Captain James Hart's horse battery posted center left. Spread between these guns, Imboden placed the tattered 58th Virginia, 54th North Carolina, and his own 18th Virginia Cavalry and 62nd Mounted Infantry, plus Delony's makeshift company from Hampton's brigade. The Southern artillery opened on the Regulars, and Graham's Federal battery responded. A blistering artillery duel erupted. Shells screamed over the open ground as the two sides launched case, shrapnel, and round shot in opposing volleys of battery fire.

As the guns dueled, Merritt deployed a wave of sharpshooters, and his Regulars pressed gamely into the Confederate line. In response, Imboden called for an advance. "As the enemy could not see the supports of our batteries, I moved the whole line forward to his full view, in single ranks, to show a long front [across their] approach." Imboden then shifted the men to make his numbers appear greater than they were. "My line passed our guns fifty or one hundred yards, where they were halted awhile, and then were withdrawn behind the hill-top again, slowly and steadily."[41] The bluff worked. Merritt thought he was facing Confederate infantry in depth and slowed his advance. Rebel rifles poured forth to help sell the ruse, and the artillery maintained a heavy fire.

Farther south, Gamble's veterans rallied following Medill's death below the Boonsboro Road and began sweeping through Rose Hill Manor. Imboden countered and sent sharpshooters from his cavalry brigade down across the Boonsboro Road to stall the advancing Federals.[42] In the meantime, Calef's Federal guns continued to hammer the Rebel lines, and his ordnance rifles were enjoying a distinct advantage over the Southern smoothbores on this end of the Rebel line. Major Benjamin Eshleman of the Washington Artillery answered by moving Captain Miller's battery of six Napoleons forward in a blistering exchange of artillery fire.[43] Gamble's Federals opened a carbine barrage in reply, allowing his troopers to rush forward and take an outbuilding flanking the advanced Southern guns. Q

Troop Confederates under Major Harry Gilmor of the 1st Maryland counterattacked and held out until relieved by Colonel George Smith's 62nd
Mounted Infantry. This allowed Eshleman's Rebel guns to continue firing,
but despite these efforts, Gamble's steady veterans continued to advance on
the flank and now threatened to roll up Imboden's right flank and break
his entire line.[44]

Southern support arrived from the river. Ammunition reached the
Rebel gunners north of the Hagerstown Pike in Captain James Hart's sector. Hart feared the far side of Imboden's line would soon break; to counter
this he ordered Captain Squires's guns of the Washington Artillery to mount
a rapid charge forward, along with a two-gun section from McClanahan's
Virginia horse battery.[45] The drivers spurred ahead, carrying the combined
guns forward at a gallop to arrive on Merritt's near flank. They opened seconds later, raking the Federal troopers with canister and shell. The sudden
barrage drove Merritt back in confusion as teamsters, walking wounded,
and Q troops advanced in the wake of the charging artillery. Delony wrote
his wife, "drove the enemy about three fourths of a mile . . . completely
flanked one of their batteries."[46] To make matters worse, Federal scouts
reported Fitz Lee's Confederate cavalry brigade would soon arrive on the
Cumberland turnpike. Merritt now had to pull his entire brigade to the rear
in order to save his right flank.[47] This put Gamble's flank in the air, and
Buford had no option but to order Gamble back as well.[48]

Imboden's unorthodox defense had worked, and not a moment too
soon as Kilpatrick now came steaming down the Hagerstown Turnpike
with Custer's Wolverines in tow. Reaching a high point in the road, the
6th Michigan turned out to form in a field beside the pike and began
deploying sharpshooters when a Rebel horse battery arrived and opened
on Custer's position.[49] Southern shells stormed in with abandon, ripping
up the ground, killing men, and rapidly forcing the Wolverines to retire.[50]
As one Federal put it, "[E]very man was under fire, and to us it became a
desperate fight for existence, and we looked anxiously for night to close
upon the scene. Had the daylight lasted another hour, we would have suffered the most disastrous defeat."[51]

The sun now lay close on the horizon, and Buford had seen his
advantage disappear in a matter of minutes. Meeting with Kilpatrick, they
assessed the situation. Merritt and Gamble were hopelessly flanked, enemy
artillery had scattered Custer, and Fitz Lee's brigade had just arrived on
the field.[52] There was nothing for it but to face about and make back for
Boonsboro. Kilpatrick fell back with Custer and sent orders for Colonel
Richmond to retreat from Hagerstown altogether.

∼

Richmond obeyed, heading south from Hagerstown on the Sharpsburg Road before joining the Williamsport Turnpike, a straight, macadamized road bordered with tall stone walls and tollhouses. Rolling pastures spread on either side, the fields dotted with farmhouses and crisscrossed with stone walls and staked rail fences.[53] Kilpatrick's retreat put Richmond in a hard spot; he now stood as the last Federal force between Stuart's brigades in Hagerstown, and it was up to Richmond to keep Stuart from piling into the rear of Custer's brigade.

Stuart fell in close on Richmond's heels; after hours of street fighting, he could finally maneuver over open ground and hoped to pin Richmond on the turnpike ahead. Stuart set Chambliss's brigade up front and put Robertson and Ferguson, moving parallel to the pike, on the fields southeast of the road.[54] Jones's brigade followed in reserve.[55]

Richmond retired down the pike with the 5th New York and Elder's battery serving as a rear guard to slow the Confederate pursuit.[56] Lieutenant Elder had served a hitch in the 2nd U.S. Artillery before the war and rose to 1st sergeant by 1858.[57] He had reenlisted in 1861, gained a commission, and been promoted to captain for gallantry at the Battle of Sharpsburg.[58] With the sun now dropping, Elder halted a two-gun section on a ridge a mile out of town, unlimbered the guns, and began lobbing shells at the Southerners as Richmond threw forward a cloud of sharpshooters. Charles McVicar, a gunner with Chew's horse battery, wrote, "They are holding their position and we have taken a stand in the pike. Our guns recoiling, bury themselves in the mud. Thought we were done for." McVicar continued, marking the range of the enemy: "Their battery is 400 yards distant. We are under a rapidly advancing line of [enemy] sharpshooters. . . . We don't mind shell but these little bees zipping by make us nervous. The cavalry charged and we are firing."[59]

As Chambliss and his troopers closed, the Federal sharpshooters withdrew, and Elder limbered up and redeployed at the next ridge, where he again opened fire. The 13th Virginia increased their pace, topped the rise, and discovered a covering squadron of Federal cavalry in the swale between the two ridges. The Federals broke east for a stand of woods off the turnpike, and the 13th gave chase as the 9th Virginia now advanced down the pike at Elder's guns in a column of fours. The Union gunners loaded canister, and the 9th Virginia split their column down the middle, forming two separate columns of twos, each wide to either side of the stone fences bordering the turnpike, with a gap between the columns as they charged forward. Elder's guns fired at twenty paces, so close the canister had not begun to spread when it struck a single trooper square in the chest. "[The] charge of canister, before escaping from the net of wire which enclosed it, struck one of our men. . . . [He] fell heavily to the ground."[60] The Confederates sprinted over the remains of their comrade and closed on the guns.

A Federal gunner knocked one of the Virginians from his horse with a staff, and the rest of the Virginians came under fire from Federal sharpshooters posted behind the fences on either side of the turnpike. The Rebels swerved as the sharpshooters fired, jumping the fence bordering the road in a ragged fashion and gaining a wheat field left of the road in loose clumps of files.[61] In the confusion, Elder's drivers charged forward, limbered the guns, and made their getaway in a brilliant display of horsemanship. "We fought over every foot of ground from Hagerstown to Williamsport," recalled a Union officer. "Every time they charged, they were met with grape and canister."[62] Richmond also praised his gun teams: "Too much credit cannot be given to Lieutenant Elder. . . . [T]he men of his battery are also deserving of special mention for their bravery and good conduct under fire."[63]

Stuart responded with Witcher's 34th Virginia and their three band Enfields. The 34th dismounted left of the pike and raked the Federals with a deadly fire that quickly cleared a number of Yankee saddles. Ferguson's men advanced as the 34th reloaded, and called for the Federals to surrender.[64] Captain Beauman of the 1st Vermont yelled back, "I don't see it," and vaulted his horse over the turnpike's wall with the remains of his squadron. He rode over a crest of rocky ground cut through with fences and vaulted the partitions as if on a fox hunt.[65] Ferguson's men couldn't keep up, and the Federals retired with Elder's guns in tow.[66]

Falling back to the next ridge, Richmond switched tactics and ordered two squadrons from the 5th New York to charge forward, screen the retreat, and stall the Confederate pursuit. Colonel James Gordon's 5th North Carolina saw the Federal attack coming, closed ranks, and spurred ahead. They crashed into the New Yorkers with revolvers blazing and shattered the Federal charge.[67] Captain James Penfield of the 5th New York rode in the front rank; his horse fell dead in the road, and Penfield suffered a hard cut from a sabre as the Tarheels stormed through the Yankee ranks from front to rear. Many Federals had their horses shot beneath them, several men were captured, and two died instantly in the countercharge by Gordon's men.[68]

Determined to buy more time for Custer and Kilpatrick, Richmond again rallied his dwindling squadrons east of the road in the last light of the day, and placed two of Elder's guns behind a stone fence bordering the pike. Stuart glassed the imposing position and called on Grumble Jones to send up fresh troops.[69] Lunsford Lomax trotted forward with his 11th Virginia Cavalry, studied the Federal position, and paused. A pair of enemy guns protruded from a tall stone fence that framed a large pasture beside the pike. From there the guns could rake the roadway, and a broad line of Federal skirmishers supported the guns, running both across the pike and behind the fence guarding the guns.[70]

Lomax formed his men and had them check the loads on their revolvers; orders circulated for all to hold their fire until they gained the enemy line. Sergeants squared the ranks a final time, and Lomax turned onto the pike in a column of fours, crested the rise, and started the charge with two hundred yards to go. Lieutenant John Blue of the 11th Virginia remembered the Federals crouching behind the wall: "Not a man could be seen, not a

Figure 21.3. Colonel Lunsford L. Lomax, Army of Northern Virginia, circa 1855. Lomax graduated West Point in 1856 and fought beside Jeb Stuart at the Battle of Solomon Fork in 1857. *Library of Congress.*

gun fired, all was silent as the grave. We well knew what this silence meant and what to expect any moment."[71]

Blue and his troopers rolled on, revolvers pointing skyward, bracing for the storm. "It appeared to me that I was riding on a line with, and looking straight into, the mouth of a twelve-pounder which protruded through the stone fence. It is surprising how rapid thoughts will follow each other when a person expects the next breath he draws may be his last." At one hundred yards, the guns erupted, and canister sprayed down the pike.

Blue's horse died on its feet, tumbling to the road and pinning Blue beneath as his comrades hurtled past. Rolling on, Lomax's men sprinted for the sharpshooters barring the pike and opened with their revolvers as they hit the enemy line. The Federals broke on contact, and the Rebels swept up a number of prisoners and enemy horses.[72]

Elder's guns, however, remained behind the stone fence bordering the pike, and their drivers now sprinted forward to pull them out. As Lomax rallied his men, he spotted two squadrons of Union cavalry moving to support the guns in the same stone-ringed pasture. The turnpike fence provided excellent cover to the Federals, and the only way through was a gap in the fence along the road.[73] Both parties bolted for the opening at the same time, the Virginians determined to take the gap and the guns beyond, and the Federals determined to cover their battery. The two sides met just inside the wall, where "the fight waxed hot and bloody."[74] Pistols flashed close and sabres thudded home in gritty collisions of men and horses. The Virginians managed to take the field, but the outnumbered Federals again won the time for Elder's drivers to limber the guns and make their escape.[75]

This attack proved the last straw for Richmond. "The enemy pressed my command so closely as to throw it into considerable confusion." Worse still, Richmond now began taking fire from Captain McGregor's Confederate horse battery, just up from Williamsport.[76] Richmond had done all anyone could expect and more. He turned on the Downsville Road and joined Kilpatrick in the Federal retreat.[77] "I retired with my command in tolerable order in the direction of Boonsborough."[78] Elder's tireless battery again formed the rear guard, trading fire with Chew's gunners into the evening, the fuses on the shells tracing bright across the twilight sky.[79] "It is 8 ½ o'clock, they are on the run," wrote Rebel gunner Charles McVicar. "We have driven them six miles; this has been a very heavy division and certainly a hard fight. One of our men, a Mr. Wright, was mortally wounded."[80]

22

BOONSBORO AND
THE SALISBURY LINE

Following the fights at Hagerstown and Williamsport, Buford, Kilpatrick, and Stuart all retired to neutral corners with one side largely frustrated and the other greatly relieved. By the morning of July 7, General Meade and General Lee were mostly of the same mind-set as their cavalry commanders. Meade still sat at Gettysburg, wading through reports, firing off dispatches, and trying to discern Lee's plans, though several things had become apparent: Lee was in retreat, the Potomac was over its banks, and a large number of enemy wagons were parked at Williamsport waiting for the river to drop. The question remained, did Lee intend to cross the Potomac to Virginia, or offer another battle above the river? If Meade could discover the correct course, he could streamline the process of transporting his supplies and better direct his infantry.

On July 6, a signal station reported the Fairfield Road clear of enemy troops, but General Sedgwick remained static east of Fairfield Pass, still under orders to avoid a general engagement. Sedgwick sent scouts forward and determined the enemy continued to hold the pass with a strong rear guard. Sedgwick's information seemed to have concerned Meade over whether Lee might linger close to South Mountain and contest the many passes in South Mountain instead of making an all-out dash for the Potomac.[1] "All evidence seems to show a movement [by the enemy] to Hagerstown and the Potomac," wrote Meade to Sedgwick, "but I apprehend they will be likely to let you alone, if you let them alone."[2] Meade recommended a non-Spartan approach and instructed Sedgwick to passively "reconnoiter in all directions, and let me know the result."[3]

On the evening of July 6, Lincoln's temper rose as he wrote General in Chief Halleck, complaining that the Army of the Potomac seemed satisfied to only drive Lee back across the Potomac rather than destroy his army and end the war.[4] Meade also drew Lincoln's ire when he halted his pursuit of Lee's army until he could determine Lee's intent. "These things all appear to me to be connected with a purpose to cover Baltimore and Washington, and to get the enemy across the river again without a further collision," complained Lincoln. "[T]hey do not appear connected with a purpose to prevent [Lee's] crossing and to destroy him."[5]

That same day, Meade received a report from John McIntosh's brigade, tracking Lee's army down to Fairfield Gap above Monterey Pass. "I proceeded with my command . . . and soon met the enemy's picket, which I drove in, capturing a dispatch showing the position of both Generals Longstreet's and Ewell's corps." McIntosh quickly forwarded this crucial intelligence on to Pleasonton and Meade: "I . . . found that, in order to reach the enemy, it became necessary for me to advance in a deep mountain gorge, where it would be impossible to use either cavalry or artillery to advantage."[6] Meade issued orders for the pursuit of Lee's army to begin the following morning. Instead of a direct pursuit through the upper mountain passes where all the advantages would favor Lee, Meade chose a second option and "determined to follow the enemy by a flank movement."[7]

Meade left McIntosh's cavalry and a supporting force of infantry to harass and pursue Lee's troops down through the mountain passes while Meade marched the greater part of his infantry down on the east side of South Mountain, and planned to cross over the mountain in the passes near Middleton, Maryland. Once west of the mountain, Meade would move to attack Lee in the Cumberland Valley. "If I can get the Army of the Potomac in hand in the valley . . . I shall give him battle."[8]

∼

Still more rain fell on July 7, turning the already flooded Potomac into a raging torrent. Downed trees rolled in the current like driftwood, and piles of debris crashed against the banks in the heavy current, prohibiting the use of even a cable ferry at Williamsport. This news, and the wrecked pontoon bridge at Falling Waters, convinced Lee to build a defensive line north of the Potomac to resist the Federal pursuit until the river dropped to a fordable level. Studying the terrain, Lee and his engineers picked a line nearly ten miles long to shield the two crossing points. Building a line of that scope would be a formidable task and take several days to complete. Lee looked to Stuart to buy the time and slow the Yankee pursuit.[9]

Stuart began shifting his troopers to comply, but he also took advantage of the stranded supply wagons at Williamsport to shoe some of his horses.[10] Despite losing the contest at Gettysburg, the Confederates had enjoyed a semi-steady stream of grain and provisions for their horses gained in Maryland and Pennsylvania by quartermasters and private soldiers alike. Many Southern artillery and cavalry horses had recently fared better than their Northern counterparts, in large part due to the close proximity of Lee's supply wagons, and Stuart's horses certainly benefited from these provisions.[11] As the rain continued, Stuart placed Robertson's remaining troopers above Hagerstown on the Smithsburg Road to scout that approach, and he set Ferguson's brigade, on his right, above Downsville to cover Falling Waters, where Longstreet's I Corps began taking positions.[12] In his center, Jones's brigade would patrol the National Road, linking Hagerstown with Funkstown and Boonsboro, as the rain continued to fall. "It may appear grand and delightful to talk of soldiering," remembered a Confederate ranker, "but the reality, sleeping in a mud hole, the rain wetting to the skin with but a filthy saddle blanket to keep out the cold is exactly the reverse."[13]

On the evening of July 7, pickets from the 7th Virginia ran into elements of the 6th U.S. Cavalry along the National Road. The 6th U.S. charged and drove in the Rebel picket, pressing the Confederates back down the roadbed. As the Federals pursued, Lieutenant Colonel Thomas Marshall countercharged the Regulars with the balance of the 7th Virginia. Still chafing from Grumble Jones's rebuke of their performance at Fairfield, Marshall put two companies into the woods on his right and still more to the left.[14] Taken unawares on multiple flanks, a forward Federal officer bungled the act of ordering a volley, and the Regulars were thrown into confusion and ran back for their reserves.[15]

The Virginians put spurs to their mounts and flew into the Federals "with great rapidity," killing and wounding a number of Regulars in the road, and putting the rest into flight along the National Road.[16] The rout continued for miles until the Federals bottlenecked at a high arcing bridge and the 7th Virginia closed on their heels. "[A]s the affrighted [Federal] men and horses swarmed upon it, numbers were crowded off and over the side, and fell headlong down into the water below."[17] A total thrashing ensued; the Federals eventually fled the bridge, but the Virginians overpursued, as cavalry often did, and came back on blown horses after losing many of their captives.[18] Grumble Jones was pleased nonetheless. "The day at Fairfield is nobly and fully avenged. The Sixth U.S. Regular Cavalry numbers among the things that were."[19] Though roughly handled, the 6th U.S. Cavalry survived to fight another day as mounted combat rarely created massed casualties. Regardless, the troopers of the 7th Virginia were glad to be out of Grumble's angry sights and back on their usual footing.

◦∾◦

On the following morning of July 8, Buford began screening the approach of General Meade's army across South Mountain and down to Boonsboro. The VI and XI Corps, commanded by generals Sedgwick and Howard, respectively, led Meade's advance. Most of Meade's army, which had been holding east of South Mountain while Meade gauged Lee's intent, now followed, and the Federal infantry slogged forward over saturated roads turned into muddy ribbons by the recent rains.[20] Despite the flooded conditions, Buford still had his orders, and he meant to clear the National Road for Meade's infantry.[21]

Likewise, Stuart moved down the National Road, intent on stalling the Federal advance. Just as Buford meant to screen Meade's army, Stuart meant to screen the remainder of Lee's army and allow these final elements to pass Hagerstown and take positions in Lee's new perimeter above the Potomac. To stall the Federals, Stuart set the brigades of Chambliss, Lee, Baker, and Jones heading down the National Road, with Jones striking the lead.[22] Moving separately from Downsville came Ferguson's brigade with their Enfield rifles.[23]

The Battle of Boonsboro began along the banks of Beaver Creek, where the flooded stream intersected the National Road. Jones's men discovered the Federal picket at the creek, but the flooded fields beyond were covered in water and maneuvering above a trot risked injuring the horses. Sharpshooters pressed forward instead and took some prisoners before the Federal picket fell back for Boonsboro.[24] A Union signal station perched on South Mountain spotted Stuart's movements and promptly flagged Buford. Orders went to Gamble, and he advanced his own dismounts on the National Road. The rest of his command remained mounted in close support with views across the open fields west of the town.[25]

As Jones's men advanced, Lieutenant Calef's six-gun battery opened fire on the Confederates, and Captain Chew's gunners opened in reply.[26] Cannon fire swept the countryside as troopers dismounted, counted fours, and filed through the water-logged fields and scattered woodlots. Carbines cracked sharply as Jones deployed east of the National Road, across from Gamble's men. Fitz Lee and Chambliss then deployed to the west opposite Devin's brigade and Merritt's Regulars.[27] "We drove the enemy back," recalled a Confederate gunner, "but they fought stubbornly . . . and contested every inch of ground."[28]

Stuart's men made repeated advances along the road and moved a battery to the west near a large barn. Calef's Federal gunners soon found the range, and "some good firing was done" causing the Southern battery to retire.[29] Undeterred, Stuart held his ground and bid his time. His goal remained the same: buy Lee time in the rear by keeping the enemy occupied in his front. The flooded fields and converging roads leading into Boonsboro slowed the Federals and aided Stuart's efforts considerably, and the roads gave Stuart a second avenue of attack as Ferguson arrived and pressed forward to flank Devin's Federals on the Union left.

As the firing increased, Kilpatrick's division came forward to support Buford, placing Custer's brigade on the Union left and holding Richmond's brigade in reserve on the right. Lieutenant Colonel Litchfield of the 7th Michigan recalled the artillery fire pouring at three squadrons supporting a Union battery: "[S]uch shelling I never saw, the Reb guns were too many and the range too good for our guns." Solid shot plowed up the ground as shells burst overhead, forward, and beyond. The heavy bombardment grew too much for one of Litchfield's junior officers, who dismounted and crouched down in fear. Litchfield rode over and quietly explained to the officer that he must remount for the sake of his men; the officer remounted.[30]

As the 1st Vermont prepared to deploy, Kilpatrick inquired how many cartridges the troopers carried. Learning they had received the standard issue of forty per man, Kilpatrick insisted each man take sixty rounds forward. This exceeded the regulation weight limit for the horses, but Kilpatrick remained adamant and loudly insisted the men take extra ammunition for what promised to be a lengthy engagement.[31] "The firing was very sharp at times," recalled one of Custer's officers, "and took on the character of skirmishing, [with] the men taking advantage of every cover that presented itself."[32]

Colonel Richmond dismounted the 18th Pennsylvania and advanced them at the double quick against a force of enemy sharpshooters rooted in a "thick piece of woods and large rocks." Richmond then directed Elder's gunners to open fire on the enemy; Richmond added another gun from Pennington's battery to the onslaught, and "the enemy soon began a precipitate retreat," allowing Richmond to take the position.[33]

Stuart countered the Federal moves by advancing Ferguson's brigade on his right with McGregor's battery in support. Ferguson's troopers ran forward, securing a position along a stone fence and opening on Devin's 17th Pennsylvania and the 6th New York in a heavy firefight across the fences. The firing escalated, and Devin's men resorted to firing their pistols when their carbines ran dry.[34] Devin quickly shuffled fresh troops into the line, and Custer's men pushed against Ferguson. "The Confederates were behind a stone fence," wrote a Michigan officer. "[W]e [were] in a piece of woods along a rail fence which ran along the edge of the timber. Between

**Figure 22.1. A period rendition of the fighting at Boonsboro from *Frank Leslie's Il-
lustrated Newspaper*, August 8, 1863. *Dickerson College*.**

was an open field."[35] Volleys rolled back and forth in a standoff; at one
point, a Rebel officer jumped atop the stone wall and exhorted his men to
advance. The quick-firing Spencers knocked him to the ground, and no
one attempted a similar act.

As the firing increased, Captain William McGregor spotted a piece of
high ground, charged his guns forward, and opened a devastating enfilade
fire upon the Federal line.[36] "[The enemy's] batteries [were] driven away
from the hill by the Napoleons of McGregor's battery," wrote Stuart.[37] The
deadly fire pouring from these guns forced a Union retreat and signaled
a serious threat to not only Boonsboro but also the passes through South
Mountain beyond.[38]

The Federal retreat prompted a reporter from the *New York Times*
to write the following: "The enemy, facile in expedients, moved in force
to the left, and made an attack upon what was then our weakest point."[39]
With his line enfiladed by Rebel guns, and his troops falling to the rear,
Buford sent an urgent request to Meade for infantry to come over the
mountain and support his deteriorating position.[40]

McGregor's gunners then came under a "plunging fire" from Pennington's Federal battery stationed on a high knoll in the Boonsboro cemetery. The ensuing duel lasted half an hour, with McGregor's smoothbores
eventually gaining the upper hand. A Federal lieutenant wrote after the
war, "Every shot you fired that missed something in my battery hit a marble
tombstone in that graveyard and the broken fragments of marble came like

hail upon my men. You were ruining us. We did not think it fair for you to shoot tombstones at us, and we left."[41]

Drifting northeast of town, Buford repositioned on high ground and Stuart's men followed, investing the woods held earlier by Custer to the west of the National Road, while Chew's battery moved forward on the east side of the road.[42] Chew's advance resulted in another gun duel between the batteries until the sun began to wane, and Federal infantry advanced over South Mountain via Turner's Gap. Upon seeing the Union foot soldiers, Stuart decided to leave while it still remained his idea, and issued orders for a withdrawal.[43]

Buford's Federals pursued immediately. Gamble's brigade pitched forward on foot, retaking the ground they lost and continuing on. "The men had run so fast that they were completely tired out, but were pleased to see General Buford shake his fat sides, as he attempted to keep up with them."[44] Kilpatrick's men joined in the Federal rush, with Custer's and Richmond's brigades retaking their former positions west of town.

Pressing after the Confederates, Colonel Richmond spotted an opportunity for a charge on the enemy column along a section of the Hagerstown Turnpike. Major William Wells of the 1st Vermont led his battalion forward and swept down upon the rear of Stuart's troopers.[45] Captain J. H. Barry of the 1st South Carolina Cavalry wheeled about and met the Yankee charge at a gallop.[46] Wells's men piled into the Southern horsemen "hilt to hilt," and the two sides mixed in a plunging jumble on the pike. "Horses and riders intermingled recklessly," the opposing troopers closed knee to knee, and the "sabres of each party . . . parried and thrust in deadly strife."[47] Major Wells engaged a pair of Confederates and received a glancing thrust across his ribs. A second blow landed across his back, and the bleeding major was pressed to the rear as his troopers fought the Rebels in a tight riot of swinging blades and cracking pistols.[48] Vermont sergeant Jerome Hatch fell pinned beneath his horse; seeing Major Wells in trouble, Hatch took aim from the ground and shot a Confederate still pressing the wounded major. Wells finally broke clear and made back for his lines.[49]

The New Englanders fell back in their major's wake. Captain Barry and his South Carolinians let them go. Lieutenant Colonel Preston, the 1st Vermont's commander, wrote, "[T]he charge was spiritedly made and sabers freely used, as the heads of my men will attest."[50] Neither side pressed the issue further. As was often the case, the mounted contest came to a close as quickly as it started.

Stuart continued pulling back along the National Road. As the last of his troops crossed Beaver Creek, a squadron of the 7th Michigan bolted forward in a horse charge. Posted at the creek was a single Blakely gun from Chew's battery, and as the Rebel gunners prepared to fire, the Yankees spotted the gun and veered off the road. Chew's gunners opened fire, timing their fuses with unerring accuracy at the zigzagging Wolverines, who sprinted and splashed across the water-logged fields.

"Never did [a] sportsman bring down his bird with more unerring shot," wrote Stuart. "In vain did it turn to the right and left. Each shell seemed drawn to the flying target with fatal accuracy."[51] Darting about in the mud, Allyne Litchfield of the 7th Michigan described the enemy fire as "brisk" in a letter to his wife. Litchfield also deadpanned a scene in the action with a veteran's sense of gallows humor. A shell burst near Colonel William Mann and unhorsed the colonel; Litchfield remarked that Colonel Mann, though unhurt, "got off his horse pretty quick"—classic horse soldier parlance for jumping out of the saddle. Litchfield then added dryly that Colonel Mann "says he was blown off."[52] Litchfield clearly held little respect for the horsemanship or fortitude of his commanding officer. Still more shells followed, and the Wolverines retreated. The Confederates turned and marched back up the National Road, no doubt cheering Chew's dead-eye gunners along the way.

Both sides claimed victory on the day. The 6th Michigan wrote succinctly, "Met the rebel General Stuart and his forces at the left of the Hagerstown Road, near Boonsborough, repulsing and routing his forces and driving them until night closed the pursuit."[53] One of Stuart's men saw it differently. "We drove the enemy back slowly, from the time the fight commenced until nearly night. . . . [T]he Yankee cavalry was reinforced with infantry and then they in turn drove us back a mile. . . . Nightfall ended the fray."[54]

~

Meanwhile, General Meade closed in on Turner's Gap with five corps from the Army of the Potomac. Many of his aides remembered this same ground from a year before when heavy fighting had rolled back and forth through the South Mountain passes in the Sharpsburg campaign. "Over this same mountain, and along this same road, we were then, as now, in close pursuit of the rebels," recalled a Pennsylvania veteran. "Let us hope for a more decisive issue."[55] Meade may well have agreed as he directed his army across the mountain. The Federal XII Corps and II Corps would secure Boonsboro and move southwest through Keedysville, with the V Corps marching for Antietam Creek. The VI Corps and I Corps would move for Funkstown on the National Road, and the XI Corps would hold in reserve. Nearly a week after Gettysburg, Meade's infantry would finally be on line, in range, and forming for a fight.

Meade wrote Halleck, "From all I can gather the enemy extends from Hagerstown to Williamsport. . . . Their cavalry and infantry pickets are advanced to the Hagerstown and Sharpsburg pike. . . . We hold Boonsborough, and our pickets, four miles in front, are in contact with the enemy." This dispatch is dated July 8 at 2:55 p.m., and Meade quite possibly heard the combat boiling between Buford and Stuart as he wrote. "The rains of yesterday and last night have made all roads but pikes impassable. Artillery and wagons are stalled; it will take time to collect them together. A large portion of the men are barefooted. Shoes will arrive at Frederick today, and will be issued as soon as possible." Meade continued, "I wish in advance to moderate the expectations of those who, in ignorance of the difficulties to be encountered, may expect too much."[56]

Halleck replied quickly: "There is reliable information that the enemy is crossing at Williamsport. The opportunity to attack his divided forces should not be lost. The president is urgent and anxious that your army should move against him by forced marches."[57]

This dispatch carried the quizzical tone Halleck often used in prior correspondence with Hooker. "My information as to the crossing of the enemy does not agree with that just received in your dispatch," replied Meade succinctly. "His whole force is in position between Funkstown and Williamsport. I have just received information that he has driven my cavalry force in front of Boonsborough." Meade was apparently receiving news from the ongoing fight nearby as he explained the situation on the ground to Halleck, perched safely back in Washington. "My army is and has been making forced marches, short of rations, and barefooted. One corps marched yesterday and last night over thirty miles. I take occasion to repeat that I will use my utmost efforts to push forward this army."[58]

"Do not understand me as expressing any dissatisfaction," placated Halleck. "I only wish to give you opinions formed from information received here. It is telegraphed from near Harper's Ferry that the enemy have been crossing for the last two days . . . that they have a bridge across. If Lee's army is so divided . . . the importance of attacking the part on this side is incalculable. Such an opportunity may never occur again."[59]

Meade would have disregarded this news. On July 5, Union general William French heard the Rebels had planked the railroad bridge at Harper's Ferry to allow wagons across it. French sent Federal cavalry, under Major H. A. Cole, who removed the planking and destroyed the

Figure 22.2. General in Chief Henry Halleck. A number of Lincoln's generals found Halleck difficult to work with. *Library of Congress*.

trestle supporting the bridge, effectively truncating all Confederate efforts at crossing the river at Harper's Ferry.[60] The following morning, July 9, Meade wrote Halleck, "I am still under the impression that Lee's whole army is between Hagerstown and Williamsport." Meade planned to cross South Mountain with his infantry and deploy more than a five-mile front from Boonsboro to Rohrersville, Maryland. "My cavalry will be pushed today well to the front, on the right and left, and I hope will collect information."[61]

～

While no doubt heartening, the future promise of infantry support at the front gave little solace to Tom Devin's troopers as they rode north on July 9 for Beaver Creek, three miles above Boonsboro. Pressing up the road, Devin had orders to cross the creek and "if practicable feel the enemy's position."[62] As Devin neared the creek, he scouted the position and threw forward a mounted skirmish line on his left to sweep ahead. Devin ordered Lieutenant Albert Vincent, 2nd U.S. Artillery, to prepare for an advance to the high ground of a ridge on the far side of the creek, which might serve as a good artillery platform.[63] Devin dismounted two additional squadrons of sharpshooters in support of Vincent and next extended his right flank to make contact with Gamble's brigade, who trailed in echelon.[64]

The advance began, and Devin pressed forward and engaged Ferguson's Confederate brigade beyond the creek. Supported by Captain Thomas Jackson's battery, Ferguson's men held the Rebel center, and to the right lay a second enemy brigade under Chambliss. A "short but sharp" fire ensued as the two sides opened fire upon one another. Cannon shells and rifle balls whistled through the air, and men from each side sprinted for a snake rail fence along a cornfield separating the combatants. Ferguson's Wildcats in the 17th Virginia won the race; they leveled a brutal volley at the Federals weaving through the cornstalks and shot down a number of Devin's men. The remaining Federals redoubled their fire, and volleys rolled back and forth through the corn and across the fence. "The air above our heads seemed to be full of splinters, bark and bullets," wrote a Rebel trooper, "but we were thus far safe . . . as the enemies' bullets mostly struck the top of the fence."[65]

Meanwhile, Vincent's drivers stormed upon the ridge, and opened a rapid fire on Chambliss's men below. Shells streamed through the Confederate ranks, and the accurate fire forced Chambliss to retire, in turn opening Ferguson's flank. Devin's troopers seized the opportunity and charged forward, rolling up Ferguson's line and forcing a Confederate retreat.

Gamble's brigade quickly joined the push, and the combined Federals swept forward for two miles, pressing the Confederates up the National Road toward Funkstown. A Confederate battery finally came into play, but the sun went down shortly after and put an end to the combat.[66] One New York trooper summed up the day's events in the flattest possible terms: "Out again. Found the rebels about 5 p.m. and made them get up and get."[67] Devin's men proudly bivouacked on the ground they'd won. Unfortunately, no Union infantry was yet in range to take advantage of the hard-won advance.

~

Back at Meade's headquarters, the telegraph kept a stream of information pouring in as Meade and his staff waded through stacks of dispatches from the Bureau of Military Intelligence. Reports of cavalry scouts, civilian sightings, interrogations of enemy deserters, and newspaper articles littered headquarters. Multiple dispatches reported Confederates bringing supplies and artillery ammunition northward, back over the Potomac and into Maryland, which made the Federals uneasy.[68]

These conflicting reports raised another question altogether. Did Lee want to fight another battle north of the Potomac, or did he mean to wait for the river to drop and return to Virginia? Whiffs of doubt began crowding Meade's orders, doubts not far removed from the cautions Hooker wrestled with at the end of his tenure. It certainly didn't help that Pleasonton's cavalry had been hard pressed these last few days by Stuart's troopers in the actions at Smithsburg, Hagerstown, Williamsport, and Boonsboro, and distracted from their principal reconnaissance duties. Meade, however, still wanted to go forward, albeit cautiously, and he wrote Halleck the following: "I propose to move on a line from Boonsborough toward . . . Hagerstown to Williamsport. . . . I shall try to keep as concentrated as the roads by which I can move will admit, so that, should the enemy attack, I can move to meet him, and, if he assumes the defensive, I can deploy as I think proper. . . . I think the decisive battle of the war will be fought in a few days."[69]

~

As dawn rose on July 10, Lee had nearly completed his defensive line before the Potomac. Running along Salisbury Ridge, it extended from Conococheague Creek to the west of Williamsport, passed behind Funkstown, and then back down to Falling Waters.[70] Colonel Porter Alexander, an artillery battalion commander and trained engineer, seemed pleased with the progress. "A fairly good line was found with its right flank on the Potomac near Downsville, passing by St. James College and resting its left on the Conococheague."[71] Though not a continuous perimeter, it offered an elevated series of positions with superior fields of fire on any advancing enemy, and forced them to traverse a lengthy series of marshy bogs and open fields.[72]

Yet despite the progress made, there remained much to improve on the perimeter. In addition, the Potomac remained over its banks, Meade's infantry was across South Mountain, and Lee expected to soon be in a pitched fight with a river at his back. He looked again to his cavalry and sent the following lines to Stuart: "We must prepare for a vigorous battle. . . . Get your men in hand, and have everything ready."[73]

On July 10, Stuart waited with his troopers beside Funkstown, Maryland, a tidy farming community perched along the north bank of Antietam Creek. Largely dismounted, his men formed a broad eastern arc about the town, with Grumble Jones's men on the far Confederate left, followed by Lee, Baker, Chambliss, Robertson, and finally Ferguson anchoring the far right flank. Three roads bisected the Southern arc. The Smithsburg Road ran northwest, and Stuart placed sharpshooters from the 4th Virginia a half mile forward of his main line, with Fitz Lee in support along with Captain Basil Manley's Battery A, 1st North Carolina Artillery. Tracking right, Chambliss covered the Beaver Creek Road, and finally Ferguson covered the National Road approaching from the south, and Stuart expected the main Federal advance to occur in this sector. Stuart placed Witcher's 34th Virginia here, well forward of the perimeter's arc, and on either side of the stone fences bordering the roadway. Chew's battery waited in support.[74]

By midmorning, Buford's 1st Division drew in range of Funkstown. On his right, Merritt's Regulars approached via the Beaver Creek Road while Gamble's brigade straddled either side of the National Road and Devin's men covered the gap between Gamble and Antietam Creek. Contact first came from Gamble's brigade when they met with a party of Rebel vedettes a mile south of the town on the National Road. Gamble's men soon counted files, dismounted, and sent the horses to the rear with the number fours. Those remaining checked the loads on their carbines and stepped forward under a light rain, no doubt encouraged by the success of Devin's brigade the day before. Instead of an easy approach, they were met with a blistering fire from Witcher's 34th Virginia.

Witcher's men enjoyed good ground, thick with hedgerows and stone fences as well as Chew's battery for support, and the Federal advance quickly bogged down. Buford called forward two sections of Graham's battery, as Devin came up on Gamble's left, and began firing into Witcher's flank. With Gamble and Devin pushing simultaneously, Witcher gave ground gradually through the morning.[75]

Growing impatient, Buford dismounted and walked to the crest of a hill to glass the halting progress of his division. While there, he presented a perfect silhouette, and one of Witcher's men sent a Minié ball ripping through the general's field blouse. The ball just missed Buford but left a string of five perfect holes through the folds of his coat.[76] Buford moved to a better spot to observe from, and his men kept pressing on, steadily driving Witcher and Chew back toward Funkstown. The Federal attack grew in pitch, and Witcher eventually retreated to Stuart's main line, where he took a strong position just left of the road, adjacent to a large barn owned by the Jacob Hauck family.[77] From this elevated barn and outbuildings, Witcher's veterans opened a withering fire that swept the ground in their front and quickly arrested the building Union advance.[78] With the support of Chew's guns, Witcher had effectively shut down the Federal push on the National Road.[79]

Now seeking a resupply of ammunition, Chew's battery withdrew to fill their limbers, and Shoemaker's battery soon ran out as well. Still drawing fire, Shoemaker's gunners laid on the ground to avoid casualties until they could rotate out and resupply. Seeing the men lying prone, Stuart inquired as to the cause, and Shoemaker told Stuart they had spent their ammunition. "Let them stand up for moral effect," ordered Stuart. The gunners stood as ordered, and Stuart became forever known as "Moral Effect" within the battery.[80]

Across the line on Buford's right, Merritt's Regulars pressed forward against Captain William Wooldridge's 4th Virginia sharpshooters in a sharp fight along the Beaver Creek Road. The contest drifted back toward Funkstown and a body of boulder-strewn trees known as Stover's Wood. Merritt's troopers took cover in the woods and there came under fire from Manley's North Carolina Battery posted in Gilbert's Field. Despite the battery fire, the Federals used these woods to move sharpshooters into a series of outbuildings and a large bank barn just four hundred yards from Stuart's line.[81]

Merritt's Regulars pressed still farther right and there managed some "telling" mounted charges down the Boonsboro Road that failed to break the Southern line but secured several prisoners in a "hand-to-hand" exchange.[82] As the scope of the fight continued to grow, Stuart realized he'd need more men to contain the growing number of Federals appearing across the fields. The closest support was from Longstreet's corps, then holding a bridge over a quiet sector of Antietam Creek.[83]

Stuart sent couriers galloping back, and one soon found Colonel William White, commanding George Anderson's infantry brigade.[84] White rode back with the courier and told Stuart he was under orders from General Evander Law to hold his current position. Stuart repeated his orders for White to move his brigade at once, and White again hesitated, saying he preferred confirmation from General Law before moving anywhere. Standing in his stirrups, Stuart categorically informed White that he, in fact, commanded this portion of the field, and "as to this man, Law, he knew nothing of him." Explained in those terms, Colonel White turned about and brought up his brigade.[85]

Across the field, Buford's men were rapidly running through their carbine ammunition. Witcher had already stopped Buford cold on his left, and Buford responded by calling on General Albion Howe of Sedgwick's VI Corps back in the rear. Up to this point, Sedgwick's infantry had taken no actual part in the fight and had, instead, parked behind the lines, where the infantry began brewing coffee, content to let the cavalry determine their own fate. "We were hard pressed by the enemy," recalled a frustrated Gamble, "and nearly all our ammunition expended, the infantry [meanwhile] pitched their shelter tents and commenced cooking and eating."[86]

This lackadaisical attitude stemmed from the fact that the infantry had no explicit orders to advance or aid the cavalry.[87] Be that as it may, Buford's men continued to burn through their ammunition, prompting Buford to ease his troopers back off the line. This left the infantry no choice but to advance and fill the troopers' former positions. Colonel Lewis A. Grant's Vermont Brigade stepped forward and replaced Gamble's men along the National Road, as well as Merritt's Regulars in Stover's Wood.

As Grant moved into position, Colonel White's Georgians arrived on the scene, and a staff officer escorted White to the front and delivered him into the hands of Fitz Lee. Happy to see support, Lee ordered White to advance his command through a defile and then deploy in view of the enemy. White objected straightaway: "I was ordered by General Lee to move forward by the flank through a narrow lane, *a la cavalry*, to within 150 yards of the enemy before deploying in line of battle."[88]

Advancing in that manner, on foot, down a channeling lane before a waiting enemy and then changing front was synonymous with high casualties, and White protested, "wishing to deploy my command [into line] before they were under fire." Fitz Lee wasn't having it and repeated his command. White went in as directed, his men carrying their muskets at right shoulder shift while the Federal infantry and artillery took the Georgians under fire. General Longstreet later said his men "had dire complaints to make of the way cavalrymen put them in columns of fours . . . when they could have advanced more rapidly and effectively in line of battle and saved half of their men lost."[89] Despite the losses, the Georgians kept coming. They absorbed the fire and pressed ahead, driving off several Federals who'd been harassing Fitz Lee's front. Unfortunately, the Georgians then suffered a volley of friendly shell fire caused by defective fuses.[90] The errant shells killed six men in one company alone and completely disordered the right side of the brigade. The stalwart Georgians redressed again and pushed on for Stover's Wood.[91]

Colonel Grant's Vermont infantry saw the Georgians coming and began kneeling behind boulders and bracing against trees. While they waited, they stacked cartridges on the ground to save time in loading. "We emptied our cartridges right out on the ground, laying the percussion caps with them and the rammers on the ground." Grant's men waited until the Georgians came to a stone fence two hundred yards out and opened a brutally accurate fire by files. The Georgians reeled under the rolling fire, but they kept coming in two crisp battle ranks and advanced to a second fence just a hundred yards from the woods. "But by this time their double line of battle had melted to almost a skirmish line," recalled a Vermonter. "[T]hey got back out of reach as quickly as possible."[92] Fitz Lee finally ordered Colonel White to desist and return to the line.[93]

The combat wound down with desultory shooting and sniping until nightfall. Casualties had been high for a minor engagement, with the Federals suffering more than 190 killed, wounded, and missing, and the Confederate casualties hovering around 280, with more than 120 men falling in White's Georgia Brigade.[94] Stretcher-bearers brought the wounded into the small town, where the surgeons set up tables in a private yard beneath some shade trees, and began cutting "arms and legs like sawing limbs from a tree."[95]

Stuart's men and mounts could hardly stand as the sun fell below the horizon.

23

FALLING WATERS

The time bought by Stuart and his troopers did not go unused. While the fighting echoed across the countryside, Lee's engineers, artillerists, and infantry continued constructing their menacing line of gun emplacements, trenches, and breastworks.[1] By July 11, the new Confederate perimeter stretched over nine miles long, originating west of Hagerstown and running east to Downsville and beyond. Cannons formed interlacing fields of fire, and the placement of the lines would force the Federals to attack across largely open ground, with much of it flooded from recent rains. As an added buffer, Hagerstown remained in Confederate hands and acted as a redan, or grand lunette, forward of the main Confederate position with the troops ready to retire at a moment's notice to the main Rebel line of entrenchments.[2] Stephens Smith of Company K, 2nd South Carolina Cavalry, took a moment behind the trenches to write his parents. "Not many of the Brooks Troop are [still] with us, we number but twelve or fifteen, some were left in Virginia, others have lost their horses and are in the rear." As he wrote Smith could hear guns in the distance. "Artillery firing is now going on, and our Army is in line of battle. Lee has a better position than he had at the Gettysburg fight and no fears are felt as to the result, though the battle will be another bloody and desperate one."[3]

Colonel Porter Alexander commanded the I Corps artillery reserve on the Confederate right and felt the new line would hold. Alexander even hoped the Federal infantry would come out and make an attack.[4] Lee, however, remained wary, and Alexander remembered watching the general's exacting involvement over the placing of troops in the new line. "I never before, and never afterward, saw him [Gen. Lee] as I thought [so] visibly anxious over an approaching action."[5]

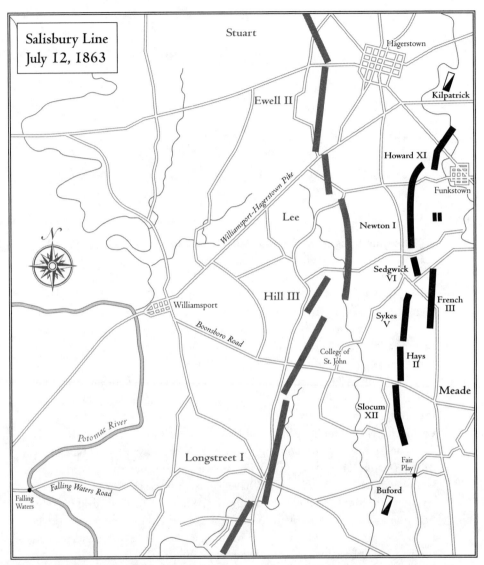

Map 17.   Salisbury Line July 12, 1863

Lee knew the survival of his army lay at stake. His engineers had done a masterful job creating this new line above the Potomac, and starting on July 5, his quartermasters began operating a single cable ferry at Williamsport that shuffled the wounded across the river into Virginia. On each return trip, the ferry carried artillery limbers back to Maryland to help replenish Lee's artillery ammunition;[6] however, one ferry operating in spurts between flooded tides could not refill all the limber chests in one week's time.[7] If the Federals did attack, Lee may not have enough ammunition to repel a lengthy, sustained attack. The solution lay in rebuilding the pontoon bridge at Falling Waters. Confederate pioneers launched a colossal effort and began stripping lumber from the river warehouses in Williamsport. Pioneers worked round the clock, constructing pontoons at Williamsport and floating them downstream to Falling Waters, where they began combining the new craft with the few surviving boats left from Major Foley's earlier raid. When the pontoon bridge became operational, Lee would have more freedom in choosing to fight or retreat.

For the past week, Meade had refitted, rerigged, and resupplied his Army of the Potomac. A week's worth of marching, shuffling, and skirmishing saw Meade's army through the Fairfield Gap and across South Mountain, to finally arrive before Lee's new lines above the Potomac. Pleasonton's cavalry led the pursuit throughout, and now pressed toward Hagerstown on the Federal right, Funkstown in the center, and Downsville on the far Federal left. As July 12 dawned, Union horse soldiers continued to press ahead. Kilpatrick's brigades swept into Hagerstown, and the Confederates retired to waiting trenches west of town. Custer's Wolverines made for the enemy breastworks and received a sudden volley. After returning the favor, the Wolverines realized they were in a poor place for mounted combat and wheeled back for the safer environs of Hagerstown proper.[8]

Kilpatrick saw it differently and ordered Custer to make another assault and clear a stone wall where enemy sharpshooters were firing upon the Federals. Custer balked, and Kilpatrick turned to Captain Jones and his escort company of Ohioans. "Go and pick up those men, use your pistols on them."[9] Jones charged forward with his company, spurred first through a gate, then a barnyard, and crossed a field at a gallop to gain the sharpshooters' flank. Union gunners launched several shells over Jones's company in support, and this fire deterred a mounted counterattack by the Confederate cavalry as the Rebel sharpshooters bolted for the protection of another wall. Jones's company caught them before they could form a line and captured twenty-six men and a lieutenant.

The escort company returned to the lines in what all agreed had almost been a deadly encounter, but for a liberal dash of good luck and an alert Federal battery. Luck or no, the unit historian still made the following entry: "This was the second time we had charged where Custer and his Michigan men had refused to go."[10]

Elsewhere that morning, Buford's troopers probed the far right of Lee's new line east of Downsville. Buford wrote that the enemy line "extends south toward the river, in a very rugged country, with many stone walls parallel to their front." Buford considered the portion beside the river to be "impracticable for any considerable force" to advance across.[11] Much like the works Custer discovered beside Hagerstown, Buford found the position well designed and formidable. Buford added the Potomac's current remained too strong and the water too high for troops to wade across the ford.[12]

Farther north, Huey's brigade from Gregg's division pushed forward near St. James College, where they found Rebel infantry in force. Calling up artillery, Huey dismounted sharpshooters and pressed ahead, driving the enemy pickets back from their first position and into a "long line of rifle pits just back from the college, and covering the ground in that vicinity." The Federals secured a few prisoners but lacked the numbers to extend their front and engage the rifle pits.[13] Eager to press ahead, Huey requested infantry support from General Henry Slocum of the XII Corps, but Slocum denied the request.[14]

Despite the scouts and gains of his cavalry, Meade appeared unwilling to bring on a general engagement against what appeared on all counts to be a stout defensive line constructed by the Confederate engineers. The day prior, Meade directed General Sedgwick to advance his brigades against Funkstown, until the enemy is "found in superior force." Once they discovered the enemy, Meade wanted them to hold their ground. Oddly enough, Federal cavalry had already reported the town clear of enemy troops.[15] Still, Meade wanted an advance, but stressed the action would be a foot reconnaissance and nothing more—even if compelled to fight by the enemy. "It is not the intention that you should support this force further than its return, [and only] if pressed." Meade wanted to locate the enemy perimeter, but without risking a counterattack or loss of ground.[16]

Meade appeared to be saving his infantry for a grand push once he had all the correct elements in place, and seemed obsessed with avoiding the slightest mistake. His hesitancy also offered little risk to the Army of the Potomac's reputation. If Meade attacked north of the Potomac and suffered a defeat, Lee could rightly claim a victory north of the river, and Meade's army would lose its champion status. These thoughts may or may not have been guiding Meade's actions up to this point. What is certain is that Meade had effectively pinned Lee's army against a flooded river, and the Army of the Potomac now stood within range to make an assault; in fact, large portions of the Rebel lines could now be seen with the naked eye from Union positions. If Meade launched a successful attack while Lee lay trapped against the river, he could possibly destroy Lee's army and end the war.

The weight of command now settled on Meade's shoulders.

On the afternoon of July 12, news arrived warranting the general's attention. In the last twenty-four hours, the Potomac River had fallen eighteen inches, meaning the ford at Williamsport could soon drop to a level allowing foot traffic. If the river fell as expected, Lee's army might begin crossing the following day. Time now became a crucial element in Meade's plans. Rather than order an attack, Meade called a council of war.[17]

The council met that evening. Meade told the members that Lee held a sound position, and Meade believed Lee had prepared for a battle. Meade added he had not yet made an ample reconnaissance, and he did not have a precise method or a point of attack yet planned. Meade stated he "was in favor of moving forward and attacking the enemy and taking the consequences." The council held a vote, and six members voted against an attack. Three members voted in favor: Oliver Howard, James Wadsworth, and Alfred Pleasonton.[18] "The opinion," continued Meade, "of the council was very largely opposed to any attack without further examination."[19]

Meade honored the vote. There would be no Federal attack on July 13. Instead, Meade would lead a small reconnaissance party to make plans for a future attack on the Confederate position.

Lee woke on the morning of July 13 fully expecting an attack by the Federals. He didn't know about Meade's council of war, and he guessed the main enemy push would come between the Boonsboro Road and the Frederick Road—across the combined fronts of Hill's and Longstreet's corps.[20] The Confederate left promised to be less active, and Lee planned to rely heavily on Stuart, directing him to make plans for leading his horse gunners forward in a charge against the Federal right flank. "I wish you to bear down on the enemy's right, endeavoring to select good positions for your horse artillery, to harass and retard them."[21]

Stuart made ready. Skirmish fire ran up and down the line throughout the morning, yet no Federal attack materialized. Hours ticked by, noon came and went, and the level of the Potomac continued to fall until the repaired pontoon bridge at Falling Waters became safe to stretch across the diminishing current. Confederate engineers launched the bridge and completed the rigging, and Lee's quartermasters began shuffling hundreds of waiting ambulances, sustenance wagons, and ordnance across the bridge. Still no Federal attack came forward, and Grumble Jones's brigade received orders to cross the river and prepare to guard the wagon trains on their way to the Shenandoah Valley.[22]

Stuart also received new orders. Come nightfall, the Confederate infantry would begin crossing the river: Ewell by wading the ford at Williamsport, Hill and Longstreet by the pontoon bridge at Falling Waters. Stuart's troopers would then man the near ten-mile front and hold the Federals at bay until dawn. Once the sun rose, Stuart's troopers would cross the river.[23]

～

While Meade conducted his July 13 reconnaissance, Judson Kilpatrick kept looking for a fight outside Hagerstown. Though the Federals already held the town, Kilpatrick continued to cast about for orders as he studied the Confederate works outside of town and the cloud of enemy skirmishers between. No orders came forth, and Kilpatrick soon looked to the 33rd Pennsylvania Militia, known as the Pennsylvania Blues. The "Blues" were green volunteers, called up by President Lincoln in response to the recent invasion. Seeking to try the militia's nerve, Kilpatrick ordered the self-styled Blues to advance against the Rebel skirmishers; however, the militia would not advance beyond the cover afforded by the houses on the outskirts of Hagerstown.[24]

Kilpatrick then sent Sergeant Hyram Judy, a flag-bearer from his escort, to lead the militia forward. Rebel skirmish fire whistled about the advancing Blues, and the militia quickly retreated to the houses ringing Hagerstown. Judy remained at the front in plain sight, and the flag quickly drew the fire of Confederate skirmishers while the militia continued to crouch behind any cover they could find. Frustrated at the balking militia, Kilpatrick ordered a charge from his 1st Brigade.[25]

Colonel Edward Sawyer of the 1st Vermont had just returned to the front following a lengthy medical absence. On his arrival, Sawyer replaced Nathaniel Richmond as the senior officer and commander of the 1st Brigade, but despite the date of his commission, Sawyer had seen little action before his absence and remained largely inexperienced. He now watched Captain William Cummings of Company D, 1st Vermont, charge forward and drive in the enemy skirmishers.[26] Following Cummings's success, either Sawyer or Kilpatrick ordered Captain Robert Schofield to take another Vermont squadron farther toward the enemy, and charge down a fence-lined road to grab a few prisoners. Supported by the Pennsylvania Blues, the squadron galloped forward and ran into a stiff gauntlet of fire. Schofield and his men continued on, drawing fire from Rebel batteries and almost reaching the enemy breastworks before a Confederate bayonet swept

Schofield from his saddle. Schofield's troopers took two Rebel prisoners in a hand-to-hand exchange and then turned for their lines after losing a number of men.[27] As the Federals retired to Hagerstown, Hyram Judy received a Rebel bullet through his knee but still returned with the flag. He died from the wound shortly after.[28]

Colonel Sawyer later made the following casual entry in his diary: "Capt. Schofield wounded and probably a prisoner. Spirited little affair. Loss of thirteen men."[29] Kilpatrick reportedly received a dispatch from Meade, wherein the commanding general claimed Kilpatrick's actions had "disarranged all his plans, as [Meade] intended attacking the enemy the next morning."[30] Meade's note purportedly launched Kilpatrick into a diatribe maligning Meade's hesitant actions, while Kilpatrick defended his own maneuvers and claimed his attacks had been necessary to check the enemy in order to hold Hagerstown. Kilpatrick then added, "I know that is not quite true, but I did not want the cowardly militia to return home without meeting the enemy."[31]

～

That evening the rain returned as the Confederate infantry started shuffling to the river. Gunners replaced cannons with "Quaker" guns made from pine logs, and Stuart's troopers moved into the trenches with their carbines.[32] "We were ordered to dismount, and we took the places of the infantry in the rifle ditches. The retreat of the army to Virginia had begun, the enemy [still] hesitating to give battle."[33] The rain increased through the night, turning the trails to the Potomac into quagmires and causing the river to rise yet again. Confusion spread everywhere, signal fires smoldered in the falling rain, and smoke ran down the lines as the Confederates slogged down to the river at Williamsport and forded the river with the water chest high and rising. Late in the night the rain lifted, and as dawn rose on July 14, the mud-crusted Army of Northern Virginia had largely completed the crossing just ahead of the rising current.

Captain William Blackford of Stuart's staff wrote, "I witnessed the passage of Ewell's corps. . . . [O]n either bank fires illuminated the scene. . . . By the bright lurid light, the long line of heads and shoulders and the dim sparkling of their musket barrels could be traced across the watery space." Stuart's cavalry crossed next, with many troopers grabbing their saddle pommels and letting their horses swim them across the rising current while holding carbines overhead. Many of the mules pulling wagons weren't as lucky, and a number drowned in the rising water and floated downstream.[34]

Already across, staff officer Frank Robertson swam back to the north side with a dispatch from Stuart for Ferguson's brigade, now serving as the rear guard at Williamsport. Stuart wanted Ferguson's people to fall back, and as Robertson rode ahead, he found Ferguson's men already heading for the river at speed: "[T]hey were coming full tilt with lots of Yankees following."[35] Union cavalry fired at Robertson as he swam back across with his mare, Miranda. "[She] plunged head under and commenced swimming, lifted again on a ledge, then another plunge." Robertson ditched his sabre to swim beside his tiring mare as the bullets splashed and skipped around them. "After sundry deep plunges, we reached the Virginia shore."[36] Robertson found Stuart watching Ferguson's troopers cross the river. A Federal shell burst amid the 14th Virginia, killing one officer and wounding two more.[37] Southern guns opened in reply, and the Northern fire ceased as the last of Ferguson's men swam the river.[38]

~

While watching the last Confederates gain the far bank at Williamsport, Buford received a dispatch. The rest of Lee's troops were still crossing five miles downriver at Falling Waters. Buford duly notified Kilpatrick to drive for Falling Waters, where Buford hoped they could pair up and pin the Confederate rear guard between their two divisions. Kilpatrick turned out quickly and arrived above Falling Waters well ahead of Buford. Rather than wait on a rival division, Kilpatrick pressed ahead on his own, eager to close with the Confederates as he pushed down Falling Waters Road.

Major Peter Weber of the 6th Michigan led the forward squadron of troops B and F, while Custer, Kilpatrick, and the rest of the 6th Michigan trailed behind with the brigade. "Kilpatrick was afraid he would not get there in time to overtake the enemy, so he spared neither man nor beast. The road was soft and miry . . . and the horses sank in the sticky mud. . . . [I]t was not possible to keep a single troop closed up in sets of fours."[39] As the Federals turned round a bend in the road, they passed a skirt of woods to reveal a large field with a farmhouse perched on the opposite side. The house sat on "a high hill, or knoll, on which an earthwork had been thrown up. Behind the earthwork a considerable force of Confederate Infantry was seen in bivouac."[40]

Kilpatrick quickly ordered his front squadron from the 6th Michigan to draw sabres and charge. Riding back in the center of Kilpatrick's column, Captain James Kidd watched his fellow troopers depart and later wrote, "[T]he audacity of the thing dazed [the enemy] for a minute, but for a minute only."[41]

~

The infantry Kilpatrick spotted were from Henry Heth's division, in A. P. Hill's III Corps. These men had exited their trenches at St. James Church that evening, and Hill had posted Heth's division here at the Donnelly farm-house as the III Corps' rear guard, while the rest of Hill's men negotiated the crowded pontoon bridge down at the river, some two miles away. Follow-ing orders, Heth established a headquarters at the farmhouse and deployed his division across the Falling Waters Road. Archer's brigade held the crest, with the 1st Tennessee beside the road, and the rest of the brigade spreading left: the 13th Alabama, 7th Tennessee, and 14th Tennessee, respectively.[42] Besides these men, another three infantry brigades spread across the line on the crest, but the Confederate gunners had already withdrawn the artillery from their emplacements and headed down to the river.[43]

In the farmhouse with Heth were several officers, including Brigadier General Johnston Pettigrew, whom Heth had questioned over the veracity of his initial scout on Gettysburg some two weeks prior.[44] When Heth's division arrived that morning, the men stacked arms, posted a few close guards, and soon fell asleep "feeling perfectly secure" that Stuart's cavalry sat between their ranks and the Federal advance.[45] Their confidence proved a falsehood. Most of the cavalry had already crossed at Williamsport, and Stuart left Fitz Lee's brigade to screen the rear guard at Falling Waters— just as Ferguson's men had done at Williamsport—and Fitz Lee's troopers should have been screening Heth's division at the Donnelly farmhouse. However, before Heth arrived Fitz Lee saw the lengthy traffic jam at the pontoon bridge and decided to move his brigade upstream and cross upstream at Williamsport instead. In his wake, Fitz Lee left two squadrons at Falling Waters to screen the pontoon bridge and inform General Hill of his actions.[46] Unfortunately, these two squadrons stayed down near the bridge by the river and crossed over with the last of Longstreet's I Corps, completely ignoring, or at best misunderstanding, their mission to screen Heth's rear guard remaining at the Donnelly farmhouse.

Believing friendly cavalry screened his front, Heth failed to post his own skirmish line, even though his division formed the last of Lee's infantry still in Maryland. This seems wildly inconsistent with the responsibilities of a division commander posted as the rear guard of a retreating army; how-ever, Heth continued to appear unconcerned at the sight of a squadron of troopers trotting their horses down Falling Waters Road. Gray mud caked the coming cavalry like every other Confederate in camp, and this may have aided in Heth's miscalculation.[47] All that changed when the mud-strewn cavalry drew sabres and spurred forward in a charge.

Heth now ordered his men to fire, but many were sleeping, and few had loaded rifles as the Federal squadron bolted up the hill.[48]

～

The Wolverines quickly gained the crest, then paired down to dash between the empty gun emplacements, shooting and slashing as they went. "The enemy dashed in, firing pistols and sabering everything in their way. Some men recovered their guns in time to fire . . . some ran away, some fought with empty pieces, some even had to recourse to stones. The din was horrible, the confusion inextricable."[49] The 1st Tennessee loaded and returned fire; other units followed, and the infantry quickly went to work. Wolverines began dropping from saddles, and many turned to avoid the musketry now building along the hill's crest.[50] Pettigrew mounted his horse to help form a defense in the growing chaos, but his mount threw him in the swirling combat.[51] Pettigrew gained his feet, pulled a revolver, and advanced at the Federals. A Union corporal shot Pettigrew through the abdomen, and a Rebel infantryman killed the corporal seconds after Pettigrew fell.[52]

The Confederates continued loading, and their numbers began to tell. Muzzles flashed across the crest shooting at anything sitting a saddle as the Rebels "made their way with the cavalry" and killed Major Peter Weber of the 6th Michigan, followed by Lieutenant Charles Bolza.[53] Lieutenant Washington Crawford fell next with his leg shattered by a Minié ball. Outnumbered five to one, the surviving Wolverines had no choice but to scatter and spur back for their reserves.

Rebel bullets followed, and many troopers didn't make it down the hill as they raced to rejoin their brigade. As the survivors returned, other elements of the 6th Michigan came riding forward, including Captain James Kidd's company. They dismounted, went into line, and engaged the enemy position with their carbines from a distance. The Confederate brigade now filled the trench and poured down fire on the Wolverines, killing many and sending a bullet through the foot of Captain Kidd. In all, the 6th Michigan lost thirty-three killed and fifty-six wounded.[54] Kilpatrick later claimed the charge of Weber's squadron "was the most gallant ever made."[55] By this point in the campaign, one would assume Kilpatrick's troopers were growing weary of funerary praises.[56]

As the rest of Custer's brigade arrived, so did Buford's 1st Division, and their combined artillery deployed and began firing at Heth's brigades on the hill. Heth held a sound position, but the guns had already left for the river with his wagons. Without artillery, Heth couldn't hold the position against two divisions of cavalry and their horse batteries. Heth wisely ordered a retreat, and his men strapped Pettigrew to a stretcher and carried him along.[57]

Figure 23.1. Alfred R. Waud's rendition of the 6th Michigan attacking General Heth's line at the Donnelly farmhouse. *Library of Congress.*

Kilpatrick, however, was far from done. Now was the moment for the cavalry to sweep forward and crush the retreating Confederates. After regrouping his troopers, he continued the pursuit, following Heth down the road and skirmishing with the enemy as the ground dropped toward the plain of the river below. Federal skirmishers began sweeping up prisoners, and Kilpatrick began to rant and curse from his saddle that Colonel Sawyer's 1st Brigade had not yet caught up with Custer's people. Seeing a mounted contingent from the 7th Michigan, Kilpatrick swiftly called them forward. Colonel Mann, the 7th's hedging commander, ordered Lieutenant Colonel Litchfield to go forward and find out what Kilpatrick wanted.

"I said I would go see the general," wrote Litchfield to his wife, "and that was the last I saw of him [Col. Mann]."[58] As Litchfield approached Kilpatrick, he passed a horse battery where a lieutenant serving the guns yelled above the din, "General, let me give them one more!"

"Well give it to them!" shouted Kilpatrick.

The round crashed forth from the cannon, and Kilpatrick screamed at Litchfield through the smoke, "Now charge them, they're running!"

Litchfield waved his men up and began dressing the ranks for a charge. "I rushed the men forward trying to close them up well—when the Gen'l, getting a little excited and in a hurry, yelled out to me. 'Take the lead of your men and go in Major.'" Though a lieutenant colonel, Litchfield didn't interrupt as Kilpatrick continued screaming his instructions at the top of his lungs: "[B]e the first man in and give them h-ll, G-d D-mn 'em!'"

Litchfield spurred forward, "intending to obey orders if it cost everything, and [I] charged up the lane just wide enough for a column of four."

Passing the Federal skirmish line, Litchfield plowed into the Confederate infantry lined along the road. "A few shots came down among us but after that no firing and I was astounded as I charged on to see them . . . throw down their arms and doff their hats till I had passed twice as many as might have taken us all prisoners."[59]

Charging on, Litchfield reached a log house where he turned his horse at a cluster of Confederates. "[R]aising my sabre I yelled at the top my voice, 'Throw down those guns!'" Every gun fell to the deck, and Litchfield looked back to discover he had only ten troopers with him as the rest had already turned out to collect those who yielded behind. The Confederates continued surrendering by the score, believing Litchfield's hard-charging vedette must be the advance of a regiment or a brigade. But as Litchfield pointed them to the rear, the Confederates realized they out-numbered his Wolverines. "By the time I got them up, the Rebs, seeing we only had a handful of cavalry among them opened fire." The victors became the vanquished as the Confederates opened on the Union horse soldiers. Litchfield skedaddled back to an orchard and ordered his men to dismount, form a line, and return fire just as reinforcements from the 7th Michigan rode up and retained many of the prisoners. It had been a close call, and Litchfield had been extremely lucky; his charge netted eleven enemy officers, four hundred men, and a stand of colors from the 55th Virginia Infantry.[60]

Buford's men also joined the pursuit, and Gamble's and Devin's troopers were soon pressing forward for the river. By now, the Con-federates had regained their cohesion, and Devin's men dismounted and advanced on foot. "We fought nearly altogether on foot," recalled a mem-ber of the 3rd West Virginia. "It was the grandest thing I was ever in. The rebels would get behind fences and we would charge on them and make them skedaddle."[61]

General Heth rode behind his men calling out, "Keep cool, men. Keep cool!" However, Heth's nervous voice and darting manner con-vinced Waylon Dunaway, a Confederate staff officer, that Heth appeared "the only hot man on the field."[62]

Nearby, men from Brokenbrough's Virginia brigade rallied to repulse Gamble's 8th Illinois after a Virginia color-bearer exclaimed, "Come on, boys; it's nothing but cavalry!"[63] The Virginians charged forward, but heavy fire from the Illinois veterans forced the Virginians back. Gamble's men were only armed with breechloaders; however, the volume of fire convinced the Virginians they were facing Spencer repeaters.[64] Bugles pealed, still more Federals charged into the mix, and the last knot of Brokenbrough's men finally surrendered to Buford's unflagging troopers.

With no other options, Waylon Dunaway cast his pistol on the ground and surrendered, angry at being sacrificed, and knowing Heth had since galloped off for the river.[65]

~

The last Confederates now fell back for the Potomac, firing and reloading on the move, with the Federal cavalry pressing sharply upon them. Watching from the south bank, Lieutenant Robertson had followed Jeb Stuart downstream to join Robert E. Lee, who sat watching the retiring Confederates on the far side of the Potomac. "We could hear musketry on the opposite side," recalled Robertson, "and soon a brigade of [Rebel] infantry appeared moving in line at the double quick, followed by a heavy skirmish line, firing as they came. Then an interval of a hundred or so yards; then a dense mass of Yanks appeared in pursuit . . . cheering and shouting."[66] Unbeknownst to Robertson, Confederate guns were hiding behind cut brush on the south bank of the river. The gunners stood, uncovered their guns, and opened on the Union sharpshooters. Parrots, Whitworths, and Napoleons unleashed a rolling volley as General Lee glassed the result.[67] The Southern guns stalled the pursuit, and no Federals attempted to ford the river. Instead, they watched the last Confederates cut the bridge loose. The pontoons swung into the current and drifted to the southern shore.

Stuart turned his mount on the road and began staging troopers to cover the retreat to Martinsburg. Undaunted, he wrote his wife, Flora, "We must invade again—it is the only path of peace. . . . General Lee's maneuvering the Yankees out of Virginia is the grandest piece of strategy ever heard of. If they [Jeff Davis and the Confederate Cabinet] had only sent 10,000 reinforcements and *plenty of ammunition* to join him here, our recrossing would have been with banners of peace."[68]

Though not a witness to the crossing, Alfred Pleasonton later stated, "It was my opinion that our army should have attacked the rebel army then at Falling Waters. . . . I was satisfied their army was short on ammunition; that they had not a sufficient supply to last for more than a three or four [hour] fight . . . [whereas] our army was well supplied."[69] Many of the rank and file of the Army of the Potomac agreed with Pleasonton. Frontline sergeant Cornelius Wheeler of the legendary Iron Brigade wrote, "If we had attacked [Lee] before he crossed the river, we might have whipped him & destroyed his army. A great mistake was made in not doing it, and to pay for it we have got to endure another campaign."[70]

General Meade had a different perspective. "I will say that if I had attacked the enemy in the position which they then occupied—he having the advantage of position and being on the defensive, his artillery in position, and his infantry behind parapets and rifle-pits—the very same reasons and causes which produced my success at Gettysburg would have operated in his favor there."[71] No one will ever know if an assault by Meade would have broken Lee's line or not, but Stuart's horse soldiers certainly helped gain the time needed to build such a formidable position.

The last of Lee's personnel, artillery, caissons, ambulances, and supply wagons now sat south of the Potomac. Remarkably, Lee's quartermasters had transported most all of the Confederate traveling wounded, some four thousand Federal prisoners, and a massive cache of supplies secured in Federal territory: some forty-five miles' worth of wagons filled in Maryland and Pennsylvania, along with an estimated twenty thousand captured horses and mules.[72] The trains included cattle, sheep, pigs, and poultry, plus corn, wheat, grain, hay, and forage—enough to feed and fuel the Confederate war effort for months to come. In a strange twist, the same supply trains that snarled Lee's rear and convinced him to continue the fight at Gettysburg also gave him the ready resources to make a rapid retreat from the Union army. Yet the supplies came at an extraordinary price. Lee's army incurred staggering losses: forty-five hundred men killed, fifteen thousand wounded, and another five thousand taken prisoner. All told the Confederates suffered twenty-eight thousand casualties out of a force of seventy thousand.[73] The Army of Northern Virginia would never fully recuperate from these massive losses.

Meade's losses were twenty-three thousand out of ninety-three thousand engaged.[74] This, too, was a serious blow to the Federal war effort, but the back-to-back victories gained at Gettysburg and Vicksburg steeled Union resolve and supplied the men and resources needed to carry the war forward. Lincoln won reelection in the fall of 1864, and the war finally ground to a halt in April 1865.

The End

EPILOGUE

HEADQUARTERS ARMY OF THE POTOMAC,
July 14, 1863, 3 p.m.

Major Woodruff,
War Department, Washington, D.C.:

The Maryland campaign is ended. Have sent to me at Harper's Ferry, as soon as practicable, all the maps you can spare of the Shenandoah Valley and the routes east of the mountains of Gordonsville.

G. K. WARREN
Brig. Gen. Vols. Engineer, Army of the Potomac[1]

Lee's recrossing of the Potomac effectively ended the Gettysburg campaign. Sharp skirmishing and maneuvering continued for another three weeks south of the river until both sides found themselves back near Brandy Station. The campaign officially closed in early August with the Confederate lines forming along the Rapidan and the Federals along the Rappahannock.

Meade drew Lincoln's wrath for not destroying Lee's army after Gettysburg. In fall 1863, Meade again tried to bring Lee to heel in the Bristoe and Mine Run campaigns, and both failed. An inquiry convened, and several officers testified Meade did not have the confidence of his men. Though dissatisfied with Meade's failure to destroy Lee along the Potomac, the inquiry committee stopped short of recommending charges against him. Historians continue to debate whether Meade would have been successful if he'd attacked Lee at Falling Waters on July 13. If a prolonged Federal attack had exhausted the Confederate ammunition, Meade may well have gained a sweeping victory. Then again, "what if" scenarios are always a slippery slope—and problematic at best.

Rather than dismiss Meade, Lincoln allowed him to keep official command of the Army of the Potomac. In March 1864, Lincoln appointed Ulysses S. Grant over Meade's head, giving Grant the first lieutenant general's commission of the war and command of all Federal armies. Grant then directed the Federal war effort in Virginia until Lee surrendered on April 9, 1865. Grant's rise also clipped the wings of Henry Halleck and relegated the former attorney to chief of staff. Halleck remained in the army, and his reputation diminished more and more as time went on.

Upon Joseph Hooker's resignation from the Army of the Potomac, he transferred to the Army of Tennessee and won a brilliant victory at the Battle of Lookout Mountain in 1863. Hooker continued to serve well in the Atlanta campaign, but after being passed over for promotion in favor of a subordinate officer, Hooker again asked to be relieved, and he accepted a transfer to the Northern Department, headquartered in Ohio. Fighting Joe retired from the army in 1868.

Alfred Pleasonton left the Army of the Potomac in 1864 and moved to the Trans-Mississippi West. He performed remarkably well in Missouri, winning a quick string of victories at Westport, Byram's Ford, Mine Creek, and Marais de Cygnes, again proving his ability to act as an active frontline commander of light cavalry. When the war ended, Pleasonton's volunteer rank of major general rolled back to his rank of major in the Regular army. Pleasonton's prior politics now caught up with him, and he watched from the sidelines as a string of his former subordinates passed above him in rank. He retired from the army in 1868, still at the rank of major, and clearly embittered over his career.

To the surprise of many, David M. Gregg resigned his commission and quit the war in January 1865. Gregg would regret his decision after the war. Hugh Judson Kilpatrick transferred to the Army of the Cumberland in 1864. Once there, he solidified his reputation as a commander who zealously engaged the enemy, but one who too often sacrificed men and horses for minor gains. After the war, Kilpatrick ran for Congress and lost. He later received an appointment as minister to Chile from President Andrew Johnson.

Sadly, John Buford did not survive the war. He died of typhoid in December 1863 at the age of thirty-seven. Upon hearing Buford would soon expire, President Lincoln promoted him to major general just hours before his death. Like Buford, fellow horse soldier Charles Town of the 1st Michigan died not in the saddle, but in a bed. The game Wolverine finally succumbed to his long battle with tuberculosis in May 1864. His commanding officer, George Custer, not only survived the war but also climbed to the rank of major general by war's end. Custer later served on the frontier with checkered results and went on to become a national martyr following his death and defeat at the Battle of Little Bighorn. Wesley Merritt also served in the Indian Wars, and rose to the regular army rank of major general in 1895.

John Irvin Gregg received a wound at the 2nd Battle of Deep Bottom, and another at Sailor's Creek in 1865. Captured at Farmville, Virginia, he gained his release three days later when Lee surrendered at Appomattox Courthouse. After the war, Gregg received command of the 8th U.S. Cavalry and served on the frontier. Former house painter Thomas Devin suffered a severe wound at Front Royal in 1864, where his troops captured two stands of colors. Like Gregg, Devin remained in the military and received a regular army commission of lieutenant colonel in the 8th Cavalry and then colonel of the 3rd U.S. Cavalry. Devin died on active duty in 1879. Irishman William Gamble survived the war, only to die of cholera in 1866 while en route to take command of the Presidio of San Francisco.

John McIntosh continued to lead his brigade after Gettysburg and lost a leg at the 3rd Battle of Winchester in 1864. He retired from the army in 1870 and, upon exiting, received a well-deserved regular army commission to brigadier general. Colonel Nathaniel Richmond of the 1st West Virginia Cavalry had a horse shot out from under him in October 1863 and badly injured his hip in the resulting fall. Richmond never fully recovered and left the army, becoming mayor of Kokomo, Indiana, after the war. Percy Wyndham, the English pugilist and adventurer who performed so well atop Fleetwood Hill, went abroad following Lee's surrender and served a stint as a mercenary in Italy. Wyndham died in 1879 while piloting a hot-air balloon of his own design near Rangoon, India.

Lieutenant Colonel Allyne Litchfield, the profound letter writer of the 7th Michigan Cavalry, was captured during the Dahlgren Raid in 1864. Papers found on a Union officer's corpse contained plans to burn Richmond, causing Litchfield and nine other prisoners to be stuffed in a seven-foot by eleven-foot cell deep in the basement of Libby Prison. Litchfield gained his release a year later; he received a brevet promotion to brigadier general but was never physically, or mentally, capable of retaking the field. Deemed insane by friends and family at the turn of the century, he lingered for another decade and died in 1911.

Federal horse gunners Alexander Pennington, Samuel Elder, and John Calef all survived the war. Pennington received command of the 3rd New Jersey Cavalry and earned a citation for gallantry at Cedar Creek in October 1864. Pennington remained in the U.S. Army and retired a brigadier general in 1899. Samuel Elder received numerous citations for bravery and rose to the rank of lieutenant colonel by the end of the war. John Calef remained in the Federal army and retired as colonel of the 1st Artillery at the turn of the century.

~

Following his return to Virginia, Lee offered his resignation to Confederate president Jefferson Davis. Davis refused to accept the resignation, and Lee continued to command the Army of Northern Virginia until he surrendered at Appomattox Courthouse on April 9, 1865. Lee entered civilian life after the war and served as president of Washington College in Lexington, Virginia. He died in 1870.

Jeb Stuart died in May 1864 from wounds received at the Battle of Yellow Tavern. Stuart fell at the front, firing at the enemy with his revolver and encouraging his men to hold the line. Several of Stuart's brigade commanders suffered similar fates the same year; James B. Gordon fell at Meadow Bridge, Grumble Jones died at the Battle of Piedmont, and John Chambliss fell along the Charles City Road.

Wade Hampton survived his Gettysburg wounds and took command of the Army of Northern Virginia's cavalry after Stuart's death. After the war, Hampton served as the governor of South Carolina, as well as two terms as a U.S. senator. Fitz Lee survived the war and served as governor of Virginia. His cousin Rooney Lee served in the Virginia state senate and the U.S. House of Representatives. John Daniel Imboden went back to practicing law in Virginia.

Following the war, John Mosby became close friends with President Ulysses S. Grant, joined the Republican Party, and served as the U.S. consul to Hong Kong. Lunsford Lomax entered civilian life at the war's end, farmed extensively, and became president of the Virginia Agriculture and Mechanical College, now known as Virginia Tech. Lomax also served in the Federal War Office, where he helped assemble and edit the *Official Records of the War of the Rebellion*. Colonel Thomas Munford survived the war and became vice president of the Lynchburg Iron, Steel and Mining Company. Pierce Young of the Cobb Legion Cavalry returned home and represented Georgia for four terms in the U.S. House of Representatives. William Delony, Young's executive officer, recovered from his sabre wounds at Hunterstown and returned to the front. Wounded again in September, Delony later died in a Union hospital. Captain Charles O'Ferrall, shot in a charge along the Trappe Road near Upperville, survived his wound and a rash of others before the war's end. After the war, O'Ferrall entered politics and served as governor of Virginia from 1894 to 1898.

Battery captains Roger Chew, William McGregor, and James Breathed each survived the war. Chew served in the West Virginia state legislature and lived well into the next century. William McGregor moved to Milam County, Texas, where he practiced law and cofounded the *Milam County Messenger*. James Breathed returned home, troubled by a painful abdominal wound received during the war. He died within five years of the surrender at Appomattox due to complications of his war wound. Gunner and avid diarist Charles McVicar went back home to Virginia, raised a family, and made his living building wagons and horse carriages in Winchester.

~

The horse soldiers and gunners of the American Civil War redefined light cavalry. The Confederacy seemed to be first to realize the potential of using the cavalry as not just a flank guard and reconnaissance resource but also a strike force capable of offensive operations. In the Gettysburg campaign, the two armies utilized their cavalry in a variety of roles: leading the advance, gathering reconnaissance, screening the enemy, launching long-range attacks, and pursuing enemy forces. By the end of the war, when Rebel forces evacuated the trenches at Petersburg, the Federal cavalry swarmed the Confederate army and helped bring the fighting to a rapid close at Appomattox.

No study of Gettysburg is complete without exploring the separate arrivals of Robert E. Lee and Jeb Stuart in Pennsylvania. Lee moved north with hopes to secure the supplies needed to keep his army operational. He also hoped to offer battle north of the Potomac under his own terms. Authors have spent much time and ink examining Stuart's ego and his need to regain his reputation either with the public or with himself, and many theories conclude these inner desires somehow guided Stuart to make errant decisions in the campaign. These are interesting concepts, but historians are not psychoanalysts.

On the evening of June 21, 1863, Stuart's cavalry still guarded the tail of Lee's army at Ashby's Gap in the Blue Ridge Mountains. Lee now wanted Stuart to cross the Potomac, sprint to the head of his army, and screen Ewell's advancing right flank through Pennsylvania. The quickest route to intersect Ewell's forward course was not back west through the Shenandoah Valley. The quickest route lay to the east—through the Federal army.

Passing the Federal army would be a risk, but multiple reports from a proven source showed the eastern course to be a viable option. In addition, Stuart's mostly unshod horses were already wearing down from a recent combination of maneuvering on macadamized roads and a lack of grain. The western route down the Shenandoah Valley would entail crossing the mountains twice, where forage was already reported in short supply. The eastern course did not require a double traverse of the mountains, and promised a faster arrival on healthier horses. Lee also recognized the strategic advantages of the eastern route; Stuart would cut the Federal lines, and this might temporarily pin Hooker in place and allow Lee's army a longer head start in Pennsylvania.

Stuart's eastern route would be a gamble—but Lee's entire campaign was a gamble. To miss this point is to misread Lee's campaign, as well as his planned use of the cavalry.

Lee divided his cavalry for different purposes. Jenkins's brigade would screen Ewell's attack on Winchester and serve as Ewell's advance across the Potomac. Imboden's brigade would screen Lee's left during the advance and collect supplies along the way. Two more brigades, Robertson's and Jones's, would watch Hooker's army in Virginia and guard the mountain passes leading to the Shenandoah Valley. Lee then wanted Stuart to take his remaining brigades across the Potomac and link up with Ewell's advancing right flank in the neighborhood of York, Pennsylvania. If Stuart could gain York quicker by passing the Federal army, panicking Washington, and retarding the Federal pursuit, then Lee judged the gamble worth the risk.

Lee could have ordered Stuart to fall in behind him, to pass west of the mountains, and Stuart would have complied. But Lee delivered no such orders, preferring Stuart make the call on his own. Stuart went east, ran into Federal troops, and suffered a series of delays. Beverly Robertson then failed to warn Lee of Hooker's army crossing the Potomac, further complicating Stuart's belated arrival.

Lee clearly missed having Stuart by his side as he entered Pennsylvania; however, Lee did not lose the Battle of Gettysburg because Stuart came late to Gettysburg. Everyone in the Army of Northern Virginia came late to the battle at Gettysburg save Henry Heth, who brought on a battle Lee hadn't intended, as evidenced by the placement of Lee's wagon trains.

Meade won the fight at Gettysburg in large part due to the actions and foresight of Buford's horse soldiers, and the resulting Federal victory placed Lee's army in a perilous position. Lee then managed a successful retreat, a retreat well screened by Stuart's cavalry, and recrossed the Potomac with a battered, but operational army.

Sadly, the war would rage on for another twenty-one months.

Appendix 1

FEDERAL ORDER OF BATTLE

Table A1.1. **Army of the Potomac, Cavalry Corps, Order of Battle, July 1–3, 1863; Maj. Gen. Alfred Pleasonton, Commanding**

Division	Brigade	Regiment
First Division Brig. Gen. John Buford	First Brigade Col. William Gamble	8th Illinois: Maj. J. Beveridge 12th Illinois (4 cos.): Col. G. Chapman 3rd Indiana (6 cos.): Col. G. Chapman 8th New York: Lt. Col. W. Markell
	Second Brigade Col. Thomas C. Devin	6th New York: Maj. W. Beardsley 9th New York: Col. W. Sackett 17th Pennsylvania: Col. J. Kellogg 3rd West Virginia (2 cos.): Capt. S. Conger
	Reserve Brigade Brig. Gen. Wesley Merritt	6th Pennsylvania: Maj. J. Haseltine 1st United States: Capt. R. Lord 2nd United States: Capt. T. Rodenbough 5th United States: Capt. J. Mason 6th United States: Capt. S. Starr

(continued)

Table A1.1.   *(continued)*

Division	Brigade	Regiment
Second Division Brig. Gen. David M. Gregg	First Brigade Col. John B. McIntosh	1st Maryland (11 cos.): Lt. Col. J. Deems Parnell (Maryland) Legion (1 co.): Capt. R. Duvall 1st Massachusetts: Lt. Col. G. Curtis 1st New Jersey: Maj. M. Beaumont 1st Pennsylvania: Col. J. Taylor 3rd Pennsylvania: Lt. Col. E. Jones 3rd Pennsylvania Heavy Artillery (serving as light. art.): Capt. W. Rank
	Second Brigade Col. Pennock Huey	2nd New York: Lt. Col. O. Harhaus 4th New York: Lt. Col. A. Pruyn 6th Ohio (10 cos.): Maj. W. Stedman 8th Pennsylvania: Capt. W. Corie
	Third Brigade Col. J. Irvin Gregg	1st Maine: Lt. Col. C. Smith 10th New York: Maj. M. Avery 4th Pennsylvania: Lt. Col. W. Doster 16th Pennsylvania: Lt. Col. J. Robison
Third Division Brig. Gen. Judson Kilpatrick	First Brigade Brig. Gen. Elon J. Farnsworth Col. Nathaniel P. Richmond	5th New York: Maj. J. Hammond 18th Pennsylvania: Lt. Col. W. Brinton 1st Vermont: Lt. Col. A. Preston 1st West Virginia (10 cos.): Col. N. Richmond; Maj C. Capehart
	Second Brigade Brig. Gen. George A. Custer	1st Michigan: Col. C. Town 5th Michigan: Col. R. Alger 6th Michigan: Col. G. Gray 7th Michigan (10 cos.): Col. W. Mann
Horse Artillery	First Brigade Capt. James M. Robertson	9th Michigan Btry.: Capt. J. Daniels 6th New York Btry.: Capt. J. Martin 2nd U.S. Btry. B & L: Lt. E. Heaton 2nd U.S. Btry. M: Lt. A. Pennington 4th U.S. Btry. E: Lt. S. Elder
	Second Brigade Capt. John Tidball	1st U.S. Btry. E & G: Capt. A. Randol 1st U.S. Btry. K: Capt. W. Graham 2nd U.S. Btry. A: Lt. J. Calef 3rd U.S. Btry. C: Lt. W. Fuller

Source: Robert N. Scott, ed., *The War of the Rebellion: A Compilation of the Official Records of the Union and Confederate Armies*, ser. 1, vol. 27, pt. 1 (Washington, DC: Government Printing Office, 1889), 166–67.

Appendix 2

CONFEDERATE ORDER OF BATTLE

Table A2.1.   Army of Northern Virginia, Cavalry, Stuart's Division, Order of Battle; Maj. Gen. J. E. B. Stuart, Commanding

Division	Brigade	Regiment
Stuart's Division	Hampton's Brigade Brig. Gen. Wade Hampton Col. L. Baker	1st North Carolina: Col. L. Baker 1st South Carolina (1 Battalion detached): Col. J. Black 1st South Carolina: Lt. Col. J. Twiggs 2nd South Carolina: Maj T. Lipscomb Cobb (Georgia) Legion: Col. P. Young Jeff Davis Legion: Lt. Col. J. Waring Phillips (Georgia) Legion: Lt. Col. W. Rich
	Fitz Lee's Brigade Brig. Gen. Fitz Lee	1st Maryland Battalion: Maj. H. Gilmor; Maj. R. Brown 1st Virginia: Col. J. Drake 2nd Virginia: Col. T. Munford 3rd Virginia: Col. T. Owen 4th Virginia: Col. W. Wickham 5th Virginia: Col. T. Rosser
	Robertson's Brigade Brig. Gen. Beverly Robertson	4th North Carolina: Col. D. Ferebee 5th North Carolina: Lt. Col. J. Gordon
	Jenkins' Brigade Brig. Gen. A. G. Jenkins Col. M. Ferguson	14th Virginia: Maj. B. Eakle 16th Virginia: Maj. J. Nounnan 17th Virginia: Col. W. French 34th Virginia Battalion: Lt. Col. V. Witcher 36th Virginia Battalion: Maj. J. Sweeney Jackson's Virginia Btry.: Capt. T. Jackson
	Jones' Brigade Brig. Gen. William E. Jones	6th Virginia: Maj. C. Flournoy 7th Virginia: Lt. Col. T. Marshall 11th Virginia: Col. L. Lomax 12th Virginia: Lt. Col. T. B. Massie*
	W. H. F. Lee's Brigade Col. J. R. Chambliss	2nd North Carolina: Capt. W. Graham 9th Virginia: Col. R. Beale 10th Virginia: Maj. R. Caskie 13th Virginia: Lt. Col. J. Phillips
	Stuart Horse Artillery Maj. R. F. Beckham	Breathed's (Virginia) Btry.: Capt. J. Breathed Chew's (Virginia) Btry.: Capt. R. Chew Griffin's (Maryland) Btry.: Capt. W. Griffin Hart's (South Carolina) Btry.: Capt. J. Hart McGregor's (Virginia) Btry.: Capt. W. McGregor Moorman's (Virginia) Btry.: Capt. M. Moorman
	Imboden's Command Brig. Gen. J. D. Imboden	18th Virginia Cavalry: Col. G. Imboden 62nd Virginia Mounted Infantry: Col. G. Smith Virginia Partisan Rangers: Capt. J. McNeill Virginia Btry.: Capt. J. McClanahan

Source: Robert N. Scott, ed., *The War of the Rebellion: A Compilation of the Official Records of the Union and Confederate Armies,* ser. 1, vol. 27, pt. 2 (Washington, DC: Government Printing Office, 1889), 290–91.

* This force was detailed elsewhere and thus is not listed in the official order of battle for Gettysburg.

Appendix 3

FEDERAL AND CONFEDERATE CASUALTIES, JULY 9–JULY 14, 1863

Casualty returns from the *Official Records* for the Army of the Potomac Cavalry Corps, Major General Alfred Pleasonton commanding, and the Army of Northern Virginia, Cavalry Division, Major General Jeb Stuart commanding, June 9–July 14, 1863.

Date and Place	Federal	Confederate
June 9		
Brandy Station	791	485
June 17–21		
Aldie, Middleburg, Upperville	821	516
June 21–30		
Haymarket, Westminster, Hanover	349	250
July 1–3		
Combined Actions at Gettysburg[1]	852	505
July 4–6		
Monterey Pass, Hagerstown, Williamsport	436	254
July 8–14		
Boonsboro, Funkstown, Falling Waters	323	216
Totals in killed, wounded, and missing.	3,572[2]	2,226[3]

These totals are approximations and shown here for comparative values. The Confederate side lacks many returns. For instance, there are no returns for the 2nd North Carolina Cavalry at Hanover and 133 casualties have been added in an attempt to correct the deficit.[4] In addition, no returns are listed for Jenkins's brigade. Numbers have been added from other sources for this brigade on July 3, but additions have not been made for other engagements in the campaign.[5]

---

1. Includes 1st Day Gettysburg, Hunterstown, Brinkerhoff Ridge, Rummel Farm, Farnsworth Brig, Merritt's Brig, and Fairfield Rd.
2. *O.R.,* vol. 27, pt. 1, 168–70. Attached infantry subtracted. *O.R.,* vol. 27, pt. 1, 171–72. Attached infantry subtracted. *O.R.,* vol. 27, pt. 1, 185–86; *O.R.,* vol. 27, pt. 1, 193.
3. *O.R.,* vol. 27, pt. 2, 345–46, 712–19.
4. Krepps, *A Strong and Sudden Onslaught,* 109–10.
5. Cole, *34th Battalion Virginia Cavalry,* 53.

NOTES

CHAPTER 1

1. Many portraits of Civil War soldiers were posed in studios and were not universally accurate renditions of the weaponry or uniforms seen at the front.

2. Immigrants did serve in the cavalry, and this was more prevalent on the Federal side, with the largest concentrations coming from Irish or Germanic backgrounds.

3. Donald Scott, "Evangelicalism, Revivalism, and the Second Great Awakening," National Humanities Center, accessed September 15, 2022, http://national humanitiescenter.org/tserve/nineteen/nkeyinfo/nevanrev.htm; "The Bible Was Used to Justify Slavery," *Washington Post*, April 30, 2019.

4. Robert F. O'Neill, "The Reidville Mutiny," *Small but Important Riots* (blog), July 10, 2019, accessed May 10, 2020, https://smallbutimportantriots .com/2019/07/10/the-readville-mutiny/.

5. George Cary Eggleston, *A Rebel's Recollections* (Bloomington: Indiana University Press, 1959), 80.

6. Also common were carbines and longer barreled rifles equipped with traditional leather slings the troopers slung diagonally across their backs. David Evans, *Sherman's Horsemen: Union Cavalry Operations in the Atlanta Campaign* (Bloomington: Indiana University Press, 1996), 45.

7. Edward G. Longacre, *General John Buford: A Military Biography* (Cambridge, MA: Da Capo, 1995), 31; James Buchanan Ballard, *William Edmondson "Grumble" Jones: The Life of a Cantankerous Confederate* (Jefferson, NC: McFarland, 2017), 31.

8. J. R. Poinsett, ed., *Cavalry Tactics: Parts 1–3* (Washington, DC: U.S. War Department; J. & G. S. Gideon, 1841).

9. These are official numbers. Numbers in the field were generally much lower.

10. J. R. Poinsett, ed., *School of the Squadron—Mounted*, part 2 of *Cavalry Tactics* (Washington, DC: U.S. War Department; J. & G. S. Gideon, 1841), 183.

11. Gregory J. W. Urwin, *The United States Cavalry: An Illustrated History 1776–1944* (Norman: University of Oklahoma Press, 1983), 54, 65, 84, 96.

12. Edward G. Longacre, *Lincoln's Cavalrymen* (Mechanicsburg, PA: Stackpole Books, 2000), 16.

13. Henry B. McClellan, *I Rode with Jeb Stuart: The Life and Campaigns of Major General J. E. B. Stuart* (New York: Da Capo, 1994), 257.

14. North Carolina provided horses for their state-funded regiments and would purchase a trooper's horse for service.

15. Some Union states provided their own horses and paid bounties to volunteer troopers, particularly at the beginning of the war.

16. Louis A. DiMarco, *War Horse: A History of the Military Horse and Rider* (Yardley, PA: Westholme, 2008), 232.

17. Laurence D. Schiller, *Of Sabres and Carbines: The Emergence of the Federal Dragoon: A Scholarly Monograph* (Saline, MI: McNaughton and Gunn for the Blue and Gray Education Society, 2001), 17.

18. Longacre, *Lincoln's Cavalrymen*, 46.

19. Deb Bennett, "Horses of the Civil War," *Equus Magazine*, June 2017.

20. Heros von Borcke and Justus Scheibert, *The Great Cavalry Battle of Brandy Station, 9 June 1863* (Winston-Salem, NC: Paelemon, 1976), 39. On a side note, von Borcke preferred riding a mule.

21. Bennett, "Horses of the Civil War."

22. Bennett, "Horses of the Civil War."

23. DiMarco, *War Horse*, 241; Longacre, *Lincoln's Cavalrymen*, 46.

24. George M. Neese, *Three Years in the Confederate Horse Artillery: Consisting of Excerpts, Where Each Touches on Matters Relating to Charlottesville, VA and Environs* (Dayton, OH: Morningside, 1988), 169–70; Justus Scheibert, *Seven Months in the Rebel States during the American War, 1863*, ed. William Stanley Hoole (Tuscaloosa: University of Alabama Press, 2009), 42.

25. Ann Norton Greene, *Horses at Work: Harnessing Power in Industrial America* (Cambridge, MA: Harvard University Press, 2008), 121, 126, 135.

26. Greene, *Horses at Work*, 132.

27. "Every Man His Own Horse Doctor," National Museum of Civil War Medicine, August 30, 2017, https://www.civilwarmed.org/animal/.

28. "The Late Skirmishes between Stuart and Pleasonton," *New York Daily Tribune*, November 10, 1862 (bracketed word by author).

29. Greene, *Horses at Work*, 135.

30. Karen E. N. Hayes, *Hands-On Horse Care: Diagnosis and First Aid* (North Pomfret, VT: Trafalgar Square, 1997), 176.

31. Susan Leigh Blackford and Charles Minor Blackford III, eds., *Letters from Lee's Army; or, Memoirs of Life in and out of the Army in Virginia during the War between the States* (Lincoln: University of Nebraska Press, 1998), 182.

32. Greene, *Horses at Work*, 158.

33. "New Estimate Raises Civil War Death Toll," *New York Times*, April 2, 2012.

34. National Sporting Library and Museum, Middleburg, Virginia.

35. Cyrus F. Boyd, *The Civil War Diary of Cyrus F. Boyd, Fifteenth Iowa Infantry, 1861–1863*, ed. Mildred Throne (Royal Oak, Auckland: Pickle Partners, 2016), 45–46; Greene, *Horses at Work*, 154.

36. Edwin Eustace Bryant, *History of the Third Regiment of Wisconsin Veteran Volunteer Infantry* (Madison, WI: Veteran Association, 1891), 169–70.

37. Borcke and Scheibert, *The Great Cavalry Battle of Brandy Station*, 38.

38. Borcke and Scheibert, *The Great Cavalry Battle of Brandy Station*, 38–39.

39. Carrie Arnold, "How Do Horses Communicate? New Signals Found," *National Geographic*, August 4, 2014.

40. Author's personal experience in fifteen years of mounted reenacting.

41. Robert F. O'Neill, *The Cavalry Battles of Aldie, Middleburg and Upperville, June 10–27, 1863*, Virginia Civil War Battle and Leaders Series (Lynchburg, VA: H. E. Howard, 1993), 55 (bracketed words by author).

42. Robert N. Scott, ed., *The War of the Rebellion: A Compilation of the Official Records of the Union and Confederate Armies*, ser. 1, vol. 27, pt. 2 (Washington, DC: Government Printing Office, 1889), 761.

CHAPTER 2

1. John Ellis, *Cavalry: The History of Mounted Warfare* (Barnsley, UK: Pen & Sword Military Classics, 2004), 10.

2. Louis A. DiMarco, *War Horse: A History of the Military Horse and Rider* (Yardley, PA: Westholme, 2012), 81, 96; David Nicolle, *Carolingian Cavalrymen, AD 768–987* (Oxford: Osprey, 2005), 10, 28.

3. Ellis, *Cavalry*, 81–84.

4. Daniel Murphy, *William Washington, American Light Dragoon* (Yardley, PA: Westholme, 2014), 22.

5. Emanuel von Warnery, Brent Nosworthy, and G. F. Koehler, *Remarks on Cavalry* (London: Constable, 1997), 4–6; Louis Edward Nolan, *Cavalry: Its History and Tactics* (Yardley, PA: Westholme, 2007), 18–22.

6. Phillip J. Haythornthwaite, *Napoleonic Cavalry* (London: Cassel, 2001), 20–22.

7. Ready-made copper percussion caps of mercury fulminate provided surer ignition, streamlined the process, and allowed for better ignition in inclement weather.

8. Daniel Murphy, "Infantry vs. Cavalry," *Journal of the American Revolution*, February 27, 2014.

9. Thomas J. Ryan and Stephen W. Sears, *Spies, Scouts, and Secrets in the Gettysburg Campaign: How the Critical Role of Intelligence Impacted the Outcome of Lee's Invasion of the North, June–July, 1863* (El Dorado Hills, CA: Savas Beatie, 2015), 18–19, 41–45; Wilbur Sturtevant Nye, *Here Come the Rebels* (Dayton, OH: Morningside, 1988), 16, 30.

10. Rory Muir, *Tactics and the Experience of Battle in the Age of Napoleon* (New Haven, CT: Yale University Press, 1998), 109–10, 129; Warnery, Nosworthy, and Koehler, *Remarks on Cavalry*, 97, 105–6.

11. Adele H. Mitchell, ed., *The Letters of Major General James E. B. Stuart* (Alexandria, VA: Stuart-Mosby Historical Society, 1990), 330–31.

12. Muir, *Tactics and the Experience of Battle*, 113–15; Daniel Murphy, "Slashing Sabres at the Rummel Farm," *America's Civil War*, January 2005, 38–45.

13. Daniel Murphy, "Shock and Awe: Mounted Combat in the Eighteenth Century," *Journal of the United States Cavalry*, June 2009, 10–13.

14. Murphy, *William Washington*, 24–25.

15. The 1840 is known today as the Wristbreaker; many collectors believe this moniker derived from the sturdier 1840 having replaced the lighter-weight 1833 Model Sabre that was judged inferior and prone to folding under stress.

16. Both the 1840 and 1860 had strong French influences in their designs rooted to Napoleon's XI Model Light Cavalry Sabre, created some fifty years before for his Hussars and lancers. As forging techniques improved, the French produced a slimmer version of this sabre, which became the 1822 French Light Cavalry Sabre. This weapon was selected in U.S. field trials to be reproduced for service in America, resulting in the U.S. Model 1840 Cavalry Sabre. The U.S. Model 1860 Light Cavalry Sabre followed twenty years later. T. T. S. Laidley, ed., *The Ordnance Manual for the Use of the Officers of the United States Army*, 3rd ed. (Philadelphia, PA: Lippincott, 1862), 224.

17. Another blade in use was the 1840 Light Artillery Sabre, which had a greater arc to the blade and was designed for cutting blows during a melee over the guns, rather than a thrust in a horse charge.

18. Muir, *Tactics and the Experience of Battle*, 108–9; Haythornthwaite, *Napoleonic Cavalry*, 30.

19. As mentioned previously, the use of sword knots prohibited the sabres from being overly sharp. Murphy, *William Washington*, 47.

20. Daniel Murphy, "Cavalry: Swords before Pistols," *Journal of the American Revolution*, February 11, 2014, https://allthingsliberty.com/author/daniel-murphy/.

21. Philip St. George Cooke, *Cavalry Tactics; or, Regulations for the Instruction, Formations, and Movements of the Cavalry of the Army and Volunteers of the United States* (Washington, DC: Government Printing Office, 1862), 207.

22. Muir, *Tactics and the Experience of Battle*, 126.

23. Warnery, Nosworthy, and Koehler, *Remarks on Cavalry*, 40.

24. DiMarco, *War Horse*, 238.

25. Mike Cox, *The Texas Rangers: Wearing the Cinco Peso, 1821–1900* (New York: Forge, 2008), 90–93.

26. Mitchell, *Letters of Major General James E. B. Stuart*, 331–32.

27. John Singleton Mosby, *Mosby's War Reminiscences: Stuart's Cavalry Campaigns* (New York: Dodd, Meade, 1898), 90, 91.

28. James Joseph Williamson, *Mosby's Rangers: A Record of the Operations of the Forty-Third Battalion of Virginia Cavalry from Its Organization to the Surrender* (New York: Sturgis & Walton, 1909; repr., 2018), 143, 85.

29. The majority of Civil War revolvers had cylinders with six chambers. Hammers could safely rest between the chambers on the cylinders, allowing for the safe carrying of a fully loaded cylinder.

30. Wiley C. Howard, *Sketch of Cobb Legion Cavalry and Some Incidents and Scenes Remembered* (Atlanta, GA: Atlanta Camp 159, S.C.V., 1901; repr., Delhi, India: Facsimile, 2013), 6.

31. F. De Brack, *Light Cavalry Outposts: Recollections* (London: W. Mitchell, 1876), 178; Muir, *Tactics and the Experience of Battle*, 114.

32. Time-Life Books, eds., *Echoes of Glory: Arms and Equipment of the Union* (Alexandria, VA: Time-Life Books, 1991), 48.

33. Jack Coggins, *Arms and Equipment of the Civil War* (Garden City, NY: Doubleday, 1962), 35–6.

34. Elliott W. Hoffman, *History of the First Vermont Cavalry Volunteers in the War of the Great Rebellion* (Baltimore, MD: Butternut and Blue, 2000), 122; John B. Bachelder, David L. Ladd, Audrey J. Ladd, and Richard A. Sauers, eds., "Letter of Col. Russell A. Alger, 9 April, 1886," in *The Bachelder Papers: Gettysburg in Their Own Words* (Dayton, OH: Morningside, 1994), 2:1298; James H. Kidd, *Personal Recollections of a Cavalryman with Custer's Michigan Cavalry Brigade in the Civil War* (1908; repr., Ionia, MI: Sentinel, 2015), 151.

35. Albert C. Manucy, *Artillery through the Ages: A Short Illustrated History of Cannon, Emphasizing Types Used in America* (Washington, DC: Government Printing Office, 1962), 9–20.

36. Robert J. Trout, *Galloping Thunder: The Story of the Stuart Horse Artillery Battalion* (Mechanicsburg, PA: Stackpole Books, 2002), 5.

37. Trout, *Galloping Thunder*, 6.

38. Craig Swain, "Artillery and Horses," *To the Sound of the Guns* (blog), accessed May 8, 2022, https://markerhunter.wordpress.com/2009/11/01/artillery-and-horses/.

39. U.S. War Department, "Instruction for Field Artillery," in *The 1864 Field Artillery Tactics: Organization, Equipment, Field Service* (Mechanicsburg, PA: Stackpole Books, 2005), 33.

40. Swain, "Artillery and Horses"; Manucy, *Artillery through the Ages*, 19–20; Coggins, *Arms and Equipment of the Civil War*, 76–77.

41. Swain, "Artillery and Horses."

42. Coggins, *Arms and Equipment of the Civil War*, 70.

43. Artillery drivers often carried revolvers for dispatching wounded horses thrashing in the traces before they could injure other horses in the team.

CHAPTER 3

1. Robert N. Scott, ed., *The War of the Rebellion: A Compilation of the Official Records of the Union and Confederate Armies*, ser. 1, vol. 25, pt. 1 (Washington, DC: Government Printing Office, 1889), 1047 (hereafter cited as *O.R.*, vol. 25); Henry B. McClellan, *I Rode with Jeb Stuart: The Life and Campaigns of Major General J. E. B. Stuart* (New York: Da Capo, 1994), 232–34.

2. Stephen W. Sears, *Chancellorsville* (Boston; New York: Houghton Mifflin, 1996), 232–33, 241.

3. Daniel Murphy, *William Washington, American Light Dragoon* (Yardley, PA: Westholme, 2014), 167–68, 177; Jim Piecuch and John H. Beakes, *"Light Horse Harry" Lee in the War for Independence* (Charleston, SC: Nautical and Aviation Publishing Company of America, 2013), 231–33.

4. Armistead Lindsey Long, *Memoirs of Robert E. Lee, His Military and Personal History: Embracing a Large Amount of Information Hitherto Unpublished* (New York; Philadelphia, PA; Washington, DC: J. M. Stoddart, 1887), 52.

5. Long, *Memoirs of Robert E. Lee*, 61.

6. Long, *Memoirs of Robert E. Lee*, 60.

7. John Salmon Ford and Stephen B. Oates, *Rip Ford's Texas* (Austin: University of Texas Press, 1987), 305–6.

8. Robert E. Lee Jr., ed., *Recollections and Letters of Robert E. Lee* (New York: Smithmark, 1995), 11, 83.

9. The war took on a personal tone for Lee when Federal troops invested his family estate at Arlington, Virginia, across the Potomac River from Washington, DC. The Federal army built three forts on his property. They would eventually declare Arlington a national cemetery and fill it with Federal dead, many of whom had died at Lee's own hand. After the war, the Lee family sued the Federal government for loss of property and received a settlement.

10. Lee, *Recollections and Letters of Robert E. Lee*, 11, 83.

11. Richard Davis Goff, *Confederate Supply* (Durham, NC: Duke University Press, 1969), 79–80.

12. Robert N. Scott, ed., *The War of the Rebellion: A Compilation of the Official Records of the Union and Confederate Armies*, ser. 1, vol. 27, pt. 2 (Washington, DC: Government Printing Office, 1889), 725 (hereafter cited as *O.R.*, vol. 27); Kent Masterson Brown, *Retreat from Gettysburg: Lee Logistics and the Gettysburg Campaign* (Chapel Hill: University of North Carolina Press, 2005), 15.

13. Brown, *Retreat from Gettysburg*, 13.

14. John Grady, "The Richmond Bread Riot," *New York Times*, April 5, 2013.

15. Brown, *Retreat from Gettysburg*, 14, 15–17.

16. *O.R.*, vol. 27, pt. 2, 305; Brown, *Retreat from Gettysburg*, 14; Harry W. Pfanz, *Gettysburg: The First Day* (Chapel Hill: University of North Carolina Press, 2001), 3.

17. Glenn Tucker, *High Tide at Gettysburg* (New York: Konecky & Konecky, 1958), 17–19; Wilbur Sturtevant Nye, *Here Come the Rebels* (Dayton, OH: Morningside, 1988), 7.

18. Nye, *Here Come the Rebels*, 42.

19. *O.R.*, vol. 27, pt. 2, 305.

20. *O.R.*, vol. 27, pt. 2, 315–16.

21. Thomas J. Ryan, "A Battle of Wits: Intelligence Operations during the Gettysburg Campaign: Part 3," *Gettysburg Magazine* 31 (n.d.); Stephen Sears, *To the Gates of Richmond: The Peninsula Campaign* (Boston, MA: Houghton Mifflin, 1992), 110–12.

22. Edward Porter Alexander, *Military Memoirs of a Confederate*, ed. Harry Williams, Civil War Centennial Series (Bloomington: University of Indiana Press, 1962), 62.

23. *O.R.*, vol. 27, pt. 3, 930–31.

24. *O.R.*, vol. 27, pt. 2, 305.

25. Adele H. Mitchell, ed., *The Letters of Major General James E. B. Stuart* (Alexandria, VA: Stuart-Mosby Historical Society, 1990), 103.

26. Mitchell, *Letters of Major General James E. B. Stuart*, 96, 99.

27. Mitchell, *Letters of Major General James E. B. Stuart*, 166.

28. Bill Yenne, *Indian Wars: The Campaign for the American West* (Yardley, PA: Westholme, 2008), 66.

29. Lomax would later command the 11th Virginia Cavalry, a regiment in Stuart's command.

30. The warrior carried an old Allen-style revolver. Mitchell, *Letters of Major General James E. B. Stuart*, 167; McClellan, *I Rode with Jeb Stuart*, 20–22.

31. Mitchell, *Letters of Major General James E. B. Stuart*, 167.

32. Mitchell, *Letters of Major General James E. B. Stuart*, 171.

33. John T. Krepps, *A Strong and Sudden Onslaught: The Cavalry Action at Hanover, Pennsylvania* (Ortanna, PA: Colecraft Industries, 2008), 84; Jeffry D. Wert, *Cavalryman of the Lost Cause: A Biography of J. E. B. Stuart* (New York: Simon & Schuster, 2009), 98.

34. W. W. Blackford, *War Years with Jeb Stuart* (New York: Scribner, 1945), 50.

35. McClellan, *I Rode with Jeb Stuart*, 255–56 (bracketed word by author).

36. Philip St. George Cooke, *Cavalry Tactics; or, Regulations for the Instruction, Formations, and Movements of the Cavalry of the Army and Volunteers of the United States* (Philadelphia, PA: Lippincott, 1862). Cooke's book stressed a single rank drill as opposed to Poinsett's double ranks.

37. George Cary Eggleston, *A Rebel's Recollections* (Bloomington: Indiana University Press, 1959), 80.

38. These particular Federal volunteers wore Zouave-styled red jackets similar in appearance to many of the Confederate volunteers decked out in red battle shirts.

39. The exact order Stuart gave was "on right into line," whereby every set of fours obliqued to the left so they would dress in on the right of each preceding set of fours. Blackford, *War Years with Jeb Stuart*, 24–25.

40. Elihu Root and Fred C. Ainsworth, eds., *The War of the Rebellion: A Compilation of the Official Records of the Union and Confederate Armies*, additions and corrections to ser. 1, vol. 5 (Washington, DC: Government Printing Office, 1902), 777 (hereafter cited as *O.R.*, vol. 5); McClellan, *I Rode with Jeb Stuart*, 42.

41. *O.R.*, vol. 5, 777; McClellan, *I Rode with Jeb Stuart*, 42.

42. Stuart and Lee had also joined forces in the capture of John Brown at Harper's Ferry before the war. Tucker, *High Tide at Gettysburg*, 13.

43. Robert N. Scott, ed., *The War of the Rebellion: A Compilation of the Official Records of the Union and Confederate Armies*, ser. 1, vol. 11, pt. 2 (Washington, DC: Government Printing Office, 1884), 514 (hereafter cited as *O.R.*, vol. 11); Alexander, *Military Memoirs of a Confederate*, 113–14.

44. McClellan, *I Rode with Jeb Stuart*, 53, 67.

45. Robert N. Scott, ed., *The War of the Rebellion: A Compilation of the Official Records of the Union and Confederate Armies*, ser. 1, vol. 19, pt. 2 (Washington, DC: Government Printing Office, 1887), 55 (hereafter cited as *O.R.*, vol. 19).

46. *O.R.*, vol. 19, pt. 2, 52–54.

47. D. B. Rea, *Sketches from Hampton's Cavalry: Embracing the Principal Exploits of the Cavalry in the Campaigns of 1862 and 1863* (Columbia: South Carolina State Press, 1864), 52.

48. *O.R.*, vol. 19, pt. 2, 58. Most estimates state Stuart captured a thousand horses; the exact number isn't known. Wade Hampton reported leaving sixty fatigued horses behind, and therefore Stuart probably left somewhere between one hundred and two hundred horses total.

49. Mitchell, *Letters of Major General James E. B. Stuart*, 268.

50. *O.R.*, vol. 19, pt. 2, 51.

51. *O.R.*, vol. 25, pt. 1, 1047; McClellan, *I Rode with Jeb Stuart,* 232–34.

52. McClellan, *I Rode with Jeb Stuart*, 235.

53. Alexander, *Military Memoirs of a Confederate*, 360.

54. *O.R.*, vol. 25, pt. 2, 820.

55. *O.R.*, vol. 27, pt. 2, 305; Joseph W. McKinney, *Brandy Station, Virginia, June 9, 1863: The Largest Cavalry Battle of the Civil War* (Jefferson, NC: McFarland, 2006), 39.

56. Wert, *Cavalryman of the Lost Cause*, 238.

57. Officially, Stuart led seven brigades but two were on detached duty while Stuart was at Culpeper.

58. Eric J. Wittenberg, *The Battle of Brandy Station: North America's Largest Cavalry Battle* (Charleston, SC: History Press, 2010), 52.

59. Robert N. Scott, ed., *The War of the Rebellion: A Compilation of the Official Records of the Union and Confederate Armies*, ser. 1, vol. 12, pt. 2 (Washington, DC: Government Printing Office, 1885), 725–26 (hereafter cited as *O.R.*, vol. 12).

60. *O.R.*, vol. 27, pt. 2, 290.

61. *O.R.*, vol. 27, pt. 2, 291.

62. Hampton purportedly killed thirteen men in hand-to-hand combat during the war. See U. R. Brooks, ed., *Butler and His Cavalry in the War of Secession 1861–1865* (Camden, SC: Gray Fox Books, n.d.), 548.

63. Robert F. O'Neill, *Chasing Jeb Stuart and John Mosby: The Union Cavalry in Northern Virginia from Second Manassas to Gettysburg* (Jefferson, NC: McFarland, 2012), 40, 42, 48.

64. *O.R.*, vol. 27, pt. 2, 290.

65. This opinion was also shared by Stonewall Jackson. Blackford, *War Years with Jeb Stuart*, 283; Edward G. Longacre, *Lee's Cavalrymen: A History of the Mounted Forces of the Army of Northern Virginia, 1861–1865* (Mechanicsburg, PA: Stackpole Books, 2002), 110; Mitchell, *Letters of Major General James E. B. Stuart*, 320.

66. *O.R.*, vol. 25, pt. 2, 819–20, 848; *O.R.*, vol. 27, pt. 2, 290.

67. Mitchell, *Letters of Major General James E. B. Stuart*, 319–20.

68. James Buchanan Ballard, *William Edmondson "Grumble" Jones: The Life of a Cantankerous Confederate* (Jefferson, NC: McFarland, 2016), 68.

69. Blackford, *War Years with Jeb Stuart*, 32–33.

70. Dobbie Edward Lambert, *Grumble: The W. E. Jones Brigade of 1863–1864* (Wahiawa, HI: Lambert Enterprises, 1992), 8; Mitchell, *Letters of Major General James E. B. Stuart*, 290–92.

71. *O.R.*, vol. 27, pt. 2, 291.

72. The Battle of Kelly's Ford occurred March 17, 1863. The Federal cavalry enjoyed much success in a surprise attack before withdrawing back across the Rappahannock River.

73. *O.R.*, vol. 27, pt. 2, 291.

74. W. A. Graham, "From Brandy Station to the Heights of Gettysburg," *News & Observer* (Raleigh, NC), February 7, 1904.

75. Company H, 4th Virginia was known as the Black Horse Troop. *O.R.*, vol. 25, pt. 2, 492, 499, 649; O'Neill, *Chasing Jeb Stuart and John Mosby*, 4, 13, 89–90, 101, 103–5; D. Michael Thomas, *Wade Hampton's Iron Scouts: Confederate Special Forces* (Charleston, SC: History Press, 2018), 35–37; Frank M. Myers, *The Comanches: A History of White's Battalion, Virginia Cavalry* (Marietta, GA: Continental, 1956), 137–39.

76. Thomas, *Wade Hampton's Iron Scouts*, 27.

77. *O.R.*, vol. 25, pt. 2, 649.

78. Jeffry D. Wert, *Mosby's Rangers* (New York: Simon & Schuster, 1991), 79.

79. McKinney, *Brandy Station*, 92–93.

CHAPTER 4

1. Stephen W. Sears, *Chancellorsville* (Boston; New York: Houghton Mifflin, 1996), 54.

2. Walter H. Hebert, *Fighting Joe Hooker* (Lincoln: University of Nebraska Press, 1999), 27; U.S. Congress, *Ex. Doc.*, 1st Session, 30th Congress, vol. 3, doc. 17, 11.

3. Hebert, *Fighting Joe Hooker*, 29 (bracketed word by author).

4. Thomas P. Lowry, *The Story the Soldiers Wouldn't Tell: Sex in the Civil War* (Mechanicsburg, PA: Stackpole Books, 1994), 148.

5. *O.R.*, vol. 11, pt. 1, 464–68.

6. John Watts de Peyster, *Personal and Military History of Phil Kearney* (New York: Rice and Gauge, 1969), 281.

7. *O.R.*, vol. 11, pt. 1, 818, 819.

8. John Michael Priest, *Antietam: The Soldiers' Battle* (New York: Oxford University Press, 1989), 86, 99.

9. *O.R.*, vol. 25, pt. 2, 239–40.

10. Edward J. Stackpole, *They Met at Gettysburg* (New York: Bonanza, 1956), 7.

11. Edwin B. Coddington, *The Gettysburg Campaign* (Norwalk, CT: Easton Press, 1998), 29.

12. Thomas J. Ryan and Stephen W. Sears, *Spies, Scouts, and Secrets in the Gettysburg Campaign: How the Critical Role of Intelligence Impacted the Outcome of Lee's Invasion of the North, June–July, 1863* (El Dorado Hills, CA: Savas Beatie, 2015), 11.

13. Some headway had been made in this regard under General John Pope's tenure in 1862.

14. *O.R.*, vol. 25, pt. 1, 1063.

15. *O.R.*, vol. 25, pt. 2, 214.

16. Federal brigadier William Averell commanded a separate wing of Stoneman's raiders, but after crossing the upper Rappahannock, he claimed to be confused by conflicting orders and performed poorly. Hooker ordered him to return to Federal lines, where his command was easily scattered by Confederate cavalry. Hooker then ordered Averell be relieved and assigned elsewhere. *O.R.*, vol. 25, pt. 1, 1076–79, 1080.

17. *O.R.*, vol. 25, pt. 2, 439, 463; *O.R.*, vol. 25, pt. 2, 320, 533.

18. *O.R.*, vol. 25, pt. 2, 547.

19. Robert F. O'Neill, *Chasing Jeb Stuart and John Mosby: The Union Cavalry in Northern Virginia from Second Manassas to Gettysburg* (Jefferson, NC: McFarland, 2012), 220–21. Hooker also scapegoated General Oliver Howard and his XI Corps for crumbling under Stonewall Jackson's flank attack; see Coddington, *The Gettysburg Campaign*, 32.

20. Edward G. Longacre, *Lincoln's Cavalrymen: A History of the Mounted Forces of the Army of Northern Virginia, 1861–1865* (Mechanicsburg, PA: Stackpole Books, 2002), 145, 147.

21. "Captain May's Report, May 10, 1846," Dragoon History, January 1, 2009, accessed June 18, 2017, https://dragoonshistory.wordpress.com/2009/01/01/resaca-de-la-palma-2/. Website is no longer active.

22. Captain May later drew criticism from his commanding officer for not directing the charge in a more efficient manner, but May countered with a successful campaign in the press where he took credit for capturing a Mexican officer his bugler had actually corralled. May was promoted to brevet lieutenant colonel more for his writing than his actions. This exchange might have affected Pleasonton later in his career.

23. Larry Tagg, *The Generals of Gettysburg: The Leaders of America's Greatest Battle* (Cambridge, MA: Da Capo, 2003), 165.

24. *O.R.*, vol. 19, pt. 2, 193–95.

25. *O.R.*, vol. 19, pt. 1, 208.

26. *O.R.*, vol. 19, pt. 1, 209–10; Matthew Forney Steele, *American Campaigns* (Washington, DC: Byron S. Adams, 1909), 1:265.

27. *O.R.*, vol. 19, pt. 1, 210.

28. *O.R.*, vol. 19, pt. 1, 211; Edward G. Longacre, *General John Buford: A Military Biography* (Cambridge, MA: Da Capo, 1995), 116.

29. Edward G. Longacre, *The Cavalry at Gettysburg: A Tactical Study of Mounted Operations during the Civil War's Pivotal Campaign, 9 June–14 July 1863* (Lincoln: University of Nebraska Press, 1986), 48.

30. *O.R.*, vol. 19, pt. 2, 367.

31. *O.R.*, vol. 19, pt. 2, 38–40.

32. *O.R.*, vol. 19, pt. 2, 42–45.

33. *O.R.*, vol. 19, pt. 2, 110, 111, 112–15.

34. Tagg, *Generals of Gettysburg*, 167; Longacre, *The Cavalry at Gettysburg*, 48.

35. *O.R.*, vol. 25, pt. 1, 773; Henry B. McClellan, *I Rode with Jeb Stuart: The Life and Campaigns of Major General J. E. B. Stuart* (New York: Da Capo, 1994), 238–40.

36. Longacre, *The Cavalry at Gettysburg*, 47; Alfred Pleasonton, "The Successes and Failures of the Battle of Chancellorsville," in *Battles and Leaders of the Civil War*, vol. 3, ed. Robert Underwood Johnson and Clarence Clough Buel (Edison, NJ: Castle, 1995), 177–80, 180n, 181; Bill Hyde, ed., *The Union Generals Speak: The Meade Hearings on the Battle of Gettysburg* (Baton Rouge: Louisiana State University Press, 2003), 134.

37. *O.R.*, vol. 25, pt. 2, 513. This was only a temporary command of undetermined length. Stoneman remained on medical leave.

38. Joseph W. McKinney, *Brandy Station, Virginia, June 9, 1863: The Largest Cavalry Battle of the Civil War* (Jefferson, NC: McFarland, 2006), 254.

39. Robert O'Neill, "For the Lack of Horses, the War Was Nearly Lost," HistoryNet, May 19, 2020, accessed August 22, 2021, https://www.historynet.com/lack-of-horses.htm.

40. Edward G. Longacre, *General John Buford: A Military Biography* (Cambridge, MA: Da Capo, 1995), 46.

41. Robert F. O'Neill, *The Cavalry Battles of Aldie, Middleburg and Upperville, June 10–27, 1863*, Virginia Civil War Battle and Leaders Series (Lynchburg, VA: H. E. Howard, 1993), 12.

42. Tagg, *Generals of Gettysburg*, 168.

43. Longacre, *General John Buford*, 49.

44. Tagg, *Generals of Gettysburg*, 168.

45. *O.R.*, vol. 12, pt. 2, 336–337, 579.

46. W. W. Blackford, *War Years with Jeb Stuart* (New York: Scribner, 1945), 134.

47. *O.R.*, vol. 12, pt. 2, 274.

48. *O.R.*, vol. 12, pt. 2, 274.

49. *O.R.*, vol. 12, pt. 2, 748.

50. Blackford, *War Years with Jeb Stuart*, 170–71; Longacre, *General John Buford*, 108.

51. Richard L. Armstrong, *7th Virginia Cavalry*, Virginia Regimental Histories Series (Lynchburg, VA: H. E. Howard, 1992), 41–42; Eric J. Wittenberg, "The Cavalry Fight at Lewis Ford August 30, 1862," Facebook, accessed March 3, 2015, https://www.facebook.com/MajorGeneralJohnBuford/posts/232495120218554.

52. William Harrison Beach, *First New York (Lincoln) Cavalry from April 19, 1861, to July 7, 1865* (n.p.: Nabu Press, 2010), 399.

53. Eric J. Wittenberg, *Union Cavalry Comes of Age: Hartwood Church to Brandy Station, 1863* (Charleston, SC: History Press, 2017), 90.

54. *O.R.*, vol. 25, pt. 1, 49.

55. Stephen B. Emerson, "Steptoe's Defeat: Battle of Tohotonimme (1858)," History Link, August 8, 2008, accessed December 26, 2015, http://www.historylink.org/index.cfm?displaypage=output.cfm&file_id=8709.

56. Tagg, *Generals of Gettysburg*, 176.

57. *O.R.*, vol. 11, pt. 2, 966–67; *O.R.*, vol. 19, pt. 2, 129–30.

58. Samuel P. Bates, *Martial Deeds of Pennsylvania* (Philadelphia, PA: T. H. Davis, 1875), 772.

59. Ryan and Sears, *Spies, Scouts, and Secrets in the Gettysburg Campaign*, 79–81.

60. Secretary of State William H. Seward and Secretary of War Edwin Stanton. *O.R.*, vol. 25, pt. 2, 510; Wilbur Sturtevant Nye, *Here Come the Rebels* (Dayton, OH: Morningside, 1988), 26; *O.R.*, vol. 25, pt. 2, 3, 8.

61. James B. Hewlett, Noah A. Trudeau, and Bryce A. Suderow, eds., *Supplement to the Official Records of the Union and Confederate Armies*, vol. 4, pt. 1, *Reports* (Wilmington, NC: Broadfoot, 1995), 474–75 (bracketed words by author).

62. *O.R.*, vol. 27, pt. 3, 32.

63. McKinney, *Brandy Station, Virginia, June 9, 1863*, 104.

64. *O.R.*, vol. 27, pt. 3, 27–28.

CHAPTER 5

1. Samuel Levis Gracey, *Annals of the Sixth Pennsylvania Cavalry* (Philadelphia, PA: E. H. Butler, 1868), 156; Eric J. Wittenberg, *The Battle of Brandy Station: North America's Largest Cavalry Battle* (Charleston, SC: History Press, 2010), 76.

2. *O.R.*, vol. 19, pt. 2, 305.

3. Henry Norton, *Deeds of Daring; or, History of the Eighth N.Y. Volunteer Cavalry, Containing a Complete Record of the Battles, Skirmishes, Marches, Etc., That the Gallant Eighth New York Cavalry Participated In, from Its Organization in November, 1861, to the Close of the Rebellion in 1865* (n.p.: Big Byte Books, 2020), 43.

4. "The Eighth Cavalry," *Rochester Daily Advertiser*, June 18, 1863; Heros von Borcke and Justus Scheibert, *The Great Cavalry Battle of Brandy Station, 9 June 1863* (Winston-Salem, NC: Paelemon, 1976), 85.

5. Joseph W. McKinney, *Brandy Station, Virginia, June 9, 1863: The Largest Cavalry Battle of the Civil War* (Jefferson, NC: McFarland, 2006), 111.

6. Robert J. Driver Jr., *1st Virginia Cavalry*, 2nd ed. (Lynchburg, VA: H. E. Howard, 1991), 61; Thomas J. Ryan and Stephen W. Sears, *Spies, Scouts, and Secrets in the Gettysburg Campaign: How the Critical Role of Intelligence Impacted the Outcome of Lee's Invasion of the North, June–July, 1863* (El Dorado Hills, CA: Savas Beatie, 2015), 14.

7. Norton, *Deeds of Daring*, 43.

8. John Buford to Lieutenant Colonel A. J. Alexander, June 13, 1863, Joseph Hooker Military Papers, Huntington Library, San Marino, CA.

9. Michael P. Musick, *6th Virginia Cavalry* (Lynchburg, VA: H. E. Howard, 1990), 38.

10. William N. McDonald, *A History of the Laurel Brigade: Originally the Ashby Cavalry of the Army of Northern Virginia and Chew's Battery*, ed. Bushrod C. Washington (Baltimore, MD: Mrs. Kate S. McDonald, 1902), 134.

11. Henry B. McClellan, *I Rode with Jeb Stuart: The Life and Campaigns of Major General J. E. B. Stuart* (New York: Da Capo, 1994), 265.

12. *O.R.*, vol. 27, pt. 1, 1044–46.

13. *O.R.*, vol. 27, pt. 2, 748–49.

14. von Borcke and Scheibert, *The Great Cavalry Battle of Brandy Station*, 78.

15. Robert J. Trout, ed., *Memoirs of the Stuart Horse Artillery Battalion: Moorman's and Hart's Batteries* (Knoxville: University of Tennessee Press, 2008), 204.

16. McClellan, *I Rode with Jeb Stuart*, 266. A prolonge was a strong rope twelve feet long with a hook at one end, a toggle on the other, and two rings in the middle for adjusting the length. The prolonge was used to quickly span the lunette of the gun carriage to the pintle hook of the limber when rapidly advancing or retreating short distances. Mark Mayo Boatner III, *The Civil War Dictionary*, rev. ed. (New York: David McKay, 1988), 673.

17. Colonel Thomas C. Devin to Captain, June 1863, Joseph Hooker Military Papers, Huntington Library, San Marino, CA.

18. *O.R.*, vol. 27, pt. 2, 748; *O.R.*, vol. 27, pt. 2, 757. The 7th Virginia was to serve as the Grand Guard that day for General Jones's brigade. They were up and already in the process of saddling horses when the Federals struck the river.

19. *O.R.*, vol. 27, pt. 2, 757.

20. Norton, *Deeds of Daring*, 44.

21. Colonel Thomas C. Devin to Captain, June 1863, Joseph Hooker Military Papers; Abner Hard, *History of the Eighth Cavalry Regiment, Illinois Volunteers, during the Great Rebellion* (Aurora, IL: n.p., 1868), 243.

22. Ezra J. Warner, *Generals in Blue: Lives of the Union Commanders* (Baton Rouge: Louisiana State University Press, 1992), 124.

23. J. R. Poinsett, ed., *School of the Squadron—Mounted*, pt. 2 of *Cavalry Tactics* (Washington, DC: U.S. War Department; J & G. S. Gideon, 1841), 100, 186; George Patton, *Patton's Cavalry Drill and Sabre Exercise* (New York: J. W. Fortune, 1861; repr., Rochelle, VA: Heartland House Press, 1990), 6–7, 45. In a column of fours, each rank of fours needed one pace, or 3 feet, between the croup of the forward file's mount and the nose of the file closer's mount. Each horse was approximately 3 yards, or 9 feet, long. Thus, each rank of four, with proper distance, was approximately 12 feet long. There are 16 (two-deep) ranks of four in one squadron. Each two-deep rank of four is 24 feet long (16 x 24 = 384 feet).

24. Colonel Thomas C. Devin to Captain, June 1863, Joseph Hooker Military Papers.

25. John Buford to Colonel Alexander, Headquarters 1st Division and Cavalry Reserve, Near Warrenton Junction, June 13, 1863, Joseph Hooker Military Papers, Huntington Library, San Marino, CA.

26. *O.R.*, vol. 27, pt. 3, 38.

27. McKinney, *Brandy Station, Virginia, June 9, 1863*, 121.

28. D. B. Rea, *Sketches from Hampton's Cavalry: Embracing the Principle Exploits of the Cavalry in the Campaigns of 1862 and 1863* (Columbia: South Carolina State Press, 1864), 88.

29. John Buford to Colonel Alexander, Headquarters 1st Division and Cavalry Reserve, Near Warrenton Junction, June 13, 1863, Joseph Hooker Military Papers; Edwin Eustace Bryant, *History of the Third Regiment of Wisconsin Veteran Volunteer Infantry, 1861–1865* (Madison, WI: Veteran Association, 1891), 170.

30. John Buford to Colonel Alexander, Headquarters 1st Division and Cavalry Reserve, Near Warrenton Junction, June 13, 1863, Joseph Hooker Military Papers.

31. Regular officers' ranks were not brevet grades issued by states, and volunteer units typically promoted their officers much faster than the regular army. This made little difference in field practice except the officers leading the U.S. regiments in the Regulars Brigade were sometimes just captains, even though they were performing as field commanders and acting in the capacity of majors, lieutenant colonels, and colonels.

32. Captain W. Merritt to "Lieutenant" in the Field, June 10, 1863, Joseph Hooker Military Papers, Huntington Library, San Marino, CA.

33. Formed as the 6th Pennsylvania, they were also known as Rush's Lancers for their early issue of pole arms. The lances had since been replaced with breech-loading carbines.

34. *O.R.*, vol. 27, pt. 2, 742.

35. Major H. G. Wheeling to Lt. James McQueston, Camp Near Catlett's Station, June 11, 1863, Joseph Hooker Military Papers, Huntington Library, San Marino, CA.

36. Gracey, *Annals of the Sixth Pennsylvania Cavalry*, 159.

37. Gracey, *Annals of the Sixth Pennsylvania Cavalry*, 159; John Buford to Alfred Pleasonton, Near Warrenton Junction, June 13, 1863, Joseph Hooker Military Papers, Huntington Library, San Marino, CA.

38. *O.R.*, vol. 27, pt. 2, 749.

39. Out on the Confederate left, Lomax made contact with a force of Federals, most likely Company D, 8th Illinois Cavalry. Lomax later wrote, "[W]e charged them, driving them back through the woods, killing and capturing several. In this charge, we passed a column of the enemy's cavalry charging our battery near the church" (*O.R.*, vol. 27, pt. 2, 762–63).

40. Charles Triplett O'Ferrall, *Forty Years of Active Service; Being Some History of the War between the Confederacy and the Union and of the Events Leading up to It, with Reminiscences of the Struggle and Accounts of the Author's Experiences of Four Years from Private to Lieutenant-Colonel and Acting Colonel in the Cavalry of the Army of Northern Virginia* (New York: Neale, 1905), 65; Gracey, *Annals of the Sixth Pennsylvania Cavalry*, 159.

41. J. R. Poinsett, ed., *School of the Squadron—Mounted*, pt. 2 of *Cavalry Tactics* (Washington, DC: U.S. War Department; J. and G. S. Gideon, 1841), 192–96. To form a squadron from a column of fours while moving at a military gallop of three hundred yards per minute (10.2 miles per hour) required the front set of fours to first advance thirty paces to the front and then break gait down to a military trot of two hundred yards per minute (6.8 miles per hour) and allow the rear ranks to come forward successively in line and form abreast, or dress, on the first set of fours. The difference in speed between the two gaits is 3.4 miles per hour, and therefore it took approximately fifty seconds to perform this maneuver on a drill field.

42. Poinsett, *School of the Squadron—Mounted*, 192–96,

43. McDonald, *A History of the Laurel Brigade*, 137; Gracey, *Annals of the Sixth Pennsylvania Cavalry*, 159.

44. Poinsett, *School of the Squadron—Mounted*, 192–96.

45. Major James F. Hart, *Philadelphia Weekly Times*, June 26, 1880; see McClellan, *I Rode with Jeb Stuart*, 267.

46. *O.R.*, vol. 27, pt. 2, 774. The 35th Battalion's unique high-pitched hoops and shouts stood out among even the Rebel yell and earned them the title of White's Comanches.

47. Trout, *Memoirs of the Stuart Horse Artillery Battalion*, 206.

48. Major H. G. Wheeling to Lt. James McQueston, Camp Near Catlett's Station, June 11, 1863, Joseph Hooker Military Papers.

49. *O.R.*, vol. 27, pt. 2, 763; Capt. George Cram to "Sir," Regimental Camp 6th Reg. Cavalry, Catlett's Station, Virginia, June 10, 1863, Joseph Hooker Military Papers, Huntington Library, San Marino, CA.

50. Dennis E. Frye, *12th Virginia Cavalry* (Lynchburg, VA: H. E. Howard, 1988), 36.

51. Louis Henry Carpenter, "Carpenter to His Father, June 11, 1863," in *Louis Henry Carpenter: Letters from the Field 1861–1865* (Philadelphia, PA: Historical Society of Pennsylvania, n.d.) (bracketed words by author).

52. Gracey, *Annals of the Sixth Pennsylvania Cavalry*, 161.

53. Capt. George Cram to "Sir," Regimental Camp 6th Reg. Cavalry, Catlett's Station, Virginia, June 10, 1863, Joseph Hooker Military Papers.

54. W. W. Blackford, *War Years with Jeb Stuart* (New York: Scribner, 1945), 213.

55. *O.R.*, vol. 27, pt. 2, 680.

56. *O.R.*, vol. 27, pt. 1, 1045.

57. Rea, *Sketches from Hampton's Cavalry*, 88; *O.R.*, vol. 27, pt. 1, 1048; *O.R.*, vol. 27, pt. 2, 722; *O.R.*, vol. 27, pt. 2, 727.

58. Vince Dooley and Samuel N. Thomas, eds., *The Legion's Fighting Bulldog: The Civil War Correspondence of William Gaston Delony, Lieutenant Colonel of Cobb's Georgia Legion Cavalry, and Rosa Delony, 1853–1863* (Macon, GA: Mercer University Press, 2017), 226.

59. Thomas Casimer Devin to Captains; Casualties in Cavalry Engagement, June 9, 1863: Names of Officers Killed, Wounded and Missing, Joseph Hooker Military Papers, Huntington Library, San Marino, CA; *O.R.*, vol. 27, pt. 2, 727; John Logan Black, *Crumbling Defenses; or, Memoirs and Reminiscences of John Logan Black* (Macon, GA: Eleanor D. McSwain, 1960), 19.

60. Thomas Casimer Devin to Captains; Casualties in Cavalry Engagement, June 9, 1863: Names of Officers Killed, Wounded and Missing, Joseph Hooker Military Papers.

61. John Buford to Colonel Alexander, Headquarters 1st Division and Cavalry Reserve, Near Warrenton Junction, June 13, 1863, Joseph Hooker Military Papers.

62. Stuart had also sent the 4th Virginia Cavalry to aid Robertson. See *O.R.*, vol. 27, pt. 2, 680.

63. Frank M. Myers, *The Comanches: A History of White's Battalion, Virginia Cavalry* (Marietta, GA: Continental, 1956), 183.

64. Myers, *The Comanches*, 183.

CHAPTER 6

1. *O.R.*, vol. 27, pt. 3, 27–28.

2. Wyndham's brigade consisted of the 1st Maryland, 1st New Jersey, and 1st Pennsylvania. Kilpatrick's brigade consisted of the 1st Maine, 2nd New York, and 10th New York. Martin's right section supported Wyndham, his left supported Kilpatrick, and the center was staged between each on the march. Russell's infantry brigade consisted of the 6th Maine; 5th New Hampshire; 56th, 81st, and 119th Pennsylvania; the 2nd and 7th Wisconsin; and Battery C, 3rd U.S. Artillery under 1st Lieutenant William Fuller.

3. D. M. M. Gregg to Colonel, Head Quarters 2nd & 3rd Cavalry Divisions, Cavalry Corps, June 12, 1863, Joseph Hooker Military Papers, Huntington Library, San Marino, CA.

4. Henry B. McClellan, *I Rode with Jeb Stuart: The Life and Campaigns of Major General J. E. B. Stuart* (New York: Da Capo, 1994), 418–21.

5. Robert F. O'Neill, *Chasing Jeb Stuart and John Mosby: The Union Cavalry in Northern Virginia from Second Manassas to Gettysburg* (Jefferson, NC: McFarland, 2012), 97.

6. McClellan, *I Rode with Jeb Stuart*, 270.

7. *O.R.*, vol. 27, pt. 1, 965; McClellan, *I Rode with Jeb Stuart*, 270; Joseph W. McKinney, *Brandy Station, Virginia, June 9, 1863: The Largest Cavalry Battle of the Civil War* (Jefferson, NC: McFarland, 2006), 156.

8. McClellan, *I Rode with Jeb Stuart*, 270.

9. This was the Federal 1st Maryland Cavalry. *O.R.*, vol. 27, pt. 1, 966. Major Charles Russell led this first advance.

10. *O.R.*, vol. 27, pt. 1, 1024. Captain Martin joined his two guns to Lieutenant Clark's section. Clark had only one functioning gun at this point.

11. *O.R.*, vol. 27, pt. 1, 966.

12. *O.R.*, vol. 27, pt. 1, 966.

13. William P. Lloyd, *History of the First Reg't Pennsylvania Reserve Cavalry, from Its Organization, August, 1861, to September, 1864: With a List of Names of All Officers and Enlisted Men Who Have Ever Belonged to the Regiment* (Salem, MA: Higginson, 1990), 55–56.

14. Charles Triplett O'Ferrall, *Forty Years of Service: Being Some History of the War between the Confederacy and the Union and of the Events Leading up to It, with Reminiscences of the Struggle and Accounts of the Author's Experiences of Four Years from Private to Lieutenant-Colonel and Acting Colonel in the Cavalry of the Army of Northern Virginia* (New York: Neale, 1904), 66.

15. McClellan, *I Rode with Jeb Stuart*, 271, n272.

16. William McDonald, *A History of the Laurel Brigade: Originally the Ashby Cavalry of the Army of Northern Virginia and Chew's Battery*, ed. Bushrod C. Washington (Baltimore, MD: Mrs. Kate S. McDonald, 1902), 140. The 12th Virginia's Company B suffered three men killed and four wounded in this first contact.

17. James Moore, *Kilpatrick and Our Cavalry, Comprising a Sketch of the Life of General Kilpatrick, with an Account of the Cavalry Raids, Engagements, and Operations*

under His Command, from the Beginning of the Rebellion to the Surrender of Johnston, by James Moore (New York: W. J. Widdleton, 1865), 58.

18. Dennis Frye, *12th Virginia Cavalry* (Lynchburg, VA: H. E. Howard, 1988), 39.

19. Frank M. Myers, *The Comanches: A History of White's Battalion, Virginia Cavalry* (Marietta, GA: Continental, 1956), 184.

20. Frye, *12th Virginia Cavalry*, 38.

21. Henry R. Pyne, *The History of the First New Jersey Cavalry* (Trenton, NJ: J. A. Breecher, 1871), 152 (bracketed word by author).

22. Frye, *12th Virginia Cavalry*, 39.

23. *O.R.*, vol. 27, pt. 2, 755.

24. Robert J. Trout, *Galloping Thunder: The Story of the Stuart Horse Artillery Battalion* (Mechanicsburg, PA: Stackpole Books, 2002), 229.

25. O'Ferrall, *Forty Years of Service*, 67; Frye, *12th Virginia Cavalry*, 39.

26. O'Ferrall, *Forty Years of Service*, 67; Frye, *12th Virginia Cavalry*, 39.

27. Samuel Toombs, *New Jersey Troops in the Gettysburg Campaign from June 5 to July 31, 1863* (Orange, NJ: Evening Mail, 1888), 57–58.

28. *O.R.*, vol. 27, pt. 1, 1054.

29. H. H. Matthews, "The Pelham-Breathed Battery," *St. Mary's Beacon*, March 16, 1905.

30. *O.R.*, vol. 27, pt. 2, 773; James F. Hart, *Philadelphia Weekly Times*, June 26, 1880.

31. Trout, *Galloping Thunder*, 229–30.

32. W. W. Blackford, *War Years with Jeb Stuart* (New York: Scribner, 1945), 217.

33. Justus Scheibert, *Seven Months in the Rebel States during the North American War, 1863*, ed. William Stanley Hoole (Tuscaloosa: University of Alabama Press, 2009), 90–91.

34. Robert J. Trout, ed., *In the Saddle with Stuart: The Story of Frank Smith Robertson of JEB Stuart's Staff* (Gettysburg, PA: Thomas Publications, 1998), 67; Robert J. Trout, *Memoirs of the Stuart Horse Artillery Battalion* (Knoxville: University of Tennessee Press, 2010), 324.

35. *O.R.*, vol. 27, pt. 2, 755.

36. *O.R.*, vol. 27, pt. 1, 1025.

37. Myers, *The Comanches*, 184.

38. One company of the 6th Virginia accompanied White's 35th Battalion in this charge.

39. *O.R.*, vol. 27, pt. 2, 769.

40. Myers, *The Comanches*, 185 (bracketed word by author).

41. Toombs, *New Jersey Troops*, 58; *O.R.*, vol. 27, pt. 1, 1025; Heros von Borcke and Justus Scheibert, "Colonel White's Report," in *The Great Cavalry Fight at Brandy Station, 9 June 1863* (Winston-Salem, NC: Paelemon, 1976), 75–77.

42. Unlike a trooper's horse outfitted with a simple saddle, battery horses wore a special harness for pulling the guns.

43. Henry C. Meyer, *Civil War Experiences under Bayard, Gregg, Kilpatrick, Custer, Raulston, and Newberry, 1862, 1863, 1864* (New York: Putnam, 1911), 28.

44. James H. Kidd, *Personal Recollections of a Cavalryman* (1908; repr., Ionia, MI: Sentinel, 2015), 166.

45. Edward G. Longacre, *The Cavalry at Gettysburg: A Tactical Study of Mounted Operations during the Civil War's Pivotal Campaign, 9 June–14 July 1863* (Lincoln: University of Nebraska Press, 1986), 53–54; Samuel J. Martin, *Kill-Cavalry: The Life of Union General Hugh Judson Kilpatrick* (Mechanicsburg, PA: Stackpole Books, 2000), 56–57.

46. Samuel Lovejoy Gillespie, *A History of Company A, First Ohio Cavalry, 1861–1865* (Columbus, OH: Lovejoy, 1898; repr., Salem, MA: Higginson, 1990), 163.

47. Kidd, *Personal Recollections*, 166.

48. *O.R.*, vol. 27, pt. 1, 1027.

49. *O.R.*, vol. 27, pt. 2, 732; Wiley C. Howard, *Sketch of the Cobb Legion Cavalry and Some Incidents and Scenes Remembered* (Atlanta, GA: Atlanta Camp 159, S.C.V., 1901; repr., Delhi, India: Facsimile, 2013), 6.

50. *O.R.*, vol. 27, pt. 2, 722.

51. Vince Dooley and Samuel N. Thomas, eds., *The Legion's Fighting Bulldog: The Civil War Correspondence of William Gaston Delony, Lieutenant Colonel of Cobb's Georgia Legion Cavalry, and Rosa Delony, 1853–1863* (Macon, GA: Mercer University Press, 2017), 218.

52. Howard, *Sketch of the Cobb Legion Cavalry*, 6; Dooley and Thomas, *The Legion's Fighting Bulldog*, 226; *O.R.*, vol. 27, pt. 2, 732.

53. *O.R.*, vol. 27, pt. 2, 733; Noble D. Preston, *History of the Tenth Regiment of Cavalry New York State Volunteers: August, 1861, to August, 1865* (New York: D. Appleton, 1892), 85.

54. *O.R.*, vol. 27, pt. 1, 1027.

55. Howard, *Sketch of the Cobb Legion Cavalry*, 7.

56. *O.R.*, vol. 27, pt. 1, 997.

57. John Logan Black, *Crumbling Defenses; or, Memoirs and Reminiscences of John Logan Black* (Macon, GA: Eleanor D. McSwain, 1960), 21.

58. *O.R.*, vol. 27, pt. 2, 728.

59. Edward P. Tobie, *History of the First Maine Cavalry, 1861–1865* (Boston: Emory & Hughes Press, 1887), 154.

60. D. B. Rea, *Sketches from Hampton's Cavalry: Embracing the Principle Exploits of the Cavalry in the Campaigns of 1862 and 1863* (Columbia: South Carolina State Press, 1864), 91.

61. *O.R.*, vol. 27, pt. 2, 722.

62. *O.R.*, vol. 27, pt. 2, 755.

63. Tobie, *History of the First Maine Cavalry*, 150–51.

64. Donald A. Hopkins, *The Little Jeff: The Jeff Davis Legion, Cavalry, Army of Northern Virginia* (Shippensburg, PA: White Mane Books, 1999), 134–35.

65. *O.R.*, vol. 27, pt. 1, 1024.

66. Richard L. Armstrong, *11th Virginia Cavalry*, Virginia Regimental Histories Series (Lynchburg, VA: H. E. Howard, 1989), 42–43.

67. Armstrong, *11th Virginia Cavalry*, 42–43; *O.R.*, vol. 27, pt. 1, 1025.

68. *O.R.*, vol. 27, pt. 2, 763.

69. McDonald, *A History of the Laurel Brigade*, 145.

CHAPTER 7

1. *O.R.*, vol. 27, pt. 3, 27–28.

2. 1st Lieutenant Alexander Cummings McWhorter Pennington was the son of a New Jersey congressman and graduate of West Point in 1860. See Mark Mayo Boatner III, *The Civil War Dictionary*, rev. ed. (New York: David McKay, 1988), 634.

3. *O.R.*, vol. 27, pt. 1, 961.

4. *O.R.*, vol. 27, pt. 2, 723.

5. *O.R.*, vol. 27, pt. 2, 729.

6. These thirty-six men were posted on a sidetrack that ran parallel with the Kirtley Road and just forward of Hansborough Mount. *O.R.*, vol. 27, pt. 2, 729.

7. Robert J. Trout, *They Followed the Plume: The Staff Officers and Headquarters Personnel of Major General J. E. B. Stuart, C.S.A.* (Mechanicsburg, PA: Stackpole Books, 1993), 111; *O.R.*, vol. 27, pt. 2, 685; Robert J. Trout, *Galloping Thunder: The Story of the Stuart Horse Artillery Battalion* (Mechanicsburg, PA: Stackpole Books, 2002), 227.

8. Henry B. McClellan, *I Rode with Jeb Stuart: The Life and Campaigns of Major General J. E. B. Stuart* (New York: Da Capo, 1994), 286.

9. The 2nd South Carolina equipment returns are missing for this particular campaign. Later returns confirm this regiment was armed with a mixture of .58 caliber and .54 caliber ammunition consistent with Enfield rifles and Austrian-manufactured Lorenz muzzle-loading weapons. It is known that other units in Hampton's brigade received Enfield rifles just prior to Brandy Station. John Logan Black, *Crumbling Defenses; or, Memoirs and Reminiscences of John Logan Black* (Macon, GA: Eleanor D. McSwain, 1960), 21.

10. John Weston, *Picket Pins and Sabers: The Civil War Letters of John Burden Weston*, ed. Robert W. Frost and Nancy D. Frost (Ashland, KY: Economy, 1971), 49.

11. U. R. Brooks, ed., *Butler and His Cavalry in the War of Secession 1861–1865* (Camden, SC: Gray Fox Books, n.d.), 166.

12. Brooks, *Butler and His Cavalry*, 166–67.

13. McClellan, *I Rode with Jeb Stuart*, 288–89.

14. *O.R.*, vol. 27, pt. 2, 729.

15. McClellan, *I Rode with Jeb Stuart*, 289.

16. *O.R.*, vol. 27, pt. 2, 744.

17. *O.R.*, vol. 27, pt. 2, 730.

18. The exact distance is unclear but appears to have been more than five hundred yards.

19. McClellan, *I Rode with Jeb Stuart*, 290–92. Knowing he was dying, Farley thanked all those who rushed to attend him. They purportedly carried him from the field with Farley clutching his severed leg to his chest.

20. *O.R.*, vol. 27, pt. 1, 962; D. M. M. Gregg to Colonel, Head Quarters 2nd & 3rd Cavalry Divisions, Cavalry Corps, June 12, 1863, Joseph Hooker Military Papers, Huntington Library, San Marino, CA.

21. D. M. M. Gregg to Colonel, Head Quarters 2nd & 3rd Cavalry Divisions, Cavalry Corps, June 12, 1863; *O.R.*, vol. 27, pt. 1, 975.

22. John Buford to Colonel A. J. Alexander, Head Quarters 1st Division and Cavalry Reserve, Near Warrenton Junction, Virginia, June 13, 1863, Joseph Hooker Military Papers, Huntington Library, San Marino, CA; Wesley Merritt to Lieutenant, Head Quarters 2nd Cavalry, in the Field, June 10, 1863, Joseph Hooker Military Papers, Huntington Library, San Marino, CA.

23. Roger H. Harrell, *The 2nd North Carolina Cavalry* (Jefferson, NC: McFarland, 2012), 119; Trout, *Galloping Thunder*, 226.

24. Joseph W. McKinney, *Brandy Station, Virginia, June 9, 1863: The Largest Cavalry Battle of the Civil War* (Jefferson, NC: McFarland, 2006), 185.

25. Mary Daughtry, *Gray Cavalier: The Life and Wars of General W. H. F. "Rooney" Lee* (Cambridge, MA: Da Capo, 2002), 135; T. F. Rodenbough, *From Everglade to Canon with the Second Dragoons, (Second United States Cavalry): An Authentic Account of Service in Florida, Mexico, Virginia, and the Indian Country, Including the Personal Recollections of Prominent Officers, with an Appendix Containing Orders, Reports and Correspondence, Military Records, Etc., Etc., Etc., 1836–1875* (New York: D. Van Nostrand, 1875), 288–89; Edward G. Longacre, *The Cavalry at Gettysburg: A Tactical Study of Mounted Operations during the Civil War's Pivotal Campaign, 9 June–14 July 1863* (Lincoln: University of Nebraska Press, 1986), 85; Daniel Murphy, "Brandy Station's Forgotten Flank," *America's Civil War*, November, 2006, 54.

26. William Graham, *Nineteenth Regiment*, vol. 2 of *Histories of the Several Regiments and Battalions from North Carolina in the Great War, 1861–1865*, ed. Walter Clark (Goldsboro, NC: Nash Brothers, 1901), 91.

27. Graham, *Nineteenth Regiment*, 91.

28. McKinney, *Brandy Station*, 186.

29. Edwin Eustace Bryant, *History of the Third Regiment of Wisconsin Veteran Volunteer Infantry 1861–1865* (Madison, WI: Veteran Association, 1891), 171.

30. Bryant, *History of the Third Regiment*, 171.

31. The captured men were from the 2nd North Carolina Cavalry.

32. John Buford to Colonel A. J. Alexander, Head Quarters 1st Division Cavalry Reserve, Near Warrenton Junction, Virginia, June 13, 1863, Joseph Hooker Military Papers.

33. G. W. Beale, *A Lieutenant of Cavalry in Lee's Army* (Baltimore, MD: Butternut and Blue, 1994), 95.

34. Beale, *A Lieutenant of Cavalry*, 95–96.

35. R. L. T. Beale, *History of the Ninth Virginia Cavalry, in the War between the States* (1899; repr., Richmond, VA: B. F. Johnson, 2010), 69; Beale, *A Lieutenant of Cavalry*, 96; Wesley Merritt to Lieutenant, Head Quarters 2nd Cavalry, in the Field, June 10, 1863, Joseph Hooker Military Papers.

36. McClellan, *I Rode with Jeb Stuart*, 282.

37. Graham, *Nineteenth Regiment*, 91; Murphy, "Brandy Station's Forgotten Flank," 54.

38. Graham, *Nineteenth Regiment*, 91–92 (bracketed word by author).

39. Robert J. Driver Jr., *10th Virginia Cavalry* (Lynchburg, VA: H. E. Howard, 1992), 37.

40. "The Cavalry Fight in Culpeper," *Richmond Daily Dispatch*, June 15, 1863.

41. Graham, *Nineteenth Regiment*, 92–93; John Buford to Colonel A. J. Alexander, Head Quarters 1st Division and Cavalry Reserve, Near Warrenton Junction, June 13, Joseph Hooker Military Papers.

42. *O.R.*, vol. 27, pt. 2, 737–738; John Buford to Colonel A. J. Alexander, Head Quarters 1st Division and Cavalry Reserve, Near Warrenton Junction, June 13, 1863, Joseph Hooker Military Papers.

43. *O.R.*, vol. 27, pt. 2, 736.

44. Ada Bruce Desper Bradshaw, ed., *Civil War Diary of Charles William McVicar* (Washington, DC: Library of Congress, 1977), 12–13.

45. McClellan, *I Rode with Jeb Stuart*, 294.

CHAPTER 8

1. *O.R.*, vol. 27, pt. 3, 58.

2. *Philadelphia Inquirer*, June 11, 1863.

3. *O.R.*, vol. 27, pt. 3, 49.

4. Federal troopers captured papers from Battery Captain Roger Chew, including a letter from someone named "Bill" writing a family member that Stuart was planning a raid into the enemy's country. It was not an official document from Stuart's command chain.

5. "Culpeper Court-House, June 8, 1863," *New York Times*, June 19, 1863. This letter was likely written by Private J. William Deck, a member of Captain Chew's Confederate horse battery.

6. *Philadelphia Inquirer*, June 11, 1863.

7. *O.R.*, vol. 27, pt. 3, 70–71 (bracketed words by author).

8. A. Pleasonton to Major General Hooker, Beverly Crossing, 9:30 p.m. June 9, 1863, Joseph Hooker Military Papers, Huntington Library, San Marino, CA.

9. *O.R.*, vol. 27, pt. 3, 70–71.

10. *O.R.*, vol. 27, pt. 2, 313.

11. Stuart did not begin crossing the Rappahannock until June 15, six days after Brandy Station. See Henry B. McClellan, *I Rode with Jeb Stuart: The Life and Campaigns of Major General J. E. B. Stuart* (New York: Da Capo, 1994), 296.

12. *O.R.*, vol. 27, pt. 3, 71.

13. *O.R.*, vol. 27, pt. 3, 71.

14. *O.R.*, vol. 27, pt. 3, 70, 71, 72, 83.

15. *O.R.*, vol. 27, pt. 3, 71.

16. Robert F. O'Neill, "For the Lack of Horses, the War Was Nearly Lost," HistoryNet, May 19, 2020, accessed September 19, 2021, https://www.historynet.com/lack-of-horses.htm.

17. *O.R.*, vol. 27, pt. 3, 58.

18. *O.R.*, vol. 27, pt. 3, 85.

19. *O.R.*, vol. 27, pt. 3, 67, 70, 71, 72.

20. *O.R.*, vol. 27, pt. 1, 38.

21. Reynolds's west wing would consist of the I, III, V, and XI Federal Corps along with the cavalry.

22. The east wing under Hooker would consist of the II, VI, and XII Federal Corps along with the Artillery Reserve.

23. *O.R.*, vol. 27, pt. 1, 38.

24. *O.R.*, vol. 27, pt. 3, 92.

25. Robert F. O'Neill, *Chasing Jeb Stuart and John Mosby: The Union Cavalry in Northern Virginia from Second Manassas to Gettysburg* (Jefferson, NC: McFarland, 2012), 125.

26. E. Prioleau Henderson, *Autobiography of Arab: Beaufort District Troop & 2nd South Carolina Cavalry 1861–1865* (Camden, SC: Gray Fox Books, 1997), 69–70; *O.R.*, vol. 25, pt. 1, 18–19.

27. Ebenezer Gould to Dear Brother, Fairfax Courthouse, April 1, 1863; see O'Neill, *Chasing Jeb Stuart and John Mosby*, 145.

28. O'Neill, "For the Lack of Horses."

29. *O.R.*, vol. 27, pt. 1, 37.

30. Halleck was keeping Stahel's men busy searching for Mosby at this point. *O.R.*, vol. 27, pt. 3, 74–75 (bracketed word by author).

31. *O.R.*, vol. 27, pt. 1, 36.

32. *O.R.*, vol. 27, pt. 1, 35.

33. *O.R.*, vol. 27, pt. 1, 34–35.

34. *O.R.*, vol. 27, pt. 1, 35.

35. *O.R.*, vol. 27, pt. 1, 35.

36. *O.R.*, vol. 27, pt. 1, 166–67; *O.R.*, vol. 27, pt. 3, 64.

37. *Richmond Examiner*, June 12, 1863.

38. Adele H. Mitchell, ed., *The Letters of James E. B. Stuart* (Alexandria, VA: Stuart-Mosby Historical Society, 1990), 324.

39. Federal troopers captured two private letters from Stuart's horse gunners, but they were not official documents as Pleasonton claimed.

40. *Richmond Daily Dispatch*, June 12, 1863.

41. Burke Davis, *Jeb Stuart, the Last Cavalier . . . with Maps by Rafael D. Palacios [with Plates, Including Portraits]* (New York: Rinehart, 1957), 313.

42. Frank M. Myers, *The Comanches: A History of White's Battalion, Virginia Cavalry* (Marietta, GA: Continental, 1956), 187.

43. Edwin B. Coddington, *The Gettysburg Campaign: A Study in Command* (Norwalk, CT: Easton Press, 1998), 655n49; *O.R.*, vol. 27, pt. 2, 290.

44. For added support, Colonel Elijah White's 35th Virginia Battalion would accompany Jenkins's command. Many of White's troopers were from Maryland and familiar with the planned route of Lee's advance north of the Potomac.

45. *O.R.*, vol. 27, pt. 2, 440, 547.

46. *O.R.*, vol. 27, pt. 3, 93.

47. *O.R.*, vol. 27, pt. 3, 101.

48. *O.R.*, vol. 27, pt. 3, 107.

49. *O.R.*, vol. 27, pt. 3, 103.

50. *O.R.*, vol. 27, pt. 1, 40.

CHAPTER 9

1. *O.R.*, vol. 27, pt. 3, 136–37.

2. *O.R.*, vol. 27, pt. 3, 186.

3. *O.R.*, vol. 27, pt. 3, 171–72.

4. Robert F. O'Neill, *Chasing Jeb Stuart and John Mosby: The Union Cavalry in Northern Virginia from Second Manassas to Gettysburg* (Jefferson, NC: McFarland, 2012), 220–21.

5. O'Neill, *Chasing Jeb Stuart and John Mosby*, 220–21. *O.R.*, vol. 12, pt. 2, 563–66.

6. O'Neill, *Chasing Jeb Stuart and John Mosby*, 221. Captain Ulric Dahlgren, an aide-de-camp of General Hooker's, later confirmed Pleasonton's part in this affair. *O.R.*, vol. 27, pt. 1, 1046.

7. *O.R.*, vol. 27, pt. 3, 172. In addition, General Stahel's Washington-based cavalry would drive west through Warrenton, Virginia, twenty miles to the south, to support Pleasonton's main push.

8. Pleasonton was familiar with the Loudoun Valley turnpikes, having sparred along these same roads with Stuart less than a year prior after the Sharpsburg campaign. *O.R.*, vol. 19, pt. 2, 107, 110, 113.

9. *O.R.*, vol. 27, pt. 3, 173.

10. The 1st Rhode Island Cavalry was also part of Kilpatrick's brigade but had been detailed elsewhere as mentioned earlier.

11. Henry B. McClellan, *I Rode with Jeb Stuart: The Life and Campaigns of Major General J. E. B. Stuart* (New York: Da Capo, 1994), 296.

12. Longstreet's corps would cross via Ashby's Gap and Snicker's Gap. *O.R.*, vol. 27, pt. 2, 315.

13. *O.R.*, vol. 27, pt. 2, 687–88.

14. *O.R.*, vol. 27, pt. 2, 687–88.

15. George Bliss, *Personal Narratives of Events in the War of the Rebellion; Being Papers Read before the Rhode Island Soldiers and Sailors Historical Society*, 4th ser., no. 1 (Providence, RI: Rhode Island Soldiers and Sailors Historical Society, 1889), 40. Official appointment to the rank of general officer eluded Munford throughout the war, and though Stuart recommended Munford for brigadier, "[h]e is a gallant soldier, a daring and skillful officer." Stuart's request for Munford's promotion was certainly less robust than his bids for his fellow graduates from West Point. See Adele H. Mitchell, ed., *The Letters of Major General James E. B. Stuart* (Alexandria, VA: Stuart-Mosby Historical Society, 1990), 274.

16. Mitchell, *The Letters of Major General James E. B. Stuart*, 270–71.

17. Larry Tagg, *The Generals of Gettysburg: The Leaders of America's Greatest Battle* (Cambridge, MA: Da Capo, 2003), 184.

18. Rosser moved to Texas before attending West Point.

19. Mitchell, *The Letters of Major General James E. B. Stuart*, 216–18.

20. Mitchell, *The Letters of Major General James E. B. Stuart*, 257.

21. Robert F. O'Neill, *The Cavalry Battles of Aldie, Middleburg and Upperville, June 10–27, 1863*, Virginia Civil War Battle and Leaders Series (Lynchburg, VA: H. E. Howard, 1993), 40.

22. *O.R.*, vol. 27, pt. 2, 739.

23. Wilbur Sturtevant Nye, *Here Come the Rebels* (Dayton, OH: Morningside, 1988), 173.

24. Joseph W. McKinney, *Brandy Station, Virginia, June 9, 1863: The Largest Cavalry Battle of the Civil War* (Jefferson, NC: McFarland, 2006), 117; Edward G. Longacre, *Lincoln's Cavalrymen: A History of the Mounted Forces of the Army of the Potomac, 1861–1865* (Mechanicsburg, PA: Stackpole Books, 2000), 155.

25. O'Neill, *The Cavalry Battles of Aldie, Middleburg and Upperville*, 39–40.

26. *O.R.*, vol. 27, pt. 2, 739, 747. Due to a shortage of carbines in the Confederacy, some of Stuart's regiments shuffled resources and designated certain squadrons for carbine work. This was the case in the 5th Virginia with Captain Boston's men.

27. *National Tribune*, June 9, 1887.

28. *O.R.*, vol. 27, pt. 3, 747.

29. O'Neill, *The Cavalry Battles of Aldie, Middleburg and Upperville*, 42.

30. *O.R.*, vol. 27, pt. 3, 747.

31. *O.R.*, vol. 27, pt. 3, 748.

32. O'Neill, *The Cavalry Battles of Aldie, Middleburg and Upperville*, 42. Stuart was outraged at Captain Boston for surrendering. Boston was later exchanged and an inquest held; upon close examination, he was cleared of all charges and returned to command. He fought the remainder of the war and was killed two days before the Confederate surrender at Appomattox.

33. *National Tribune*, June 9, 1887.

34. *O.R.*, vol. 27, pt. 2, 740–41.

35. Henry H. Matthews, "The Pelham-Breathed Battery," part 11, *Saint Mary's Beacon*, April 13, 1905.

36. O'Neill, *The Cavalry Battles of Aldie, Middleburg and Upperville*, 48.

37. O'Neill, *The Cavalry Battles of Aldie, Middleburg and Upperville*, 49.

38. *O.R.*, vol. 27, pt. 2, 740.

39. *O.R.*, vol. 27, pt. 2, 743.

40. *O.R.*, vol. 27, pt. 2, 740.

41. *O.R.*, vol. 27, pt. 2, 746.

42. Mathews, "The Pelham-Breathed Battery," *Saint Mary's Beacon*, April 13, 1905.

43. Chauncey F. Worthington, ed., *A Cycle of Adams Letters, 1861–1865* (New York: Houghton Mifflin, 1920), 2:36–37.

44. O'Neill, *The Cavalry Battles of Aldie, Middleburg and Upperville*, 51–52.

45. Di Cesnola received a citation from the U.S. Army Congressional Medal of Honor Society: "Was present, in arrest, when, seeing his regiment fall back, he rallied his men, accompanied them, without arms, in a second charge, and in recognition of his gallantry was released from arrest. He continued in the action at the head of his regiment until he was desperately wounded and taken prisoner" ("Louis Palma di Cesnola," Congressional Medal of Honor Society, accessed November 2, 2022, https://www.cmohs.org/recipients/louis-p-di-cesnola).

46. O'Neill, *The Cavalry Battles of Aldie, Middleburg and Upperville*, 51–52.

47. Private Scruggs and Private Wade of the 2nd Virginia Cavalry are credited with capturing Colonel di Cesnola.

48. *O.R.*, vol. 27, pt. 2, 741–43.

49. A modern tour of the battlefield reveals a steep bowl the 2nd Virginia would have traversed to attack the dismounted 1st Massachusetts. Modern erosion may have altered this terrain feature, but it is possible that the 2nd Virginia was temporarily hidden from the view of the 1st Massachusetts by the depth of the bowl as the 2nd Virginia pursued the 4th New York and approached the dismounted Federal line.

50. George Tucker Brooke, *Autobiography of Sergeant George Tucker Brooke, Co. B 2nd Virginia Cavalry* (Richmond: Virginia Historical Society, 1907), 27–30.

51. Worthington, *A Cycle of Adams Letters*, 36–37.

52. Edward P. Tobie, *History of the First Maine Cavalry, 1861–1865* (Boston, MA: Emery & Hughes, 1887), 162.

53. Brooke, *Autobiography of Sergeant George Tucker Brooke*, 28.

54. John Weston, *Picket Pins and Sabers: The Civil War Letters of John Burden Weston*, ed. Robert W. Frost and Nancy D. Frost (Ashland, KY: Economy, 1971), 50 (bracketed word by author).

55. Weston, *Picket Pins and Sabers*, 49, 51.

56. *O.R.*, vol. 27, pt. 2, 743; Edward G. Longacre, *Lee's Cavalrymen: A History of the Mounted Forces of the Army of Northern Virginia, 1861–1865* (Mechanicsburg, PA: Stackpole Books, 2002), 198.

57. O'Neill, *The Cavalry Battles of Aldie, Middleburg and Upperville*, 60; Tobie, *History of the First Maine Cavalry*, 161. Tobie's book claims this was the 4th's colors.

58. Tobie, *History of the First Maine Cavalry*, 162.

59. Nathan Webb (1st Maine Cavalry), Nathan Webb Diary, University of Michigan, Michigan Historical Collections, Bentley Historical Library, Ann Arbor, Michigan; O'Neill, *The Cavalry Battles of Aldie, Middleburg and Upperville*, 62–63.

60. *O.R.*, vol. 27, pt. 2, 741.

CHAPTER 10

1. *O.R.*, vol. 27, pt. 1, 962.

2. While convalescing, Rooney Lee was captured by Federal cavalry and held in Federal prisons until his release in 1864.

3. *O.R.*, vol. 25, pt. 1, 85, 86.

4. Larry Tagg, *The Generals of Gettysburg: The Leaders of America's Greatest Battle* (Cambridge, MA: Da Capo, 2003), 365.

5. R. L. T. Beale, *History of the Ninth Virginia Cavalry, in the War between the States* (1899; repr., Richmond, VA: B. F. Johnson, 2010), 70.

6. Beale, *History of the Ninth Virginia Cavalry*, 70; G. W. Beale, *A Lieutenant of Cavalry in Lee's Army* (Baltimore, MD: Butternut and Blue, 1994), 100.

7. Henry B. McClellan, *I Rode with Jeb Stuart: The Life and Campaigns of Major General J. E. B. Stuart* (New York: Da Capo, 1994), 303–4.

8. *O.R.*, vol. 27, pt. 1, 964. Frederic Denison, *Sabres and Spurs: The First Regiment Rhode Island Cavalry, 1861–1865: Its Origin, Marches, Scouts, Skirmishes, Raids,*

Battles, Sufferings, Victories, and Appropriate Official Papers; with the Roll of Honor and Roll of the Regiment (Providence, RI: First Rhode Island Veteran Association, 1876), 233.

9. John Singleton Mosby, *Stuart's Cavalry in the Gettysburg Campaign* (London: Forgotten Books, 2012), 71.

10. W. W. Blackford, *War Years with Jeb Stuart* (New York: Scribner, 1945), 159–60.

11. Justus Scheibert, *Seven Months in the Rebel States during the North American War, 1863*, ed. William Stanley Hoole (Tuscaloosa: University of Alabama Press, 2009), 42.

12. Blackford, *War Years with Jeb Stuart*, 159–61.

13. Heros von Borcke, *Memoirs of the Confederate War for Independence* (Philadelphia, PA: J. B. Lippincott, 1867), 416 (bracketed word by the author).

14. Robert F. O'Neill, *The Cavalry Battles of Aldie, Middleburg and Upperville, June 10–27, 1863*, Virginia Civil War Battle and Leaders Series (Lynchburg, VA: H. E. Howard, 1993), 72.

15. Denison, *Sabres and Spurs*, 233–34.

16. "Wounded," *Fayetteville Observer*, July 2, 1863. Accessed online 10/18/2015. Miraculously, McNeill survived this wound only to die while again leading his regiment in a charge at Chamberlain's Run, in March 1865.

17. von Borcke, *Memoirs of the Confederate War for Independence*, 427.

18. *O.R.*, vol. 27, pt. 1, 963.

19. Denison, *Sabres and Spurs*, 233–34; Paul B. Means, *Additional Sketch Sixty-Third Regiment (5th Cavalry)*, vol. 3 of *Histories of the Several Regiments and Battalions from North Carolina, in the Great War, 1861–1865*, ed. Walter Clark (Goldsboro, NC: Nash Brothers, 1901), 563.

20. *O.R.*, vol. 27, pt. 1, 963.

21. Beale, *History of the Ninth Virginia Cavalry*, 70; Beale, *A Lieutenant of Cavalry in Lee's Army*, 100.

22. Beale, *A Lieutenant of Cavalry in Lee's Army*, 101.

23. Denison, *Sabres and Spurs*, 236, 237–39; *O.R.*, vol. 27, pt. 1, 1055.

24. Duffié went on to serve in the Department of West Virginia, where he vowed to bring John Mosby back to Washington in chains. Instead Duffié was captured by John Mosby's Rangers in October 1864 and served a lengthy stint in a Confederate prison. His acting commander requested he be dismissed from service.

25. Jeffry D. Wert, *Cavalryman of the Lost Cause: A Biography of J. E. B. Stuart* (New York: Simon & Schuster, 2009), 97.

26. Jeffry D. Wert, *Mosby's Rangers* (New York: Simon & Schuster, 1991) 30.

27. Robert F. O'Neill, *Chasing Jeb Stuart and John Mosby: The Union Cavalry in Northern Virginia from Second Manassas to Gettysburg* (Jefferson, NC: McFarland, 2012), 223.

28. Mosby, *Stuart's Cavalry in the Gettysburg Campaign*, 64–67; John Singleton Mosby, *Mosby's War Reminiscences: Stuart's Cavalry Campaigns* (New York: Dodd, Mead, 1898), 165–68.

29. *O.R.*, vol. 27, pt. 2, 689.

30. McClellan, *I Rode with Jeb Stuart*, 306.

31. *O.R.*, vol. 27, pt. 2, 689.

32. *O.R.*, vol. 27, pt. 1, 50.

33. *O.R.*, vol. 27, pt. 1, 906–7 (bracketed words by author).

34. *O.R.*, vol. 27, pt. 1, 907. This was later amended to 305 total casualties. See *O.R.*, vol. 27, pt. 1, 171.

35. *O.R.*, vol. 27, pt. 1, 45.

36. *O.R.*, vol. 27, pt. 1, 47.

37. *O.R.*, vol. 27, pt. 1, 47.

38. *O.R.*, vol. 27, pt. 1, 908.

39. *O.R.*, vol. 27, pt. 1, 908.

40. John L. Smith, ed., *History of the 118th Pennsylvania Volunteers, Corn Exchange Regiment from Their First Engagement at Antietam to Appomattox* (Philadelphia, PA: J. L. Smith, 1905), 225.

41. *O.R.*, vol. 27, pt. 1, 976.

42. Eric J. Wittenberg, *The Battle of Brandy Station: North America's Largest Cavalry Battle* (Charleston, SC: History Press, 2010), 43.

43. *O.R.*, vol. 27, pt. 1, 975–76.

44. Henry C. Meyer, *Civil War Experiences under Bayard, Gregg, Kilpatrick, Custer, Raulston, and Newberry, 1862, 1863, 1864* (New York: Putnam, 1911), 36–38 (bracketed words by author).

45. William E. Doster, *Lincoln and Episodes of the Civil War* (New York: Putnam, 1915), 210–11.

46. Edward P. Tobie, *History of the First Maine Cavalry, 1861–1865* (Boston: Emory & Hughes, 1887), 166–68.

47. *O.R.*, vol. 27, pt. 1, 976.

48. Robert J. Trout, *Memoirs of the Stuart Horse Artillery Battalion*, Vol. 2 86–87. The battery endured the flying shards until finally ordered to change position.

49. Beale, *A Lieutenant of Cavalry in Lee's Army*, 102. O'Neill, *The Cavalry Battles of Aldie, Middleburg and Upperville*, 106.

50. Smith, *History of the 118th Pennsylvania*, 224–25.

51. Beale, *A Lieutenant of Cavalry in Lee's Army*, 102.

52. *O.R.*, vol. 27, pt. 2, 689.

53. Wilbur Sturtevant Nye, *Here Come the Rebels* (Dayton, OH: Morningside, 1988), 194.

54. Trout, *Memoirs of the Stuart Horse Artillery Battalion*, Vol. 2 87. These revolving side hammer carbines had a high rate of fire but were slow to reload. Special care had to be taken or they could chain fire with all chambers in the cylinder igniting at once.

55. Roger H. Harrell, *The 2nd North Carolina Cavalry* (Jefferson, NC: McFarland, 2012), 136.

56. Blackford, *War Years with Jeb Stuart*, 218–19.

57. *O.R.*, vol. 27, pt. 2, 69; Trout, *Memoirs of the Stuart Horse Artillery Battalion*, 87.

58. *O.R.*, vol. 27, pt. 1, 909.

59. *New York Times*, June 24, 1863.

60. Nye, *Here Come the Rebels*, 194–95.

CHAPTER 11

1. *O.R.*, vol. 27, pt. 1, 911 (bracketed word by author).

2. *O.R.*, vol. 27, pt. 1, 911.

3. *O.R.*, vol. 27, pt. 1, 911 (bracketed word by author).

4. *O.R.*, vol. 27, pt. 1, 921.

5. Letter, "Daniel Pulis to Dear Parents, Camp Near Aldie, VA, June 23, 1863," Rochester Historical Society, Rochester, NY (bracketed words by author).

6. Henry B. McClellan, *I Rode with Jeb Stuart: The Life and Campaigns of Major General J. E. B. Stuart* (New York: Da Capo, 1994), 306–8.

7. Hampton met Stahel's forces in a driving downpour. The storm delayed the Federal advance, night set in, and the Federals retired thinking they were vastly outnumbered. *O.R.*, vol. 27, pt. 1, 910; *O.R.*, vol. 27, pt. 2, 689; *O.R.*, vol. 27, pt. 3, 208; McClellan, *I Rode with Jeb Stuart*, 307.

8. *O.R.*, vol. 27, pt. 2, 690.

9. *O.R.*, vol. 27, pt. 2, 750.

10. *O.R.*, vol. 27, pt. 2, 357; Longstreet's corps entered the Shenandoah Valley two days prior but now turned back and held ready to support Stuart against this predicted Federal push.

11. U. R. Brooks, ed., *Butler and His Cavalry in the War of Secession 1861–1865* (Camden, SC: Gray Fox Books, n.d.), 174; Robert J. Trout, *Galloping Thunder: The Story of the Stuart Horse Artillery Battalion* (Mechanicsburg, PA: Stackpole Books, 2002), 266.

12. D. B. Rea, *Sketches from Hampton's Cavalry: Embracing the Principle Exploits of the Cavalry in the Campaigns of 1862 and 1863* (Columbia: South Carolina State Press, 1864), 98.

13. Trout, *Galloping Thunder*, 266.

14. Brooks, *Butler and His Cavalry*, 176.

15. Robert J. Trout, *Memoirs of the Stuart Horse Artillery Battalion*, 211.

16. *Detroit Advertiser and Tribune*, July 1, 1863.

17. This was the first gun lost in battle by Stuart's horse artillery. The piece was a Blakely rifled cannon, an English import purchased by Wade Hampton with his own funds.

18. Edward G. Longacre, *The Cavalry at Gettysburg: A Tactical Study of Mounted Operations during the Civil War's Pivotal Campaign, 9 June–14 July 1863* (Lincoln: University of Nebraska Press, 1986), 91; Ezra J. Warner, *Generals in Blue: Lives of the Union Commanders* (Baton Rouge: Louisiana State University Press, 1992), 165.

19. *O.R.*, vol. 27, pt. 1, 920–22, 932–33.

20. *O.R.*, vol. 27, pt. 2, 690.

21. *O.R.*, vol. 27, pt. 1, 911.

22. Trout, *Galloping Thunder*, 267.

23. John Logan Black, *Crumbling Defenses; or, Memoirs and Reminiscences of John Logan Black* (Macon, GA: Eleanor D. McSwain, 1960), 25; W. W. Blackford, *War Years with Jeb Stuart* (New York: Scribner, 1945), 221; Brooks, *Butler and His Cavalry*, 178.

24. Black, *Crumbling Defenses*, 25–27; Robert F. O'Neill, *The Cavalry Battles of Aldie, Middleburg and Upperville, June 10–27, 1863*, Virginia Civil War Battle and Leaders Series (Lynchburg, VA: H. E. Howard, 1993), 126–27; Trout, *Galloping Thunder*, 268.

25. *O.R.*, vol. 27, pt. 2, 690.

26. Brooks, *Butler and His Cavalry*, 177; Trout, *Galloping Thunder*, 267.

27. O'Neill, *The Cavalry Battles of Aldie, Middleburg and Upperville*, 126–27.

28. O'Neill, *The Cavalry Battles of Aldie, Middleburg and Upperville*, 147–48.

29. *O.R.*, vol. 27, pt. 1, 921.

30. McClellan, *I Rode with Jeb Stuart*, 311.

31. S. A. J. Creekmore, *Diary of Sergeant S. A. J. Creekmore, Company C, Jeff Davis Legion* (Jackson: Mississippi Department of Archives and History, n.d.), n.p. (bracketed words by author).

32. *Detroit Free Press*, July 2, 1863.

33. O'Neill, *The Cavalry Battles of Aldie, Middleburg and Upperville*, 149.

34. Creekmore, *Diary of Sergeant S. A. J. Creekmore*.

35. The Reserves Brigade was here composed of the 1st, 2nd, 5th, and 6th U.S. Regular Cavalry.

36. Tattnal Paulding, *Diary of Lieutenant Tattnal Paulding*, courtesy of Dr. James Milgram, Chicago, IL.

37. Isaac Rothermel Dunkelberger Memoir, Michael J. Winey Collection, United States Army Heritage Education Center, Carlisle, PA.

38. McClellan, *I Rode with Jeb Stuart*, 311–12.

39. Rea, *Sketches from Hampton's Cavalry*, 100.

40. Creekmore, *Diary of Sergeant S. A. J. Creekmore*, n.p.

41. Adele H. Mitchell, *The Letters of Major General James E. B. Stuart* (Alexandria, VA: Stuart-Mosby Historical Society, 1990), 326. John Esten Cooke, *Wearing of the Gray: Being Personal Portraits, Scenes and Adventures of the War* (New York: E. B. Treat, 1867), 238; *Philadelphia Weekly Times*, February 21, 1880.

42. Vince Dooley and Samuel N. Thomas, eds., *The Legion's Fighting Bulldog: The Civil War Correspondence of William Gaston Delony, Lieutenant Colonel of Cobb's Georgia Legion Cavalry, and Rosa Delony, 1853–1863* (Macon, GA: Mercer University Press, 2017), 233; McClellan, *I Rode with Jeb Stuart*, 311–12; *Philadelphia Weekly Times*, July 20, 1878.

43. Isaac Rothermel Dunkelberger Memoir, Michael J. Winey Collection (bracketed word by author); G. N. Saussy, "Upperville's Cavalry Battle," *Watson's Jeffersonian Magazine* 4, no. 4 (April 1910): 334.

44. Ida Powell Dulany, *In the Shadow of the Enemy: The Civil War Journal of Ida Powell Dulany*, ed. Mary L. Mackall and Steven F. Meserve (Knoxville: University of Tennessee Press, 2009), 88 (bracketed words by author).

45 *O.R.*, vol. 27, pt. 1, 185; *O.R.*, vol. 27, pt. 1, 922. In the *Official Records*, Buford lists the total losses in killed, wounded, and captured for the 1st U.S. Cavalry at Upperville as fifty-three. Saussy, "Upperville's Cavalry Battle"; Brooks, *Butler and His Cavalry*, 180.

46. McClellan, *I Rode with Jeb Stuart*, 311; Brooks, *Butler and His Cavalry*, 180.

47. Letter, "Stephens Calhoun Smith to Dear Father & Mother. Near Williams-port, MD. 12 July, 1863," Duke University.

48. *O.R.*, vol. 27, pt. 1, 947. Hampton mistakenly identified dismounts from the 5th and 6th Regulars as Federal infantry.

49. *O.R.*, vol. 27, pt. 2, 776; Saussy, "Upperville's Cavalry Battle," 335.

CHAPTER 12

1. *O.R.*, vol. 27, pt. 1, 921.

2. *O.R.*, vol. 27, pt. 1, 921.

3. Colonel Lomax with sharpshooters from the 11th and 12th Virginia was trailing behind Jones's brigade, acting as a rear guard, and repeatedly engaging the enemy.

4. This fence corner was still present in August 2020 when the author led a horse tour of this ground courtesy of the property owners and the Virginia Piedmont Heritage Association.

5. *O.R.*, vol. 27, pt. 1, 933; G. W. Beale, *A Lieutenant of Cavalry in Lee's Army* (Baltimore, MD: Butternut and Blue, 1994), 104; Ada Bruce Desper Bradshaw, ed., *Civil War Diary of Charles William McVicar* (Washington, DC: Library of Congress, 1977), 14–15; Stewart Bell Jr. Archives, Handley Library, Winchester, VA.

6. Roger H. Harrell, *The 2nd North Carolina Cavalry* (Jefferson, NC: McFarland, 2012), 141; John Heritage Bryan Papers, Private Collection no. 6, North Carolina Division of Archives and History, Raleigh, NC.

7. *O.R.*, vol. 27, pt. 1, 933.

8. R. L. T. Beale, *History of the Ninth Virginia Cavalry, in the War between the States* (1899; repr., Richmond, VA: B. F. Johnson, 2010), 74.

9. *O.R.*, vol. 27, pt. 2, 751; Harrell, *The 2nd North Carolina Cavalry*, 142.

10. Captain Chew was an outstanding gunner and an aggressive officer who once led his own raid behind enemy lines to capture Federal horses for his battery. See *O.R.*, vol. 25, pt. 1, 145.

11. William N. McDonald, *A History of the Laurel Brigade: Originally the Ashby Cavalry of the Army of Northern Virginia and Chew's Battery*, ed. Bushrod C. Washington (Baltimore, MD: Mrs. Kate S. McDonald, 1902), 150.

12. Harrell, *The 2nd North Carolina Cavalry*, 142.

13. Bradshaw, *Civil War Diary of Charles William McVicar*, 14–15.

14. McDonald, *A History of the Laurel Brigade*, 150–51.

15. Bradshaw, *Civil War Diary of Charles William McVicar*, 14–15. This small field and its supporting walls did not survive into the twenty-first century and may have only been a simple ox yard or holding pen.

16. *O.R.*, vol. 27, pt. 2, 751; Bradshaw, *Civil War Diary of Charles William McVicar*, 14–15; McDonald, *A History of the Laurel Brigade*, 150–51. One of Chew's guns, a rifled English Blakely, was retired after the Battle of Brandy Station. Scholarship suggests Chew had a twenty-four-pound Howitzer, a Napoleon, and an additional rifled Blakely at Upperville; see Robert J. Trout, *Galloping Thunder: The*

Story of the Stuart Horse Artillery Battalion (Mechanicsburg, PA: Stackpole Books, 2002), 696n30, 699n1. Chew may have also acquired a rifled piece taken from Martin's Federal battery by Jones's brigade/Lomax's 11th Virginia during the fight at Fleetwood Heights. Exactly which guns were used here on the Trappe Road is also a guess, but smoothbores and rifled pieces were generally paired alike when possible.

17. *O.R.*, vol. 27, pt. 1, 933; Bradshaw, *Civil War Diary of Charles William McVicar*, 14–15.

18. Bradshaw, *Civil War Diary of Charles William McVicar*, 14–15.

19. Abner Hard, *History of the Eighth Cavalry Regiment, Illinois Volunteers, during the Great Rebellion* (Aurora, IL: n.p., 1868), 251.

20. James Joseph Williamson, *Mosby's Rangers: A Record of the Forty-Third Battalion of the Virginia Cavalry from Its Organization to the Surrender* (New York: Sturgis & Walton, 1909; repr., 2018), 47. Ranger James Williamson counted thirty-one dead horses in a single heap the day after the battle; a second account claimed forty-five.

21. Hard, *History of the Eighth Cavalry Regiment*, 251.

22. *O.R.*, vol. 27, pt. 1, 921.

23. Bradshaw, *Civil War Diary of Charles William McVicar*, 14–15; *O.R.*, vol. 27, pt. 1, 933; William Graham, *Nineteenth Regiment*, vol. 2 of *Histories of the Several Regiments and Battalions from North Carolina in the Great War, 1861–1865*, ed. Walter Clark (Goldsboro, NC: Nash Brothers, 1901), 96; *O.R.*, vol. 27, pt. 1, 933.

24. Hard, *History of the Eighth Cavalry Regiment*, 252.

25. George M. Neese, *Three Years in the Confederate Horse Artillery: Consisting of Excerpts, Where Each Touches on Matters Relating to Charlottesville, VA and Environs* (Dayton, OH: Morningside, 1988), 182.

26. Trout, *Galloping Thunder*, 271; Beale, *History of the Ninth Virginia Cavalry*, 74.

27. Bradshaw, *Civil War Diary of Charles William McVicar*, 14–15; *O.R.*, vol. 27, pt. 2, 766.

28. Bradshaw, *Civil War Diary of Charles William McVicar*, 14–15.

29. *O.R.*, vol. 27, pt. 2, 766; Lucy Rebecca Buck, *Sad Earth, Sweet Heaven: The Diary of Lucy Rebecca Buck*, ed. William P. Buck (Birmingham, AL: Cornerstone, 1973), 205–6.

30. Robert F. O'Neill, *The Cavalry Battles of Aldie, Middleburg and Upperville, June 10–27, 1863*, Virginia Civil War Battle and Leaders Series (Lynchburg, VA: H. E. Howard, 1993), 141 (bracketed words by author).

31. *O.R.*, vol. 27, pt. 2, 751.

32. The charging Federal cavalry may have masked the fire of their own sharpshooters behind the Thomas walls at this time.

33. Neese, *Three Years in the Confederate Horse Artillery*, 182; Harrell, *The 2nd North Carolina Cavalry*, 142.

34. *O.R.*, vol. 27, pt. 2, 751; Bradshaw, *Civil War Diary of Charles William McVicar*, 14–15; Neese, *Three Years in the Confederate Horse Artillery*, 183.

35. Bradshaw, *Civil War Diary of Charles William McVicar*, 14–15; Neese, *Three Years in the Confederate Horse Artillery*, 183.

36. *O.R.*, vol. 27, pt. 2, 751.

37. Beale, *History of the Ninth Virginia Cavalry*, 74–75.

38. Michalowski's section was from Captain Graham's Battery K, 2nd U.S. Artillery.

39. Beale, *A Lieutenant of Cavalry*, 104 (bracketed words by author).

40. McDonald, *A History of the Laurel Brigade*, 151.

41. Bradshaw, *Civil War Diary of Charles William McVicar*, 16.

42. Graham, *Nineteenth Regiment*, 96.

43. Bradshaw, *Civil War Diary of Charles William McVicar*, 16.

44. "The Late Skirmishes between Stuart and Pleasonton," *New York Daily Tribune*, November 10, 1862.

45. Edward P. Tobie, *History of the First Maine Cavalry, 1861–1865* (Boston: Emory & Hughes, 1887), 169.

46. Robert F. O'Neill, *Chasing Jeb Stuart and John Mosby: The Union Cavalry in Northern Virginia from Second Manassas to Gettysburg* (Jefferson, NC: McFarland, 2012), 234.

47. O'Neill, *The Cavalry Battles of Aldie, Middleburg and Upperville*, 155.

48. Tobie, *History of the First Maine Cavalry*, 171.

49. Tobie, *History of the First Maine Cavalry*, 171.

50. Paul B. Means, *Additional Sketch Sixty-Third Regiment (5th Cavalry)*, vol. 3 of *Histories of the Several Regiments and Battalions from North Carolina, in the Great War, 1861–1865*, ed. Walter Clark (Goldsboro, NC: Nash Brothers, 1901), 567.

51. Charles Gardner Memoirs, Civil War Times Illustrated Collection, U.S. Army Center of Military History, Carlisle, PA; O'Neill, *The Cavalry Battles of Aldie, Middleburg and Upperville*, 158.

52. Trout, *Galloping Thunder*, 273; Neese, *Three Years in the Confederate Horse Artillery*, 183–84.

53. Trout, *Galloping Thunder*, 273.

54. *O.R.*, vol. 27, pt. 1, 912.

55. Letter, "Daniel Pulis to Dear Parents, Camp Near Aldie, VA, June 23, 1863," Rochester Historical Society, Rochester, NY.

56. *O.R.*, vol. 27, pt. 1, 913.

CHAPTER 13

1. Thomas Marshall, *Thomas Marshall, an Aide de Camp of Lee*, ed. Sir Frederick Maurice (Boston, MA: Little, Brown, 1927), Stratford Hall, Lee Family Digital Archive.

2. *O.R.*, vol. 27, pt. 3, 923.

3. Henry B. McClellan, *I Rode with Jeb Stuart: The Life and Campaigns of Major General J. E. B. Stuart* (New York: Da Capo, 1994), 317.

4. W. W. Blackford, *War Years with Jeb Stuart* (New York: Scribner, 1945), 110.

5. *O.R.*, vol. 27, pt. 3, 915.

6. Wilbur Sturtevant Nye, *Here Come the Rebels* (Dayton, OH: Morningside, 1988), 313.

7. Marshall, *Thomas Marshall, an Aide de Camp of Lee*, 203 (bracketed words by author).

8. R. Shepard Brown, *Stringfellow of the Fourth* (New York: Crown, 1960), 197.

9. Mosby wrote that he planned to reach Rowser's Ford by 11:00 p.m. on June 9. Thus, Stuart, who was more than fifty miles away at Culpeper, would have ordered Mosby to make this assault well before June 9; see John Singleton Mosby, *Mosby's War Reminiscences: Stuart's Cavalry Campaigns* (New York: Dodd, Mead, 1898), 159.

10. Mosby meant to make the attack on June 9 but was delayed.

11. Rowser's Ford was more than fifty miles from Culpeper, so Stuart had to have ordered Mosby to make the assault well before the Battle of Brandy Station on June 9.

12. *O.R.*, vol. 27, pt. 3, 915.

13. *O.R.*, vol. 27, pt. 3, 914.

14. Ewell's troops that crossed the mountains did not cross through Emmitsburg as Lee states; instead, they crossed to the east side of South Mountain via Cashtown Pass.

15. *O.R.*, vol. 27, pt. 2, 316.

16. *O.R.*, vol. 27, pt. 3, 914–15 (bracketed words by author).

17. Mosby, *Mosby's War Reminiscences*, 174–75.

18. *O.R.*, vol. 27, pt. 3, 923 (bracketed words by author).

19. Edward J. Stackpole, *They Met at Gettysburg* (New York: Bonanza, 1956), 47.

20. Mark Nesbitt, *Saber and Scapegoat: J. E. B. Stuart and the Gettysburg Controversy* (Mechanicsburg, PA: Stackpole Books, 1994), 65. Though Lee expected Hooker to pursue the Army of Northern Virginia across the Potomac, Lee had not ruled out the possibility of Hooker turning south and attacking Richmond, Lee's supply line, or a portion of Lee's columns.

21. *O.R.*, vol. 11, pt. 2, 514.

22. Blackford, *War Years with Jeb Stuart*, 226.

23. *O.R.*, vol. 27, pt. 3, 927–28.

24. General Lee seemed to favor these men more than Stuart, and both officers were brought back under Stuart's command for the current campaign on Lee's orders rather than Stuart's. Adele H. Mitchell, ed., *The Letters of Major General James E. B. Stuart* (Alexandria, VA: Stuart-Mosby Historical Society, 1990), 319–22; *O.R.*, vol. 25, pt. 2, 836–37; Mitchell, *Letters of Major General James E. B. Stuart*, 272; *O.R.*, vol. 25, pt. 2, 788–89, 820.

25. Stackpole, *They Met at Gettysburg*, 49–50.

26. John Singleton Mosby, *Stuart's Cavalry in the Gettysburg Campaign* (London: Forgotten Books, 2012), 81; Mosby, *Mosby's War Reminiscences*, 173.

27. Mosby, *Mosby's War Reminiscences*, 173.

28. Mosby, *Stuart's Cavalry in the Gettysburg Campaign*, 76.

29. Mosby, *Mosby's War Reminiscences*, 173.

30. Mosby, *Mosby's War Reminiscences*, 179.

31. *O.R.*, vol. 27, pt. 2, 297 (bracketed words by author).

32. John W. Peake, "Recollections of a Boy Cavalryman," *Confederate Veteran Magazine* 34 (1926): 261.

33. W. A. Graham, "From Brandy Station to the Heights of Gettysburg," *News & Observer* (Raleigh, NC), February 7, 1904.

34. *O.R.*, vol. 27, pt. 2, 689.

35. *O.R.*, vol. 27, pt. 3, 927.

36. Blackford, *War Years with Jeb Stuart*, 277.

37. McClellan, *I Rode with Jeb Stuart*, 317; Blackford, *War Years with Jeb Stuart*, 110.

38. All six guns came from Stuart's artillery battalion. Four of the guns were from Captain Breathed's battery, and the remaining two from Captain McGregor's battery. Overall command of the Confederate artillery was under Major Robert Beckham.

39. Mosby, *Mosby's War Reminiscences*, 174.

40. Mosby, *Stuart's Cavalry in the Gettysburg Campaign*, 77 (bracketed words by author).

41. Mosby, *Mosby's War Reminiscences*, 180–81; James Joseph Williamson, *Mosby's Rangers: A Record of the Operations of the Forty-Third Battalion of Virginia Cavalry from Its Organization to the Surrender* (New York: Sturgis & Walton, 1909; repr., 2018), 47–48; Robert F. O'Neill, *Chasing Jeb Stuart and John Mosby: The Union Cavalry in Northern Virginia from Second Manassas to Gettysburg* (Jefferson, NC: McFarland, 2012), 239. Mosby would eventually enter Pennsylvania entirely separate of Stuart's forces. Unable to link with Lee's command, the partisan commander captured several hundred head of cattle and kidnapped twelve African Americans, whom he took back to Virginia.

42. *O.R.*, vol. 27, pt. 2, 692.

43. *O.R.*, vol. 27, pt. 3, 306.

44. Robert J. Trout, *Galloping Thunder: The Story of the Stuart Horse Artillery Battalion* (Mechanicsburg, PA: Stackpole Books, 2002), 279.

45. *O.R.*, vol. 27, pt. 3, 284, 285, 294, 306; Mosby, *Mosby's War Reminiscences*, 192–93.

46. McClellan, *I Rode with Jeb Stuart*, 321.

47. *O.R.*, vol. 27, pt. 2, 693.

48. McClellan, *I Rode with Jeb Stuart*, 322.

49. Beginning north of the Potomac in the state of Maryland, South Mountain is the local name for the continuation of the Blue Ridge Mountains. The term *South Mountain* is used in Maryland and parts of Pennsylvania. Both the Blue Ridge Mountains and South Mountain are part of the greater Appalachian Mountain chain running from Maine to Georgia.

50. Pleasonton's troopers did in fact move for and seize these lower passes over South Mountain beginning on June 25, 1863. *O.R.*, vol. 27, pt. 3, 305–6, 312; Nye, *Here Come the Rebels*, 313.

51. *O.R.*, vol. 27, pt. 2, 693 (bracketed words by author); Blackford, *War Years with Jeb Stuart*, 277.

52. *O.R.*, vol. 27, pt. 3, 914, 923.

53. *O.R.*, vol. 27, pt. 2, 693.

54. Eric J. Wittenberg and J. David Petruzzi, *Plenty of Blame to Go Around: Jeb Stuart's Controversial Ride to Gettysburg* (New York: Savas Beatie, 2011), 15; Donald A. Hopkins, *The Little Jeff: The Jeff Davis Legion, Cavalry, Army of Northern Virginia* (Shippensburg, PA: White Mane Books, 1999), 144.

55. McClellan, *I Rode with Jeb Stuart*, 323; Wittenberg and Petruzzi, *Plenty of Blame to Go Around*, 16.

56. O.R., vol. 27, pt. 2, 693.

57. Graham, "From Brandy Station to the Heights of Gettysburg"; R. L. T. Beale, *History of the Ninth Virginia Cavalry, in the War between the States* (1899; repr., Richmond, VA: B. F. Johnson, 2010), 77.

58. J. B. Jones, *A Rebel War Clerk's Diary*, vol. 1, ed. James L. Robertson Jr. (Lawrence: University Press of Kansas, 2015), 326.

59. Had this crucial dispatch been entered in the official records assembled after the war, it may well have altered many postwar perspectives on Stuart's performance in the campaign.

60. McClellan, *I Rode with Jeb Stuart*, 323.

61. Blackford, *War Years with Jeb Stuart*, 277.

62. McClellan, *I Rode with Jeb Stuart*, 323.

CHAPTER 14

1. O.R., vol. 27, pt. 3, 333.

2. O.R., vol. 27, pt. 3, 244–45.

3. O.R., vol. 27, pt. 3, 305–6, 312.

4. O.R., vol. 27, pt. 1, 908.

5. John Singleton Mosby, *Mosby's War Reminiscences: Stuart's Cavalry Campaigns* (New York: Dodd, Mead, 1898), 171–72.

6. Robert F. O'Neill, *Chasing Jeb Stuart and John Mosby: The Union Cavalry in Northern Virginia from Second Manassas to Gettysburg* (Jefferson, NC: McFarland, 2012), 237.

7. O.R., vol. 27, pt. 3, 334–35.

8. O.R., vol. 27, pt. 3, 335.

9. Alfred Pleasonton to Brigadier General John Farnsworth, June 23, 1863, Alfred Pleasonton Papers, Manuscripts Division, Library of Congress, Washington, DC.

10. O.R., vol. 27, pt. 1, 51.

11. Alfred Pleasonton to Brigadier General John Farnsworth, June 23, 1863.

12. O.R., vol. 27, pt. 3, 258–59.

13. O.R., vol. 19, pt. 1, 208; Alfred Pleasonton to Seth Williams, June 15, 1863, Joseph Hooker Military Papers, Huntington Library, San Marino, CA.

14. Alfred Pleasonton to Brigadier General John Farnsworth, June 23, 1863.

15. Letter, "Elon Farnsworth to Dear General, Headquarters Cavalry Corps, June 23, 1863," Alfred Pleasonton Papers, Manuscripts Division, Library of Congress, Washington, DC.

16. *O.R.*, vol. 27, pt. 1, 59–60.

17. Also transferred were the 2nd Pennsylvania, as well as companies A and C of the 1st Ohio Cavalry.

18. *O.R.*, vol. 27, pt. 3, 373.

19. Bill Hyde, ed., *The Union Generals Speak: The Meade Hearings on the Battle of Gettysburg* (Baton Rouge: Louisiana State University Press, 2003), 242.

20. *O.R.*, vol. 27, pt. 1, 60.

21. O'Neill, *Chasing Jeb Stuart and John Mosby*, 252.

22. Hyde, *The Union Generals Speak*, 7; Larry Tagg, *The Generals of Gettysburg: The Leaders of America's Greatest Battle* (Cambridge, MA: Da Capo, 2003), 3.

23. Tagg, *The Generals of Gettysburg*, 2.

24. George Gordon Meade, *The Life and Letters of George Gordon Meade*, 2 vols. (New York: Scribner, 1913), 1:345, http://www.latinamericanstudies.org/civil-war/The_life_and_letters_of_George_Gordon_Meade-1.pdf.

25. Edwin B. Coddington, *The Gettysburg Campaign: A Study in Command* (Norwalk, CT: Easton Press, 1998), 214.

26. This reply certainly seems plausible given the bickering that transpired in the final weeks of Hooker's tenure. Coddington, *The Gettysburg Campaign*, 37.

27. *O.R.*, vol. 27, pt. 1, 15, 61–62.

28. *O.R.*, vol. 27, pt. 1, 61.

29. *O.R.*, vol. 27, pt. 1, 61–62.

30. *O.R.*, vol. 27, pt. 1, 63.

31. *O.R.*, vol. 27, pt. 3, 400.

32. *O.R.*, vol. 27, pt. 1, 913, 943.

33. *O.R.*, vol. 27, pt. 3, 400.

34. *O.R.*, vol. 27, pt. 1, 67.

35. Henry B. McClellan, *I Rode with Jeb Stuart: The Life and Campaigns of Major General J. E. B. Stuart* (New York: Da Capo, 1994), 324–25.

36. W. W. Blackford, *War Years with Jeb Stuart* (New York: Scribner, 1945), 278.

37. *O.R.*, vol. 27, pt. 3, 340.

38. *O.R.*, vol. 27, pt. 2, 695; *O.R.*, vol. 27, pt. 3, 2381–82; McClellan, *I Rode with Jeb Stuart*, 326; Jeffry D. Wert, *Cavalryman of the Lost Cause: A Biography of J. E. B. Stuart* (New York: Simon & Schuster, 2009), 272; Kent Masterson Brown, *Meade at Gettysburg: A Study in Command* (Chapel Hill: University of North Carolina Press, 2021), 59–60.

39. W. A. Graham, "From Brandy Station to the Heights of Gettysburg," *News & Observer* (Raleigh, NC), February 7, 1904.

40. Graham, "From Brandy Station to the Heights of Gettysburg."

41. Graham, "From Brandy Station to the Heights of Gettysburg."

42. Fitz Lee's men caused significant damage to this vital rail line between Baltimore and Harper's Ferry. On June 29, the 1st Delaware Cavalry suffered sixty-seven men killed, wounded, and captured in a sharp skirmish at Westminster while the 4th Virginia lost two men killed. This action was similar to the fight at Fairfax Courthouse on June 27 where Federal troops opened with a bold charge and were then defeated by superior numbers.

43. Wilbur Sturtevant Nye, *Here Come the Rebels* (Dayton, OH: Morningside, 1988), 322.

44. Roger H. Harrell, *The 2nd North Carolina Cavalry* (Jefferson, NC: McFarland, 2012), 155.

45. G. R. Prowell, *Encounter at Hanover: Prelude to Gettysburg* (Shippensburg, PA: White Mane, 1994), 65.

46. Harrell, *The 2nd North Carolina Cavalry*, 155; Robert J. Trout, *Galloping Thunder: The Story of the Stuart Horse Artillery Battalion* (Mechanicsburg, PA: Stackpole Books, 2002), 281, 283.

47. *O.R.*, vol. 27, pt. 2, 695.

48. John T. Krepps, *A Strong and Sudden Onslaught: The Cavalry Action at Hanover Pennsylvania* (Ortanna, PA: Colecraft Industries, 2008), 41.

49. Prowell, *Encounter at Hanover*, 61.

50. There were two sections of two Confederate guns near Chambliss's brigade, one from Captain McGregor and one from Captain Breathed. The initial artillery shots fired were most likely launched by McGregor's section. Krepps, *A Strong and Sudden Onslaught*, 61, 107.

51. Krepps, *A Strong and Sudden Onslaught*, 42.

52. Krepps, *A Strong and Sudden Onslaught*, 42.

53. Prowell, *Encounter at Hanover*, 65.

54. Harrell, *The 2nd North Carolina Cavalry*, 157; George A. Rummel, *Cavalry on the Roads to Gettysburg: Kilpatrick at Hanover and Hunterstown* (Shippensburg, PA: White Mane, 2000), 388–89; Prowell, *Encounter at Hanover*, 71.

55. Elliott Hoffman and Horace K. Ide, "The First Vermont Cavalry in the Gettysburg Campaign," *Gettysburg* 14 (January 1996).

56. Letter from William Payne to Fitzhugh Lee, May 12, 1871. Brake Collection, United States Army Military History Institute, Carlisle, PA.

57. Graham, "From Brandy Station to the Heights of Gettysburg."

58. Krepps, *A Strong and Sudden Onslaught*, 55; Blackford, *War Years with Jeb Stuart*, 226; Robert J. Driver Jr., *10th Virginia Cavalry* (Lynchburg, VA: H. E. Howard, 1992), 39.

59. "Forgotten Warrior," *North and South Magazine* 2, no. 7 (September 1999): 85–86. Payne's total of twenty-three reflects men who were ready to ride on fit horses.

60. Krepps, *A Strong and Sudden Onslaught*, 50.

61. Harrell, *The 2nd North Carolina Cavalry*, 158.

62. R. L. T. Beale, *History of the Ninth Virginia Cavalry, in the War between the States* (1899; repr., Richmond, VA: B. F. Johnson, 2010), 83.

63. *O.R.*, vol. 27, pt. 1, 1008; Rummel, *Cavalry on the Roads to Gettysburg*, 245–46.

64. Rummel, *Cavalry on the Roads to Gettysburg*, 247.

65. Blackford, *War Years with Jeb Stuart*, 226 (bracketed words by author).

66. Rummel, *Cavalry on the Roads to Gettysburg*, 255; see Krepps, *A Strong and Sudden Onslaught*, 107.

67. Henry H. Matthews, "Pelham-Breathed Battery: The Raid into Maryland, Hanover and Carlisle, PA., up to and including Gettysburg," *St. Mary's Beacon,* April 20, 1905.

68. Trout, *Galloping Thunder,* 281; G. W. Beale, *A Lieutenant of Cavalry in Lee's Army* (Baltimore, MD: Butternut and Blue, 1994), 114; Harrell, *The 2nd North Carolina Cavalry,* 160.

69. Krepps, *A Strong and Sudden Onslaught,* 107; Robert J. Trout, *Memoirs of the Stuart Horse Artillery Battalion,* vol. 2, *Breathed's and McGregor's Batteries* (Knoxville: University of Tennessee Press, 2010), 95.

70. Krepps, *A Strong and Sudden Onslaught,* 59.

71. O.R., vol. 27, pt. 1, 999; Rummel, *Cavalry on the Roads to Gettysburg,* 276–79; James H. Kidd, *Personal Recollections of a Cavalryman with Custer's Michigan Cavalry Brigade in the Civil War* (1908; repr., Ionia, MI: Sentinel, 2015), 127; J. Robertson, *Michigan in the War* (Lansing, MI: W. S. George, 1882), 580; Krepps, *A Strong and Sudden Onslaught,* 67–69.

72. McClellan, *I Rode with Jeb Stuart,* 328–29.

73. James McClure, *East of Gettysburg: A Gray Shadow Crosses York County, PA* (York, PA: York Daily Record/York County Heritage Trust, 2003), 88; O.R., vol. 27, pt. 2, 709; Eric J. Wittenberg and J. David Petruzzi, *Plenty of Blame to Go Around: Jeb Stuart's Controversial Ride to Gettysburg* (New York: Savas Beatie, 2011), 120.

74. Harrell, *The 2nd North Carolina Cavalry,* 161.

75. O.R., vol. 27, pt. 1, 987; Krepps, *A Strong and Sudden Onslaught,* 94.

76. O.R., vol. 27, pt. 2, 696.

77. Beale, *A Lieutenant of Cavalry,* 114.

78. Susan Leigh Blackford and Charles Minor Blackford III, eds., *Letters from Lee's Army; or, Memoirs of Life in and out of the Army in Virginia during the War between the States* (Lincoln: University of Nebraska Press, 1998), 194; Krepps, *A Strong and Sudden Onslaught,* 85, 88.

79. Wert, *Cavalryman of the Lost Cause,* 271.

80. O.R., vol. 27, pt. 2, 696.

81. O.R., vol. 27, pt. 2, 696.

82. O.R., vol. 27, pt. 2, 697.

CHAPTER 15

1. O.R., vol. 27, pt. 2, 464–65; John Harper Dawson, *Wildcat Cavalry: A Synoptic History of the Seventeenth Virginia Cavalry Regiment of the Jenkins-McCausland Brigade in the War between the States* (Dayton, OH: Morningside, 1982), 22.

2. O.R., vol. 27, pt. 2, 466–67.

3. O.R., vol. 27, pt. 2, 316.

4. O.R., vol. 27, pt. 2, 307.

5. Charles Marshall, "Events Leading Up to the Battle of Gettysburg," address before Confederate Veterans Association of Washington, DC, January 1896, in

Southern Historical Society Papers, ed. R. A. Brock (Richmond, VA: Southern Historical Society, 1894), 22:226–27.

6. Robertson did not start moving for Lee's army until June 29, the day after Harrison informed Lee of the Federal advance. *O.R.*, vol. 27, pt. 2, 751–52.

7. *O.R.*, vol. 27, pt. 2, 298; *O.R.*, vol. 27, pt. 2, 307.

8. *O.R.*, vol. 27, pt. 3, 305–6, 312; Lee's line of communication with Virginia was also his route to procure additional ammunition. Marshall, "Events Leading Up to the Battle of Gettysburg," 226–27.

9. *O.R.*, vol. 27, pt. 2, 307 (bracketed words by author).

10. Harry W. Pfanz, *Gettysburg: The Second Day* (Chapel Hill: University of North Carolina Press, 1987), 3.

11. Edwin B. Coddington, *The Gettysburg Campaign: A Study in Command* (Norwalk, CT: Easton Press, 1998), 196–97, 181.

12. *O.R.*, vol. 25, pt. 1, 886, 889; Larry Tagg, *The Generals of Gettysburg: The Leaders of America's Greatest Battle* (Cambridge, MA: Da Capo, 2003), 340.

13. Pettigrew was a brilliant student and slated early on for a professor's slot at the Naval Observatory in Washington, DC. He later entered the legal profession and practiced law in Baltimore, Maryland, and Charleston, South Carolina. Tagg, *The Generals of Gettysburg*, 343.

14. Walter Clark, ed., *Histories of the Several Regiments and Battalions from North Carolina in the Great War, 1861–1865* (Raleigh: State of North Carolina, 1901), 5:115.

15. Harry W. Pfanz, *Gettysburg: The First Day* (Chapel Hill: University of North Carolina Press, 2001), 27; Clark, *Histories of the Several Regiments*, 5:115–17; *O.R.*, vol. 27, pt. 2, 637.

16. Clark, *Histories of the Several Regiments*, 5:116.

17. Clark, *Histories of the Several Regiments*, 5:115.

18. Pfanz, *Gettysburg: The First Day*, 28.

19. *O.R.*, vol. 27, pt. 1, 923.

20. Pfanz, *Gettysburg: The First Day*, 39.

21. *O.R.*, vol. 27, pt. 1, 923–24.

22. *O.R.*, vol. 27, pt. 3, 458; *O.R.*, vol. 27, pt. 3, 416, 418–21; Pfanz, *Gettysburg: The First Day*, 48.

23. Aaron B. Jerome, "Buford on Oak Hill," in *The Decisive Conflicts of the Late Civil War or Slaveholders' Rebellion*, by John Watts de Peyster (New York: MacDonald, 1867), 151–52.

24. Buford's two brigades under Gamble and Devin did not have Spencer repeating carbines. They were issued a mixture of Sharps, Burnside, Smith, Gallager, Ballard, and Morrill carbines. All were breechloaders; none were repeaters. Burt Kummorow, "Small Arms in the Cavalry Regiments of the Army of the Potomac during the Gettysburg Campaign," Ordnance Records in U.S. Archives, Washington, DC, 1962.

25. *O.R.*, vol. 27, pt. 1, 923, 924.

26. Thomas G. Day, "Opening the Battle of Gettysburg," *National Tribune*, July 30, 1903 (bracketed word by author).

27. Kummorow, "Small Arms in the Cavalry."

28. This was Major William Pegram's artillery battery. *O.R.*, vol. 27, pt. 2, 637; Eric J. Wittenberg, *The Devil's to Pay: John Buford at Gettysburg: A History and Walking Tour* (El Dorado Hills, CA: Savas Beatie, 2018), 85.

29. Day, "Opening the Battle of Gettysburg."

30. John H. Calef, "Gettysburg Notes: The Opening Gun," *Journal of the Military Services Institution of the United States*, Jan./Feb., 1907, 40–57.

31. Kummorow, "Small Arms in the Cavalry Regiments"; Hillman Allyn Hall, William B. Besley, and Gilbert Guion Wood, *History of the Sixth New York Cavalry: (Second Ira Harris Guard) Second Brigade—First Division—Cavalry Corps, Army of the Potomac, 1861–1865* (Salem, MA: Higginson, 2005), 138.

32. John B. Bachelder, David L. Ladd, Audrey J. Ladd, and Richard A. Sauers, eds., *The Bachelder Papers: Gettysburg in Their Own Words* (Dayton, OH: Morningside, 1994), 1:329.

33. Bachelder et al., *The Bachelder Papers*, 1:329.

34. Tagg, *The Generals of Gettysburg*, 170–71, 349, 352.

35. Pfanz, *Gettysburg: The First Day*, 77–78.

36. Chris Mackowski, Kristopher D. White, and Daniel T. Davis, *Fight like the Devil: The First Day at Gettysburg, July 1, 1863* (El Dorado Hills, CA: Savas Beatie, 2015), 32; Edward G. Longacre, *General John Buford: A Military Biography* (Cambridge, MA: Da Capo, 1995), 194.

37. *O.R.*, vol. 27, pt. 2, 607, 638.

38. Wilbur Sturtevant Nye, *Here Come the Rebels* (Dayton, OH: Morningside, 1988), 41.

39. Pfanz, *Gettysburg: The First Day*, 149. Ewell and a number of his officers were confused by the latest round of orders with its "indefinite phraseology" sent out by Lee's chief of staff William Marshall. Ewell and his staff found them to be vague and unclear.

40. Harry W. Pfanz, *Gettysburg: Culp's Hill and Cemetery Hill* (Chapel Hill: University of North Carolina Press, 1993), 35; Robert J. Trout, *They Followed the Plume: The Staff Officers and Headquarters Personnel of Major General J. E. B. Stuart, C.S.A.* (Mechanicsburg, PA: Stackpole Books, 1993), 270–71.

41. *O.R.*, vol. 27, pt. 2, 444.

42. Coddington, *The Gettysburg Campaign*, 289–93; *O.R.*, vol. 27, pt. 2, 444–45, 468–69, 552–54.

43. Author's private tour with Gettysburg Battlefield licensed guide Eric Lindblade. Wittenberg, *The Devil's to Pay*, 133–37.

44. Day, "Opening the Battle of Gettysburg."

45. Daniel W. Pulis to his parents, July 6, 1863; Edward G. Longacre, *Lincoln's Cavalrymen: A History of the Mounted Forces of the Army of the Potomac, 1861–1865* (Mechanicsburg, PA: Stackpole, 2000), 187.

46. Day, "Opening the Battle of Gettysburg."

47. Upon Ewell's initial attack, his troopers had been shelled by their own artillery firing from Cemetery Hill and were forced to retire under this "persistent" fire. *O.R.*, vol. 27, pt. 1, 939.

48. *O.R.*, vol. 27, pt. 1, 927; *O.R.*, vol. 27, pt. 1, 934; *O.R.*, vol. 27, pt. 1, 939; Longacre, *General John Buford*, 195–96.

49. *O.R.*, vol. 27, pt. 2, 308.

50. Pfanz, *Gettysburg: The First Day*, 275.

51. *O.R.*, vol. 27, pt. 2, 445.

52. *O.R.*, vol. 27, pt. 2, 317–18, 607, 613; Pfanz, *Gettysburg: The First Day*, 319–20.

53. *O.R.*, vol. 27, pt. 2, 444; Pfanz, *Gettysburg: Culp's Hill and Cemetery Hill*, 72–80.

54. Mackowski, White, and Davis, *Fight like the Devil*, appendix E.

CHAPTER 16

1. *O.R.*, vol. 27, pt. 3, 466.

2. Harry W. Pfanz, *Gettysburg: The Second Day* (Chapel Hill: University of North Carolina Press, 1998), 58.

3. *O.R.*, vol. 27, pt. 3, 1086; *O.R.*, vol. 27, pt. 1, 939; H. P. Moyer, *History of the Seventeenth Regiment, Pennsylvania Volunteer Cavalry; or, One Hundred and Sixty-Second in the Line of Pennsylvania Volunteer Regiments: War to Suppress the Rebellion, 1861–1865* (1911; repr., Salem, MA: Higginson, 1998), 51; Hillman Allyn Hall, William B. Besley, and Gilbert Guion Wood, *History of the Sixth New York Cavalry: (Second Ira Harris Guard) Second Brigade—First Division—Cavalry Corps, Army of the Potomac, 1861–1865* (Salem, MA: Higginson, 2005), 142–43.

4. *O.R.*, vol. 27, pt. 1, 923.

5. *O.R.*, vol. 27, pt. 1, 1058–59.

6. This glaring mistake would contribute to Sickles's famous repositioning of his troops later that day. James A. Hessler and Britt C. Isenberg, *Gettysburg's Peach Orchard: Longstreet, Sickles, and the Bloody Fight for the "Commanding Ground" along the Emmitsburg Road* (El Dorado Hills, CA: Savas Beatie, 2019), 73.

7. *O.R.*, vol. 27, pt. 1, 914–16.

8. *O.R.*, vol. 27, pt. 2, 307.

9. Pfanz, *Gettysburg: The Second Day*, 22.

10. J. A. Early, "Causes of the Defeat of General Lee's Army at the Battle of Gettysburg: Opinions of Leading Confederate Soldiers," in *Southern Historical Society Papers*, ed. J. William Jones (Richmond, VA: Southern Historical Society, 1877), 4:60.

11. *O.R.*, vol. 27, pt. 2, 308.

12. S. A. Cunningham, ed., *Confederate Veteran* (Nashville, TN: Cunningham, 1913), 23:508.

13. *O.R.*, vol. 27, pt. 2, 318–19.

14. Armistead Lindsey Long, *Memoirs of Robert E. Lee, His Military and Personal History: Embracing a Large Amount of Information Hitherto Unpublished* (New York; Philadelphia, PA; Washington, DC: J. M. Stoddart, 1887), 281.

15. Long, *Memoirs of Robert E. Lee*, 281.

16. Long, *Memoirs of Robert E. Lee*, 281.

17. John W. Thomason Jr., *Jeb Stuart* (New York: Scribner, 1930), 440; Mark Nesbitt, *Saber and Scapegoat: J. E. B. Stuart and the Gettysburg Controversy* (Mechanicsburg, PA: Stackpole Books, 1994), 89.

18. Nesbitt, *Saber and Scapegoat*, 89–91.

19. J. B. Jones, *A Rebel War Clerk's Diary*, ed. James L. Robertson Jr. (Lawrence: University Press of Kansas, 2015), 1:326. Henry McClellan claimed Stuart also sent a dispatch from Haymarket warning Lee of the Federal movements to the river. See Henry B. McClellan, *I Rode with Jeb Stuart: The Life and Campaigns of Major General J. E. B. Stuart* (New York: Da Capo, 1994), 321.

20. *O.R.*, vol. 27, pt. 3, 914–15.

21. *O.R.*, vol. 27, pt. 3, 913.

22. McClellan, *I Rode with Jeb Stuart*, 336.

23. *O.R.*, vol. 27, pt. 3, 947–48.

24. Unpublished manuscript by David Gregg McIntosh describing a dinner party held on February 24, 1887. David Gregg McIntosh Papers, Virginia Historical Society, Richmond VA.

25. *O.R.*, vol. 27, pt. 2, 692–97.

26. *O.R.*, vol. 27, pt. 2, 308, 697.

27. R. L. T. Beale, *History of the Ninth Virginia Cavalry, in the War between the States* (1899; repr., Richmond, VA: B. F. Johnson, 2010), 86.

28. George A. Rummel, *Cavalry on the Roads to Gettysburg: Kilpatrick at Hanover and Hunterstown* (Shippensburg, PA: White Mane, 2000), 111; J. Robertson, *Michigan in the War* (Lansing, MI: W. S. George, 1882), 761, 838, 878.

29. Michael Phipps, *"Come on, You Wolverines!" Custer at Gettysburg* (Gettysburg, PA: Farnsworth House Military Impressions, 1995), 13–15.

30. Rummel, *Cavalry on the Roads to Gettysburg*, 111.

31. Rummel, *Cavalry on the Roads to Gettysburg*, 126.

32. Robert F. O'Neill, *Chasing Jeb Stuart and John Mosby: The Union Cavalry in Northern Virginia from Second Manassas to Gettysburg* (Jefferson, NC: McFarland, 2012), 12, 181.

33. Grabbing one's wide-brimmed hat in hand before a gallop was a common occurrence for any horse soldier wanting to keep his cover. Modern readers can easily verify this in a car by driving down the road at twenty miles an hour with the window open.

34. Eric J. Wittenberg and J. David Petruzzi, *Plenty of Blame to Go Around: Jeb Stuart's Controversial Ride to Gettysburg* (New York: Savas Beatie, 2011), 164.

35. Harriet Bey Mesic, *Cobb's Legion Cavalry: A History and Roster of the Ninth Georgia Volunteers in the Civil War* (Jefferson, NC: McFarland, 2011), 79.

36. Ralph Kirshner, *The Class of 1861: Custer, Ames, and Their Classmates after West Point* (Carbondale: Southern Illinois University Press, 1999), 10.

37. Hampton sent to Stuart for artillery support, but Breathed's horses were exhausted and their caissons near empty; instead, a battery was found from Ewell's corps, that of Captain Charles Green's battery of the Louisiana Guard Artillery. Robert J. Trout, *Galloping Thunder: The Story of the Stuart Horse Artillery Battalion* (Mechanicsburg, PA: Stackpole Books, 2002), 290.

38. Wittenberg and Petruzzi, *Plenty of Blame*, 167; Fredrick Whitaker, *A Popular Life of Gen. George A. Custer* (New York: Sheldon, 1876), 173.

39. Mesic, *Cobb's Legion Cavalry*, 79.

40. *O.R.*, vol. 27, pt. 2, 724.

41. Whitaker, *A Popular Life*, 174; Wittenberg and Petruzzi, *Plenty of Blame*, 173.

42. Wiley C. Howard, *Sketch of the Cobb Legion Cavalry and Some Incidents and Scenes Remembered* (Atlanta, GA: Atlanta Camp 159, S.C.V., 1901; repr., Delhi, India: Facsimile, 2013), 8–9.

43. Phipps, *"Come on, You Wolverines!,"* 28 (bracketed word by author).

44. Vince Dooley and Samuel N. Thomas, eds., *The Legion's Fighting Bulldog: The Civil War Correspondence of William Gaston Delony, Lieutenant Colonel of Cobb's Georgia Legion Cavalry, and Rosa Delony, 1853–1863* (Macon, GA: Mercer University Press, 2017), 238.

45. Mesic, *Cobb's Legion Cavalry*, 80.

46. *O.R.*, vol. 27, pt. 1, 992.

47. John Harper Dawson, *Wildcat Cavalry: A Synoptic History of the Seventeenth Virginia Cavalry Regiment of the Jenkins-McCausland Brigade in the War between the States* (Dayton, OH: Morningside, 1982), 25; Bert H. Barnett, "'. . . Our Position Was Finely Adapted to Its Purpose . . .': The Guns of Cemetery Hill," *Gettysburg Seminar Papers* (2019): 244–45.

48. Dawson, *Wildcat Cavalry*, 81.

49. Colonel Ferguson was also missing from the front lines on the following day in the fighting at the Rummel farm. John B. Bachelder, David L. Ladd, Audrey J. Ladd, and Richard A. Sauers, eds., "Letter of Lt. Col. Vincent A. Witcher," in *The Bachelder Papers: Gettysburg in Their Own Words* (Dayton, OH: Morningside, 1994), 2:1239.

50. *O.R.*, vol. 27, pt. 2, 518.

51. *O.R.*, vol. 27, pt. 2, 518.

52. U.S. Army Pennsylvania Cavalry 3rd Regiment, *History of the Third Pennsylvania Cavalry* (Philadelphia, PA: Franklin, 1905), 295.

53. Nobel D. Preston, *History of the Tenth Regiment of Cavalry New York State Volunteers: August, 1861, to August, 1865* (New York: D. Appleton, 1892), 108.

54. Campbell Brown, *Campbell Brown's Civil War: With Ewell and the Army of Northern Virginia* (Baton Rouge: Louisiana State University Press, 2001), 219.

55. Brown, *Campbell Brown's Civil War*, 220; Eric J. Wittenberg, *Protecting the Flank at Gettysburg: The Battles for Brinkerhoff's Ridge and East Cavalry Field, July 2–3, 1863* (El Dorado Hills, CA: Savas Beatie, 2013), 30.

56. Preston, *History of the Tenth Regiment of Cavalry*, 112.

57. "Report of Captain William E. Miller," in Bachelder et al., *Bachelder Papers*, 2:1262.

58. *O.R.*, vol. 27, pt. 2, 518–19.

CHAPTER 17

1. *O.R.*, vol. 27, pt. 2, 320.

2. Jeff Toalson, ed., *Send Me a Pair of Old Boots and Kiss My Little Girls: The Civil War Papers of Richard and Mary Watkins* (New York: Universe, 2009), 201.

3. *O.R.*, vol. 27, pt. 2, 697.

4. *O.R.*, vol. 27, pt. 2, 697.

5. John B. Bachelder, David L. Ladd, Audrey J. Ladd, and Richard A. Sauers, eds., "Letter of Captain William A. Graham," in *The Bachelder Papers: Gettysburg in Their Own Words*, vols. 1–3 (Dayton, OH: Morningside, 1994), 1373.

6. Colonel John L. Black of the 1st South Carolina had been detached with one battalion to scout for Longstreet's I Corps. "Letter of Col. John L. Black, " in Bachelder et al., *Bachelder Papers*, 1239–43.

7. H. H. Matthews, "The Pelham-Breathed Battery," *St. Mary's Beacon*, April 20, 1905.

8. *O.R.*, vol. 27, pt. 2, 699; Robert J. Trout, *Galloping Thunder: The Story of the Stuart Horse Artillery Battalion* (Mechanicsburg, PA: Stackpole Books, 2002), 291.

9. Michael Phipps, *"Come on, You Wolverines!" Custer at Gettysburg* (Gettysburg, PA: Farnsworth House Military Impressions, 1995), 37.

10. *O.R.*, vol. 27, pt. 2, 698; James H. Kidd, *Personal Recollections of a Cavalryman with Custer's Michigan Cavalry Brigade in the Civil War* (1908; repr., Ionia, MI: Sentinel, 2015), 149.

11. *O.R.*, vol. 27, pt. 2, 698, 699.

12. Henry B. McClellan, *I Rode with Jeb Stuart: The Life and Campaigns of Major General J. E. B. Stuart* (New York: Da Capo, 1994), 337.

13. *O.R.*, vol. 25, pt. 1, 52.

14. *O.R.*, vol. 25, pt. 1, 49, 52.

15. Mark Mayo Boatner III, *The Civil War Dictionary*, rev. ed. (New York: Random House, 1988), 534. The 1st Massachusetts, also part of this brigade, was still out of commission following the fight at Aldie on June 17.

16. *O.R.*, vol. 27, pt. 1, 956 (bracketed words by author).

17. The report came from a Union signal station atop Cemetery Hill. Noble D. Preston, *History of the Tenth Regiment of Cavalry New York State Volunteers: August, 1861, to August, 1865* (New York: D. Appleton, 1892), 116.

18. *O.R.*, vol. 27, pt. 1, 956.

19. "Detailed Strength and Casualty Numbers for the Army of the Potomac in the Battle of Gettysburg," Stone Sentinels, Gettysburg National Military Park; George A. Rummel, *Cavalry on the Roads to Gettysburg: Kilpatrick at Hanover and Hunterstown* (Shippensburg, PA: White Mane, 2000), appendix F.

20. *O.R.*, vol. 27, pt. 1, 1051. These skirmishers were under the command of Major Hugh Janeway. Henry R. Pyne, *The History of the First New Jersey Cavalry (Sixteenth Regiment, New Jersey Volunteers)* (Trenton, NJ: J. A. Breecher, 1871), 164.

21. *O.R.*, vol. 27, pt. 1, 1051 (bracketed word by author).

22. Scott C. Cole, *34th Battalion Virginia Cavalry* (Lynchburg, VA: H. E. Howard, 1993), 5, 12, 20.

23. Trout, *Galloping Thunder*, 292.

24. Trout, *Galloping Thunder*, 293 (bracketed words by author).

25. Author's conversation with Daniel Hoffman, the former owner of the Rummel farm property, September 2003; "Letter of Lt. Col. Vincent A. Witcher," in Bachelder et al., *Bachelder Papers*, 2:1237.

26. Cole, *34th Battalion Virginia Cavalry*, 48.

27. Cole, *34th Battalion Virginia Cavalry*, 49; "Letter of Lt. James Chester, 27 Nov. 1884," in Bachelder et al., *Bachelder Papers*, 1079.

28. *O.R.*, vol. 27, pt. 2, 699.

29. "Letter of Brig. Gen. Fitzhugh Lee, 7 May 1877," in Bachelder et al., *Bachelder Papers*, 3:1377.

30. *O.R.*, vol. 27, pt. 2, 697, 699.

31. *O.R.*, vol. 27, pt. 2, 699.

32. *O.R.*, vol. 27, pt. 2, 724.

33. Cole, *34th Battalion Virginia Cavalry*, 49.

34. Trout, *Galloping Thunder*, 293.

35. "Letter of Private Theodore J. Dimitry, 13 May 1886," in Bachelder et al., *Bachelder Papers*, 3:1381.

36. "Luther S. Trowbridge to Gov. R. A. Alger, Feb. 19, 1886," in Bachelder et al., *Bachelder Papers*, 1207.

37. "Letter of Captain James Chester to Lt. William Brooke-Rawle," in Bachelder et al., *Bachelder Papers*, 1:655.

38. *O.R.*, vol. 27, pt. 1, 957; J. Robertson, ed., *Michigan in the War* (Lansing, MI: W. S. George, 1882), 583.

39. "Letter of Lt. William R. Gaines, 1st Lt. Company B, 14th Virginia Cavalry," in Bachelder et al., *Bachelder Papers*, 3:1446.

40. *O.R.*, vol. 27, pt. 2, 698.

41. "Letter of Lt. Col. V. A. Witcher," in Bachelder et al., *Bachelder Papers*, 2:1238.

42. "Letter of Lt. Col. V. A. Witcher," in Bachelder et al., *Bachelder Papers*, 2:1293.

43. *O.R.*, vol. 27, pt. 2, 698; R. T. L. Beale, *History of the Ninth Virginia Cavalry, in the War between the States* (1899; .repr., Richmond, VA: B. V. Johnson, 2010), 87; Robert K. Krick, *9th Virginia Cavalry*, Virginia Regimental History Series (Lynchburg, VA: H. E. Howard, 1982), 24.

44. "Letter of Thomas T. Munford, 11 Feb. 1886," in Bachelder et al., *Bachelder Papers*, 2:1201.

45. "Letter of Col. William A. Morgan," in Bachelder et al., *Bachelder Papers*, 2:1278.

46. Lieutenant Brooke-Rawle stated the 3rd Pennsylvania did not charge against this first Confederate advance. "Statement of Lt. William Brooke-Rawle," in Bachelder et al., *Bachelder Papers*, 1:658; "Letter of Lt. James Lee, CO. F, 2nd VA Cavalry," in Bachelder et al., *Bachelder Papers*, 2:1113; "Col. Thomas T. Munford to Maj. Henry B. McClellan," in Bachelder et al., *Bachelder Papers*, 2:1117; "Letter of Thomas T. Munford," in Bachelder et al., *Bachelder Papers*, 2:1201; "Letter of

Sgt Elliot G. Fishburne," in Bachelder et al., *Bachelder Papers*, 2:1286; "Letter of S. S. Murrill," in Bachelder et al., *Bachelder Papers*, 3:1378; Robert J. Driver Jr., *1st Virginia Cavalry*, 2nd ed., Virginia Regimental Histories Series (Lynchburg, VA: H. E. Howard, 1991), 66.

47. "Letters of Lt. James Chester," in Bachelder et al., *Bachelder Papers*, 2:1078, 1089.

48. General Gregg had mistakenly relieved the 1st Maryland and ordered Custer's brigade to this position. The Virginians charged Chester's guns as these changes were still under way. "Letter of Col. John B. McIntosh," in Bachelder et al., *Bachelder Papers*, 2:1124; "Letter of B. G. Garrett, 24 July 1884," in Bachelder et al., *Bachelder Papers*, 2:1115; "Statement of Sgt. Elliot G. Fishburne," in Bachelder et al., *Bachelder Papers*, 2:1286.

49. "Letters of Lt. James Chester," in Bachelder et al., *Bachelder Papers*, 2:1078, 1089; *O.R.*, vol. 27, pt. 1, 977.

50. The 7th Michigan was the regimental command of Colonel William Mann. Robertson, *Michigan in the War*, 583; "Letter of Col. John B. McIntosh," in Bachelder et al., *Bachelder Papers*, 2:1124. It was this forward movement by Custer's 7th Michigan that prompted Stuart to order Chambliss forward in a mounted charge across the Rummel farm. *O.R.*, vol. 27, pt. 2, 698.

51. *O.R.*, vol. 27, pt. 1, 957 (bracketed word by author). *O.R.*, vol. 27, pt. 1, 1051. Colonel McIntosh agreed with General Gregg's assessment.

52. Henry C. Meyer, *Civil War Experiences under Bayard, Gregg, Kilpatrick, Custer, Raulston, and Newberry, 1862, 1863, 1864* (New York: Putnam, 1911), 50.

53. "Statement of Sgt. Elliot G. Fishburne," in Bachelder et al., *Bachelder Papers*, 2:1286; "Letter of Sgt. C. W. Chick," in Bachelder et al., *Bachelder Papers*, 3:1340–41.

54. *O.R.*, vol. 27, pt. 2, 698; "Letter of Lt. James I. Lee," in Bachelder et al., *Bachelder Papers*, 2:1113; "Letter of Lt. Edward Burgh," in Bachelder et al., *Bachelder Papers*, 2:1110; "Col. Thomas T. Munford to Maj. Henry B. McClellan," in Bachelder et al., *Bachelder Papers*, 2:1117; "Letter of James W. Biggs," in Bachelder et al., *Bachelder Papers*, 3:1343; "Letter of S. S. Murrill," in Bachelder et al., *Bachelder Papers*, 3:1378.

55. "Letter of James W. Biggs," in Bachelder et al., *Bachelder Papers*, 3:1343.

56. "Letter of Col. William Morgan, April 1886," in Bachelder et al., *Bachelder Papers*, 2:1280.

57. Phipps, *"Come on, You Wolverines!,"* 43–44.

58. "Luther S. Trowbridge to Gov. R. A. Alger, Feb. 19, 1886," in Bachelder et al., *Bachelder Papers*, 2:1207.

59. "Report of Capt. William Miller," in Bachelder et al., *Bachelder Papers*, 2:1266.

60. "Lieutenant Colonel Allyne Litchfield to My Dear Wife, Boonsboro July 7, 1863," Litchfield-French Papers, Shannon Wait Manuscripts Division, William Clements Library, University of Michigan.

61. "Lieutenant Colonel Allyne Litchfield to My Dear Wife, Boonsboro July 7, 1863."

62. "Letter of Lt. George G. Briggs," in Bachelder et al., *Bachelder Papers*, 2:1257. Lieutenant Briggs's account stands in contrast to Colonel James Kidd's later account, but Briggs was an actual participant of this event whereas Kidd was only a distant witness from a thousand yards away. See Kidd, *Personal Recollections*, 154.

63. *O.R.*, vol. 27, pt. 2, 698; Beale, *History of the Ninth Virginia Cavalry*, 87; Krick, *9th Virginia Cavalry*, 24.

64. Beale, *History of the Ninth Virginia Cavalry*, 88; "To Recover the Flag," *National Tribune*, March 4, 1897; "Vincent Witcher to Sec. of War, 27 March, 1887," in Bachelder et al., *Bachelder Papers*, 3:1482.

65. "Letter of James W. Biggs," in Bachelder et al., *Bachelder Papers*, 3:1343. Biggs wrote that they made their sprint during Hampton's charge, but that was sometime later; the author thinks he is confused with Chambliss's charge, which came earlier and from the same direction.

66. "Letter of Captain William W. Rogers, 14 March 1886," in Bachelder et al., *Bachelder Papers*, 2:1223.

67. "Notes of a Conversation with Lt. Junius B. Jones of Colonel John R. Chambliss Jr., 13th Virginia Cavalry Staff, 30 August 1866," in Bachelder et al., *Bachelder Papers*, 1:210. Fortunately, Captain Newhall survived his wound and the war.

68. "Letter of Captain William Miller," in Bachelder et al., *Bachelder Papers*, 2:1268.

69. "Letter of Col. Russell Alger," in Bachelder et al., *Bachelder Papers*, 2:1300.

70. McClellan, *I Rode with Jeb Stuart*, 344; "Letter of Col. Russell Alger," in Bachelder et al., *Bachelder Papers*, 2:1300; "Letter of Maj. Luther S. Trowbridge, 19 Feb. 1886," in Bachelder et al., *Bachelder Papers*, 2:1208.

71. The force covering Green's battery may have been Captain Frederick F. Smith's, Company G, 17th Virginia Cavalry. "Letter of Lt. Col. Vincent A. Witcher," in Bachelder et al., *Bachelder Papers*, 2:1290, 1296n173, 1296n194; "Letter of Pvt. Theodore J. Dimitry," in Bachelder et al., *Bachelder Papers*, 3:1381.

72. *O.R.*, vol. 27, pt. 2, 724–25.

73. McClellan, *I Rode with Jeb Stuart*, 344.

74. *O.R.*, vol. 27, pt. 2, 725. Hampton states the Cobb Legion did not take part in this charge. There was only one battalion of the 1st South Carolina at Rummel's farm. The rest of the 1st South Carolina was posted on the far flank of the battlefield.

75. "Statement of Sgt. Fishbourne," in Bachelder et al., *Bachelder Papers*, 2:1286.

76. *O.R.*, vol. 27, pt. 2, 724–25; *O.R.*, vol. 27, pt. 2, 697.

77. "Letter of Capt. William E. Miller, 29 March, 1886," in Bachelder et al., *Bachelder Papers*, 2:1266.

78. "Letter of Capt. William Miller, 29 March, 1866," in Bachelder et al., *Bachelder Papers*, 2:1266.

79. Edward G. Longacre, *Lincoln's Cavalrymen: A History of the Mounted Forces of the Army of the Potomac, 1861–1865* (Mechanicsburg, PA: Stackpole Books, 2000), 197.

80. Hamilton and Woodruff each commanded a gun section in Pennington's Battery A. "Letter of Lt. Carle A. Woodruff, 14 December 1884," in Bachelder

et al., *Bachelder Papers*, 2:1088; "Letter of Frank B. Hamilton, 12 Dec. 1884," in Bachelder et al., *Bachelder Papers*, 2:1086.

81. "Letter of Lt. Carle A. Woodruff, 14 December 1884," in Bachelder et al., *Bachelder Papers*, 2:1088.

82. George N. Saussy, "Campaigning with Jeb Stuart," *Watson's Jeffersonian Magazine* 13, no. 1 (May 1911): 64.

83. "Letter from Captain Amasa E. Matthews, 11 June, 1887," in Bachelder et al., *Bachelder Papers*, 3:1491.

84. The 1st North Carolina had recently suffered significant losses in their field commanders; Lieutenant Colonel Gordon had been reassigned to command the 5th North Carolina two weeks prior, and Major Whitaker fell at Fairfax Courthouse on June 27.

85. Robertson, *Michigan in the War*, 583; *O.R.*, vol. 27, pt. 1, 977. The author believes this clash occurred at the Michigan monument along Gregg Avenue at East Cavalry field.

86. "Letter from Captain Amasa E. Matthews, 11 June, 1887," in Bachelder et al., *Bachelder Papers*, 3:1492.

87. "Letter from Captain Amasa E. Matthews, 11 June, 1887," in Bachelder et al., *Bachelder Papers*, 3:1492.

88. "Letter from Captain Amasa E. Matthews, 11 June, 1887," in Bachelder et al., *Bachelder Papers*, 3:1492.

89. Edward E. Miller, "The Cavalry Battle Near Gettysburg," Gettysburg National Military Park files, Gettysburg, PA.

90. "Letter of Capt. William Miller," in Bachelder et al., *Bachelder Papers*, 2:1267; Wilbur Sturtevant Nye, *Here Come the Rebels* (Dayton, OH: Morningside, 1988), 204.

91. Letter from P. J. Malone to John Logan Black, 6 January, 1867, "Charge of Black's Cavalry Regiment at Gettysburg," *Southern Historical Society Papers* 16.

92. *O.R.*, vol. 27, pt. 2, 775; Richard M. Coffman, *Going Back the Way They Came: A History of the Phillips Georgia Legion Cavalry Battalion* (Macon, GA: Mercer University Press, 2011), 45–46.

93. "Letter from Stephens Calhoun Smith to Dear Father and Mother, Near Williamsport, MD. July 12, 1863," Stephens Calhoun Smith Papers, Duke University, copy of typed transcript in Gettysburg National Military Park. Smith wrote, "It was my fate this day for the first time in the war to kill a man with my sabre."

94. "Letter from Captain Amasa E. Matthews, 11 June, 1887," in Bachelder et al., *Bachelder Papers*, 3:1492.

95. "Letter from Captain Amasa E. Matthews, 11 June, 1887," in Bachelder et al., *Bachelder Papers*, 3:1493.

96. *O.R.*, vol. 27, pt. 1, 998.

97. "Letter from Captain Amasa E. Matthews, 11 June, 1887," in Bachelder et al., *Bachelder Papers*, 3:1493.

98. D. B. Rea, *Sketches from Hampton's Cavalry: Embracing the Principle Exploits of the Cavalry in the Campaigns of 1862 and 1863* (Columbia: South Carolina State Press, 1864), 116.

99. "Letter of Colonel William A. Morgan," in Bachelder et al., *Bachelder Papers*, 2:1281; "Statement of Sgt. Fishbourne," in Bachelder et al., *Bachelder Papers*, 2:1286, 3:1379; "Statement of Lt. John M. Jordan," in Bachelder et al., *Bachelder Papers*, 3:1376.

100. "Letter of S. S. Murrill," in Bachelder et al., *Bachelder Papers*, 3:1378.

101. "Letter of Maj. Luther S. Trowbridge," in Bachelder et al., *Bachelder Papers*, 2:1208; "Letter of Colonel Russel A. Alger," in Bachelder et al., *Bachelder Papers*, 1:247; "Lieutenant Colonel Allyne Litchfield to My Dear Wife, Boonsboro July 7, 1863."

102. Manly Wade Wellman, *Giant in Gray: A Biography of Wade Hampton of South Carolina* (Dayton, OH: Morningside, 1988), 120.

103. "Letter of Col. William A. Morgan, April 1886," in Bachelder et al., *Bachelder Papers*, 2:1282.

104. "Letter of Colonel Vincent A. Witcher," in Bachelder et al., *Bachelder Papers*, 2:1238. The force opposing Miller may have been the 2nd North Carolina later covering the batteries of Breathed and McGregor. W. A. Graham, "From Brandy Station to the Heights of Gettysburg," *News & Observer* (Raleigh, NC), February 7, 1904; William Graham, *Nineteenth Regiment*, vol. 2 of *Histories of the Several Regiments and Battalions from North Carolina in the Great War, 1861–1865*, ed. Walter Clark (Goldsboro, NC: Nash Brothers, 1901), 98; Thomas Holbrook, "William Edward Miller, Captain, Company H, 3rd Pennsylvania Cavalry," in *Unsung Heroes of Gettysburg: Programs of the Fifth Annual Gettysburg Seminar* (Gettysburg, PA: Gettysburg National Military Park, 1996).

105. "Report of Capt. William Miller," in Bachelder et al., *Bachelder Papers*, 2:1267–68. Miller later received a Medal of Honor for his actions in this battle.

106. "Letter of Lieutenant William Brooke-Rawle, 17 June 1880," in Bachelder et al., *Bachelder Papers*, 1:659.

107. "Report of Capt. William Miller," in Bachelder et al., *Bachelder Papers*, 2:1267.

108. "Letter from Captain Amasa E. Matthews, 11 June, 1887," in Bachelder et al., *Bachelder Papers*, 3:1493.

109. McClellan, *I Rode with Jeb Stuart*, 341; Trout, *Galloping Thunder*, 294; "Francis Halsey Wigfall to Louis T. Wigfall, July 7, 1863," n35, 710; *O.R.*, vol. 27, pt. 1, 957; *O.R.*, vol. 27, pt. 2, 698; Graham, *Nineteenth Regiment*, 98; "Letter of Captain William A. Graham," in Bachelder et al., *Bachelder Papers*, 3:1374.

110. Matthews, "The Pelham-Breathed Battery," *St. Mary's Beacon*, April 20, 1905.

111. "Letter of Lt. James Chester," in Bachelder et al., *Bachelder Papers*, 2:1080; "Letter of Colonel Vincent A. Witcher," in Bachelder et al., *Bachelder Papers*, 2:1230, 2:1238; "Letter of Lt. Phillip P. Johnston," in Bachelder et al., *Bachelder Papers*, 2:1225, Matthews, "The Pelham-Breathed Battery," *St. Mary's Beacon*, April 20, 1905; McClellan, *I Rode with Jeb Stuart*, 345.

112. *O.R.*, vol. 27, pt. 1, 957; Robertson, *Michigan in the War*, 583.

113. *O.R.*, vol. 27, pt. 2, 698.

114. Kidd, *Personal Recollections*, 160; James Henry Avery, *Under Custer's Command: The Civil War Journal of James Henry Avery*, comp. Karla Jean Husby, ed. Eric

J. Wittenberg (Washington, DC: Potomac Books, 2006), 38; "Letter of Lt. James Chester," in Bachelder et al., *Bachelder Papers*, 2:1091.

115. *O.R.*, vol. 27, pt. 2, 699.

116. Driver, *1st Virginia Cavalry*, 67.

CHAPTER 18

1. Eric J. Wittenberg, *Gettysburg's Forgotten Cavalry Actions: Farnsworth's Charge, South Cavalry Field, and the Battle of Fairfield, July 3, 1863* (New York: Savas Beatie, 2011), 113.

2. *O.R.*, vol. 27, pt. 1, 943, 947.

3. Wittenburg, *Gettysburg's Forgotten Cavalry Actions*, 111.

4. Sidney Morris Davis, *Common Soldier, Uncommon War: Life as a Cavalryman in the Civil War* (Bethesda, MD: J. H. Davis Jr., 1993–1994), 420; Randy Steffen, *The Horse Soldier 1776–1943: The United States Cavalryman: His Uniforms, Arms, Accoutrements, and Equipments* (Norman: University of Oklahoma Press, 1977), 1:72.

5. War Record of Samuel H. Starr, Samuel Starr Papers, Missouri Historical Society, St. Louis, MO.

6. Donald C. Caughey and Jimmy J. Jones, *The 6th United States Cavalry in the Civil War: A History and Roster* (Jefferson, NC: McFarland, 2013), 12.

7. Caughey and Jones, *The 6th United States Cavalry*, 102.

8. Davis, *Common Soldier, Uncommon War*, 428.

9. *O.R.*, vol. 27, pt. 2, 751–52.

10. The 12th Virginia Cavalry was left in Virginia on detached duty.

11. *O.R.*, vol. 27, pt. 2, 752.

12. T. J. Young, "The Battle of Fairfield, Pennsylvania," *Confederate Veteran* 5 (1893): 251.

13. John Blue, *Hanging Rock Rebel: Lieutenant John Blue's War in West Virginia and the Shenandoah Valley*, ed. Daniel P. Oates (Shippensburg, PA: Burd Street Press, 1994), 203.

14. William N. McDonald, *A History of the Laurel Brigade: Originally the Ashby Cavalry of the Army of Northern Virginia and Chew's Battery*, ed. Bushrod C. Washington (Baltimore, MD: Mrs. Kate S. McDonald, 1902), 155.

15. *O.R.*, vol. 27, pt. 2, 752.

16. George M. Neese, *Three Years in the Confederate Horse Artillery: Consisting of Excerpts, Where Each Touches on Matters Relating to Charlottesville, VA and Environs* (Dayton, OH: Morningside, 1988), 181.

17. Tattnall Paulding, *Diary of Lieutenant Tattnall Paulding*, courtesy of Dr. James Milgram, Chicago IL.

18. McDonald, *A History of the Laurel Brigade*, 155 (bracketed word by author).

19. McDonald, *A History of the Laurel Brigade*, 156.

20. *O.R.*, vol. 27, pt. 2, 756 (bracketed word by author).

21. Young, "The Battle of Fairfield, Pennsylvania."

22. William H. Carter, *From Yorktown to Santiago with the Sixth U.S. Cavalry* (Baltimore, MD: Lord Baltimore Press, 1900), 97–98; James McDowell to Colonel Don Caldwell, April 6, 1895, George Platt Medal of Honor file, National Archives.

23. Caughey and Jones, *The 6th U.S. Cavalry*, 110.

24. John H. Connell, "A Cavalry Fight: A Confederate Tells of the Collision between the 7th VA and the 6th U.S. Cavalry," *National Tribune*, April 30, 1891 (bracketed words by author).

25. Caughey and Jones, *The 6th United States Cavalry*, 117; *O.R.*, vol. 27, pt. 1, 948. Lieutenant Nicholas Nolan claimed 8 officers and 290 enlisted men were killed, wounded, or missing. Starr survived the wound to his skull and an amputation of his arm in captivity. Remarkably, he received a promotion to brevet colonel and was exchanged the following November.

26. Neese, *Three Years in the Confederate Horse Artillery*, 188.

27. Franklin Aretas Haskell, *The Battle of Gettysburg* (Columbia, SC: Big Byte Books, 2016), 60; *O.R.*, vol. 27, pt. 3, 524; Jeffry D. Wert, *Gettysburg Day Three* (New York: Simon & Schuster, 2001), 174.

28. John B. Bachelder, David L. Ladd, Audrey J. Ladd, and Richard A. Sauers, eds., "Letter of Maj. Gen. George Meade," in *The Bachelder Papers: Gettysburg in Their Own Words*, vols. 1–3 (Dayton, OH: Morningside, 1994), 1:379.

29. "Letter of Maj. Gen. George Meade," in Bachelder et al., *Bachelder Papers*, 1:379.

30. "Letter of Maj. Gen. George Meade," in Bachelder et al., *Bachelder Papers*, 1:379; Wert, *Gettysburg, Day Three*, 207.

31. "Letter of Lt. John Egan to George Meade Jr.," in Bachelder et al., *Bachelder Papers*, 1:389.

32. Haskell, *The Battle of Gettysburg*, 76; Thomas J. Ryan and Stephen W. Sears, *Spies, Scouts, and Secrets in the Gettysburg Campaign: How the Critical Role of Intelligence Impacted the Outcome of Lee's Invasion of the North, June–July, 1863* (El Dorado Hills, CA: Savas Beatie, 2015), 337.

33. Bill Hyde, ed., *The Union Generals Speak: The Meade Hearings on the Battle of Gettysburg* (Baton Rouge: Louisiana State University Press, 2003), 141, 179, 233.

34. Hyde, *The Union Generals Speak*, 218.

35. *O.R.*, vol. 27, pt. 1, 943.

36. Isaac Rothermel Dunkelberger Memoir, Michael J. Winey Collection, National Archives (bracketed word by author).

37. Roughly handled at Upperville, three guns of Hart's battery had been repaired at Martinsburg. "Letter of Capt. James F. Hart, March 3, 1886," in Bachelder et al., *Bachelder Papers*, 2:1215–16.

38. *O.R.*, vol. 27, pt. 1, 943; "Letter of Capt. James F. Hart, March 5, 1886," in Bachelder et al., *Bachelder Papers*, 2:1217.

39. *O.R.*, vol. 27, pt. 2, 397, 402–3; "Letter of Brig. Gen. Evander M. Law," in Bachelder et al., *Bachelder Papers*, 1:495–96, 2:1370–71.

40. Lieutenant Samuel S. Elder, Battery E, 4th U.S. Artillery, and Captain William M. Graham, Battery K, 1st U.S. Artillery.

41. The two batteries were commanded by Captain James Reilly and Captain William K. Bachman. *O.R.*, vol. 27, pt. 2, 355; "Letter of Capt. James A. Reilly," in Bachelder et al., *Bachelder Papers*, 3:1873.

42. Andie Custer, "Into the Mouth of Hell," *Blue & Gray* 23, no. 1 (Spring 2006): 6–22.

43. Hyde, *The Union Generals Speak*, 111.

44. *O.R.*, vol. 27, pt. 1, 1005; "Annals of the War: The Campaign of Gettysburg," *Philadelphia Weekly Times*, January 19, 1878.

45. Captain Henry C. Parsons, Company L, 1st Vermont Cavalry, speech, July 3, 1913.

46. Captain Henry C. Parsons, Company L, 1st Vermont Cavalry, speech, July 3, 1913.

47. Eli Holden, "Farnsworth's Death," *National Tribune*, September 15, 1892.

48. *O.R.*, vol. 19, pt. 1, 208.

49. *O.R.*, vol. 27, pt. 1, 1013.

50. *O.R.*, vol. 27, pt. 1, 1013.

51. Custer, "Into the Mouth of Hell."

52. *Galveston Weekly News*, October 21, 1863 (bracketed word by author).

53. *New York Times*, July 3, 1913.

54. *New York Times*, July 30, 1863.

55. *Galveston Weekly News*, October 21, 1863 (bracketed words by author).

56. Custer, "Into the Mouth of Hell."

57. "Letter of Sgt. Thomas J. Grier," in Bachelder et al., *Bachelder Papers*, 3:1542–44.

58. *O.R.*, vol. 27, pt. 1, 1011, 1012.

59. Wittenberg, *Gettysburg's Forgotten Cavalry Actions*, 60.

60. Jeffrey D. Stocker, ed., *From Huntsville to Appomattox: R. T. Coles's History of 4th Regiment, Alabama Volunteer Infantry, C.S.A., Army of Northern Virginia* (Knoxville: University of Tennessee Press, 1996), 111–12.

61. *Galveston Weekly News*, October 21, 1863.

62. "Letter of Brigadier General Evander M. Law," in Bachelder et al., *Bachelder Papers*, 1:497.

63. "Letter of Colonel William C. Oates," in Bachelder et al., *Bachelder Papers*, 1:466.

64. Custer, "Into the Mouth of Hell." Confederates described this officer as having blond hair and wearing a white havelock head covering. Lieutenant Cushman had blond hair and was wearing a silk neckerchief pinned to his cap. Farnsworth had dark hair, and a *New York Times* reporter described him as wearing a slouched hat during the charge.

65. Custer, "Into the Mouth of Hell." Cushman was found on the battlefield the day after and survived the wound, which entered his right cheek, pushed up through the roof of his mouth, and exited his face beneath his left eye. Such a wound is consistent with a self-inflicted pistol shot.

66. *O.R.*, vol. 27, pt. 1, 993 (bracketed words by author).

67. Custer, "Into the Mouth of Hell," sidebar, "Captain Parson's *Battles & Leaders* Account," 10.

68. Custer, "Into the Mouth of Hell," sidebar, "Captain Parson's *Battles & Leaders* Account," 10.

CHAPTER 19

1. *O.R.*, vol. 27, pt. 2, 360, 608.
2. Kent Masterson Brown, *Retreat from Gettysburg: Lee Logistics and the Gettysburg Campaign* (Chapel Hill: University of North Carolina Press, 2005), 70–74.
3. *O.R.*, vol. 27, pt. 2, 311.
4. *O.R.*, vol. 27, pt. 2, 311.
5. *O.R.*, vol. 27, pt. 2, 699, 700.
6. *O.R.*, vol. 27, pt. 2, 699; *O.R.*, vol. 27, pt. 3, 568, 546.
7. Robert Underwood Johnson and Clarence Clough Buel, *Battles and Leaders of the Civil War*, pt. 1 (Boulder, CO: Bibliolife, 2010), 3:420–29 (bracketed word by author).
8. Johnson and Buel, *Battles and Leaders of the Civil War*, 3:420–29.
9. Johnson and Buel, *Battles and Leaders of the Civil War*, 3:420–29; R. E. Lee, *The Wartime Papers/with Connective Narratives by Clifford Dowdey and Maps by Samuel H. Bryant*, ed. Clifford Dowdey and Louis H. Manarin (Boston; Toronto: Little, Brown, 1961), 538.
10. Brown, *Retreat from Gettysburg*, 93.
11. Michael P. Musick, *6th Virginia Cavalry* (Lynchburg, VA: H. E. Howard, 1990), 45.
12. *O.R.*, vol. 27, pt. 1, 489.
13. William Harrison Beach, *First New York (Lincoln) Cavalry from April 19, 1861, to July 7, 1865* (n.p.: Nabu Press, 2010), 269.
14. *O.R.*, vol. 27, pt. 3, 524.
15. Beach, *First New York (Lincoln) Cavalry*, 270.
16. *O.R.*, vol. 27, pt. 3, 514.
17. Bill Hyde, ed., *The Union Generals Speak: The Meade Hearings on the Battle of Gettysburg* (Baton Rouge: Louisiana State University Press, 2003), 170; *O.R.*, vol. 27, pt. 1, 151, 187.
18. *O.R.*, vol. 27, pt. 3, 524; Brown, *Retreat from Gettysburg*, 45, 47.
19. *O.R.*, vol. 27, pt. 3, 495, 523; *O.R.*, vol. 27, pt. 2, 466. Meade had not planned on fighting at Gettysburg. Instead, he'd hoped to fight at Pipe Creek, Maryland, closer to the railhead at Westminster, and this is where his supplies had been staged and were now stranded.
20. *O.R.*, vol. 27, pt. 3, 524, 543, 545.
21. *O.R.*, vol. 27, pt. 3, 517–18, 531.
22. There was no direct rail line from Westminster to Frederick.
23. *O.R.*, vol. 27, pt. 1, 916, 928, 967, 977, 993. Also joining Kilpatrick was Colonel Pennock Huey's brigade from Gregg's 2nd Division, containing the 2nd and 4th New York, 6th Ohio, and 8th Pennsylvania.
24. *O.R.*, vol. 27, pt. 1, 916.

25. Andie Custer, "Into the Mouth of Hell," *Blue & Gray* 23, no. 1 (Spring 2006): 19.

26. James H. Kidd, *Personal Recollections of a Cavalryman with Custer's Michigan Cavalry Brigade in the Civil War* (1908; repr., Ionia, MI: Sentinel, 2015), 167–68.

27. Kidd, *Personal Recollections*, 168.

28. Kidd, *Personal Recollections*, 169.

29. Robert J. Trout, *Memoirs of the Stuart Horse Artillery Battalion*, 56; O.R., vol. 27, pt. 1, 998; O.R., vol. 27, pt. 2, 764.

30. Paul B. Means, *Additional Sketch Sixty-Third Regiment (5th Cavalry)*, vol. 3 of *Histories of the Several Regiments and Battalions from North Carolina, in the Great War, 1861–1865*, ed. Walter Clark (Goldsboro, NC: Nash Brothers, 1901), 534, 569; D. B. Rea, *Sketches from Hampton's Cavalry: Embracing the Principle Exploits of the Cavalry in the Campaigns of 1862 and 1863* (Columbia: South Carolina State Press, 1864), 119.

31. Means, *Additional Sketch Sixty-Third Regiment*, 570; Chris J. Hartley, *Stuart's Tarheels: James B. Gordon and His North Carolina Cavalry* (Baltimore, MD: Butternut and Blue, 1996), 242.

32. Rea, *Sketches from Hampton's Cavalry*, 119 (bracketed word by author).

33. "Operations of Our Cavalry: The Michigan Cavalry Brigade," *New York Times*, August 6, 1863; O.R., vol. 27, pt. 1, 998.

34. Rea, *Sketches from Hampton's Cavalry*, 119 (bracketed word by author).

35. Means, *Additional Sketch Sixty-Third Regiment*, 570.

36. O.R., vol. 27, pt. 1, 994.

37. Henry B. McClellan, *I Rode with Jeb Stuart: The Life and Campaigns of Major General J. E. B. Stuart* (New York: Da Capo, 1994), 353 (bracketed word by author).

38. Kidd, *Personal Recollections*, 169 (bracketed word by author).

39. Kidd, *Personal Recollections*, 170–71.

40. Brown, *Retreat from Gettysburg*, 132.

41. O.R., vol. 27, pt. 2, 753.

42. William McDonald, *A History of the Laurel Brigade: Originally the Ashby Cavalry of the Army of Northern Virginia and Chew's Battery*, ed. Bushrod C. Washington (Baltimore, MD: Mrs. Kate S. McDonald, 1902), 157.

43. McClellan, *I Rode with Jeb Stuart*, 354.

44. O.R., vol. 27, pt. 2, 753.

45. McClellan, *I Rode with Jeb Stuart*, 355.

46. Brown, *Retreat from Gettysburg*, 134.

47. O.R., vol. 27, pt. 1, 994.

48. O.R., vol. 27, pt. 1, 1019.

49. Samuel Lovejoy Gillespie, *A History of Company A, First Ohio Cavalry, 1861–1865* (Columbus, OH: Lovejoy, 1898; repr., Salem, MA: Higginson, 1990), 155–56.

50. Gillespie, *A History of Company A*, 157–58.

51. O.R., vol. 27, pt. 1, 1019.

52. Gillespie, *A History of Company A*, 158.

53. *Wheeling Daily Intelligencer*, July 15, 1863; Steven A. Cunningham and Beth A. White, "The Ground Trembled as They Came: The 1st West Virginia Cavalry in the Gettysburg Campaign," in "Gettysburg: Regimental Leadership and Command," ed. Mark A. Snell and Theodore Savas, *Civil War Regiments* 6, no. 3 (1999): 77.

54. Brown, *Retreat from Gettysburg*, 138.

55. Gillespie, *A History of Company A*, 158. Many of Stuart's troopers lacked carbines. The escort company may have mainly suffered revolver fire, accounting for the horses' continued progress.

56. Letter, "George M. Emack to My Dear Dora, Shepherdstown, VA, July 21, 1863," courtesy of the Monterey Pass and Battlefield Museum, Waynesboro, PA; Brown, *Retreat from Gettysburg*, 137; McClellan, *I Rode with Jeb Stuart*, 355; *O.R.*, vol. 27, pt. 2, 753.

57. Gillespie, *A History of Company A*, 158–59. Major Capehart of the 1st West Virginia would later receive the Medal of Honor for driving home one of the most memorable horse charges of the war. See Congressional Medal of Honor File, Major Charles E. Capehart, 1st West Virginia Cavalry, April 7, 1898, Record Group 94, Records of the Adjutant General's Office, 1762–1984, Washington, DC.

58. *O.R.*, vol. 27, pt. 2, 715; Robert J. Driver Jr., *The 1st and 2nd Rockbridge Artillery*, Virginia Regimental Histories Series (Lynchburg, VA: H. E. Howard, 1987), 44–45.

59. Brown, *Retreat from Gettysburg*, 137.

60. Gillespie, *A History of Company A*, 159.

61. *O.R.*, vol. 27, pt. 1, 994.

62. Estimates varied greatly. A newspaper article in the *Wheeling Intelligencer* claimed one hundred wagons and 1,250 prisoners. Gillespie's *The History of Company A* claimed three hundred wagons, fifteen ambulances, and 1,300 prisoners. Kilpatrick's After Action Report stated nine-tenths of Ewell's wagons and 1,360 prisoners. Kilpatrick was clearly in error on the wagon count.

63. This route to Smithsburg had been used earlier by Lieutenant Colonel Preston, 1st Vermont Cavalry. *O.R.*, vol. 27, pt. 1, 994.

CHAPTER 20

1. Kilpatrick sent the 1st Vermont Cavalry to again strike the Rebel train suspected at Leitersburg on the night of July 4. The New Englanders followed their orders, but when they reached Leitersburg on the morning of July 5, they found only stragglers and no wagons. This gap in the train, no doubt caused by Kilpatrick's operations on Monterey, caused the 1st Vermont to move on, and they rode to Hagerstown farther south with the same result. They didn't link back with Kilpatrick until the early morning hours of July 6. Elliott W. Hoffman, *History of the First Vermont Cavalry Volunteers in the War of the Great Rebellion* (Baltimore, MD: Butternut and Blue, 2000), 119.

2. Kent Masterson Brown, *Retreat from Gettysburg: Lee Logistics and the Gettysburg Campaign* (Chapel Hill: University of North Carolina Press, 2005), 179.

3. *O.R.*, vol. 27, pt. 1, 994. The Federals kept eight forges and several ambulances.

4. *O.R.*, vol. 27, pt. 1, 971; *O.R.*, vol. 27, pt. 1, 994.

5. Robert Underwood Johnson and Clarence Clough Buel, *Battles and Leaders of the Civil War* (Edison, NJ: Castle, 1995), 3:420–29.

6. Johnson and Buel, *Battles and Leaders of the Civil War*, 3:420–29 (bracketed words by author).

7. Johnson and Buel, *Battles and Leaders of the Civil War*, 3:420–29.

8. *O.R.*, vol. 27, pt. 2, 311; *O.R.*, vol. 27, pt. 2, 699.

9. Johnson and Buel, *Battles and Leaders of the Civil War*, 3:420–29.

10. Johnson and Buel, *Battles and Leaders of the Civil War*, 3:420–29.

11. *O.R.*, vol. 27, pt. 1, 993, 994.

12. John A. Miller, "The Road to Smithsburg," *War Returns to South Mountain* (blog), March 22, 2010, accessed June 11, 2021, https://southmountaincw.word press.com/2010/03/22/the-road-to-smithsburg/.

13. This was Merritt's Federal brigade, as it moved down through Lewistown, modern-day Thurmont, on the way to Frederick, Maryland. *O.R.*, vol. 27, pt. 1, 943.

14. Stuart mistakenly wrote Cooperstown, not Creagerstown, in his After Action Report (AAR). *O.R.*, vol. 27, pt. 2, 700; Miller, "The Road to Smithsburg."

15. *O.R.*, vol. 27, pt. 2, 700. Stuart does not name these routes in his AAR. Today the direct route Ferguson took roughly follows the modern Foxville Road, and the route Stuart and Chambliss selected follows modern-day Raven's Rock Road.

16. R. L. T. Beale, *History of the Ninth Virginia Cavalry, in the War between the States* (1899; repr., Richmond, VA: B. F. Johnson, 2010), 90.

17. *O.R.*, vol. 27, pt. 2, 700.

18. Lieutenant William D. Fuller, Battery C., 3rd U.S. Artillery.

19. Beale, *History of the Ninth Virginia Cavalry*, 91.

20. *O.R.*, vol. 27, pt. 1, 1009.

21. James H. Kidd, *Personal Recollections of a Cavalryman with Custer's Michigan Cavalry Brigade in the Civil War* (1908; repr., Ionia, MI: Sentinel, 2015), 173; *O.R.*, vol. 27, pt. 1, 998.

22. Kidd, *Personal Recollections*, 173.

23. *O.R.*, vol. 27, pt. 1, 994.

24. *O.R.*, vol. 27, pt. 1, 995.

25. *O.R.*, vol. 27, pt. 2, 701.

26. In *Fightin' Tom Rosser, C.S.A.*, authors Millard K. Bushong and Dean M. Bushong state that Jones offered his resignation to Stuart here for failing to better protect the wagons in Monterey Pass. This is hard to confirm with certainty. If true, Stuart refused Jones's resignation. See Millard K. Bushong and Dean M. Bushong, *Fightin' Tom Rosser, C.S.A.* (Shippensburg, PA: Beidel, 1983), 59; Douglas Southall Freeman, *Lee's Lieutenants* (New York: Simon & Schuster, 1995), 3:213, 3:60n41.

27. *O.R.*, vol. 27, pt. 2, 606, 608, 615; *O.R.*, vol. 27, pt. 2, 361; *O.R.*, vol. 27, pt. 2, 448, 471–72.

28. *O.R.*, vol. 27, pt. 3, 532.

29. *O.R.*, vol. 27, pt. 3, 538; Bill Hyde, ed., *The Union Generals Speak: The Meade Hearings on the Battle of Gettysburg* (Baton Rouge: Louisiana State University Press, 2003), 112.

30. Kent Masterson Brown, *Meade at Gettysburg: A Study in Command* (Chapel Hill: University of North Carolina Press, 2012), 322, 332–33.

31. Hyde, *The Union Generals Speak*, 112.

32. Anson Haines, *The 15th Regiment: New Jersey Volunteers* (New York: Jenkins & Thomas, 1883), 96.

33. "After Gettysburg: Pursuing Lee to the Potomac," *New York Daily Tribune*, July 1, 1888, 11.

34. Haines, *The 15th Regiment*, 98.

35. *O.R.*, vol. 27, pt. 2, 472.

36. Haines, *The 15th Regiment*, 98.

37. *O.R.*, vol. 27, pt. 1, 117; *O.R.*, vol. 27, pt. 1, 663.

38. Dana B. Shoaf, "On the March Again at Daybreak: Major John I. Nevin and the 93rd Pennsylvania Infantry," in "Gettysburg: Regimental Leadership and Command," ed. Mark A. Snell and Theodore Savas, *Civil War Regiments* 6, no. 3 (1999): 127.

CHAPTER 21

1. Abner Hard, *History of the Eighth Cavalry Regiment, Illinois Volunteers, during the Great Rebellion* (Aurora, IL: n.p., 1868), 260.

2. Isaac R. Dunkelberger Papers, Michael Winey Collection.

3. *O.R.*, vol. 27, pt. 1, 928; *O.R.*, vol. 27, pt. 1, 995.

4. Formerly Elon Farnsworth's brigade.

5. Colonel Pennock Huey's brigade still lacked horses after the Loudoun Valley campaign and would hold as a skeleton reserve. *O.R.*, vol. 27, pt. 1, 995; Kent Masterson Brown, *Retreat from Gettysburg: Lee Logistics and the Gettysburg Campaign* (Chapel Hill: University of North Carolina Press, 2005), 220.

6. *O.R.*, vol. 27, pt. 2, 701.

7. *O.R.*, vol. 27, pt. 2, 701.

8. *O.R.*, vol. 27, pt. 1, 995; *O.R.*, vol. 27, pt. 1, 928; Bradley M. Gottfried, *The Maps of the Cavalry in the Gettysburg Campaign* (El Dorado Hills, CA: Savas Beatie, 2020), 151.

9. Elements of the 2nd and 4th North Carolina cavalry were also present.

10. Frank A. Bond, "Company A, First Maryland Cavalry," *Confederate Veteran* 6 (1898): 78.

11. Eric J. Wittenberg, "Colonel Nathaniel P. Richmond," folder 3, accessed May 23, 2021, https://www.fold3.com/memorial/632318856/nathaniel-richmond/stories.

12. Brown, *Retreat from Gettysburg*, 224; *O.R.*, vol. 27, pt. 1, 1010.

13. *O.R.*, vol. 27, pt. 2, 701.

14. George M. Neese, *Three Years in the Confederate Horse Artillery: Consisting of Excerpts, Where Each Touches on Matters Relating to Charlottesville, VA and Environs* (Dayton, OH: Morningside, 1988), 194.

15. *O.R.*, vol. 27, pt. 1, 1010.

16. Steven A. Cunningham and Beth A. White, "The Ground Trembled as They Came," in "Gettysburg: Regimental Leadership and Command," ed. Mark A. Snell and Theodore Savas, *Civil War Regiments* 6, no. 3 (1999): 79.

17. *O.R.*, vol. 27, pt. 1, 1006.

18. R. L. T. Beale, *History of the Ninth Virginia Cavalry, in the War between the States* (1899; repr., Richmond, VA: B. F. Johnson, 2010), 92.

19. Bond, "Company A, First Maryland Cavalry."

20. Bond, "Company A, First Maryland Cavalry."

21. Robert J. Trout, *Memoirs of the Stuart Horse Artillery Battalion: Moorman's and Hart's Batteries* (Knoxville: University of Tennessee Press, 2008), 56.

22. Samuel St. Clair, "The Fight at Hagerstown," in *History of the Eighteenth Regiment of Cavalry Pennsylvania Volunteers*, ed. Publication Committee of the Regimental Association (New York: Wynkoop Hallenbeck Crawford, 1909), 95.

23. W. W. Jacobs, "Custer's Charge: Little Hagerstown, the Scene of Bloody Strife," *National Tribune*, August 27, 1897.

24. "Captain Charles Snyder, Company F, 1st Michigan Cavalry," *New York Times*, August 6, 1863.

25. Elliott W. Hoffman, *History of the First Vermont Cavalry Volunteers in the War of the Great Rebellion* (Baltimore, MD: Butternut and Blue, 2000), 120 (bracketed word by author).

26. St. Clair, "The Fight at Hagerstown," 95.

27. Theophilus F. Rodenbough, "Historical Sketch," in Publication Committee of the Regimental Association, *History of the Eighteenth Regiment of Cavalry Pennsylvania Volunteers*, 18.

28. *O.R.*, vol. 27, pt. 2, 581.

29. Eric J. Wittenberg, J. David Petruzzi, and Michael F. Nugent, *One Continuous Fight: The Retreat from Gettysburg and the Pursuit of Lee's Army of Northern Virginia, July 4–14, 1863* (El Dorado Hills, CA: Savas Beatie, 2013), 116.

30. Hoffman, *History of the First Vermont Cavalry*, 120–21.

31. Robert Underwood Johnson and Clarence Clough Buel, *Battles and Leaders of the Civil War* (Edison, NJ: Castle, 1995), 3:420–29.

32. Wiley C. Howard, *Sketch of Cobb Legion Cavalry and Some Incidents and Scenes Remembered* (Atlanta, GA: Atlanta Camp 159, S.C.V., 1901; repr., Delhi, India: Facsimile, 2013), 9; Vince Dooley and Samuel N. Thomas, eds., "Will Delony to Rosa Delony, Near Gettysburg, Pennsylvania, 4 July, 1863," in *The Legion's Fighting Bulldog: The Civil War Correspondence of William Gaston Delony, Lieutenant Colonel of Cobb's Georgia Legion Cavalry, and Rosa Delony, 1853–1863* (Macon, GA: Mercer University Press, 2017), 239.

33. Colonel J. M. Stone of the 2nd Mississippi also commanded a Q troop in the battle outside Williamsport.

34. Brown, *Retreat from Gettysburg*, 236.

35. Susan Leigh Blackford and Charles Minor Blackford III, eds., *Letters from Lee's Army; or, Memoirs of Life in and out of the Army in Virginia during the War between the States* (Lincoln: University of Nebraska Press, 1998), 189.

36. *O.R.*, vol. 27, pt. 1, 935.

37. John H. Worsham, *One of Jackson's Foot Cavalry; His Experience and What He Saw during the War 1861–1865, Including a History of "F Company,"* Richmond, Va., *21st Regiment Virginia Infantry, Second Brigade, Jackson's Division, Second Corps, A.N.V.* (1912; repr., New York: Neale, 1992), 150–51.

38. Worsham, *One of Jackson's Foot Cavalry,* 152.

39. Brown, *Retreat from Gettysburg,* 245.

40. Hard, *History of the Eighth Cavalry Regiment,* 261; Worsham, *One of Jackson's Foot Cavalry,* 107.

41. Robert Underwood Johnson and Clarence Clough Buel, *Battles and Leaders of the Civil War,* pt. 1 (Boulder, CO: Bibliolife, 2010), 3:420–29 (bracketed words by author).

42. Imboden's sharpshooters were from the 18th Virginia Cavalry, McNeill's Rangers, and 62nd Mounted Infantry.

43. *O.R.*, vol. 27, pt. 2, 437; Wittenberg, Petruzzi, and Nugent, *One Continuous Fight,* 132. The Washington Artillery Battery was divided into two six-gun batteries. One was commanded by Major Benjamin Esherman, and the second by Captain Charles Squires.

44. Harry Gilmor, *Four Years in the Saddle,* ed. Daniel Carroll Toomey (New York: Harper & Brothers, 1866; repr., Baltimore, MD: Butternut and Blue, 1986), 101–2.

45. Johnson and Buel, *Battles and Leaders of the Civil War,* 3:420–29; *O.R.*, vol. 27, pt. 2, 437–38; Brown, *Retreat from Gettysburg,* 248.

46. "Will Delony to Rosa Delony, Williamsport, 7 July 1863," in Dooley and Thomas, *The Legion's Fighting Bulldog,* 240.

47. *O.R.*, vol. 27, pt. 2, 438; *O.R.*, vol. 27, pt. 1, 928.

48. *O.R.*, vol. 27, pt. 1, 928; *O.R.*, vol. 27, pt. 1, 935.

49. Recent scholarship suggests this was William McGregor's battery. See Robert J. Trout, *Memoirs of the Stuart Horse Artillery Battalion,* vol. 2, *Breathed's and McGregor's Batteries* (Knoxville: University of Tennessee Press, 2010), 212n202, 212n203, 212n205.

50. James H. Kidd, *Personal Recollections of a Cavalryman with Custer's Michigan Cavalry Brigade in the Civil War* (1908; repr., Ionia, MI: Sentinel, 2015), 175–76.

51. Samuel Levis Gracey, *Annals of the Sixth Pennsylvania Cavalry* (Philadelphia, PA: E. H. Butler, 1868), 184.

52. *O.R.*, vol. 27, pt. 1, 971.

53. *O.R.*, vol. 27, pt. 2, 702.

54. It's not clear if General Robertson was present or not. He may have stayed in Hagerstown. Stuart only mentions James B. Gordon and the 5th North Carolina in his After Action Report.

55. Paul B. Means, *Additional Sketch Sixty-Third Regiment (5th Cavalry),* vol. 3 of *Histories of the Several Regiments and Battalions from North Carolina, in the Great War,*

1861–1865, ed. Walter Clark (Goldsboro, NC: Nash Brothers, 1901), 570; Beale, *History of the Ninth Virginia Cavalry*, 93.

56. *O.R.*, vol. 27, pt. 1, 1010.

57. *Harrisburg Telegraph*, April 7, 1885.

58. *O.R.*, vol. 19, pt. 1, 344.

59. Ada Bruce Desper Bradshaw, ed., *Civil War Diary of Charles William McVicar* (Washington, DC: Library of Congress, 1977), 19 (bracketed word by author).

60. Beale, *History of the Ninth Virginia Cavalry*, 94 (bracketed words by author).

61. Beale, *History of the Ninth Virginia Cavalry*, 94; *O.R.*, vol. 27, pt. 2, 702; *O.R.*, vol. 27, pt. 1, 1006.

62. *Wheeling Daily Intelligencer*, July 15, 1863.

63. *O.R.*, vol. 27, pt. 1, 1006.

64. Captain Woodward of Company M, 1st Vermont died instantly from a bullet through his forehead. Lieutenant Stewart and Sergeant Hill fell wounded and were left behind. Elliot W. Hoffman, ed., *A Vermont Cavalryman in War and Love: The Civil War Letters of Brevet Major General William Wells and Anna Richardson* (Lynchburg, VA: Schroeder, 2007), 184–85.

65. "The Vermont Cavalry in the Last Campaign," *Burlington Free Press*, July 24, 1863.

66. *O.R.*, vol. 27, pt. 2, 702.

67. Means, *Additional Sketch Sixty-Third Regiment*, 570; H. H. Matthews, "From Gettysburg to Hagerstown, Williamsport and Back to the Rappahannock," *St. Mary's Beacon*, April 27, 1905.

68. Stuart claimed Gordon deserved a special commendation in leading this charge. *O.R.*, vol. 27, pt. 2, 702; James Allen Penfield, *The 1863–1864 Civil War Diary of Captain James Penfield, 5th New York Volunteer Cavalry, Company H* (Crown Point, NY: Penfield Foundation, 1999), 71.

69. *O.R.*, vol. 27, pt. 2, 702.

70. William McDonald, *A History of the Laurel Brigade: Originally the Ashby Cavalry of the Army of Northern Virginia and Chew's Battery*, ed. Bushrod C. Washington (Baltimore, MD: Mrs. Kate S. McDonald, 1902), 160–61.

71. John Blue, *Hanging Rock Rebel: Lt. John Blue's War in West Virginia and the Shenandoah Valley*, ed. Daniel P. Oates (Shippensburg, PA: Burd Street Press, 1994), 207.

72. Blue, *Hanging Rock Rebel*, 207; *O.R.*, vol. 27, pt. 2, 764; *O.R.*, vol. 27, pt. 2, 702.

73. *O.R.*, vol. 27, pt. 2, 764.

74. McDonald, *A History of the Laurel Brigade*, 162.

75. The Union paid a high price for the guns. Lomax took a hundred prisoners combined between the fight for the turnpike and the later combat for the guns. See *O.R.*, vol. 27, pt. 2, 764.

76. Trout, *Memoirs of the Stuart Horse Artillery Battalion*, 2:212n202, 212n203, 212n205.

77. *O.R.*, vol. 27, pt. 2, 702.

78. *O.R.*, vol. 27, pt. 1, 1006.

79. *O.R.*, vol. 27, pt. 1, 1006.

80. Bradshaw, *Diary of Charles William McVicar*, 19.

CHAPTER 22

1. *O.R.*, vol. 27, pt. 3, 555; *O.R.*, vol. 27, pt. 3, 556.

2. *O.R.*, vol. 27, pt. 3, 558.

3. *O.R.*, vol. 27, pt. 3, 558.

4. Also at play were the larger politics within the general officers of the Army of the Potomac. West Pointers tended to be socially conservative Democrats, and their views didn't necessarily line up with Lincoln's Republican Party platform. Lincoln selected Meade partially because Meade tended to avoid politics and steer clear of the typical intrigues surrounding high command. Yet Meade remained a member of the Democratic Party, and many Democrats in the Federal army felt that the war should end by a vote and a reconciliation of all the states at a treaty table. Lincoln, however, and the Republicans wanted a complete, unconditional surrender of all states in revolt; therefore, the annihilation of Lee's army better suited their political strategy.

5. *O.R.*, vol. 27, pt. 3, 567.

6. *O.R.*, vol. 27, pt. 1, 967.

7. *O.R.*, vol. 27, pt. 1, 117–18.

8. *O.R.*, vol. 27, pt. 1, 80.

9. *O.R.*, vol. 27, pt. 2, 703.

10. George M. Neese, *Three Years in the Confederate Horse Artillery: Consisting of Excerpts, Where Each Touches on Matters Relating to Charlottesville, VA and Environs* (Dayton, OH: Morningside, 1988), 196.

11. Kent Masterson Brown, *Meade at Gettysburg: A Study in Command* (Chapel Hill: University of North Carolina Press, 2021), 312.

12. *O.R.*, vol. 27, pt. 2, 703.

13. Thomas J. Ryan and Richard R. Schaus, *"Lee Is Trapped and Must Be Taken": Eleven Fateful Days after Gettysburg, July 4–14, 1863* (El Dorado Hills, CA: Savas Beatie, 2021), 71.

14. *O.R.*, vol. 27, pt. 2, 761.

15. Sidney Morris Davis, *Common Soldier, Uncommon War: Life as a Cavalryman in the Civil War*, ed. Charles F. Cooney (Bethesda, MD: J. H. Davis Jr., 1994), 447.

16. *O.R.*, vol. 27, pt. 2, 761.

17. Davis, *Common Soldier, Uncommon War*, 447 (bracketed word by author).

18. *O.R.*, vol. 27, pt. 2, 761.

19. *O.R.*, vol. 27, pt. 2, 754.

20. *O.R.*, vol. 27, pt. 3, 587.

21. *O.R.*, vol. 27, pt. 1, 118; *O.R.*, vol. 27, pt. 3, 601.

22. Colonel Lawrence Baker of the 1st North Carolina continued to command Hampton's brigade.

23. Stuart left Imboden to cover Williamsport and Robertson to cover Hagerstown. See *O.R.*, vol. 27, pt. 2, 703.

24. *O.R.*, vol. 27, pt. 2, 703.

25. *O.R.*, vol. 27, pt. 1, 935.

26. *O.R.*, vol. 27, pt. 1, 1033.

27. *O.R.*, vol. 27, pt. 1, 940–41; *O.R.*, vol. 27, pt. 2, 703.

28. Neese, *Three Years in the Confederate Horse Artillery*, 197.

29. *O.R.*, vol. 27, pt. 1, 1033.

30. "Lieutenant Colonel Allyn Litchfield to My Dear Wife, Boonsboro July 9, 1963," Litchfield-French Papers, Shannon Wait Manuscripts Division, William Clements Library, University of Michigan.

31. Elliott W. Hoffman, *History of the First Vermont Cavalry Volunteers in the War of the Great Rebellion* (Baltimore, MD: Butternut and Blue, 2000), 122.

32. James H. Kidd, *Personal Recollections of a Cavalryman with Custer's Michigan Cavalry Brigade in the Civil War* (1908; repr., Ionia, MI: Sentinel, 2015), 178 (bracketed word by author).

33. *O.R.*, vol. 27, pt. 1, 1007.

34. *O.R.*, vol. 27, pt. 1, 941.

35. Kidd, *Personal Recollections*, 178 (bracketed words by author).

36. *O.R.*, vol. 27, pt. 2, 703.

37. *O.R.*, vol. 27, pt. 2, 703 (bracketed words by author).

38. *O.R.*, vol. 27, pt. 1, 935, 1033.

39. *New York Times*, July 12, 1863.

40. *O.R.*, vol. 27, pt. 3, 602, 603.

41. Robert J. Trout, *Galloping Thunder: The Story of the Stuart Horse Artillery Battalion* (Mechanicsburg, PA: Stackpole Books, 2002), 309.

42. Kidd, *Personal Recollections*, 179; *O.R.*, vol. 27, pt. 1, 1033.

43. *O.R.*, vol. 27, pt. 2, 703.

44. Abner Hard, *History of the Eighth Cavalry Regiment, Illinois Volunteers, during the Great Rebellion* (Aurora, IL: n.p., 1868), 263.

45. *O.R.*, vol. 27, pt. 1, 1007.

46. D. B. Rea, *Sketches from Hampton's Cavalry: Embracing the Principle Exploits of the Cavalry in the Campaigns of 1862 and 1863* (Columbia: South Carolina State Press, 1864), 122.

47. Rea, *Sketches from Hampton's Cavalry*, 122.

48. Rea, *Sketches from Hampton's Cavalry*, 122.

49. Elliott W. Hoffman, ed., *A Vermont Cavalryman in War and Love: The Civil War Letters of Brevet Major General William Wells and Anna Richardson* (Lynchburg, VA: Schroeder, 2007), 186.

50. *O.R.*, vol. 27, pt. 1, 1015.

51. *O.R.*, vol. 27, pt. 2, 704 (bracketed word by author).

52. "Lieutenant Colonel Allyne Litchfield to My Dear Wife, Boonsboro July 9, 1963."

53. *O.R.*, vol. 27, pt. 1, 999.

54. Neese, *Three Years in the Artillery*, 197.

55. William Henry Locke, *The Story of the Regiment, by William Henry Locke* (Philadelphia, PA: Lippincott, 1868), 249.

56. *O.R.*, vol. 27, pt. 1, 84.

57. *O.R.*, vol. 27, pt. 1, 84.

58. *O.R.*, vol. 27, pt. 1, 85.

59. *O.R.*, vol. 27, pt. 1, 85.

60. *O.R.*, vol. 27, pt. 1, 489; *O.R.*, vol. 27, pt. 3, 572.

61. *O.R.*, vol. 27, pt. 1, 86.

62. *O.R.*, vol. 27, pt. 1, 941.

63. Lieutenant Albert O. Vincent commanded a section of Lieutenant Edward Heaton's combined Battery B/L of the 2nd U.S. Artillery. *O.R.*, vol. 27, pt. 1, 941, 1021.

64. *O.R.*, vol. 27, pt. 1, 941.

65. Eric J. Wittenberg, J. David Petruzzi, and Michael F. Nugent, *One Continuous Fight: The Retreat from Gettysburg and the Pursuit of Lee's Army of Northern Virginia, July 4–14, 1863* (El Dorado Hills, CA: Savas Beatie, 2013), 203.

66. Neese, *Three Years in the Artillery*, 197.

67. *O.R.*, vol. 27, pt. 1, 941; Henry Norton, *Deeds of Daring; or, History of the Eighth N.Y. Volunteer Cavalry, Containing a Complete Record of the Battles, Skirmishes, Marches, Etc., That the Gallant Eighth New York Cavalry Participated In, from Its Organization in November, 1861, to the Close of the Rebellion in 1865* (Salem, MA: Higginson, 1998), 47.

68. *O.R.*, vol. 27, pt. 1, 87.

69. *O.R.*, vol. 27, pt. 1, 86.

70. John Thomas Scharf, *History of Western Maryland* (Philadelphia, PA: Louis H. Everts, 1882), 1:280.

71. Edward Porter Alexander, *Military Memoirs of a Confederate*, ed. Harry Williams, Civil War Centennial Series (Bloomington: Indiana University Press, 1962), 439.

72. Kent Masterson Brown, *Retreat from Gettysburg: Lee Logistics and the Gettysburg Campaign* (Chapel Hill: University of North Carolina Press, 2005), 294.

73. *O.R.*, vol. 27, pt. 3, 991.

74. *O.R.*, vol. 27, pt. 2, 704; Bradley M. Gottfried, *The Maps of the Cavalry in the Gettysburg Campaign* (El Dorado Hills, CA: Savas Beatie, 2020), 160–61.

75. Scott C. Cole, *34th Battalion Virginia Cavalry* (Lynchburg, VA: H. E. Howard, 1993), 54; Joseph R. Stonebraker, *A Rebel of '61* (New York: Wyncoop Hallenbeck Crawford, 1899), 53; *O.R.*, vol. 27, pt. 1, 936; *O.R.*, vol. 27, pt. 1, 942; *O.R.*, vol. 27, pt. 1, 1033.

76. Hard, *History of the Eighth Cavalry Regiment*, 264.

77. Stonebraker, *Rebel of '61*, 53.

78. *O.R.*, vol. 27, pt. 1, 1033.

79. The reinforcements came from the 14th and 16th Virginia Cavalry as well as the 36th Virginia Cavalry Battalion. Cole, *34th Battalion Virginia Cavalry*, 54; *O.R.*, vol. 27, pt. 2, 704.

80. Trout, *Galloping Thunder*, 313–14.

81. *O.R.*, vol. 27, pt. 2, 704; Stonebraker, *Rebel of '61*, 53.

82. *O.R.*, vol. 27, pt. 1, 944.

83. Brown, *Retreat from Gettysburg*, 301.

84. White had commanded Anderson's brigade since the third day of Gettysburg.

85. *O.R.*, vol. 27, pt. 2, 398.

86. *O.R.*, vol. 27, pt. 1, 936 (bracketed word by author).

87. *O.R.*, vol. 27, pt. 1, 929.

88. *O.R.*, vol. 27, pt. 2, 398–99.

89. James Longstreet, *From Manassas to Appomattox: Memoirs of the Civil War in America* (Philadelphia, PA: Lippincott, 1896), 428 (bracketed words by author).

90. Colonel White's After Action Report claimed this fire came from the Stuart horse artillery. A native of Funkstown, Joseph Stonebreaker, who witnessed the battle and was an officer in Lee's army, claimed the errant shell came from Manley's battery.

91. *O.R.*, vol. 27, pt. 2, 398.

92. "After Gettysburg: Pursuing Lee to the Potomac: The Experiences of a Vermont Veteran," *New York Tribune*, July 1, 1888, 11.

93. Stonebraker, *Rebel of '61*, 54; *O.R.*, vol. 27, pt. 2, 398.

94. Brown, *Retreat from Gettysburg*, 306; *O.R.*, vol. 27, pt. 1, 931; *O.R.*, vol. 27, pt. 2, 399, 716.

95. Stonebreaker, *Rebel of '61*, 55.

CHAPTER 23

1. Elliott W. Hoffman, *History of the 1st Vermont Cavalry Volunteers in the War of the Great Rebellion* (Baltimore, MD: Butternut and Blue, 2000), 123.

2. *O.R.*, vol. 27, pt. 2, 704–5.

3. Letter, "Stephens Calhoun Smith to Dear Father & Mother, Near Williamport, MD. 12 July, 1863," Duke University (bracketed word by author).

4. Edward Porter Alexander, *Fighting for the Confederacy: The Papers and Recollections of General Edward Porter Alexander*, ed. Gary W. Gallagher (Chapel Hill: University of North Carolina Press, 1989), 271.

5. Edward Porter Alexander, *Military Memoirs of a Confederate*, ed. Harry Williams, Civil War Centennial Series (Bloomington: Indiana University Press, 1962), 439.

6. Kent Masterson Brown, *Retreat from Gettysburg: Lee Logistics and the Gettysburg Campaign* (Chapel Hill: University of North Carolina Press, 2005), 321–23.

7. *O.R.*, vol. 27, pt. 2, 309.

8. James Henry Avery, *Under Custer's Command: The Civil War Journal of James Henry Avery*, comp. Karla Jean Husby, ed. Eric J. Wittenberg (Washington, DC: Potomac Books, 2002), 43.

9. Samuel Lovejoy Gillespie, *A History of Company A, First Ohio Cavalry, 1861–1865* (1898; repr., Salem, MA: Higginson, 1990), 169.

10. Gillespie, *A History of Company A*, 169.

11. *O.R.*, vol. 27, pt. 3, 656–57.

12. *O.R.*, vol. 27, pt. 3, 657–58.

13. *O.R.*, vol. 27, pt. 3, 660.

14. Bill Hyde, ed., *The Union Generals Speak: The Meade Hearings on the Battle of Gettysburg* (Baton Rouge: Louisiana State University Press, 2003), 142.

15. *O.R.*, vol. 27, pt. 3, 648.

16. *O.R.*, vol. 27, pt. 3, 648 (bracketed words by author).

17. Hyde, *The Union Generals Speak*, 116.

18. The vote was cast by the following generals: James Wadsworth, William Hays, William French, George Sykes, John Sedgwick, Oliver Howard, John Slocum, A. A. Humphreys, and Alfred Pleasonton.

19. Hyde, *The Union Generals Speak*, 117.

20. *O.R.*, vol. 27, pt. 3, 998.

21. *O.R.*, vol. 27, pt. 3, 998.

22. *O.R.*, vol. 27, pt. 2, 302, 310; *O.R.*, vol. 27, pt. 2, 762, 765.

23. *O.R.*, vol. 27, pt. 2, 323.

24. Gillespie, *A History of Company A*, 165.

25. Colonel Preston, the senior officer in the brigade, had just arrived at the front and replaced Nathaniel Richmond of the 1st West Virginia as commander of the 1st Brigade.

26. Elliot W. Hoffman, ed., *A Vermont Cavalryman in War and Love: The Civil War Letters of Brevet Major General William Wells and Anna Richardson* (Lynchburg, VA: Schroeder, 2007), 188.

27. Hoffman, *A Vermont Cavalryman in War and Love*, 186–87.

28. Gillespie, *A History of Company A*, 165–66.

29. Hoffman, *A Vermont Cavalryman in War and Love*, 187.

30. Gillespie, *History of Company A*, 166; Letter, Lieutenant Colonel Allyne Litchfield to My Dear Wife, "Bivouac between Williamsport and Falling Waters July 14 1863," Litchfield-French Papers, Shannon Wait Manuscripts Division, William Clements Library, University of Michigan (bracketed word by author).

31. Gillespie, *History of Company A*, 166.

32. S. Roger Keller, *Crossroads of War: Washington County, Maryland, in the Civil War* (Shippensburg, PA: Burd Street Press, 1997), 68.

33. Thomas J. Ryan and Richard R. Schaus, *"Lee Is Trapped and Must Be Taken": Eleven Fateful Days after Gettysburg, July 4–14, 1863* (El Dorado Hills, CA: Savas Beatie, 2021), 236 (bracketed word by author).

34. W. W. Blackford, *War Years with Jeb Stuart* (New York: Scribner, 1945), 116.

35. Frank Robertson Reade, *In the Saddle with Stuart: The Story of Frank Smith Robertson of Jeb Stuart's Staff*, ed. Robert J. Trout (Gettysburg, PA: Thomas, 1998), 86.

36. Reade, *In the Saddle with Stuart*, 86 (bracketed word by author).

37. Eric J. Wittenberg, J. David Petruzzi, and Michael F. Nugent, *One Continuous Fight: The Retreat from Gettysburg and the Pursuit of Lee's Army of Northern Virginia, July 4–14, 1863* (El Dorado Hills, CA: Savas Beatie, 2013), 279.

38. Reade, *In the Saddle with Stuart*, 86.

39. James H. Kidd, *Personal Recollections of a Cavalryman with Custer's Michigan Cavalry Brigade in the Civil War* (1908; repr., Ionia, MI: Sentinel, 2015), 183.

40. Kidd, *Personal Recollections*, 183; George F. Franks III, *The Battle of Falling Waters 1863: Custer, Pettigrew, and the End of the Gettysburg Campaign* (North Charleston, SC: George F. Franks III, 2013), 47.

41. Kidd, *Personal Recollections*, 183.

42. Archer's brigade was now headed by Lieutenant Colonel S. G. Shephard.

43. Franks, *Battle of Falling Waters*, 27–28.

44. Pettigrew's North Carolinians had gone on to distinguish themselves at McPherson's Ridge on July 1 and again on July 3 when they attacked beside Pickett's division and briefly planted Confederate colors on the stone wall at the foot of the Federal line. This two-day performance came at a price, and Pettigrew's 26th North Carolina had suffered a casualty rate of 89 percent. *O.R.*, vol. 27, pt. 2, 289; Eric Lindblade and James Hessler, "Johnston Pettigrew and the Gettysburg Campaign," *The Battle of Gettysburg Podcast*, season 1, episode 10, November 6, 2019.

45. *O.R.*, vol. 27, pt. 2, 644.

46. *O.R.*, vol. 27, pt. 2, 705.

47. *O.R.*, vol. 27, pt. 2, 648.

48. *O.R.*, vol. 27, pt. 2, 644.

49. James Caldwell, *The History of a Brigade of South Carolinians* (Philadelphia, PA: King and Baird, 1886), 107.

50. *O.R.*, vol. 27, pt. 2, 648.

51. Prior to this Pettigrew had reportedly "received a severe contusion to his hand on the 3d, but would not report off duty." This may have hindered Pettigrew's riding and shooting abilities on July 14. *O.R.*, vol. 27, pt. 2, 644.

52. Franks, *Battle of Falling Waters*, 48.

53. *O.R.*, vol. 27, pt. 2, 648.

54. Kidd, *Personal Recollections*, 185–86.

55. *O.R.*, vol. 27, pt. 1, 990.

56. Kidd, *Personal Recollections*, 167.

57. Pettigrew died from his wound three days later near Bunker Hill, West Virginia.

58. Litchfield letter, July 14, 1863, "Bivouac between Williamsport and Falling Waters July 14 1863" (bracketed words by author).

59. Litchfield letter, July 14, 1863, "Bivouac between Williamsport and Falling Waters July 14 1863" (bracketed word by author).

60. Litchfield letter, July 14, 1863, "Bivouac between Williamsport and Falling Waters July 14 1863."

61. "Letter from Frederick, MD, W.S. Company C, 3rd [West] Va. Cavalry," *Wheeling Daily Intelligencer*, July 27, 1863.

62. Waylon Fuller Dunaway, *Reminiscences of a Rebel* (New York: Neale, 1913), 98.

63. Abner Hard, *History of the Eighth Cavalry Regiment, Illinois Volunteers, during the Great Rebellion* (Aurora, IL: n.p., 1868), 265.

64. Dunaway, *Reminiscences of a Rebel*, 98–99.

65. Dunaway, *Reminiscences of a Rebel*, 99–100.

66. Reade, *In the Saddle with Stuart*, 86.

67. O.R., vol. 27, pt. 1, 942 (bracketed word by author).

68. Adele Mitchell, ed., *The Letters of Major General James E. B. Stuart* (Alexandria, VA: Stuart-Mosby Historical Society, 1990), 328 (bracketed words by author).

69. Hyde, *The Union Generals Speak*, 142 (bracketed word by author).

70. Ryan and Schaus, *"Lee Is Trapped and Must Be Taken,"* 273 (bracketed word by author).

71. Hyde, *The Union Generals Speak*, 118.

72. Brown, *Retreat from Gettysburg*, 384–87.

73. Mark Mayo Boatner III, *The Civil War Dictionary*, rev. ed. (New York: David McKay, 1988), 339.

74. O.R., vol. 27, pt. 1, 187.

EPILOGUE

1. O.R., vol. 27, pt. 1, 691.

BIBLIOGRAPHY

Alexander, Edward Porter. *Fighting for the Confederacy: The Papers and Recollections of General Edward Porter Alexander.* Edited by Gary W. Gallagher. Chapel Hill: University of North Carolina Press, 1989.

———. *Military Memoirs of a Confederate.* Edited by Harry Williams. Civil War Centennial Series. Bloomington: Indiana University Press, 1962.

Armistead, Lindsay Long. *Memoirs of Robert E. Lee: His Military and Personal History Embracing a Large Amount of Information Hitherto Unpublished. Together with Incidents Relating to His Private Life Subsequent to the War. Collected and Ed. with the Assistance of Marcus. J. Wright. Illustr. [Robert Edward Lee].* New York: J. M. Stoddart, 1887.

Armstrong, Richard L. *11th Virginia Cavalry.* Virginia Regimental Histories Series. Lynchburg, VA: H. E. Howard, 1989.

———. *7th Virginia Cavalry.* Virginia Regimental Histories Series. Lynchburg, VA: H. E. Howard, 1992.

Arnold, Carrie. "How Do Horses Communicate? New Signals Found." *National Geographic*, August 4, 2014.

Avery, James Henry. *Under Custer's Command: The Civil War Journal of James Henry Avery.* Compiled by Karla Jean Husby. Edited by Eric J. Wittenberg. Washington, DC: Potomac Books, 2002.

Bachelder, John B., David L. Ladd, Audrey J. Ladd, and Richard A. Sauers, eds. *The Bachelder Papers: Gettysburg in Their Own Words.* Vols. 1–3. Dayton, OH: Morningside, 1994.

Ballard, James Buchanan. *William Edmondson "Grumble" Jones: The Life of a Cantankerous Confederate.* Jefferson, NC: McFarland, 2017.

Barnett, Bert H. "'. . . Our Position Was Finely Adapted to Its Purpose , . .': The Guns of Cemetery Hill." *Gettysburg Seminar Papers* (2019): 231–60.

Bates, Samuel P. *Martial Deeds of Pennsylvania.* Philadelphia, PA: T. H. Davis, 1875.

Beach, William Harrison. *First New York (Lincoln) Cavalry from April 19, 1861, to July 7, 1865.* N.p.: Nabu Press, 2010.

Beale, G. W. *A Lieutenant of Cavalry in Lee's Army.* Baltimore, MD: Butternut and Blue, 1994.

Beale, R. L. T. *History of the Ninth Virginia Cavalry, in the War between the States.* 1899. Reprint, Richmond, VA: B. F. Johnson, 2010.

Bennett, Deb. "Horses of the Civil War." *Equus Magazine,* June 2017.

Black, John Logan. *Crumbling Defenses; or, Memoirs and Reminiscences of John Logan Black.* Macon, GA: Eleanor D. McSwain, 1960.

Blackford, Susan Leigh, and Charles Minor Blackford III, eds. *Letters from Lee's Army; or, Memoirs of Life in and out of the Army in Virginia during the War between the States.* Lincoln: University of Nebraska Press, 1998.

Blackford, W. W. *War Years with Jeb Stuart.* New York: Scribner, 1945.

Bliss, George. *Personal Narratives of Events in the War of the Rebellion; Being Papers Read before the Rhode Island Soldiers and Sailors Historical Society.* 4th ser., no. 1. Providence, RI: Rhode Island Soldiers and Sailors Historical Society, 1889.

Blue, John. *Hanging Rock Rebel: Lt. John Blue's War in West Virginia and the Shenandoah Valley.* Edited by Daniel P. Oates. Shippensburg, PA: Burd Street Press, 1994.

Boatner, Mark Mayo, III. *The Civil War Dictionary.* Rev. ed. New York: David McKay, 1988.

Bond, Frank A. "Company A, First Maryland Cavalry." *Confederate Veteran* 6 (1898): 78.

Boyd, Cyrus F. *The Civil War Diary of Cyrus F. Boyd, Fifteenth Iowa Infantry, 1861–1863.* Edited by Mildred Throne. Royal Oak, Auckland: Pickle Partners, 2016.

Bradshaw, Ada Bruce Desper, ed. *Civil War Diary of Charles William McVicar.* Washington, DC: Library of Congress, 1977.

Brock, R. A., ed. *Southern Historical Society Papers.* Vol. 22. Richmond, VA: Southern Historical Society, 1894.

———. *Southern Historical Society Papers.* Vol. 23. Richmond, VA: Southern Historical Society, 1895.

Brooke, George Tucker. *Autobiography of Sergeant George Tucker Brooke, Co. B 2nd Virginia Cavalry.* Richmond: Virginia Historical Society, 1907.

Brooks, U. R., ed. *Butler and His Cavalry in the War of Secession 1861–1865.* Camden, SC: Gray Fox Books, n.d.

Brown, Campbell. *Campbell Brown's Civil War: With Ewell and the Army of Northern Virginia.* Edited by Terry L. Jones. Baton Rouge: Louisiana State University Press, 2001.

Brown, Kent Masterson. *Meade at Gettysburg: A Study in Command.* Chapel Hill: University of North Carolina Press, 2021.

———. *Retreat from Gettysburg: Lee Logistics and the Gettysburg Campaign.* Chapel Hill: University of North Carolina Press, 2005.

Brown, R. Shepard. *Stringfellow of the Fourth.* New York: Crown, 1960.

Bryant, Edwin Eustace. *History of the Third Regiment of Wisconsin Veteran Volunteer Infantry, 1861–1865.* Madison, WI: Veteran Association, 1891.

Buck, Lucy Rebecca. *Sad Earth, Sweet Heaven.* Edited by William P. Buck. Birmingham, AL: Cornerstone, 1973.

Bushong, Millard K., and Dean M. Bushong. *Fightin' Tom Rosser, C.S.A.* Shippensburg, PA: Beidel, 1983.

Caldwell, James. *The History of a Brigade of South Carolinians.* Philadelphia, PA: King and Baird, 1886.

Calef, John H. "Gettysburg Notes: The Opening Gun," *Journal of the Military Services Institution of the United States,* Jan./Feb., 1907, 40–57.

Carpenter, Louis Henry. *Louis Henry Carpenter: Letters from the Field 1861–1865.* Philadelphia, PA: Historical Society of Pennsylvania, n.d.

Carter, William H. *From Yorktown to Santiago with the Sixth U.S. Cavalry.* Baltimore, MD: Lord Baltimore Press, 1900.

Caughey, Donald C., and Jimmy J. Jones. *The 6th United States Cavalry in the Civil War: A History and Roster.* Jefferson, NC: McFarland, 2013.

Clark, Walter, ed. *Histories of the Several Regiments and Battalions from North Carolina in the Great War, 1861–1865.* Vol. 5. Raleigh: State of North Carolina, 1901.

Coddington, Edwin B. *The Gettysburg Campaign: A Study in Command.* Norwalk, CT: Easton Press, 1998.

Coffman, Richard M. *Going Back the Way They Came: A History of the Phillips Georgia Legion Cavalry Battalion.* Macon, GA: Mercer University Press, 2011.

Coggins, Jack. *Arms and Equipment of the Civil War.* Garden City, NY: Doubleday, 1962.

Cole, Scott C. *34th Battalion Virginia Cavalry.* Lynchburg, VA: H. E. Howard, 1993.

Cooke, John Esten. *Wearing of the Gray: Being Personal Portraits, Scenes and Adventures of the War.* New York: E. B. Treat, 1867.

Cooke, Philip St. George. *Cavalry Tactics; or, Regulations for the Instruction, Formations, and Movements of the Cavalry of the Army and Volunteers of the United States.* Washington, DC: Government Printing Office, 1862.

Cox, Mike. *The Texas Rangers: Wearing the Cinco Peso, 1821–1900.* New York: Forge, 2008.

Creekmore, S. A. J. *Diary of Sergeant S. A. J. Creekmore, Company C, Jeff Davis Legion.* Jackson: Mississippi Department of Archives and History, n.d.

Cunningham, S. A., ed. *Confederate Veteran.* Vol. 23. Nashville, TN: Cunningham, 1913.

Cunningham, Steven A., and Beth A. White. "The Ground Trembled as They Came." In "Gettysburg: Regimental Leadership and Command," edited by Mark A. Snell and Theodore Savas. Issue, *Civil War Regiments* 6, no. 3 (1999): 79.

Custer, Andie. "Into the Mouth of Hell." *Blue & Gray* 23, no. 1 (Spring 2006): 6–22.

Daughtry, Mary. *Gray Cavalier: The Life and Wars of General W. H. F. "Rooney" Lee.* Cambridge, MA: Da Capo, 2002.

Davis, Burke. *Jeb Stuart, the Last Cavalier . . . with Maps by Rafael D. Palacios [with Plates, Including Portraits].* New York: Rinehart, 1957.

Davis, Sidney Morris. *Common Soldier, Uncommon War: Life as a Cavalryman in the Civil War.* Edited by Charles F. Cooney. Bethesda, MD: J. H. Davis Jr., 1994.

Dawson, John Harper. *Wildcat Cavalry: A Synoptic History of the Seventeenth Virginia Cavalry Regiment of the Jenkins-McCausland Brigade in the War between the States.* Dayton, OH: Morningside, 1982.

De Brack, F. *Light Cavalry Outposts: Recollections.* London: W. Mitchell, 1876.

Denison, Frederic. *Sabres and Spurs: The First Regiment Rhode Island Cavalry in the Civil War, 1861–1865: Its Origin, Marches, Scouts, Skirmishes, Raids, Battles, Sufferings, Victories, and Appropriate Official Papers; with the Roll of Honor and Roll of the Regiment.* Providence: First Rhode Island Veteran Association, 1876.

de Peyster, John Watts. *The Decisive Conflicts of the Late Civil War or Slaveholders' Rebellion.* New York: MacDonald, 1867.

———. *Personal and Military History of Phil Kearney.* New York: Rice and Gauge, 1969.

DiMarco, Louis A. *War Horse: A History of the Military Horse and Rider.* Yardley, PA: Westholme, 2012.

Dooley, Vince, and Samuel N. Thomas, eds. *The Legion's Fighting Bulldog: The Civil War Correspondence of William Gaston Delony, Lieutenant Colonel of Cobb's Georgia Legion Cavalry, and Rosa Delony, 1853–1863.* Macon, GA: Mercer University Press, 2017.

Doster, William E., and Alfred Whital. *Lincoln and Episodes of the Civil War.* New York: Putnam, 1915.

Driver, Robert J., Jr. *The 1st and 2nd Rockbridge Artillery.* Virginia Regimental Histories Series. Lynchburg, VA: H. E. Howard, 1987.

———. *1st Virginia Cavalry.* 2nd ed. Lynchburg, VA: H. E. Howard, 1991.

———. *10th Virginia Cavalry.* Virginia Regimental Histories Series. Lynchburg, VA: H. E. Howard, 1992.

Dulany, Ida Powell. *In the Shadow of the Enemy: The Civil War Journal of Ida Powell Dulany.* Edited by Mary L. Mackall and Steven F. Meserve. Knoxville: University of Tennessee Press, 2010.

Dunaway, Waylon Fuller. *Reminiscences of a Rebel.* New York: Neale, 1913.

Early, J. A. "Causes of the Defeat of General Lee's Army at the Battle of Gettysburg: Opinions of Leading Confederate Soldiers." In *Southern Historical Society Papers.* Vol 4. Edited by J. William Jones. Richmond, VA: Southern Historical Society, 1877.

Eggleston, George Cary. *A Rebel's Recollections.* Bloomington: Indiana University Press, 1959.

Ellis, John. *Cavalry: The History of Mounted Warfare.* Barnsley, UK: Pen & Sword Military Classics, 2004.

Emerson, Stephen B. "Steptoe's Defeat: Battle of Tohotonimme (1858)." History Link, August 8, 2008. Accessed December 26, 2015. http://www.historylink. org/index.cfm?displaypage=output.cfm&file_id=8709.

Evans, David. *Sherman's Horsemen: Union Cavalry Operations in the Atlanta Campaign.* Bloomington: Indiana University Press, 1996.

Ford, John Salmon, and Stephen B. Oates. *Rip Ford's Texas.* Austin: University of Texas Press, 1987.

Franks, George F., III. *The Battle of Falling Waters 1863: Custer, Pettigrew, and the End of the Gettysburg Campaign.* North Charleston, SC: George F. Franks III, 2013.

Frye, Dennis E. *12th Virginia Cavalry.* Lynchburg, VA: H. E. Howard, 1988.

Gillespie, Samuel Lovejoy. *A History of Company A, First Ohio Cavalry, 1861–1865.* Columbus, OH: Lovejoy, 1898. Reprint, Salem, MA: Higginson, 1990.

Gilmor, Harry. *Four Years in the Saddle.* Edited by Daniel Carroll Toomey. New York: Harper & Brothers, 1866. Reprint, Baltimore, MD: Butternut and Blue, 1986.

Goff, Richard Davis. *Confederate Supply.* Durham, NC: Duke University Press, 1969.

Gottfried, Bradley M. *The Maps of the Cavalry in the Gettysburg Campaign.* El Dorado Hills, CA: Savas Beatie, 2020.

Gracey, Samuel Levis. *Annals of the Sixth Pennsylvania Cavalry.* Philadelphia, PA: E. H. Butler, 1868.

Graham, William. *Nineteenth Regiment.* Vol. 2 of *Histories of the Several Regiments and Battalions from North Carolina in the Great War, 1861–1865,* edited by Walter Clark. Goldsboro, NC: Nash Brothers, 1901.

Greene, Ann Norton. *Horses at Work: Harnessing Power in Industrial America.* Cambridge, MA: Harvard University Press, 2008.

Haines, Anson. *The 15th Regiment: New Jersey Volunteers.* New York: Jenkins & Thomas, 1883.

Hall, Hillman Allyn, William B. Besley, and Gilbert Guion Wood. *History of the Sixth New York Cavalry: (Second Ira Harris Guard) Second Brigade—First Division—Cavalry Corps, Army of the Potomac, 1861–1865.* Salem, MA: Higginson, 2005.

Hard, Abner. *History of the Eighth Cavalry Regiment, Illinois Volunteers, during the Great Rebellion.* Aurora, IL: n.p., 1868.

Harrell, Roger H. *The 2nd North Carolina Cavalry.* Jefferson, NC: McFarland, 2012.

Hartley, Chris J. *Stuart's Tarheels: James B. Gordon and His North Carolina Cavalry.* Baltimore, MD: Butternut and Blue, 1996.

Haskell, Franklin Aretas. *The Battle of Gettysburg.* Columbia, SC: Big Byte Books, 2016.

———. *The Battle of Gettysburg: A Soldier's First-Hand Account.* Mineola, NY: Dover, 2003.

Hayes, Karen E. N. *Hands-On Horse Care: Equine Health Care, Diagnosis and First Aid.* North Pomfret, VT: Trafalgar Square, 1997.

Haythornthwaite, Phillip J. *Napoleonic Cavalry.* London: Cassell, 2001.

Hebert, Walter H. *Fighting Joe Hooker.* Lincoln: University of Nebraska Press, 1999.

Henderson, E. Prioleau. *Autobiography of Arab: Beaufort District Troop & 2nd South Carolina Cavalry 1861–1865.* Camden, SC: Gray Fox Books, 1997.

Hessler, James A., and Britt C. Isenberg. *Gettysburg's Peach Orchard: Longstreet, Sickles, and the Bloody Fight for the "Commanding Ground" along the Emmitsburg Road.* El Dorado Hills, CA: Savas Beatie, 2019.

Hewlett, James B., Noah A. Trudeau, and Bryce A. Suderow, eds. *Supplement to the Official Records of the Union and Confederate Armies.* Vol. 4. Part 1, *Reports.* Wilmington, NC: Broadfoot, 1995.

Hoffman, Elliott W. *History of the First Vermont Cavalry Volunteers in the War of the Great Rebellion.* Baltimore, MD: Butternut and Blue, 2000.

———, ed. *A Vermont Cavalryman in War and Love: The Civil War Letters of Brevet Major General William Wells and Anna Richardson.* Lynchburg, VA: Schroeder, 2007.

Hoffman, Elliott, and Horace K. Ide. "The First Vermont Cavalry in the Gettysburg Campaign." *Gettysburg* 14 (January 1996).

Holbrook, Thomas. "William Edward Miller, Captain, Company H, 3rd Pennsylvania Cavalry." In *Unsung Heroes of Gettysburg: Programs of the Fifth Annual Gettysburg Seminar.* Gettysburg, PA: Gettysburg National Military Park, 1996.

Hopkins, Donald A. *The Little Jeff: The Jeff Davis Legion, Cavalry, Army of Northern Virginia.* Shippensburg, PA: White Mane Books, 1999.

Howard, Wiley C. *Sketch of the Cobb Legion Cavalry and Some Incidents and Scenes Remembered.* Atlanta, GA: Atlanta Camp 159, S.C.V., 1901. Reprint, Delhi, India: Facsimile, 2013.

Hyde, Bill, ed. *The Union Generals Speak: The Meade Hearings on the Battle of Gettysburg.* Baton Rouge: Louisiana State University Press, 2003.

Johnson, Robert Underwood, and Clarence Clough Buel. *Battles and Leaders of the Civil War.* Vol. 3. Part 1. Boulder, CO: Bibliolife, 2010.

Jones, J. B. *A Rebel War Clerk's Diary.* Vol. 1. Edited by James L. Robertson Jr. Lawrence: University Press of Kansas, 2015.

Jones, J. William, ed. *Southern Historical Society Papers.* Vol. 4. Richmond, VA: Southern Historical Society, 1877.

Keller, S. Roger. *Crossroads of War: Washington County, Maryland, in the Civil War.* Shippensburg, PA: Burd Street Press, 1997.

Kidd, James H. *Personal Recollections of a Cavalryman with Custer's Michigan Cavalry Brigade in the Civil War.* 1908. Reprint, Ionia, MI: Sentinel, 2015.

Kirshner, Ralph. *The Class of 1861: Custer, Ames, and Their Classmates after West Point.* Carbondale: Southern Illinois University Press, 1999.

Krepps, John T. *A Strong and Sudden Onslaught: The Cavalry Action at Hanover, Pennsylvania.* Ortanna, PA: Colecraft Industries, 2008.

Krick, Robert K. *9th Virginia Cavalry.* Virginia Regimental History Series. Lynchburg, VA: H. E. Howard, 1982.

Kummorow, Bert. "Small Arms in the Cavalry Regiments of the Army of the Potomac during the Gettysburg Campaign." Ordnance Records in U.S. Archives, Washington, DC, 1962.

Laidley, T. T. S., ed. *The Ordnance Manual for the Use of the Officers of the United States Army.* 3rd ed. Philadelphia, PA: Lippincott, 1862.

Lambert, Dobbie Edward. *Grumble: The W. E. Jones Brigade of 1863–1864.* Wahiawa, HI: Lambert Enterprises, 1992.

Lee, R. E. *The Wartime Papers/with Connective Narratives by Clifford Dowdey and Maps by Samuel H. Bryant.* Edited by Clifford Dowdey and Louis H. Manarin. Boston; Toronto: Little, Brown, 1961.

Lee, Robert E., Jr., ed. *Recollections and Letters of Robert E. Lee.* New York: Smithmark, 1995.

Lindblade, Eric, and James Hessler. "Johnston Pettigrew and the Gettysburg Campaign." *The Battle of Gettysburg Podcast.* Season 1. Episode 10. November 6, 2019.

Lloyd, William P. *History of the First Reg't. Pennsylvania Reserve Cavalry, from Its Organization, August, 1861, to September, 1864: With a List of Names of All Officers and Enlisted Men Who Have Ever Belonged to the Regiment.* Salem, MA: Higginson, 1990.

Locke, William Henry. *The Story of the Regiment, by William Henry Locke.* Philadelphia, PA: Lippincott, 1868.

Long, Armistead Lindsey. *Memoirs of Robert E. Lee, His Military and Personal History: Embracing a Large Amount of Information Hitherto Unpublished.* New York; Philadelphia, PA; Washington, DC: J. M. Stoddart, 1887.

Longacre, Edward G. *The Cavalry at Gettysburg: A Tactical Study of Mounted Operations during the Civil War's Pivotal Campaign, 9 June–14 July 1863.* Lincoln: University of Nebraska Press, 1986.

———. *General John Buford: A Military Biography.* Cambridge, MA: Da Capo, 1995.

———. *Lee's Cavalrymen: A History of the Mounted Forces of the Army of Northern Virginia, 1861–1865.* Mechanicsburg, PA: Stackpole Books, 2002.

———. *Lincoln's Cavalrymen: A History of the Mounted Forces of the Army of the Potomac, 1861–1865.* Mechanicsburg, PA: Stackpole Books, 2000.

Longstreet, James. *From Manassas to Appomattox: Memoirs of the Civil War in America.* Philadelphia, PA: Lippincott, 1896.

Lowry, Thomas P. *The Story the Soldiers Wouldn't Tell: Sex in the Civil War.* Mechanicsburg, PA: Stackpole Books, 1994.

Mackowski, Chris, Kristopher D. White, and Daniel T. Davis. *Fight like the Devil: The First Day at Gettysburg, July 1, 1863.* El Dorado Hills, CA: Savas Beatie, 2015.

Manucy, Albert C. *Artillery through the Ages: A Short, Illustrated History of Cannon, Emphasizing Types Used in America.* Washington, DC: Government Printing Office, 1962.

Marshall, Charles. "Events Leading Up to the Battle of Gettysburg." Address before Confederate Veterans Association of Washington, DC, January 1896. In *Southern Historical Society Papers.* Vol. 22. Edited by R. A. Brock. Richmond, VA: Southern Historical Society, 1894.

Marshall, Thomas. *Thomas Marshall, an Aide de Camp of Lee.* Edited by Sir Frederick Maurice. Boston, MA: Little, Brown, 1927. Stratford Hall, Lee Family Digital Archive.

Martin, Samuel J. *Kill-Cavalry: The Life of Union General Hugh Judson Kilpatrick.* Mechanicsburg, PA: Stackpole Books, 2000.

McClellan, Henry B. *I Rode with Jeb Stuart: The Life and Campaigns of Major General J. E. B. Stuart.* New York: De Capo, 1994.

McClure, James. *East of Gettysburg: A Gray Shadow Crosses York County, PA.* York, PA: York Daily Record/York County Heritage Trust, 2003.

McDonald, William N. *A History of the Laurel Brigade: Originally the Ashby Cavalry of the Army of Northern Virginia and Chew's Battery*. Edited by Bushrod C. Washington. Baltimore, MD: Mrs. Kate S. McDonald, 1902.

McKinney, Joseph W. *Brandy Station, Virginia, June 9, 1863: The Largest Cavalry Battle of the Civil War*. Jefferson, NC: McFarland, 2006.

Meade, George Gordon. *The Life and Letters of George Gordon Meade*. Vol. 1. New York: Scribner, 1913. http://www.latinamericanstudies.org/civil-war/The_life_and_letters_of_George_Gordon_Meade-1.pdf.

———. *The Life and Letters of George Gordon Meade: Major-General United States Army*. Vol. 2. New York: Scribner, 1913.

Means, Paul B. *Additional Sketch Sixty-Third Regiment (5th Cavalry)*. Vol. 3 of *Histories of the Several Regiments and Battalions from North Carolina, in the Great War, 1861–1865*, edited by Walter Clark. Goldsboro, NC: Nash Brothers, 1901.

Mesic, Harriet Bey. *Cobb's Legion Cavalry: A History and Roster of the Ninth Georgia Volunteers in the Civil War*. Jefferson, NC: McFarland, 2011.

Meyer, Henry C. *Civil War Experiences under Bayard, Gregg, Kilpatrick, Custer, Raulston, and Newberry, 1862, 1863, 1864*. New York: Putnam, 1911.

Miller, Francis Trevelyan, and Robert S. Lanier, eds. *The Photographic History of the Civil War in Ten Volumes*. Vol. 4, *The Cavalry*. New York: Review of Reviews, 1911.

Miller, John A. "The Road to Smithsburg." *War Returns to South Mountain* (blog), March 22, 2010. Accessed June 11, 2021. https://southmountaincw.wordpress.com/2010/03/22/the-road-to-smithsburg/.

Mitchell, Adele H., ed. *The Letters of Major General James E. B. Stuart*. Alexandria, VA: Stuart-Mosby Historical Society, 1990.

Moore, James. *Kilpatrick and Our Cavalry, Comprising a Sketch of the Life of General Kilpatrick, with an Account of the Cavalry Raids, Engagements, and Operations under His Command, from the Beginning of the Rebellion to the Surrender of Johnston, by James Moore*. New York: W. J. Widdleton, 1865.

Mosby, John Singleton. *Mosby's War Reminiscences: Stuart's Cavalry Campaigns*. New York: Dodd, Mead, 1898.

———. *Stuart's Cavalry in the Gettysburg Campaign*. London: Forgotten Books, 2012.

Moyer, H. P. *History of the Seventeenth Regiment, Pennsylvania Volunteer Cavalry; or, One Hundred and Sixty-Second in the Line of Pennsylvania Volunteer Regiments: War to Suppress the Rebellion, 1861–1865*. 1911. Reprint, Salem, MA: Higginson, 1998.

Muir, Rory. *Tactics and the Experience of Battle in the Age of Napoleon*. New Haven, CT: Yale University Press, 1998.

Murphy, Daniel. "Brandy Station's Forgotten Flank." *America's Civil War*, November 2006, 54.

———. "Cavalry: Swords before Pistols." *Journal of the American Revolution*, February 11, 2014. https://allthingsliberty.com/author/daniel-murphy/.

———. "Infantry vs. Cavalry." *Journal of the American Revolution*, February 27, 2014.

————. "Shock and Awe: Mounted Combat in the Eighteenth Century." *Journal of the United States Cavalry*, June 2009, 10–13.

————. "Slashing Sabres at the Rummel Farm." *America's Civil War*, January 2005, 38–45.

————. *William Washington, American Light Dragoon*. Yardley, PA: Westholme, 2014.

Musick, Michael P. *6th Virginia Cavalry*. Lynchburg, VA: H. E. Howard, 1990.

Myers, Frank M. *The Comanches: A History of White's Battalion, Virginia Cavalry*. Marietta, GA: Continental, 1956.

Neese, George M. *Three Years in the Confederate Horse Artillery: Consisting of Excerpts, Where Each Touches on Matters Relating to Charlottesville, VA and Environs*. Dayton, OH: Morningside, 1988.

Nesbitt, Mark. *Saber and Scapegoat: J. E. B. Stuart and the Gettysburg Controversy*. Mechanicsburg, PA: Stackpole Books, 1994.

Nicolle, David. *Carolingian Cavalrymen, AD 768–987*. Oxford: Osprey, 2005.

Nolan, Louis Edward. *Cavalry: Its History and Tactics*. Yardley, PA: Westholme, 2007.

Norton, Henry. *Deeds of Daring; or, History of the Eighth N.Y. Volunteer Cavalry, Containing a Complete Record of the Battles, Skirmishes, Marches, Etc., That the Gallant Eighth New York Cavalry Participated In, from Its Organization in November, 1861, to the Close of the Rebellion in 1865*. N.p.: Big Byte Books, 2020.

Nye, Wilbur Sturtevant. *Here Come the Rebels*. Dayton, OH: Morningside, 1988.

O'Ferrall, Charles Triplett. *Forty Years of Active Service; Being Some History of the War between the Confederacy and the Union and of the Events Leading up to It, with Reminiscences of the Struggle and Accounts of the Author's Experiences of Four Years from Private to Lieutenant-Colonel and Acting Colonel in the Cavalry of the Army of Northern Virginia*. New York: Neale, 1904.

O'Neill, Robert F. *The Cavalry Battles of Aldie, Middleburg and Upperville, June 10–27, 1863*. Virginia Civil War Battle and Leaders Series. Lynchburg, VA: H. E. Howard, 1993.

————. *Chasing Jeb Stuart and John Mosby: The Union Cavalry in Northern Virginia from Second Manassas to Gettysburg*. Jefferson, NC: McFarland, 2012.

————. "For the Lack of Horses, the War Was Nearly Lost." HistoryNet, May 19, 2020. Accessed September 19, 2021. https://www.historynet.com/lack-of-horses.htm.

————. "The Reidville Mutiny." *Small but Important Riots* (blog), July 10, 2019. Accessed May 10, 2020. https://smallbutimportantriots.com/2019/07/10/the-readville-mutiny/.

Patton, George. *Patton's Cavalry Drill and Sabre Exercise*. New York: J. W. Fortune, 1861. Reprint, Rochelle, VA: Heartland House Press, 1990.

Peake, John W. "Recollections of a Boy Cavalryman." *Confederate Veteran Magazine* 34 (1926): 261.

Penfield, James Allen. *The 1863–1864 Civil War Diary of Captain James Penfield, 5th New York Volunteer Cavalry, Company H*. Crown Point, NY: Penfield Foundation, 1999.

Pfanz, Harry W. *Gettysburg: Culp's Hill and Cemetery Hill*. Chapel Hill: University of North Carolina Press, 1993.

————. *Gettysburg: The First Day*. Chapel Hill: University of North Carolina Press, 2001.

————. *Gettysburg: The Second Day*. Chapel Hill: University of North Carolina Press, 1987.

Phipps, Michael. *"Come on, You Wolverines!" Custer at Gettysburg*. Gettysburg, PA: Farnsworth House Military Impressions, 1995.

Piecuch, Jim, and John H. Beakes. *"Light Horse Harry" Lee in the War for Independence*. Charleston, SC: Nautical and Aviation Publishing Company of America, 2013.

Poinsett, J. R., ed. *Cavalry Tactics*. Parts 1–3. Washington, DC: U.S. War Department; J & G. S. Gideon, 1841.

————, ed. *School of the Squadron—Mounted*. Part 2 of *Cavalry Tactics*. Washington, DC: U.S. War Department; J. & G. S. Gideon, 1841.

Preston, Noble D. *History of the Tenth Regiment of Cavalry, New York State Volunteers: August, 1861, to August, 1865*. New York: D. Appleton, 1892.

Priest, John Michael. *Antietam: The Soldiers' Battle*. New York: Oxford University Press, 1989.

Prowell, G. R. *Encounter at Hanover: Prelude to Gettysburg*. Shippensburg, PA: White Mane, 1994.

Pyne, Henry R. *The History of the First New Jersey Cavalry (Sixteenth Regiment, New Jersey Volunteers)*. New Brunswick, NJ: J. A. Beecher, 1871.

Rea, D. B. *Sketches from Hampton's Cavalry: Embracing the Principle Exploits of the Cavalry in the Campaigns of 1862 and 1863*. Columbia: South Carolina State Press, 1864.

Reade, Frank Robertson. *In the Saddle with Stuart: The Story of Frank Smith Robertson of Jeb Stuart's Staff*. Edited by Robert J. Trout. Gettysburg, PA: Thomas, 1998.

Robertson, J. *Michigan in the War*. Lansing, MI: W. S. George, 1882.

Rodenbough, Theophilus F. *From Everglade to Canon with the Second Dragoons, (Second United States Cavalry): An Authentic Account of Service in Florida, Mexico, Virginia, and the Indian Country, Including the Personal Recollections of Prominent Officers, with an Appendix Containing Orders, Reports and Correspondence, Military Records, Etc., Etc., Etc., 1836–1875*. New York: D. Van Nostrand, 1875.

————. "Historical Sketch." In *History of the Eighteenth Regiment of Cavalry Pennsylvania Volunteers*, edited by the Publication Committee of the Regimental Association. New York: Wynkoop Hallenbeck Crawford, 1909.

Root, Elihu, and Fred C. Ainsworth, ed. *The War of the Rebellion: A Compilation of the Official Records of the Union and Confederate Armies*, Additions and Correction to Ser. 1. Vol. 5. Washington, DC: Government Printing Office, 1902.

Rummel, George A. *Cavalry on the Roads to Gettysburg: Kilpatrick at Hanover and Hunterstown*. Shippensburg, PA: White Mane, 2000.

Ryan, Thomas J. "A Battle of Wits: Intelligence Operations during the Gettysburg Campaign: Part 3." *Gettysburg Magazine* 31 (n.d.).

Ryan, Thomas J., and Richard R. Schaus. *"Lee Is Trapped and Must Be Taken": Eleven Fateful Days after Gettysburg, July 4–14, 1863.* El Dorado Hills, CA: Savas Beatie, 2021.

Ryan, Thomas J., and Stephen W. Sears. *Spies, Scouts, and Secrets in the Gettysburg Campaign: How the Critical Role of Intelligence Impacted the Outcome of Lee's Invasion of the North, June–July, 1863.* El Dorado Hills, CA: Savas Beatie, 2015.

Saussy, George N. "Campaigning with Jeb Stuart." *Watson's Jeffersonian Magazine* 13, no. 1 (May 1911): 64.

———. "Upperville's Cavalry Battle." *Watson's Jeffersonian Magazine* 4, no. 4 (April 1910): 334.

Scharf, John Thomas. *History of Western Maryland.* Philadelphia, PA: Louis H. Everts, 1882.

Scheibert, Justus. *Seven Months in the Rebel States during the North American War, 1863.* Edited by William Stanley Hoole. Tuscaloosa: University of Alabama Press, 2009.

Schiller, Laurence D. *Of Sabres and Carbines: The Emergence of the Federal Dragoon: A Scholarly Monograph.* Saline, MI: McNaughton and Gunn for the Blue and Gray Education Society, 2001.

Scott, Donald. "Evangelicalism, Revivalism, and the Second Great Awakening." National Humanities Center. Accessed September 15, 2022. http://national humanitiescenter.org/tserve/nineteen/nkeyinfo/nevanrev.htm.

Scott, Robert N., ed. *The War of the Rebellion: A Compilation of the Official Records of the Union and Confederate Armies.* Ser. 1. Vol. 11. Parts 1–3. Washington, DC: Government Printing Office, 1884.

———, ed. *The War of the Rebellion: A Compilation of the Official Records of the Union and Confederate Armies.* Ser. 1. Vol. 12. Parts 1–3. Washington, DC: Government Printing Office, 1885.

———, ed. *The War of the Rebellion: A Compilation of the Official Records of the Union and Confederate Armies.* Ser. 1. Vol. 19. Parts 1–2. Washington, DC: Government Printing Office, 1887.

———, ed. *The War of the Rebellion: A Compilation of the Official Records of the Union and Confederate Armies.* Ser. 1. Vol. 25. Parts 1–2. Washington, DC: Government Printing Office, 1889.

———, ed. *The War of the Rebellion: A Compilation of the Official Records of the Union and Confederate Armies.* Ser. 1. Vol. 27. Parts 1–3. Washington, DC: Government Printing Office, 1889.

———, ed. *The War of the Rebellion: A Compilation of the Official Records of the Union and Confederate Armies.* Ser. 1. Vol. 29. Part 1. Washington, DC: Government Printing Office, 1889.

Sears, Stephen W. *Chancellorsville.* Boston; New York: Houghton Mifflin, 1996.

———. *To the Gates of Richmond: The Peninsula Campaign.* Boston, MA: Houghton Mifflin, 1992.

Shoaf, Dana B. "On the March Again at Daybreak: Major John I. Nevin and the 93rd Pennsylvania Infantry." In "Gettysburg: Regimental Leadership and Command," edited by Mark A. Snell and Theodore Savas. Issue, *Civil War Regiments* 6, no. 3 (1999).

Smith, John L., ed. *History of the 118th Pennsylvania Volunteers, Corn Exchange Regiment from Their First Engagement at Antietam to Appomattox.* Philadelphia, PA: J. L. Smith, 1905.

Stackpole, Edward J. *They Met at Gettysburg.* New York: Bonanza, 1956.

St. Clair, Samuel. "The Fight at Hagerstown." In *History of the Eighteenth Regiment of Cavalry Pennsylvania Volunteers*, edited by the Publication Committee of the Regimental Association. New York: Wynkoop Hallenbeck Crawford, 1909.

Steele, Matthew Forney. *American Campaigns.* Vol. 1. Washington, DC: Byron S. Adams, 1909.

Steffen, Randy. *The Horse Soldier 1776–1943: The United States Cavalryman: His Uniforms, Arms, Accoutrements, and Equipments.* Vol. 1. Norman: University of Oklahoma Press, 1977.

St. George Cooke, Phillip. *Cavalry Tactics; or, Regulations for the Instruction, Formations, and Movements of the Cavalry of the Army and Volunteers of the United States.* Philadelphia, PA: Lippincott, 1862.

Stocker, Jeffrey D., ed. *From Huntsville to Appomattox: R. T. Coles's History of 4th Regiment, Alabama Volunteer Infantry, C.S.A., Army of Northern Virginia.* Knoxville: University of Tennessee Press, 1996.

Stonebraker, Joseph R. *A Rebel of '61.* New York: Wynkoop Hallenbeck Crawford, 1899.

Swain, Craig. "Artillery and Horses." *To the Sound of the Guns* (blog). Accessed May 8, 2022. https://markerhunter.wordpress.com/2009/11/01/artillery-and-horses/.

Tagg, Larry. *The Generals of Gettysburg: The Leaders of America's Greatest Battle.* Cambridge, MA: Da Capo, 2003.

Thomas, D. Michael. *Wade Hampton's Iron Scouts: Confederate Special Forces.* Charleston, SC: History Press, 2018.

Thomason, John W., Jr. *Jeb Stuart.* New York: Scribner, 1930.

Time-Life Books, eds. *Echoes of Glory: Arms and Equipment of the Union.* Alexandria, VA: Time-Life Books, 1991.

Toalson, Jeff, ed. *Send Me a Pair of Old Boots and Kiss My Little Girls: The Civil War Papers of Richard and Mary Watkins.* New York: Universe, 2009.

Tobie, Edward P. *History of the First Maine Cavalry, 1861–1865.* Boston: Emory & Hughes, 1887.

Toombs, Samuel. *New Jersey Troops in the Gettysburg Campaign from June 5 to July 31, 1863.* Orange, NJ: Evening Mail, 1888.

Trout, Robert J. *Galloping Thunder: The Story of the Stuart Horse Artillery Battalion.* Mechanicsburg, PA: Stackpole Books, 2002.

———, ed. *In the Saddle with Stuart: The Story of Frank Smith Robertson of JEB Stuart's Staff.* Gettysburg, PA: Thomas Publications, 1998.

———, ed. *Memoirs of the Stuart Horse Artillery Battalion.* Vol. 2, *Breathed's and McGregor's Batteries.* Knoxville: University of Tennessee Press, 2010.

———, ed. *Memoirs of the Stuart Horse Artillery Battalion: Moorman's and Hart's Batteries.* Knoxville: University of Tennessee Press, 2008.

———. *They Followed the Plume: The Staff Officers and Headquarters Personnel of Major General J. E. B. Stuart, C.S.A.* Mechanicsburg, PA: Stackpole Books, 1993.

Tucker, Glenn. *High Tide at Gettysburg.* New York: Konecky & Konecky, 1958.

Urwin, Gregory J. W. *The United States Cavalry: An Illustrated History, 1776–1944.* Norman: University of Oklahoma Press, 1983.

U.S. Army Pennsylvania Cavalry 3rd Regiment. *History of the Third Pennsylvania Cavalry.* Philadelphia, PA: Franklin, 1905.

U.S. War Department. "Instruction for Field Artillery." In *The 1864 Field Artillery Tactics: Organization, Equipment, Field Service.* 1864. Reprint, Mechanicsburg, PA: Stackpole Books, 2005.

von Borcke, Heros. *Memoirs of the Confederate War for Independence.* Philadelphia, PA: Lippincott, 1867.

von Borcke, Heros, and Justus Scheibert. "Colonel White's Report." In *The Great Cavalry Fight at Brandy Station, 9 June 1863.* Winston-Salem, NC: Paelemon, 1976.

———. *The Great Cavalry Battle of Brandy Station, 9 June 1863.* Winston-Salem, NC: Paelemon, 1976.

von Warnery, Karl Emanuel, Brent Nosworthy, and G. F. Koehler. *Remarks on Cavalry.* London: Constable, 1997.

Warner, Ezra J. *Generals in Blue: Lives of the Union Commanders.* Baton Rouge: Louisiana State University Press, 1992.

Wellman, Manly Wade. *Giant in Gray: A Biography of Wade Hampton of South Carolina.* Dayton, OH: Morningside, 1988.

Wert, Jeffry D. *Cavalryman of the Lost Cause: A Biography of J. E. B. Stuart.* New York: Simon & Schuster, 2009.

———. *Gettysburg, Day Three.* New York: Simon & Schuster, 2001.

———. *Mosby's Rangers.* New York: Simon & Schuster, 1991.

Weston, John. *Picket Pins and Sabers: The Civil War Letters of John Burden Weston.* Edited by Robert W. Frost and Nancy D. Frost. Ashland, KY: Economy, 1971.

Whitaker, Fredrick. *A Popular Life of Gen. George A. Custer.* New York: Sheldon, 1876.

Williamson, James Joseph. *Mosby's Rangers: A Record of the Operations of the Forty-Third Battalion of Virginia Cavalry from Its Organization to the Surrender.* New York: Sturgis & Walton, 1909. Reprint, 2018.

Wittenberg, Eric J. *The Battle of Brandy Station: North America's Largest Cavalry Battle.* Charleston, SC: History Press, 2010.

———. "The Cavalry Fight at Lewis Ford August 30, 1862." Facebook. Accessed March 3, 2015. https://www.facebook.com/MajorGeneralJohnBuford/posts/232495120218554.

———. "Colonel Nathaniel P. Richmond." Folder 3. Accessed May 23, 2021. https://www.fold3.com/memorial/632318856/nathaniel-richmond/stories.

———. "The Devil's to Pay," Gen. John Buford, USA. Gettysburg, PA: Farnsworth House Military Impressions, 1995.

———. *The Devil's to Pay: John Buford at Gettysburg: A History and Walking Tour.* El Dorado Hills, CA: Savas Beatie, 2018.

———. *Gettysburg's Forgotten Cavalry Actions: Farnsworth's Charge, South Cavalry Field, and the Battle of Fairfield, July 3, 1863.* New York: Savas Beatie, 2013.

———. *Protecting the Flank at Gettysburg: The Battles for Brinkerhoff's Ridge and East Cavalry Field, July 2–3, 1863.* El Dorado Hills, CA: Savas Beatie, 2013.

———. *Union Cavalry Comes of Age: Hartwood Church to Brandy Station, 1863.* Charleston, SC: History Press, 2017.

Wittenberg, Eric J., and J. David Petruzzi. *Plenty of Blame to Go Around: Jeb Stuart's Controversial Ride to Gettysburg.* New York: Savas Beatie, 2011.

Wittenberg, Eric J., J. David Petruzzi, and Michael F. Nugent. *One Continuous Fight: The Retreat from Gettysburg and the Pursuit of Lee's Army of Northern Virginia, July 4–14, 1863.* El Dorado Hills, CA: Savas Beatie, 2013.

Worsham, John H. *One of Jackson's Foot Cavalry; His Experience and What He Saw during the War 1861–1865, Including a History of "F Company," Richmond, Va., 21st Regiment Virginia Infantry, Second Brigade, Jackson's Division, Second Corps, A.N.V.* 1912. Reprint, New York: Neale, 1992.

Worthington, Chauncey, F., ed. *A Cycle of Adams Letters, 1861–1865.* Vol. 2. New York: Houghton Mifflin, 1920.

Yenne, Bill. *Indian Wars: The Campaign for the American West.* Yardley, PA: Westholme, 2008.

Young, T. J. "The Battle of Fairfield, Pennsylvania." *Confederate Veteran* 5 (1893): 251.

NEWSPAPERS

Detroit Advertiser and Tribune
Detroit Free Press
Fayetteville Observer
Galveston Weekly News
Gettysburg Compiler
Hanover Herald
National Tribune
New York Daily Tribune
New York Times
Philadelphia Inquirer
Philadelphia Weekly Times
Raleigh News and Observer
Richmond Dispatch
Richmond Examiner
Richmond Sentinel
Rochester Daily Union and Advertiser
St. Mary's Beacon
Washington Post
Wheeling Daily Intelligencer

PERIODICALS

America's Civil War
Blue and Gray Magazine
Confederate Veteran Magazine
Equus Magazine
Gettysburg Magazine
Journal of the American Revolution
Journal of the United States Cavalry
National Geographic
North and South Magazine
Virginia Magazine of Biography and History
Watson's Jeffersonian Magazine

LIBRARIES AND SPECIAL COLLECTIONS

Bentley Historical Library, University of Michigan
Clements Library, University of Michigan
Dickinson College
Duke University
Handley Library, Winchester Virginia
Historical Society of Pennsylvania
Huntington Library
Library of Congress
Mississippi Department of Archives & History
National Archives
New York Historical Society Museum and Library
North Carolina Division of Archives and History
Queens College/University of New York
Rochester Historical Society
United States Army Heritage and Education Center
Virginia Historical Society

INDEX

415